Welfare Policy for the 1990s

Welfare Policy for the 1990s

Edited by Phoebe H. Cottingham
and David T. Ellwood

Harvard University Press
Cambridge, Massachusetts
London, England
1989

Library of Congress Cataloging-in-Publication Data

Welfare policy for the 1990s / edited by Phoebe H.
   Cottingham and David T. Ellwood.
      p.   cm.
   Bibliography: p.
   Includes index.
   ISBN 0-674-94905-6 (alk. paper)
   1. Public welfare—United States.   2. Public
welfare—Law and legislation—United States.
I. Cottingham, Phoebe H.   II. Ellwood, David T.
HV95.W454   1989
361'.973—dc19   88-38182
                                        CIP

Contents

Abbreviations

AFDC	Aid to Families with Dependent Children
AFDC-U	Aid to Families with Dependent Children-Unemployed Parent
APWA	American Public Welfare Association
CBO	Congressional Budget Office
CCP	Comprehensive Competencies Program
CDBG	Community Development Block Grant (program)
CETA	Comprehensive Employment and Training Act
CPI	Consumer Price Index
CPS	Current Population Surveys (Census Bureau)
CSAP	Child Support Assured Payment
CSAS	Child Support Assurance System
CWEP	Community Work Experience Program
DIME	Denver Income Maintenance Experiment
DOA	Department of Agriculture
DOL	Department of Labor
EITC	Earned Income Tax Credit
EOPP	Employment Opportunity Pilot Project
ESL	English as a Second Language
ET	Employment and Training (program) (or Massachusetts ET)
ETA	Employment and Training Administration
FAP	Family Assistance Plan
GAIN	Greater Avenues for Independence (program)

GED	General Equivalency Diploma
HEW	Health, Education, and Welfare
HHS	Health and Human Services (Department of)
HUD	Housing and Urban Development
JEDI	Jobs for Employable Dependent Individuals (Act)
JOBS	Job Opportunities and Basic Skills (training program)
JTPA	Job Training Partnership Act
LIHEAP	Low Income Home Energy Assistance Program
MCPI	Medical Consumer Price Index
MDRC	Manpower Demonstration Research Corporation
MPR	Mathematica Policy Research
NLS	National Longitudinal Survey (of labor market behavior)
NMCUES	National Medical Care Utilization and Expenditure Survey
OBRA	Omnibus Budget Reconciliation Act (various years)
OCSE	Office of Child Support Enforcement
OFA	Office of Family Assistance
OJT	On-the-Job Training
PBJI	Program for Better Jobs and Incomes
PCE	Personal Consumption Expenditures
PSE	Public Service Experience
PSID	Panel Study of Income Dynamics (Michigan)
SIME	Seattle Income Maintenance Experiment
SIPP	Survey of Income and Program Participation (by the Census Bureau)
SSBG	Social Services Block Grant (or title XX)
SSI	Supplemental Security Income
TEFAP	Temporary Emergency Food Assistance Program
WIC	(The supplemental food program for) Women, Infants, and Children
WIN	Work Incentive (program)
WPA	Works Progress Administration

Welfare Policy for the 1990s

Introduction

Phoebe H. Cottingham

The new welfare reform legislation had its origins in changes in the political climate in the 1970s as well as changes in the demographic composition and economic status of families. For the past two decades, poverty in America has shifted most markedly from the aged to children and their mothers. In part this shift reflected rapid increases in Social Security benefits for the aged. But it also reflected profound changes in the family composition and labor market participation patterns of groups that historically suffered more poverty than the rest of Americans: blacks, Hispanics, and women.

In the early years of the Reagan administration, welfare reform was well down on the list of priorities. In its closing year the reform was again perceived as a pressing concern. Specific changes in the welfare system have just been legislated; it remains to be seen how far-reaching and effective they will be. To be sure, everyone agrees on the fundamental objectives of welfare reform—to reduce poverty and dependence and to encourage economic self-sufficiency—but the consensus wavers on the concrete ways to bring them about. In this fluid context, the purpose of this book is to bring together three types of new knowledge: research on poverty and income-support mechanisms; practical and applied research on state welfare initiatives; and perspectives on the values and attitudes that surrounded the debate about welfare reform. The focus is on tangible policy options and on the major themes and issues that have surfaced in the debates.

The Reform Debate

The discussion of welfare has focused mainly on the Aid to Families with Dependent Children (AFDC) system, which provides income support for nearly 12 million women and children in poverty. This government program (first called Aid to Dependent Children) began under the Social Security Act of 1935 as a form of social insurance for dependent children deprived of parental support "by reason of the death, continued absence from the home, or physical or mental incapacity of a parent." Payments under the system were expected principally to aid children of widows and to fill the gap until the survivor's insurance became effective.

During the last fifty years, however, the number of AFDC recipients grew (especially in the postwar period) from 900,000 children in 1950 to 2,400,000 in 1960, and 3,700,000 in 1987. By the mid 1980s the AFDC system was costing $17.7 billion (1986), of which $15.8 billion represented direct benefit payments to recipients. This was almost 20 percent of the approximately $90 billion being spent annually through the national welfare system, which provides government support to able-bodied adults of working age and their children who qualify for income-conditioned assistance programs such as Medicaid, Food Stamps, Housing Assistance, and so on.

While the AFDC system has expanded, the most serious problem, it now seems, is not the burden on the taxpayers per se. The costs of AFDC have not been rising, nor have there been increases recently in the aggregate number of people supported by welfare. Indeed, AFDC participation rates among the eligible population have fallen in the last decade. The primary motivation for reforming the welfare system is to change the conditions of long-term poverty among children and reduce the social isolation and separation between families with working parents and those with nonworking parents dependent on welfare. A social equation is under dispute.

There seem to be only two ways of promoting economic independence for AFDC families: encourage or help the mothers find employment, and get absent parents of children on welfare to provide more support for those children and their mothers. The public policy question from this perspective is whether economic independence is a realistic objective for significant numbers of those currently receiving welfare, and if it is, how best to do it. (Robert Reischauer sorts out the probable practical consequences in Chapter 1.)

Reducing Dependency and Poverty

The AFDC system is intended to provide temporary family income support in the absence of a working parent. For most recipients it does offer transitional financial assistance during times of marital disruption or, in the case of some single mothers, during periods of unemployment. For an increasing number, however, it has become a long-term support system, especially among very young, unmarried mothers.

This raises the question of whether there are alternative policies for providing income support to this population or reducing their need for income support. The epidemic of poverty among minority children—over 50 percent now experience a home environment dependent on welfare for a significant portion of their early years—and the increasing rates of poverty among American children overall have prompted a national search for policies and programs that offer alternatives to welfare for single-parent family income. (In Chapter 2 Sheldon Danziger offers an anatomy of poverty and discusses the role of government programs in reducing poverty among different populations, including children and single parents.)

Poverty and the Inner City

An important component in the welfare reform debate has been poverty trends in the inner city. Some analysts believe that it is not the welfare system per se that is at fault for the increasing numbers of children in poverty. Structural changes in the older urban core have produced new and larger concentrations of persistently poor populations that appear isolated from jobs and mainstream institutions. (William Julius Wilson and Loïc Wacquant examine the issues related to urban inner core poverty in Chapter 3.)

Changes in the welfare system may thus have little effect on populations living in new urban conditions. Far more massive social and economic policies may be needed that complement the reform of education, child care, and job training systems to transform the social environment. These policies, however, are beyond the immediate concern of those whose responsibility is to manage the existing welfare system. But they loom as a worrisome backdrop.

Reform, Employment, and Income

The welfare reform debate has benefited from research on the employment and earnings effects of programs aimed at welfare recipients. Some of this research is encouraging regarding the likely impact of welfare reform, but it also suggests that some programs have limited effect. (See the discussion by Gary Burtless in Chapter 4.) So far, the evidence regarding the impact of welfare reform comes from earlier voluntary demonstrations aimed at improving employment among long-term AFDC recipients who did not have very young children, and from studies of low-cost mandatory programs developed in state workfare demonstrations designed to reach large numbers of AFDC recipients. The latter programs were not targeted on the young mother with very young children. Nevertheless, these studies offer an important policy baseline.

The early experimental demonstration programs of intensive, voluntary employment and training interventions for welfare recipients showed that such programs can result in sizable gains in employment and earnings. For example, employment rates rose 8.5 percentage points, and earnings as much as $1,500 a year in the first such experimental program for AFDC recipients (Supported Work). In a more recent experiment, earnings gains averaged $1,100 a year for AFDC recipients who participated in an intensive training-employment program (the AFDC Health Aide Demonstration). The long-term economic benefits to the participants and the savings to taxpayers significantly outweighed the high initial public costs of these intensive service programs.

More recent evaluations of lower-cost mandatory programs, such as job search, find much smaller, and in some cases negligible, employment and earnings impacts for participants. Under the Omnibus Budget Reconciliation Act (OBRA) of 1981, state agencies experimented with strategies that would move AFDC recipients off welfare and into work, or into preparation for work. State work-welfare programs that required AFDC recipients to register, engage in job search, or even perform unpaid work in a community agency in return for AFDC payments have had only modest short-run effects on earnings (at most $560 a year, but typically much less). Short-run effects on employment are even less impressive than the earnings effects, suggesting that those who exit from AFDC into jobs through the low-cost workfare programs would typically have found some employment without the program, although they would not have achieved the higher wage rates. It is important to note that some subgroups in the AFDC population may be getting slightly better jobs through these programs than what they would have found otherwise, and increased attention to these groups appears warranted. While these work-welfare programs have only a modest impact on earnings, they are nevertheless cost-effective, even over the short term. Thus, even though dependency is not reduced on the scale hoped for through these programs, there are net gains to society from these efforts.

Evaluations of mandatory workfare programs have not so far measured their longer term impacts. Moreover, the early mandatory workfare programs did not reach the long-term dependency population that has as its core younger, never-married mothers with very young children. Still under assessment are newer mandatory state work-welfare programs that attempt to offer full services to AFDC recipients. These programs, it appears, are costing more, but may have stronger impacts than the first low-cost workfare programs, judging by the findings on the more expensive, full service voluntary programs that brought important gains in not only employment but earnings. Such programs require much higher outlays of public resources (and well before the hope of any return) to obtain this reduction in poverty and welfare dependency. (The estimated costs of different types of welfare-employment interventions are compared by Craig Thornton in Chapter 9.)

Long-Term Recipients

During the 1980s the reduction in federal outlays for income support programs has stimulated a fresh look at who is poor and why. New studies identified two major types of welfare recipients: (1) short-term recipients who average less than two years on AFDC and move on and off as a transition between jobs or marriages; (2) long-term recipients who average eight to ten years of dependency, often beginning their welfare experience with giving birth out of wedlock while a teenager. (Douglas Besharov discusses the differences between the two groups in Chapter 5.)

Targeting within universal programs raises questions of stigma, equity, effectiveness, and institutional setting. For example, some urge targeting interventions on low-income teenage mothers before they become long-term recipients, while others fear that targeting of services would reward early childbearing. We need to continue our efforts not only to better understand who is dependent on welfare and why but also to identify more effective ways to deliver services that are appropriate to the needs of individual welfare recipients. We have much to learn about how to target services more effectively.

Support Services

We have limited evidence to document the barriers to employment presented by child care, basic skill deficiencies, and the stress of family responsibilities, and whether services designed to fill those gaps are in fact effective.

Traditionally, employment training programs have been viewed as the social response to basic skills problems. However, recent experiences in the new mandatory program environment are revealing a mismatch between the basic skills of many AFDC recipients and the skills requirements of training programs and jobs, especially jobs that pay enough to improve family income. The issue is whether improving the basic skills of AFDC recipients can be accomplished most effectively through short-term remediation programs, or in more traditional educational settings. (Gary Walker addresses this point in his note to Chapter 4.)

The accessibility and affordability of child care is another issue that must be considered in designing policies, if reducing dependency through employment is to be a serious goal. No rigorous evidence is yet available to document the extent to which child care is a barrier to self-sufficiency, yet there are hints from pilot studies designed to improve child development that quality preschool programs may in fact reduce the AFDC dependency of the mothers of the children involved. (Denise Polit and Joseph O'Hara provide an extensive review of this area in Chapter 6.)

Increasing medical costs have heightened the importance of Medicaid for poor families. This fact, combined with a general social concern with protecting the health of our population, has led to proposals to extend Medicaid benefits to working poor families. Others have proposed that mandatory employer coverage of health care be part of a welfare reform package.

These social and support services components of potential welfare reform programs and policies may be important in terms of the central goal of welfare reform—reducing dependency. They may also be important in meeting other social objectives such as reducing poverty and improving child development outcomes linked to parental education, child-care settings, and health services.

Institutional Effects

Remarkably little is known about how the welfare system interacts with other social institutions with which welfare recipients must be in contact. Much research and evaluation is going on to add to our understanding of the potential effects of different work, training, and employment strategies on employment, earnings, and welfare receipt. It is now becoming increasingly clear that the administrative organization and institutional structures of the welfare system interact in numerous ways with many other social institutions (the courts, the child support system, to name a few). (In Chapter 7, Demetra Nightingale discusses the intergovernmental and interprogram relations that will be perturbed in varying degrees by welfare reform and in turn influence the achievement of reform objectives.) Research into the types and extent of these interactions has been neglected. Such information is badly needed and can be expected to contribute importantly to our knowledge of how the welfare system (and other systems) in fact mediate the expected impacts of program activities on recipients.

Child Support

The primary nonwelfare strategies are those that increase the income transfers to AFDC families from absent parents of children in the household. Child support is attractive as a target for nonwelfare systemic change. Some urge that child support be expanded into a mixed private-public system for assuring a universal child allowance, independent of the work status of the custodial parent. (Robert Lerman reviews these options in detail in Chapter 8.)

The welfare system has always been obligated to try to increase the establishment of support orders and the collection of child support. However, the administrative costs of doing so relative to the short-run reductions in transfer income thus obtained have hampered this strategy. Changes in the child-support system potentially could have substantial returns in terms of long-run reductions in poverty among AFDC recipients. Estimates of the additional income to AFDC recipients range up to an average of $3,000 a year, on the assumption that all fathers of AFDC children had child-support obligations averaging 25 percent of income, which they fully paid. This is in sharp contrast to the average child-support payment, which was $225 in 1984.

In view of the administrative costs and changes needed to bring the maximum contribution from noncustodial fathers into the AFDC households, there is enormous interest in finding ways to introduce the structural changes of such a universal system, while at the same time adding a contribution by the government to children in single-parent families (either all children or only those with support orders). Such a contribution, called child-support assurance payments, could include modest means tests, but in any event would provide modest transfer income to supplement low-wage job income in such households and could even encourage welfare recipients to seek employment.

But as is true for all the nonwelfare policies that might reduce dependency or poverty, there are conflicts over the introduction of another universal system. Such systems expand the beneficiary class to large numbers of people and increase public outlays. Therefore, the payout or benefit level will tend to be relatively low and thus have, correspondingly, less impact on the very poor. The beneficiaries are numerous, however, so such programs are popular and stigma is correspondingly reduced.

Nonwelfare Strategies

Welfare reform will not succeed in making substantial inroads into poverty or dependency unless it is linked to or made parallel with other systemic changes. (David Ellwood summarizes the major alternatives in the conclusion.) Nonwelfare strategies include: (1) increasing the transfer income to AFDC households through such means as child support or child assurance, child allowances, and refundable tax credits; (2) improving the economic position of the working poor, by adding such general benefits as mandatory employer health insurance, child care subsidization, or increases in the minimum wage; (3) improving the job holding capacities of AFDC recipients through reform of the mainstream systems for education, training, child care, and other support services. Each of these strategies, while having potentially modest effects as a single strategy, may, in combination, significantly alter the current imbalance of the equation in favor of targeted intervention. These nonwelfare strategies also generally have a larger beneficiary population than AFDC families and, therefore, will have less of a labeling effect than do welfare policies.

Within the existing system, reduction in poverty among those most likely to be highly dependent on AFDC may be achievable only with straightforward increases in benefits. This would obviously increase program costs and would tend to discourage recipients from seeking employment and self-sufficiency. In the short term, an increase in benefits would lead to reductions in the number of poor families, but more families will likely be dependent on AFDC support for longer periods of time. This dilemma of welfare reform within the existing system's objectives may, in the end, force changes in other institutions that are unforeseen in the 1980s debate.

The Welfare Reform Legislation: Directions for the Future

Robert D. Reischauer

After a hiatus of nearly a decade, welfare reform reappeared on the nation's policy agenda in February 1986, when President Reagan announced in his State of the Union Message that his administration would reexamine the existing welfare system and formulate a strategy for its reform. In response to this announcement, a number of other interested parties joined the administration in launching studies of ways to reform the welfare system during 1986.[1]

The reports that followed revealed a surprising degree of consensus about the major shortcomings of the existing system and the general directions that reform should take. Conservatives, moderates, and liberals agreed that the breakdown of the family, out-of-wedlock births, and inadequate inner-city educational systems were generating a class of welfare recipients that was likely to be dependent for long periods of time. They also concluded that the current system was doing little to help these recipients become more self-sufficient, and that a reformed system should be based on the concept of reciprocal responsibilities under which both the government and the recipients had clear obligations. Finally, most agreed that states should be given greater discretion over certain aspects of welfare policy.

These diagnoses and general prescriptions for reform were translated into concrete legislative proposals during 1987.[2] For the most part, these proposals were incremental in design and modest in scope. When compared to the two major welfare reform initiatives of the 1970s, the Family Assistance Plan (FAP) and the Program for Better Jobs and Incomes (PBJI), they hardly merited the label "reform"; "revision" would have been more appropriate. The limited nature of the remedies contrasted with the dire diagnoses—diagnoses which implied that only significant structural reform could be effective.

Even these limited responses revealed significant disagreements among those concerned with welfare policy. While there was little dispute over broad objectives or goals, the proponents of reforms disagreed sharply over the specific steps needed to implement the general aims. Conservatives, moderates, and liberals could not agree on what obligations should be imposed on recipients, which recipients should be required to participate in work-oriented programs, how much latitude should be given to states, and whether benefits should be raised and expanded.

These disagreements, together with the pall cast by the budget deficit, slowed legislative action on welfare reform. The House of Representatives passed a relatively liberal welfare reform bill in December 1987 and the Senate followed suit with a more conservative bill in June 1988. After three months of difficult negotiations which, at times, seemed to reach unresolvable impasses, the Conference Committee hammered out a compromise bill (the Family Support Act of 1988) just as the 100th Congress prepared for final adjournment in late September 1988. This bill, which the Senate (96 to 1) and the House (347 to 53) passed by overwhelming majorities, was also acceptable to President Reagan, who signed it in October.

The passage of the Family Support Act was accompanied by an outpouring of enthusiastic rhetoric and hyperbole to the effect that it represented landmark legislation, a policy revolution, and a radically new approach to the welfare problem. A more dispassionate judgment would conclude that the changes made by this legislation were quite modest. While they represented important shifts of policy emphasis and direction, they will not, by themselves, provide long-run solutions to the nation's problems of poverty and dependency. Future administrations and Congresses will thus be compelled to revisit the same policy battleground.

This is not likely to occur for several years, however, because most politicians and policy makers will want to give the modest reforms enacted in 1988 a chance to show whether they can make any noticeable difference. Nevertheless, several developments almost guarantee that welfare reform will return to the nation's policy agenda sometime in the early 1990s. One of these will be the need to fine-tune or adjust the 1988 reforms when states encounter problems trying to implement the legislation's child-support and work components. A second driving force behind a renewed reform effort will be the research findings that will come from the welfare experiments that are already under way in several states and the demonstration projects called for in the 1988 legislation. Reformers will want to incorporate these findings immediately into policy. Finally, a number of the more controversial provisions of the Family Support Act are scheduled to expire in the late 1990s, thus ensuring a continuing debate over whether their demise should be hastened or delayed.

When welfare reform does reemerge as a priority issue, the policy environment, areas of disagreement, and strategies and options that are considered will be similar to those that characterized the debate leading up to the enactment of the Family Support Act of 1988. It is therefore important to understand the dynamics of this latest round of welfare reform if one is to consider how these forces will affect future policy debates.

The New Policy Environment

The recent welfare policy debate took place in a different environment from that of the 1970s and early 1980s. One difference was the emergence of more tolerant public attitudes toward the poor and welfare programs. Historically, the public has expressed ambivalent attitudes toward the poor and little support for welfare programs. Exceptional stories of welfare recipients driving luxury cars and using Food Stamps to purchase filet mignon and of women bearing children solely to obtain added AFDC benefits have been gullibly accepted by the public as the norm. The Reagan administration tapped these antiwelfare feelings to support its 1981 welfare program cuts, which, it argued, would root out fraud, waste, and abuse, and target assistance more effectively.

Public opinion polls suggest that attitudes toward the poor and welfare programs became more sympathetic as the 1980s progressed. In the words of one group of observers, "From the last half of 1981 through the present there has been a striking liberal rebound, in which opinions appear to have returned to the levels of the period before the conservative shift began in the 1970s" (Shapiro et al., 1987).[3] The same liberal shift can be seen in public responses to questions concerning desirable ways to cut the budget deficit; while a majority of the population was willing to cut poverty programs to reduce the deficit in the early 1980s, few Americans advocate reduced spending for the poor in the late 1980s.[4]

Congress reflected these views by protecting means-tested entitlement programs from the automatic Gramm-Rudman-Hollings budget cuts, by increasing appropriations for some low-income programs in an era of budget stringency, and by considering welfare reform at a time when fiscal retrenchment was the order of the day.

The extent to which policy makers will want to address welfare issues in a more fundamental way anytime soon will depend, in part, on whether the new-found sympathy for the poor that emerged during the 1980s was ephemeral or has a more permanent basis. To the degree that this liberal sentiment rests on the symbolic role into which poverty policies were cast, it may be short-lived. Like defense policy, support for poverty programs came to be a test of one's attitudes toward the Reagan administration. Opponents potrayed it as one that cared little for the poor and downtrodden. The rise in the poverty rate, the growth of income inequality, and government efforts to cut welfare programs provided some credence to this characterization. Therefore, sympathy for the poor may have risen when the popularity of the administration fell during the Iran-Contra, Noriega, and Meese difficulties. If so, this sympathy could begin to evaporate after Reagan leaves office in 1989.

However, it is possible that the growing public sympathy for the poor may have a more permanent basis and therefore represent a source of support for more fundamental welfare reform. The sharp increases in the poverty population and the poverty rate over the 1978 to 1983 period profoundly troubled many Americans. While the situation has improved since 1983, there were more poor Americans in 1987 (32.5 million) and the poverty rate was higher (13.5 percent) than at any time during the 1970s. As the economy has strengthened and the unemployment rate has fallen, the gap between the poor and the rest of society has become more disturbing.

Increasing sympathy for the poor may also be related to the growth of two particularly vulnerable population groups: the homeless and poor children. Although the homeless probably represent less than one-quarter of one percent of the population, the attention the media have paid to this problem ensures that all Americans who read a newspaper or watch television have been exposed, in a sympathetic manner, to the plight of this group.[5] In addition, many residents of America's large metropolitan areas have, with understandable discomfort, come face to face with the homeless on the streets, in subway, bus, or train stations, or in the lobbies of public buildings.

The appalling incidence of poverty among children has also raised public concern. Roughly one-fifth of all children were poor in 1987, a fraction that has increased significantly since the early 1970s.[6] Close to half of all children probably experience at least one year of poverty before they reach their eighteenth birthday.[7] Such widespread childhood poverty could affect the nation's economic future, for, as numerous studies have shown, childhood poverty not only imposes immediate deprivation but also reduces future life prospects of the affected child. Today's poor children will be the American workers of tomorrow, who will not only need to compete with the Koreans, Taiwanese, Japanese, and Germans, but will also have to support the retirement benefits of the baby boom generation.

A second important difference in policy environment is that welfare supports a less adequate life style today than was the case in the early 1970s. The real value of the benefits provided by the major cash and in-kind means-tested programs peaked in the mid-1970s and then fell (see Panel B of Table 1.1). By 1986 they were some 15 percent below the levels reached a decade earlier.

Not only have real benefit levels dwindled, but participation rates have also fallen. Some 63 percent of female-headed families with children received some AFDC benefits in 1973; by 1986 participation had declined to under 45 percent (see Panel A of Table 1.1). This decline cannot be explained by a reduction in the incidence of need among female-headed families; 32.2 percent of such families were poor in 1973 and 34.6 percent were poor in 1986. Rather, reduced real benefit levels and other factors explain the drop in participation.

The benefits and coverage of the existing welfare system have eroded both because states have failed to raise benefits to keep pace with inflation and because the federal government tightened welfare eligibility conditions in 1981. As a result of this retrenchment, there has been no traditional welfare "crisis" to provide an impetus for reform—welfare caseloads have not been rising rapidly nor have welfare budgets been exploding. In fact, over the past decade, the welfare rolls and aggregate real welfare budgets have shown little growth (see Panels C and D of Table 1.1).

A third way in which the environment of the welfare reform debate has changed over the past decade relates to the continuing fracturing of the structure of the American family. Divorce, separation, female-headed families, and out-of-wedlock births are not as unusual nor as stigmatized as they were in the past. The proportion of families with children that are headed by women has risen from 8.5 percent in 1960 to 19.3 percent

Table 1.1. Welfare participation rates, benefit levels, recipients, and budgets, 1969–1986

	1969	1973	1977	1981	1983	1985	1986
Participation rates							
AFDC[a]	42%	63%	57%	53%	45%	43%	44%
AFDC and							
Food Stamps	22	43	42	n.a.	38	n.a.	n.a.
Medicaid	88	89	85	76	74	70	69
Real monthly benefits[b]							
AFDC[c]	$515	$485	$485	$410	$387	$396	$401
Food Stamps[c]	233	218	246	221	244	237	234
Medicaid[d]	111	140	147	130	114	113	112
Sum[e]	705	698	733	638	629	627	627
Recipients[f]							
AFDC basic	5,788	10,481	10,449	10,279	9,515	9,665	9,890
AFDC-U	336	557	659	881	1,144	1,129	1,101
Food Stamps	n.a.	12,200	17,100	22,400	23,000	21,300	20,900
Medicaid[g]	9,330	12,725	14,463	14,768	14,885	14,939	15,678
Budgets							
AFDC[h]	$10,638	$17,546	$19,800	$17,510	$16,934	$17,107	$17,575
Food Stamps[h]	652	5,089	9,243	13,716	13,725	12,797	12,540
Medicaid[i]	5,492	9,060	11,170	10,626	10,100	9,850	10,102

Sources: The first two sections are from Moffitt (1987), table 3, revised October 1987, except for several numbers for 1983, 1985, and 1986, which were provided by Moffitt separately. The last two sections are from U.S. House of Representatives, Committee on Ways and Means (1987), and from unpublished data from the Department of Health and Human Services and the Department of Agriculture.

a. Participation of female-headed families in the basic AFDC program. Adjusted for CPS subfamily coding errors.

b. In 1982 dollars deflated by the implicit price deflator for personal consumption expenditures (PCE) or the medical care component of the CPI (MCPI).

c. Maximum paid to a family of four with no other income.

d. Average of payments for nonaged and nondisabled adults and children per adult deflated by the MCPI.

e. Food Stamps plus 70 percent of AFDC plus Medicaid.

f. Average monthly number of recipients by fiscal year, in thousands.

g. Unduplicated number of dependent children and adults in families with dependent children, in thousands.

h. Federal and state expenditures for benefits and administration deflated by the PCE, in thousands of 1986 dollars.

i. Medicaid expenditures for dependent children and adults in families with dependent children, in thousands of 1986 dollars deflated by the MCPI.

in 1986 (see Table 1.2). Demographers have estimated that more than half of all marriages occurring in the 1980s will end in divorce and that over half of all children will live some period of time in a female-headed family before their eighteenth birthday.[8] Despite the legalization of abortion in 1973, the prevalence of out-of-wedlock births has increased. While only one child in twenty was born out of wedlock in 1960, one in five was in the mid-1980s.

These changes have altered the social attitudes and values that are relevant to the welfare reform debate. Divorce and out-of-wedlock birth are now more socially accepted, and the public is more familiar with and understanding of the difficulties encountered by many single parents.

A fourth difference in policy environment between the present and the past relates to society's expectations concerning the participation of mothers with young children in the labor force. In 1960 most women with young children did not work outside the home, and they were not expected to. This held for both married and unmarried mothers (see Table 1.3). Therefore, a benefit program that permitted women with no

Table 1.2. Female-headed families with children and out-of-wedlock births, 1960–1986

	1960	1970	1980	1985	1986
Female-headed families (percentage of families with children under 18)					
Total	8.5%	10.2%	17.5%	19.3%	19.3%
White	6.7	7.9	13.4	15.0	15.2
Black	24.2	30.6	46.8	49.9	47.6
Out-of-wedlock births (percentage of all births)					
Total	5.3%	10.7%	18.4%	22.0%	23.4%
White	2.3	5.7	11.0	14.5	15.7
Black	21.6[a]	37.6	55.2	60.1	61.2
Rate per 1,000 unmarried women					
Total	21.6	26.4	29.4	32.8	34.2
White	9.2	13.8	17.6	21.8	23.0
Black	98.3[a]	95.5	81.4	78.8	80.9

Sources: U.S. Bureau of the Census, Current Population Reports, P-20, nos. 419, 411, 366, 218, and 106, table 1; *Census of the Population: 1960,* Subject Report: Families, PC(Z)-4A; *Statistical Abstract of the United States: 1988,* table 87. Also, unpublished data from the National Center for Health Statistics.

a. Includes other nonwhite racial groups.

Table 1.3. Labor force participation rates of women with children, 1960–1987

	1960	1970	1980	1986	1987
All women with children	30.4%[a]	52.9%[a]	56.6%	62.8%	64.7%
Married women					
Youngest child < 6	18.6	30.3	45.0	53.8	56.8
Youngest child ⩾ 6	39.0	49.2	61.8	68.4	70.6
Separated women					
Youngest child < 6	n.a.	45.4	52.2	57.4	55.1
Youngest child ⩾ 6	n.a.	60.6	66.6	70.6	72.6
Divorced women					
Youngest child < 6	n.a.	63.3	68.3	73.8	70.5
Youngest child ⩾ 6	n.a.	82.4	82.3	84.7	84.5
Never-married women					
Youngest child < 6	n.a.	n.a.	44.1	47.5	49.9
Youngest child ⩾ 6	n.a.	n.a.	67.6	65.9	64.1
Widowed women					
Youngest child < 6	n.a.	36.8	44.7	46.4	38.5
Youngest child ⩾ 6	n.a.	55.3	60.7	57.5	60.1

Sources: U.S. Bureau of the Census, *Statistical Abstract of the United States, 1987,* table 654, and U.S. Department of Labor Bulletin no. 2175, table 56, p. 125. B.L.S. News Release USDL 86-345, August 20, 1986; USDL 84-321, July 26, 1984; USDL 87-345 August 12, 1987, table 3. Department of Labor, B.L.S., Special Labor Force Report, *Marital and Family Characteristics of Workers, March 1960,* April 1961, table G.

a. Excludes never-married women.

income to stay home and care for their children was relatively uncontroversial because it conformed to the behavior pattern of the majority.

By the 1980s this was no longer the case. Public opinion polls indicate that most Americans feel that it is both appropriate and desirable for mothers to work outside the home—a sentiment that reflects reality with a vengeance. Well over half of women with children under six participated in the labor force in 1986, although many worked less than full time, full year. Over two-thirds of those with older children participated in the labor force. The proportion of divorced mothers is particularly high. Hence the premise underlying the basic AFDC program has begun to diverge increasingly from the social norm. This has undoubtedly undermined public support for this program.

A fifth difference between the contemporary policy environment and the past is that the analytical basis for policy decisions is much sounder now, thanks to a spate of recent research. This work, much of it based on several longitudinal data bases, has provided a new understanding of the dynamics of poverty and welfare. For example, policy makers now know a good deal about the relative importance of the various events that are associated with the initiation and termination of poverty spells, more about how long various types of people are likely to remain poor or welfare dependent, and more about the intergenerational transmission of dependency.[9]

Another body of research has shed light on the effectiveness of low-cost programs designed to facilitate the employment of welfare recipients.[10] The researchers have measured the costs and benefits of various work-oriented programs, examined the types of recipients for whom these programs seem to be the most effective, and analyzed the conditions that seem to be the most conducive to the success of such efforts.

A final way in which the policy environment is different today than it was in the past is locus of policy innovation. In theory, welfare policy has always been the joint responsibility of the federal and state governments. However, for the period extending from the mid-1950s through 1980, the federal government was the unquestioned source of policy change. In many ways states appeared content to act as subcontractors executing federal policy. Many elected state officials did not pay a great deal of attention to welfare policy, and state welfare bureaucracies often seemed to interact more with HEW than with interested parties at the state level.

This pattern changed in 1981, when the federal government began to withdraw from welfare policy. The rhetoric and actions of the Reagan administration sent a clear signal to the states that welfare was not an important priority of the federal government. First, the administration cut back welfare programs through the Omnibus Budget Reconciliation Act of 1981 (OBRA). Then, through its New Federalism initiatives, the administration attempted to shift the entire responsibility for AFDC and Food Stamps onto the states.

As the federal welfare budget was scaled back and HHS ceased to be a source of policy change, the locus of innovation shifted to state capitals. This development was facilitated by the administration's belief that the states should be given greater latitude to experiment. To a greater extent than before, governors and state legislators began to take an interest in welfare issues. Some concluded that there was political mileage to be gained from designing and implementing identifiable state-specific reforms. They devoted considerable time, energy, and political capital to these efforts. Federal policy makers have to accept the fact that they can no longer monopolize policy innovation in this area.

Major Choices for the Future

The most fundamental choice for future antipoverty policy will be to decide how much effort to devote to further reforms of the welfare system and how much to changes in broader policies that would indirectly affect the well-being of welfare recipients. The welfare system exists largely as a last recourse, one that picks up the pieces when other systems and institutions fail. Failures in the educational system, in marriages and families, and in labor markets are the major systemic causes of welfare dependency. Resources can be devoted to strengthening these institutions and systems in the hope that doing so will reduce the burden on the welfare system in the long run.

The list of possible initiatives of this sort is long, but their effects are uncertain. More resources could be devoted to programs that try to reduce out-of-wedlock births, which are associated with 30 percent of new welfare cases and an even higher proportion of those beginning a period of long-term dependency (see Bane and Ellwood, 1983; and Ellwood, 1986). Similarly, more of an effort could be made to strengthen the educational systems that serve youth from low-income families. This might mean increasing the budgets of the Head Start and Chapter 1 programs or pursuing more radical educational reforms such as year-around schooling for disadvantaged children.

Some of the negative consequences of the changes in American family structure could be ameliorated by strengthening the child support system. Policies could be adopted to raise the proportion of children covered by support awards, increase award levels, and ensure that awards are paid. For the past decade, state and federal policies have been moving in these directions. The Family Support Act of 1988 contains a number of significant measures along these lines, but much more could be done. For example, the government could assure that all children living in single-parent families received a minimum level of child support even when low earnings, unemployment, or imprisonment left the noncustodial parent with insufficient resources to pay an adequate amount.[11]

The labor market for single mothers and young men with few skills could be improved through a range of policies. JTPA and Job Corps training programs could be expanded and better targeted. The unemployment compensation system, which provided benefits to fewer than one-third of the unemployed in 1987 (versus one-half during the 1974 to 1980 period), could be liberalized. The minimum wage, which has been frozen at $3.35 per hour since January 1981, could be raised and the Earned Income Tax Credit (EITC) could be increased and varied by family size. More radical options, such as Senator Paul Simon's (1987) proposal to establish a guaranteed jobs program, could be pursued.

Steps also could be taken to reduce the barriers that are thought to stand between many welfare recipients and the world of work. For example, day care could be expanded, either through an expansion of the Title XX grant program or through a restructuring of the dependent-care tax credit to make it refundable for those with no tax liability. Health insurance could be extended to workers who lacked coverage, either by allowing uncovered workers to buy into a scaled-down Medicaid program or by requiring employers to contribute to basic health insurance coverage for all of their workers.[12]

In theory, policies such as these should complement, not compete with, direct reforms of the welfare system. Policies that raise the living standard of the nondependent poor are essential because this living standard inevitably limits the improvements that can be made in the welfare system. Politically, it is difficult to devote significant resources to the dependent population when little is being done for the working poor, a group that is behaving according to society's norms. Except on a temporary basis, the welfare population cannot be offered a set of benefits and opportunities that support a standard of living that exceeds that of the working poor. Moreover, if the low-income population at large is not significantly better off than the population on welfare, one cannot expect welfare recipients to strive for self-sufficiency. Unfortunately, the complementary approach rarely is followed because both budgetary and leadership resources are scarce.

A broad strategy of reform that does not focus on the narrow welfare programs has obvious advantages. One strength of this approach is that it is less likely to engender a public backlash because it does not appear to concentrate resources on the dependent population. Because a broader group benefits from the nonwelfare approach, a political constituency can be developed to support such policies. Efforts to reform the welfare system directly have never been able to marshall much voter support.

Even those who would be affected by reform only in their tax bills would be more sympathetic to the wider approach because it reinforces mainstream values and behavior and appears to be directed at a broad group that is viewed as more deserving than the narrow welfare population. Although nonwelfare strategies tend to be expensive because they must serve a larger clientele, much of the cost can be shifted out of the public budget and onto employers, consumers, and noncustodial parents. The weakness of these policies is that they have an uncertain and less immediate impact on the dependent population than do direct changes in the means-tested programs.

For the most part, the 1986–1988 welfare reform effort did not put a significant emphasis on nonwelfare approaches. Numerous nonwelfare policies that could have affected the dependent population came before the 100th Congress, but they were not adopted and were never considered as integral parts of welfare reform. Among these were proposals to raise the minimum wage, to expand child-care programs, to vary the EITC by family size, and to augment JTPA education and training efforts. While the Family Support Act of 1988 did expand child care, health insurance, and education and training services, eligibility for these enriched services was restricted to welfare recipients rather than to the broader, low-income population. The one exception to this pattern was the area of child support where stronger policies affecting all Americans became an integral component of welfare reform.[13]

As the various provisions of the Family Support Act are phased in over the 1989 to 1994 period, the focus of reformers' efforts may shift to nonwelfare approaches. However, at some point their concerns will gravitate back to the welfare programs where future reform efforts are likely to be bedeviled by the same major unresolved areas of policy dispute that defined the 1986–1988 debate. The first of these was the question of whether anything should be done to raise benefits and make welfare more uniformly available across the various states. A second involved the controversy over whether the new work orientation should be framed as an opportunity that is available to recipients or as an obligation that recipients must fulfill. A final area of dispute was the degree of latitude that states should be given to devise alternative welfare programs.

Benefits

A major dispute during the 1986–1988 debate centered on whether benefits should be improved. The liberals, concerned with the erosion of real benefit levels and the persistence of huge interstate differences in benefits, have long regarded some benefit enhancement as the litmus test of real reform. In addition, liberals and moderates have considered it essential that all states be required to provide coverage for intact families through the AFDC-U program. Conservatives have argued that a welfare reform promoting work and self-sufficiency should not lead to an increase in dependency. Higher benefits, they point out, will increase the caseload and make it more difficult for those receiving welfare to find a job that improves their financial situation. In addition, benefit increases tend to be very expensive, absorbing resources that might be spent more productively on efforts to enhance the employability of recipients.

This debate is primarily one of values; data can be marshaled to support or undercut both positions. Advocates of increases point out that welfare benefits have declined in real value and are well below the poverty threshold, the level that society has established as its minimal acceptable living standard. In 1986, the median state's AFDC and Food Stamp benefit for a family of four was 65 percent of the poverty level. Only six states provided benefits that exceeded 80 percent of the poverty threshold, while nine offered benefits that fell below 55 percent of this level.

Opponents of benefit increases point out that the case for them may be less compelling than suggested by the data indicating real declines, because many, but far from all, welfare recipients have benefited from recent expansions in other means-tested programs such as low-income housing, WIC, school lunches and low-income energy assistance. For example, the fraction of AFDC cases that receive some form of housing subsidy has risen from about 14 percent in 1973 to 21 percent in 1986. In addition, it is clear that welfare recipients have not suffered alone in recent years: other relevant groups of Americans have also experienced substantial deterioration in their living standards (see Table 1.4). For example, the real median earnings of a group that is most comparable to welfare mothers—young working women who have not completed high school—fell significantly between 1973 and the early 1980s. The standard of living of these low-skilled workers has perhaps deteriorated by as much as that of the welfare recipients if one considers the increased payroll and income taxes these women have to pay. Those holding minimum-wage jobs and even those earning the average private-sector hourly wage found their real incomes falling over this period.

The Family Support Act of 1988 did virtually nothing to improve ben-

Table 1.4. Indices of real AFDC benefits, earnings, hourly wages, and unemployment compensation, 1973–1986 (1973 = 100)

	1973	1977	1981	1983	1985	1986
AFDC[a]	100	100	85	80	82	83
Minimum wage[b]	100	107	109	100	93	91
Earnings[c]	100	95	88	90	106	98
Hourly wage[d]	100	97	99	92	94	94
Unemployment compensation[e]	100	100	95	100	96	100

a. Maximum benefit for a family of four from Table 2.1.

b. Minimum wage deflated by the implicit price deflator for personal consumption expenditures (PCE).

c. Real median earnings of women aged 25–34 with 1 to 3 years of high school who worked full-time, full-year. Deflated by the PCE deflator. From U.S. Bureau of the Census, *Current Population Reports*, P-60, and unpublished numbers. Because earnings data were not tabulated in 1973, the base figure was estimated by multiplying the total income of such women by .952, which was the ratio of earnings to total income for such women over the period 1975–1978.

d. Average hourly earnings of all private nonagricultural workers adjusted for overtime in manufacturing and interindustry employment shifts. Deflated by the CPI. From *The Economic Report of the President,* January 1987, table B-41.

e. Average weekly unemployment benefit deflated by the PCE deflator. From U.S. Department of Labor, *Unemployment Insurance Statistics,* monthly, and *Annual Report of the Secretary of Labor.*

efits.[14] Therefore this issue remains very much alive among many of those who are concerned with welfare policy. But should a new opportunity to reform the welfare system develop, advocates will find it difficult to raise benefits in an efficient manner. This is because the states, not the federal government, are responsible for setting benefit levels and, under the current system, must pay a portion of the costs associated with any benefit increase.[15] There is no simple mechanism through which the federal government can ensure that federal resources intended for benefit increase actually end up raising benefit levels. One possible approach would be to increase the federal matching rate for the costs associated with future state benefit increases.[16] However, it is inevitable that a large portion of the added federal costs associated with such an inducement would reimburse states for the costs of benefit increases that they would have granted in the absence of enhanced matching rates.[17]

Of course, the federal government could attempt to raise the standards of living of welfare recipients directly by increasing Food Stamp benefits, over which it has complete control. However, even this approach raises several difficulties. First, states could respond by slowing the pace at which they raise AFDC benefits, thus offsetting the federal action. There is evidence that states responded this way in the 1970s, when the Food Stamp and Medicaid programs were expanded (Moffitt, 1987). Second, Food Stamp increases are much more expensive than equivalent AFDC increases because there are far more Food Stamp recipients and many more persons are made eligible by an equal dollar increase in benefit levels. Furthermore, a greater fraction of the additional benefits would go to households with relatively higher incomes.

In addition to benefit increases, liberals and conservatives have been divided over whether states should be required to provide AFDC coverage to two-parent families with an unemployed breadwinner. Liberals argue that such a mandate is a matter of basic equity; poor children in two-parent families should not have to suffer more than those in single-parent families. They also believe that such a mandate would represent sensible family policy; after all, family dissolution should not be a prerequisite for receiving welfare. Although researchers have found little or no evidence to support the proposition, many liberals participating in the policy debate argue that a universal and more generous AFDC-U program will increase marriage rates and decrease divorce, separation, and out-of-wedlock birth rates.[18]

Conservatives, while clearly troubled by these pro-family arguments, contend that states should retain the flexibility to decide whether or not to offer AFDC-U coverage. They also point out that, contrary to the liberals' assertion, marital instability could increase if the AFDC-U program were expanded. Evidence supporting this position came from the evaluations of the Seattle-Denver income maintenance experiments of the 1970s. Although recent reevaluation of this evidence has found no strong effects on marriage, other research suggests that the impact of AFDC-U on families is still an open question.[19]

The Family Support Act of 1988 settled on an uneasy compromise with respect to AFCD-U. All states will be required to establish AFDC-U programs by FY1991. But the issue will be revisited because this requirement will terminate, unless it is extended, after eight years. Those states that did not offer AFDC-U when the Act was passed will be allowed to limit the duration of the AFDC-U benefits they provide to eligible families to as little as six months in any twelve-month period; the remaining 27 states and the District of Columbia will be required to offer eligible families benefits for the full year.[20] The extension of AFDC-U, while symbolically very important, will not have a major impact on the shape of the nation's welfare system. This is because jurisdictions containing about 62 percent of the nation's total population, 58 percent of its poor population, and 73 percent of its basic AFDC caseload already offer this program. For the most part, the states that will be required to establish an AFDC-U program are ones with low benefit levels and stringent eligibility rules, so that relatively few people will be affected by this benefit expansion.

Notably absent from the legislation considered by the 100th Congress was any effort to reduce the interstate variation in benefit levels. This should not be taken as a sign that this perennial inequity of the American welfare system has been reduced in recent years. By various measures (see Table 1.5) interstate discrepancies seem to be as great today as they were in the past. The variance of AFDC benefits across states was as large in the mid-1980s as it was a decade earlier. While the spread of the Food Stamp program reduced the disparity in the combined AFDC/Food Stamp benefits a bit in the early 1970s, it has changed little since the mid-1970s.

Liberals have long supported policies to even out welfare benefits. Why, they have argued, should a child born to an impoverished unwed mother in Alabama have an AFDC benefit that is one-fifth that of a similar

Table 1.5. Measures of interstate variation in welfare benefits, 1970–1986

	1970	1975	1980	1985	1986
Variance					
AFDC (3 persons)	n.a.	33	34	34	n.a.
AFDC (4 persons)	36	34	36	33	n.a.
AFDC/Food Stamps (3 persons)	n.a.	19	19	18	n.a.
AFDC/Food Stamps (4 persons)	21	19	19	17	n.a.
Range (AFDC 4 persons)					
High state	330 (CT)	453 (MI)	563 (CA/NY)	676 (NY)	706 (NY)
Low state	70 (MS)	60 (MS)	120 (MS)	120 (MS)	144 (MS)

Source: Peterson and Rom (1987).

child living in Wisconsin? Besides this obvious inequity, those who want to reduce interstate payment differences argue that benefit disparities foster inefficient interstate migration and that the fear of such migration and other competitive factors cause the states to set their benefits at suboptimal levels.[21]

Conservatives have tended to accept the current benefit diversity, arguing that true federalism requires that states retain the authority to set welfare levels. Such freedom is important in a diverse nation in which wages, labor market conditions, the cost of living, values, political cultures, and incomes differ greatly.[22]

Because benefit levels are set by the states, there is little the federal government can do to standardize them short of federalizing all or some portion of the program. While the federal matching rate could be increased for all the states, this may not reduce disparities if states with high benefits are more responsive to such inducements than states with low benefit levels. Because existing benefits appear to reflect differences in state preferences rather than differences in their ability to pay for welfare, it would be difficult to limit enhanced matching rates to states with the lowest benefits.[23] Moreover, many of the states that have the lowest benefit levels already enjoy the highest federal matching rates; Mississippi, the state with the lowest payment level for a family of four, has the highest federal matching rate (78.42 percent).

Liberals have long advocated a minimum federal benefit level. However, this type of reform has had little political appeal for two reasons. A national minimum that was set at a moderate level would impose significant added costs either on the affected states or on the federal government; if it was set at a low level, however, few states would be affected and many of them would be opposed to the change.[24]

Work as an Opportunity or an Obligation?

A second major area of disagreement in the welfare reform debate was the controversy over work. All agreed that work has intrinsic value; that it can help welfare recipients develop a sense of self-respect, self-confidence, and identity in our work-oriented society. There was also a consensus that more should be done to try to make welfare recipients more self-sufficient. The dispute centered on how to do this—how much emphasis to place on carrots and how much on sticks.

The JOBS (Job Opportunities and Basic Skills Training Program) portion of the Family Support Act provided an apparent resolution of this dispute. But the compromise that was reached is unlikely to be very durable. When states implement their JOBS programs over the next few years, they will face very different budget, administrative, and political constraints. As a result, some will emphasize a conservative approach, others will go off on a more liberal tack. These differences will rekindle the debate over the efficacy and appropriateness of the two approaches when Congress, as it inevitably will, attempts to fine tune the work portions of the 1988 welfare reform legislation.

At its roots, the disagreement concerning work derives from different perceptions concerning why welfare recipients are not doing more to find employment and help themselves. Liberals tend to stress the failings of society or "the system": the suitable jobs are too few, the pay and working conditions of available jobs are inadequate; the recipients lack the education needed for a decent job; day-care and transportation difficulties preclude employment; and the available jobs do not provide adequate health insurance. Conservatives tend to stress the behavioral deficiencies of the individual. They argue that the values of many recipients are dysfunctional and that people won't work or get the necessary training and education unless there is a clear expectation for them to do so.

This dispute manifested itself in several hard-fought battles over the specific design of the work component of the Family Support Act. The major issues in contention involved the questions of who should be expected to participate in the welfare-employment programs, what activities participants should be offered, what support services should be made available to participants, what jobs participants should be required to accept, and what level of participation should the states be required to maintain.[25]

In general, the liberal position has been that welfare-employment programs should first serve those who volunteer and, to the extent there is still capacity, participation should be required only of those who have no preschool (under six) children and no problem that would make participation a burden. The activities offered participants should include a full range of services such as job counseling, assessments of employment readiness, job search assistance, basic skills training, English as a second language (ESL), remedial education, advanced education, skills training, job readiness training, on-the-job training, work supplementation, and short-term community work experience (CWEP). The participant, with the assistance of a case manager, should be free to choose the course action that she feels would be most likely to lead to greater self-sufficiency.

The liberal agenda calls for a full range of support services. For example, participants should be guaranteed adequate day care, reimbursement for transportation and work-related expenses, and suffer no loss of health insurance (Medicaid) coverage. At the same time, the jobs and training positions filled by recipients should not lead to the displacement, direct or indirect, of other workers. Participants should not be expected to take jobs that pay below the minimum wage or jobs that pay below normal pay scales. Nor should they be forced to take jobs that leave them worse off than they were when they were dependent on welfare; this comparison should include the value of Medicaid. Participation requirements should take a back seat to providing meaningful training of the sort that will lead to the long-term self-sufficiency of the participants. Since these activities are expensive, their implementation may mean serving a relatively small portion of the caseload.

Conservatives believe that the most important consequence of reform should be to communicate clearly to welfare recipients that society expects them to get into the mainstream workforce. Once there, they will develop the self-discipline and motivation that will lead to self-sufficiency. As many recipients as possible, even those with very young children, should be required to participate in some constructive activity, at least part-time. Early participation is essential both because it makes society's expectations clear and because it will reduce the possibility that those with young children will become entrapped by a dependent mindset during the period before they are required to participate. Such work requirements are also only fair considering that a majority of mothers with very young children now participate in the labor force.[26]

Recipients should be required to participate in activities that lead quickly to job placement. While long-term education and training activities may seem attractive, the majority of welfare recipients have not been successful in classroom situations and subjecting them to the learning environment again is not likely produce significant results. What they need is a bit of doing, including unlimited CWEP for those who cannot find private-sector jobs. The appropriate course of activities should be determined by an experienced case manager who knows the individual's potential and the conditions of the local labor market.

Conservatives agree that support services are a vital component of any program that hopes to get welfare recipients into the labor force.

However, they are not as prescriptive as the liberals. For example, they would provide working welfare mothers with help to meet whatever day-care arrangements the mother chose, not just those that were licensed or met certain standards of adequacy. After all, public authorities should not dictate to the poor when middle-class mothers have the discretion to make such decisions for themselves. Conservatives worry less than liberals do about the pay, working conditions, and benefits of the jobs that recipients should be required to accept. They point out that a large number of Americans are employed in low-wage jobs that have poor working conditions and offer no fringe benefits; it would be unrealistic to expect many welfare recipients to do better considering their lack of education, work experience, and skills. While displacement of low-paid workers should be avoided, it is impossible to ensure that this condition is met. Participation requirements should be set quite high. If only a few are required to participate, they will soon be labeled the "chumps," the culture will remain one of avoidance, and expectations and attitudes among recipients will not change. Low participation requirements will also tempt some states to establish minimal programs so as to save money.

The debate over work initiatives involves not only values and perceptions of the dependent population, but also matters of costs, administrative feasibility, and efficacy. If done thoroughly, the liberal approach could be quite expensive. Day-care services can cost $3,000 per child per year; a comprehensive course of training might cost another $4,000; transportation and work-related expenses might add $1,000; and case management could add $300.[27] The liberal program could also be quite difficult to implement. It requires coordination among many agencies that have not cooperated constructively in the past. The task of guiding welfare recipients through education, training, and jobs programs, and providing them with the appropriate support services, is a very complex one, far more difficult than the current task of determining eligibility and writing checks. Such enlightened case management would require the retraining and expansion of the existing staffs of most welfare agencies, and complex, computerized client tracking systems that do not now exist. Moreover, there is no definitive evidence that such an approach will work and be cost-effective.[28]

While the conservative approach would clearly be cheaper and more manageable, it is not likely to have a dramatic impact on the shape of the welfare system. Research evidence suggests that low-budget work programs of the sort that have been established in many states since 1981 are cost-effective and generate increases in the employment and earnings of participants and reductions in welfare expenditures, but the magnitudes of these impacts are quite modest.[29] Even the most effective of the low-cost welfare employment programs appear to have little impact on certain types of recipients; for example, on those who were the most and least self-sufficient in the past and on AFDC-U cases (Friedlander and Long, 1987). In addition, the evidence from the demonstrations indicates that welfare employment programs may not be able to raise earnings or employment in chronically weak labor markets or when the national economy is in recession (Friedlander et al., 1986). Moreover, the evidence suggests that programs that offer few services and rely heavily on sanctions to ensure high participation rates will not only fail to increase participants' earnings and employment but also may leave them financially worse off (Friedlander et al., 1987).

The work-related portions of the Family Support Act represent a somewhat uneasy mix of liberal and conservative approaches. The participation requirements and sanctions follow a fairly conservative path, while the service provisions go in a more liberal direction. An AFDC recipient whose youngest child is three or older and who is not otherwise exempted is required to participate in the state's JOBS program.[30] These programs must offer a wide range of activities that includes education, job skills training, job readiness activities, job development and placement, and two of four work activities (job search, on-the-job training, work supplementation, and CWEP). One adult member of each AFDC-U family is required to participate in sixteen hours of work activity a week.

Once they are fully phased in (FY1995 for AFDC and FY1997 for AFDC-U), the caseload participation requirements will be fairly stringent. An average of one-fifth of eligible AFDC recipients and three-quarters of eligible AFDC-U families must participate each month or the federal government will reduce its cost sharing for the JOBS program. Federal matching funds will also be reduced if states do not concentrate their expenditures on long-term recipients, young mothers with limited education and work experience, and certain other target groups.

Benefits will be reduced for recipients who refuse to participate in JOBS as well as those who refuse to accept a reasonable employment opportunity. However, recipients cannot be required to accept a job that would reduce their net cash (not in-kind) income, nor one that requires unreasonable travel, and physical or other burdens. For the first nine months of any CWEP assignment, the wage rate need not exceed the applicable minimum wage.

States are required to conduct an initial assessment of each participant's education and employment skills and use this information, along with consultations with the client, to develop an employability plan. While individual contracts that lay out the client's obligations and the state's responsibilities are permitted, they are not required. Neither is case management.

The Family Support Act mandates a fairly liberal array of support services and transitional benefits. States are required to offer child care to JOBS participants. However, they can choose virtually any arrangement, ranging from giving cash to the mother to establishing agency-run centers, to fulfill this obligation. States are also required to reimburse JOBS participants for the cost of transportation and other work-related supportive services. Families that cease to be eligible for welfare benefits because their earnings have increased are eligible for child-care assistance and Medicaid coverage for a twelve-month period. States are required to charge an income-related fee for the former and are permitted to do so for the latter during the second six months.

State Flexibility in Welfare Policy

Policy makers have long disagreed about the degree of latitude that states should be permitted when they devise new approaches to welfare. Traditionally, states have been able to make minor modification in the design of their welfare programs only if granted a specific waiver by federal authorities under Section 1115 of the Social Security Act. Until recently, these waivers were granted very sparingly and only for incremental changes and short-term demonstrations. However, in 1987 and 1988 several states as well as the Reagan administration wanted to initiate experiments of a more radical nature. Through both the Section 1115 provision and special legislative authority, states such as California, New Jersey, New York, Washington, Ohio, and Wisconsin were given permission to modify existing federal policy in fairly fundamental ways.

The questions of how much experimentation to permit and under what conditions thus became major issues of contention during the 1986–1988 welfare reform debate. But in the end, these questions were left unresolved when the Conference Committee decided to drop the language dealing with state experimentation from the Family Support Act.[31] This, together with the impact of the current state experiments, will ensure that these questions will be part of the next welfare reform debate. It is, therefore, worth reviewing the arguments on both sides.

Conservatives have generally supported more unconstrained state flexibility as long as such experimentation does not lead to increased federal spending or much larger welfare caseloads. Liberals have favored experimentation only under certain limited conditions. They want assurances that the new approaches do not reduce the benefits available to current or potential recipients. Unlike conservatives, they do not object to experimentation that increases caseload or federal welfare costs.[32]

Four arguments have been used to support the case for increased state experimentation. First, it is clear that the current system is not a smashing success and that experts cannot offer a guaranteed, tested alternative that would work better. State experimentation is one way to learn about policies that might be more effective than current ones. The limited demonstrations of the sort mounted in the past are useful, but they have not led to breakthroughs; fundamentally different approaches may be required. Such approaches may involve major changes in attitudes, expectations, and agency behavior that can only be accomplished through large-scale experiments run on a state-wide basis.

A second argument that has been used for years to support the position that states should have considerable latitude to design their own welfare programs invokes the great diversity that characterizes the nation. The average recipient in Oregon is quite different from the average recipient in Mississippi with respect to age, education, number of children, prior work experience, and race (U.S. Department of Health and Human Services, 1986). The labor market conditions in Connecticut contrast sharply with those of West Virginia. Even within a single state, sharp differences exist; unskilled year-around jobs are more available in Boston than they are in rural western Massachusetts. The values and political culture of New York differ significantly from those of Indiana. The capabilities of states' welfare bureaucracies also vary greatly. Considering all these differences, it may not make much sense to impose the same programmatic design everywhere. The most effective and appropriate approaches may be ones that adapt at least partially to the conditions prevalent in different regions of the country.

Federalism is the third perennial argument used to buttress the case for greater state flexibility. If the United States is a true federal republic, states should have the authority to design the programs that they operate, especially when they are required to pay a large portion of the programs' costs from their own tax revenues. Currently, many states are little more than subcontractors operating programs that are designed and specified down to the most minute detail by legislators and bureaucrats in Washington, who are far from the front lines and often insensitive to problems of implementation.

The experience of the last few years is the final argument used to support the case for greater state flexibility. When the Reagan administration withdrew the federal government from its traditional role of initiator of innovation and change in welfare policy, states moved in. At first, state activity was limited to the modest welfare-employment initiatives authorized by OBRA. As state confidence and capacity grew, more major reforms have developed. In the work area, Governor Dukakis of Massachusetts and Governor Deukmejian of California have mounted comprehensive programs. Wisconsin adopted a major child-support initiative. The states of New Jersey and Washington have formulated comprehensive alternative approaches to the existing welfare programs. All this ferment and activity suggest that the states now have the creativity, capacity, and will to be given greater freedom to set their own welfare policies.

Many, primarily among the liberals, are leery of any great increase in the latitude states have over welfare policy. They fear that a change of this sort may be a veiled attempt to shred an already tattered safety net. In part, this opposition comes from the Reagan administration's enthusiastic support for giving states almost unlimited freedom to experiment; the administration was not trusted by advocates of the poor because it had repeatedly tried to cut back federal welfare programs and to transfer the responsibility for them to the states.

The opponents fear that increases in the ability of states to design their own programs will mark the end of the entitlement nature of welfare programs and the gradual reduction in federal spending for programs that help the poor. The more radical plans would have the federal government provide a block grant to those states opting to design their own welfare systems. The size of the grant would be equal to projected costs under the old program structure. Some persons who would have received benefits under the old program structure could be denied aid under the new state plan, and client rights might not be protected. Benefit disparities across states could increase. As time went on and economic and social conditions changed, the federal block grant could diverge significantly from the federal expenditures that would have taken place under the old program structure. If this occurred, the state's new programs could result in either a serious reduction in benefits for the poor or a higher burden on state taxpayers.

Liberals also oppose expanded state flexibility because of the past behavior of some states. Faced with budget difficulties, some states might use their greater discretion over welfare policy to cut these politically weak programs disproportionately or to serve as a rationale for inaction. While a number of states initiated thoughtful reforms during the 1981–1988 period, most did little to enhance the self-sufficiency of their recipients. Overall, fewer than 7 percent of recipients participated in a job search or CWEP program in 1987 (U.S. House of Representatives, The Committee on Ways and Means, 1988).

A future compromise in this area of dispute is possible, because some of the opposition to granting states more authority related to a basic mistrust of the Reagan administration's motives. As his presidency recedes into history, a consensus could develop around granting states broadened authority for fundamental state experiments, which preserve the entitlement nature of current antipoverty programs. The catch, of course, is that such a policy, invariably, would cost additional money.

The liberals' fear that some states might use such authority to cut back antipoverty efforts may prove exaggerated. Almost all of the innovative activity to date has been undertaken by states that seem willing to devote more, not less, resources to the poor. A state that sought to use its authority to cut back programs sharply would probably face a firestorm of controversy at the federal, if not the state, level. State politicians would find this to be politically damaging. Furthermore, by controlling benefit levels, states already possess the most effective means of cutting back their welfare programs.

Future welfare reform efforts will have to grapple with the issues that dominated the debate of 1986–1988, namely with the adequacy of benefits, the emphasis of the work programs, and the degree of policy discretion to leave with the states. Several other equally contentious issues could emerge. One of these might be the extent to which AFDC benefits should be used to supplement earnings. This issue could rise to the fore if significant numbers of JOBS participants are only able to secure jobs which provide marginal incomes. Another potentially divisive issue that could emerge involves the degree to which eligibility for Medicaid, child care, and other support services should be restricted to those on or working their way off of AFDC. Inevitably, pressure will mount to extend the transition period during which JOBS participants can utilize these services. But this will only serve to underline the fact that many non-dependent working poor lack comparable benefits.

Constraints Confronting Future Efforts to Reform Welfare

Enactment of the Family Support Act of 1988 is likely to put the issue of welfare reform on the back burner for several years. However, the intractable nature of the poverty problem as well as the inevitable need to modify this legislation to take account of experience and new knowledge will force policy makers to deal with these issues sometime in the near future. When this happens, the executive branch will find itself seriously constrained by the budget deficit and by a number of lesser obstacles. Among these are the diminished capacity of the executive branch to formulate welfare proposals, the balkanization of authority over welfare on Capitol Hill, and the difficulties inherent in integrating welfare policy with policies designed to help the poor overall.

The Budget Deficit

Significant welfare reform costs money. Despite the wishes of many in Congress and the Executive, the existing welfare system cannot be much improved without spending a good deal more, at least in the short run. This conclusion holds whether one's view of an improved system entails more adequate benefits and enhanced support services, increased work activity, or education and training for recipients.[33] Research evidence suggests, but does not assure, that spending on investment-oriented welfare reform policies might result in lower welfare expenditures in the long run.

Because of the budget deficit, political leaders responsible for the 1988 welfare reform effort had to practice modern alchemy; they mixed together a number of low-cost initiatives and proclaimed that they would achieve a grand objective. The limited nature of the 1988 legislation is best illustrated by the CBO's estimate that it will add only $3.3 billion to federal welfare spending over the FY1989–93 period. This amounts to only a tiny fraction of normal spending growth that is projected to occur in the AFDC, Food Stamp, and Medicaid programs.

Deficit considerations affected the shape, substance, and timing of the 1988 legislation. Early efforts to establish a national minimum AFDC benefit and an EITC that varied by family size were dropped because of their costs. Consideration of welfare was delayed numerous times because legislators were reluctant to take up a spending initiative when retrenchment was the order of the day. Moreover, the legislators with primary responsibility for welfare reform, members of the Ways and Means and Finance committees, faced congested calendars and conflicting responsibilities insofar as they also played major roles in the effort to reduce the deficit.

Future efforts to reform the welfare system will face the same budget-related constraints that affected the 1988 legislation. For at least the next five years, the major issue before the nation will be deficit reduction. Under the Gramm-Rudman-Hollings restrictions, tax increases and spending cuts amounting to at least $121 billion will have to be approved by FY1993. Mounting a significant welfare reform initiative when other domestic and military spending is being curtailed and taxes are being raised will be a politically difficult task, and the hardship of tackling it will tempt any president to pursue welfare reform more through rhetoric than through substance.

Rebuilding the Executive Branch's Policy Capacity

At a far less decisive level, a new administration that decides to mount a welfare reform effort will be hampered by the diminished capacity of the executive branch. From the days of OEO through 1981, the executive branch of the federal government was the unquestioned center of policy expertise on welfare issues. HHS, DOL, HUD and DOA all had large staffs of policy analysts working on welfare reform. These agencies funded a substantial amount of related academic and private-sector research through grants and contracts.

When the Reagan administration decided to scale back the federal antipoverty effort and shift it to the states, much of this capacity was cut back or allowed to wither away. Today, most of these experts are scattered across numerous universities, "think tanks," consulting companies, and congressional agencies. An administration that wants to mount a significant welfare reform initiative will need to rebuild the executive branch's policy capacity so that it can compete with these external centers of expertise.

The Balkanization of Authority on Capitol Hill

Strong presidential leadership is an important ingredient to successful welfare reform. When the president does not take the lead, the issue can lose its focus and coherence on Capitol Hill because authority over welfare issues is fragmented in Congress among a number of subcommittees.[34] Each is led by an individual with a slightly different perspective and clientele. Each chairman is, understandably, a jealous guardian of his subcommittee's jurisdiction and anxious to put his own distinctive stamp on any piece of welfare reform legislation.

Coordination is difficult and is hampered by interstaff rivalries and lack of communication. In general, much effort goes into avoiding confrontation. Sometimes this has meant drafting an admittedly incomplete or limited proposal. For example, the waiver authority contained in S. 1511 was restricted to programs under the jurisdiction of the Senate Finance Committee to avoid the possible delay and controversy associated with joint referral. At other times, skirting unresolved rivalries may mean including conflicting provisions in a single bill.

If a new administration wants to embark on a meaningful reform of the welfare system, it will have to reassert a greater degree of executive-branch control over this policy area. In the Senate, where there has been a tendency to follow the lead of Senator Moynihan, one of the nation's leading thinkers on welfare issues, this may be only a moderately complex task. In the House, where strong competing centers of authority exist, exerting strong executive leadership will be more difficult.

Meshing Welfare Policy with Mainstream American Life

A new administration that is interested in welfare reform will need to integrate welfare policies with those directed at the nondependent population. As long as welfare policies did not emphasize education, training, and employment, they were separated from the primary activities of mainstream America. This is no longer the case now that the Family Support Act has shifted the focus to enhancing recipient self-sufficiency, jobs, training, and educational opportunities. To avoid a political backlash, care will have to be taken to integrate new welfare policies with those available for the working poor. Welfare mothers cannot be provided better day-care benefits, richer education and training opportunities, jobs with higher pay, or more adequate medical coverage than those that are available to citizens who have struggled at marginal jobs to support their families. Programs aimed at improving the lot of nondependent low-income Americans will have to be an integral part of the next welfare reform effort.

Conclusion

Two major decisions will come up at the next round of welfare reform. The first will be the choice between elevating antipoverty policy to the level of a major initiative or continuing the incremental, low-profile approach that characterized the decade and a half that preceded enactment of the Family Support Act of 1988. The second decision will be whether to pursue the objective directly through changes in the means-tested programs or to follow an indirect approach that involves modifying nonwelfare policies that affect the welfare population.

Two arguments can be made to support the position that welfare reform should be made into a major initiative. First, the problems of poverty and dependence are sufficiently entrenched that they are not likely to be affected significantly by further modest or incremental policy changes. This is particularly true in the depressed, inner-city ghetto neighborhoods. Without the high level of attention that comes with a major initiative, political and budgetary constraints are likely to permit only marginally effective responses.

The second line of argument is made up of the several factors that suggest that the late 1980s and early 1990s represent a propitious time to mount a major assault on poverty and dependency. First, more than at any time in the recent past, the nation appears to be concerned with the plight of the disadvantaged. The media have reflected this public interest by highlighting the plight of the homeless, the emergence of an underclass, the growth of out-of-wedlock births, and the economic vulnerability of low-skilled Americans. It is possible that with strong presidential leadership, the public may be willing to support major initiatives directed at the disadvantaged.

Second, labor market conditions for entry level and low-skilled workers should improve over the next decade, making it a good time to stress employment-related programs. Over the past decade and a half, competition in these labor markets has been intense as the baby boom generation has flooded into the workforce, the labor force participation rate of women has increased rapidly, and the number of new immigrants has surged. However, over the next decade, the number of young persons entering the labor force will shrink, the rate at which female labor force participation rises will diminish, and the number of low-skilled immigrants entering the nation might decline as the effects of the 1986 Immigration Reform Act are felt.

A third hopeful factor is the recent evidence that drug usage may have peaked and may be declining among many groups. Another meliorative development is that state and local political leaders and business groups have turned their attention to improving the schools, particularly those that have served the disadvantaged population so poorly. Thus many of the ingredients needed to mount and sustain a major redirection of policy are available.

If the administration decides to launch a major assault on poverty and dependency, the current political and budget circumstances suggest that it would be best to place the primary emphasis on the indirect or non-welfare approach. For one thing, this approach could generate broad political support among people who have had a difficult time weathering the economic turbulence of the past fifteen years. Serious efforts to reduce the budget deficits through tax increases and spending cuts could slow the economy down and make a broad segment of the less educated and skilled population feel more vulnerable. Already there is widespread concern over such issues as job security, the erosion of real wages, insufficient health insurance coverage, the cost and quality of educational opportunities available to children, the prevalence of drugs, the lack of affordable child care, and the cost of housing.

A second advantage of placing primary emphasis on nonwelfare policies is that much of the costs of such an approach could be borne by the private sector, by state and local taxpayers, and by individuals. The problem posed by the federal budget deficit may thus be surmountable. For example, a comprehensive strategy might include an increase in the minimum wage, mandates on employers to provide some form of basic health insurance coverage for all their workers, an expansion of early childhood education in the public schools, and a significant strengthening of the child support system. None of these policies would require large increases in federal expenditures.[35]

The nonwelfare approach also promises to be less divisive because it would help low-income families that are not dependent on welfare as well as those that are, and because it would reinforce mainstream values.

An expansion of the Head Start program, an enhancement of the dependent-care tax credit, and a family-size adjustment in the EITC would provide substantial assistance to the low-income working population while increasing the incentive of welfare recipients to enter the workforce.

A major, overall initiative to reduce poverty and dependency should not preclude further modest and incremental reforms in welfare programs. In fact, changes in non-welfare programs could both enhance the effectiveness of the Family Support Act and make possible more adequate benefit levels. This could happen if the policies listed above increased the opportunities available to the low-skilled workers and improved their standards of living, thus providing welfare recipients with a greater incentive to seek the nondependent life.

Reducing both poverty and dependency will be a difficult task. From the 1950s through the mid-1970s the various administrations successfully reduced the incidence of poverty, but rates of dependency rose. Since the mid-1970s dependency rates have fallen in some programs, but the poverty rate has risen. There is a good possibility that the Family Support Act may cut dependency still further but do little to reduce poverty. Although bringing down the rates of both may not be easy, we know a great deal more about the dynamics of poverty, the consequences of dependency, and the effectiveness of government programs than we did a decade ago. If the new knowledge were combined with enlightened political leadership and a stable economy, there would be some reason to be optimistic about the nation's ability to meet its responsibilities toward the poor.

· T W O ·

Fighting Poverty and Reducing
Welfare Dependency

Sheldon Danziger

For many demographic groups, the outlook for reducing poverty in the late 1980s remains severe. Even if the current economic recovery continues until the end of the decade, poverty for all persons will decline only to the levels of the late 1970s. And poverty rates as officially measured for minority children, white children living in single-parent families, minority elderly persons, and elderly white widows all now exceed 20 percent. A national poverty rate of 20 percent led President Johnson to declare the War on Poverty, a broad range of social and labor market interventions that placed little emphasis on welfare.[1]

The current high poverty rates have not yet led to a renewed antipoverty effort. Today's active welfare reform debate in the academic and policy arenas has no antipoverty counterpart. Most welfare reforms currently before Congress or state legislatures will have small antipoverty effects. They should, if successful, reduce dependency and provide enhanced social and labor market services to welfare recipients; to that extent they represent an improvement over the status quo.

But if we are to reduce poverty significantly over the next decade, we must fight it directly, as well as seek to reduce welfare dependency.[2] Such an effort should focus on the diverse needs of all of the poor and should include reforms in these systems: taxation, child support, education, employment and training, and health insurance. In this context, welfare reform is but one of many antipoverty strategies. The other reforms outside of welfare will help many current welfare recipients, but they will also aid many poor and near-poor families who now receive little or no public assistance.

Reducing poverty, which was an important priority of the welfare reform proposals of the 1969–1979 decade, does not appear as a goal of most current proposals. This may reflect a major lesson learned from two decades of poverty research—that the poor are a diverse group and that no single program or policy can address all of their needs. I do not fault any specific welfare reform proposal, but the fact that welfare reform is not being packaged as one part of a comprehensive antipoverty strategy.

Most analysts and policy makers now avoid the simple statements that characterized the antipoverty policy debates of the late 1960s and early 1970s. Those debates typically viewed the poor either as victims of their own inadequacies, often mired in a culture of poverty, or as victims of societal deficiencies such as inadequate schooling, lack of labor market opportunities, and discrimination. Social critics today show an appreciation of the diversity of the poverty population—an awareness that the polar views of individual inadequacies and societal inequities each apply to only a small portion of the poverty population. The poverty problem of the elderly widow differs from that of the family whose head seeks full-time work but finds only sporadic employment; the poverty of the family head who works full time at low wages differs from that of the family head who receives welfare and either cannot find a job or does not find it profitable to seek work.

A consensus has emerged in the mid-1980s that only the elderly or others who are not expected to work, such as the disabled, should receive increased access to or higher welfare benefits; cash welfare should not be extended to the working poor. This represents a dramatic shift from the consensus of the 1970s that cash welfare benefits should be universally available (for example, in Nixon's FAP and Carter's PBI). Unfortunately, most current welfare reform proposals do not provide nonwelfare alternatives to address the needs of the working poor.[3] Rather, they seek to remove long-term welfare recipients from the welfare rolls and to replace their welfare benefits with earnings. Too few proposals seek to ensure that those earnings—or some combination of earnings and public benefits—are at least near the poverty line. If successful, these reforms will reduce welfare dependency but not poverty.

Welfare reform has remained an elusive goal of public policy for more than two decades, and it is unclear whether we can expect this situation to change. An optimist may argue that if the current incremental approach to reform is successful, it will be a necessary first step toward a renewed antipoverty effort—for it can begin to move the long-term, nonworking welfare dependents onto a ladder whose first rung contains the working poor, and which offers an eventual escape from poverty. By turning a welfare check into a paycheck—even if at first the amount of the check is unchanged—these programs would transform nonworking, poor welfare recipients into the working poor. Then, according to the optimistic scenario, welfare programs will be viewed more favorably by the public. And once employed, former recipients will benefit from the types of nonwelfare reform policies that are needed to reduce poverty in a meaningful way.

Most current welfare reform proposals target long-term welfare recipients; they offer no aid to the working poor or to the many short-term welfare recipients. Long-term welfare recipients do have the most difficult poverty problems, but they account for only about a fifth of all the officially poor and about half of all welfare recipients. This targeting strategy can effectively reach one of the poorest groups: black children. About three-quarters of poor black children receive welfare in a given year and about half of them are long-term welfare recipients.[4]

In addition to neglecting the diverse needs of many of the poor, an emphasis on welfare reform leads us to underestimate the potential for funding other antipoverty policies. For example, the Family Support Act of 1988 will spend only modest amounts to reform AFDC (see Chapter 1), reflecting concerns with reducing the deficit. In sharp contrast, the additional funds being directed to the working poor in the form of tax relief by the Tax Reform Act of 1986 are many times larger.[5] Because welfare is so unpopular, the funds available to reform it are likely to remain small, whereas many nonwelfare policies to aid the poor command broad public support. This is an additional reason for emphasizing comprehensive antipoverty policies.

The political problems of launching a major antipoverty effort are substantial. The budget deficit imposes considerable restraint on the scope of nonwelfare as well as welfare expenditures. Furthermore, the efficacy of antipoverty programs has been questioned. The following two statements from President Reagan are representative:

> With the coming of the Great Society, government began eating away at the underpinnings of the private enterprise system. The big taxers and big spenders in the Congress had started a binge that would slowly change the nature of our society and, even worse, it threatened the character of our people . . . By the time the full weight of Great Society programs was felt, economic progress for America's poor had come to a tragic halt.

(Remarks before the National Black Republican Council, September 15, 1982.)

In 1964, the famous War on Poverty was declared. And a funny thing happened. Poverty, as measured by dependency, stopped shrinking and then actually began to grow worse. I guess you could say, "poverty won the war." Poverty won, in part, because instead of helping the poor, government programs ruptured the bonds holding poor families together. (Radio address, February 15, 1986.)

These views are typical of a number of recent attacks (of which Murray, 1984, is the most famous) on the programs of the War on Poverty and the Great Society. They are misguided, for several reasons. First, they tend to treat welfare recipients in female-headed families as representative of the entire poverty population and as having received large and increasing amounts of public aid. Second, they ignore the major success of the War on Poverty and Great Society—namely, that most of the increased social spending was targeted on the elderly and yielded a dramatic decline in their poverty rate. Third, they neglect the poverty problems caused by economic stagnation since the early 1970s and the uneven distribution of the benefits of economic growth in the current recovery.

To document these points, I will review trends in family incomes and poverty, emphasizing the antipoverty effects of economic growth and government policies. I will then focus on poverty and income transfer recipiency among children, emphasizing the diversity of the poverty population and showing who is aided by welfare programs and who is not. Next I review the evidence on persistent poverty and welfare receipt and show that, because the poverty of black children is so persistent and their welfare receipt so pervasive, current reforms, however modest, would, if implemented and successful, aid them disproportionately. I conclude with a set of antipoverty reforms that would reduce poverty without increasing welfare dependency and could be financed without greatly increasing the deficit.

Trends in Family Incomes and Poverty

Recent trends in family incomes and poverty stand in sharp contrast with those of the 1950s and 1960s.[6] Median family income (column 1, Table 2.1) adjusted for inflation grew by about 40 percent between 1949 and

Table 2.1. Family incomes, poverty, and unemployment, selected years, 1949–1986

Year	Median family income (1985 $) (1)	Official poverty rate, all persons (2)	Unemployment rate (3)	Cash transfers per household (1985 $) (4)
1949	$14,021	34.3%[a]	5.9%	$ 832
1954	16,678	27.3[a]	5.5	1,059
1959	19,993	22.4	5.5	1,676
1964	22,783	19.0	5.2	2,060
1969	27,680	12.1	3.5	2,465
1974	28,145	11.2	5.6	3,249
1979	29,029	11.7	5.8	3,626
1985	27,735	14.0	7.2	3,693
1986	28,904	13.6	7.0	n.a.

Sources: U.S. Bureau of the Census, Current Population Reports, P-60, for first two columns; U.S. Council of Economic Advisers, *Economic Report of the President* for third column; Danziger and Gottschalk (1985) for fourth column.

a. Estimate based on unpublished tabulations from March CPS by Gordon Fisher, U.S. Department of Health and Human Services.

1959 and by about 40 percent between 1959 and 1969. Poverty as officially measured (column 2) dropped by about 10 percentage points during each decade. In fact, between 1949 and 1969, real year-to-year changes in the median (not shown) were positive 16 times, unchanged twice, and negative only once. The period since 1969, especially since 1974, is one of stagnation. Real median family income in 1985 was at about the same level as in 1969, and poverty was higher.[7] Since 1969, there have been eight positive year-to-year changes in the median, two years of no change, and six years of negative changes. And unemployment throughout the 1980s has been high by historical standards.

These macroeconomic conditions refuted two key expectations of the planners of the War on Poverty and Great Society. They thought that poverty could be alleviated against a background of healthy economic growth because the business cycle could be controlled. This was a reasonable assumption at the time, as median family income growth was positive for each year from 1958 to 1969. They also believed that economic growth taking place in an economy with low unemployment rates, and with antidiscrimination policies and education and training programs in operation, would at least be proportional, with all incomes rising at about the same rate. At best, income growth for the poor would exceed the average rate, further reducing poverty. Instead, since the early 1970s income inequality has increased. Incomes have grown less than average for the poorest families and more than average for the richest (see Danziger, 1986, and U.S. Congressional Budget Office, 1988).

This pattern emerged despite the increase in government income transfer payments (column 4 of Table 2.1 and Figure 2.1). Cash transfers per household doubled between 1949 and 1959 and then almost doubled again by 1974. But after 1974, almost all the growth in transfers was in social insurance (top graph in Figure 2.1) and not in public assistance (welfare) programs (bottom of Figure 2.1). In fact, most of the increased federal social spending over the past twenty years is accounted for by the expansion and indexation of social security benefits and the introduction and expansion of Medicare, Medicaid, and the SSI program, which provide disproportionate benefits to the elderly. Ellwood and Summers (1986) show that spending on welfare, housing, Food Stamps, and Med-

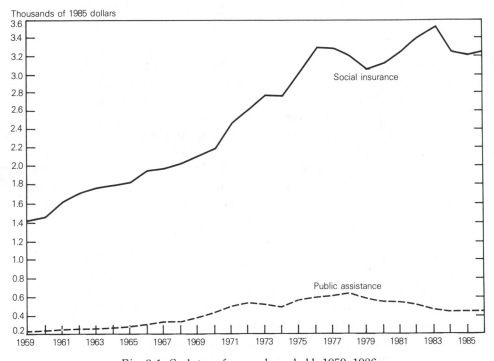

Fig. 2.1. Cash transfers per household, 1959–1986

icaid for those who are neither aged nor disabled made up only 11.9 percent of total social welfare expenditures in 1980, a figure dwarfed by the 66.0 share of spending on social security, Medicare, and other programs for the elderly. As a result, over the period from 1969 to 1985 poverty among the elderly diminished substantially, and they experienced increases in median family income that differ greatly from the trends shown in Table 2.1 for all persons and all families.

While spending on the elderly increased throughout the period, spending on children has declined in recent years. Welfare receipt among poor children increased rapidly after declaration of the War on Poverty. Less than 15 percent of poor children in 1960 received welfare benefits. This increased to about 20 percent in 1965, about 50 percent in 1969, peaked at over 80 percent in 1973, and fell to about 50 percent in the mid-1980s (U.S. House of Representatives, Committee on Ways and Means, 1985).

Since 1973, a smaller percentage of poor children have received welfare benefits because of economic and program changes. Economic changes increased the number of poor children, and program changes left fewer eligible to receive benefits. The first program change resulted from legislative inaction—states allowed benefits to be eroded by the high inflation rates of the 1970s. The second resulted from rule changes implemented in the early years of the Reagan Administration that made it difficult for people to receive welfare if they worked on a regular basis.

The story which emerges from this review is that the early period of declining poverty was due to strong economic growth, declining unemployment rates, and increased government spending. After the mid-1970s, rising unemployment and stagnating family incomes raised poverty by more than social spending, now growing at a much slower rate, could reduce it. Households that received little in the way of government transfers and were most affected by market conditions, particularly those with children, fared much worse than average (Danziger and Gottschalk, 1985), while elderly households that received large amounts of transfers and were mostly insulated from market conditions fared rather well (Smolensky, Danziger, and Gottschalk, 1988).

Family income growth for the poor was much slower in recent years than in the two decades following World War II because of poor macroeconomic performance, increased income inequality, and reduced government benefits. In addition, taxes on the poor increased steadily from the mid-1970s through 1986. The three devices in the personal income tax that protect the poor from taxation—the personal exemption, the zero bracket amount, and the earned-income tax credit—were all eroded by inflation over this period and were not affected by the 1981 tax cuts. In 1975 a family of four with earnings at the poverty line paid 1.3 percent of its income in federal personal income and payroll (employee share) taxes; by 1985 this had increased to 10.5 percent, an amount sufficient to offset the value of any Food Stamps the family might have received. The Tax Reform Act of 1986 has eliminated federal income taxes for most of the poor: for example, a family of four with earnings at the poverty line receives a tax credit equal to about 5 percent of its income. It pays 2.3 percent of its income in taxes after paying the employee share of the payroll tax. The Act thus offsets the increased tax burden of the past decade, but does nothing to further compensate the poor for the declines in earnings and government benefits of the same period.

The Impact of Welfare and Nonwelfare Transfers on Poor Children

A detailed examination of the poverty rates and welfare recipiency of families with children will be illuminating, both because their poverty rates are higher than those of most adults and because concern for their well-being has provided the impetus for current welfare reform efforts. Table 2.2 shows, for male-headed and female-headed families with children, the trends in poverty and the antipoverty impacts of major cash income transfer programs. The antipoverty impacts of cash social insurance (column 4) and public assistance (column 5) transfers are measured by the percentage of the pretransfer poor (column 1) these programs remove from poverty. The calculations are done sequentially, so that all social insurance benefits are first added to pretransfer incomes, yielding the prewelfare poverty rate in column 2. Then welfare transfers are added, yielding the official poverty rate in column 3 (see the Appendix for a discussion).[8]

Poverty rates are almost five times higher for persons in female-headed than in male-headed families. But the poverty trends are similar—declines occur from the late 1960s to the late 1970s and increases occur thereafter. As a result, the 1985 rate was very similar to the 1967 rate for each group.

Cash social insurance transfers removed a greater percentage of pre-transfer poor persons from poverty in all years than did cash public assis-

Table 2.2. Poverty rates and the antipoverty impact of cash transfers, for persons living in families with children, selected years, 1967–1985

Year	Pretransfer poverty rate (1)	Prewelfare poverty rate (2)	Official poverty rate (3)	% of pretransfer poor removed from poverty by:	
				Cash social insurance[a] (4)	Cash public assistance[b] (5)
Male-headed families					
1967	11.5%	10.3%	10.0%	10.4%	2.6%
1972	9.6	8.0	7.4	16.7	6.3
1977	10.2	7.9	7.2	22.6	6.9
1979	9.6	7.8	7.2	18.8	6.3
1982	14.5	11.8	11.3	18.6	3.5
1985	12.6	10.7	10.2	15.1	4.0
Female-headed families					
1967	58.8	52.4	49.1	10.9	5.6
1972	60.9	55.3	47.9	9.2	12.2
1977	57.2	51.4	45.3	10.1	10.7
1979	53.5	48.6	43.3	9.2	10.0
1982	58.5	54.2	51.3	7.4	5.0
1985	54.5	50.7	48.3	7.0	4.4

Source: Computations from March CPS computer tapes.

a. Cash social insurance transfers include Social Security, railroad retirement, unemployment compensation, workers' compensation, government employee pensions, and veterans' pensions and compensation. Figure defined as ((column 2 − column 1)/column 1) × 100.

b. Cash public assistance transfers include AFDC, SSI, and general assistance. Figure defined as ((column 3 − column 2)/column 1) × 100.

tance transfers, because a greater portion of the pretransfer poor received them and because the average social insurance benefit was higher. For these same reasons, their effects were larger in all years for male-headed than female-headed families with children.

The antipoverty effects of both types of transfers had increased between the late 1960s and late 1970s, but have declined over the last decade. Total benefits from cash transfers plus Food Stamps per poor child fell by about 12 percent between 1975 and 1983 (U.S. House of Representatives, Committee on Ways and Means, 1985). Column 5 of Table 2.2 shows that between 1972 and 1985 there was a particularly large decline in the antipoverty effect of cash public assistance for female-headed families with children. In 1972, 7.4 percent in this category were taken out of poverty (55.3–47.9 percent); in 1985 only 2.4 percent (50.7–48.3 percent) were affected. If the antipoverty effect of cash welfare assistance in 1985 had been at its 1972 level, then their official rate in 1985 would have been 44.0 percent instead of 48.3 percent. And if current welfare reform proposals could raise the antipoverty effect of welfare to 20 percent (which is likely to be an upper-bound estimate), the official poverty rate for this group would still be about 40 percent.

Figure 2.2 contrasts the antipoverty impacts of all cash transfers (the sum of columns 4 and 5 in Table 2.2) among families with children with those for the elderly. The effects for the elderly were much greater in every year and rose over the entire period. In any recent year almost all of the elderly poor received cash transfers, while about a third of the nonelderly poor received none; and per capita transfers to the elderly from social security were much larger than those to the nonelderly, particularly from welfare programs (Danziger and Weinberg, 1986).

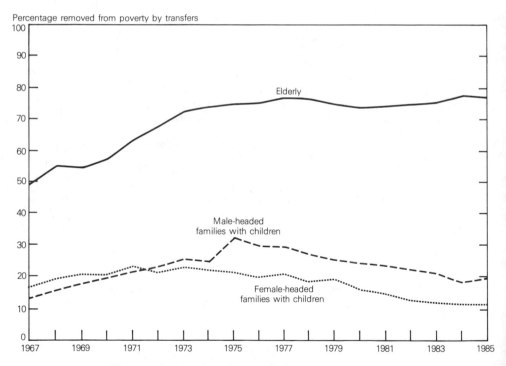

Fig. 2.2. Antipoverty effects of cash transfers, 1967–1985

How much of the recent increase in poverty can be attributed to the three factors discussed above—disappointing macroeconomic performance, declining income transfer benefits, and increasing federal taxation of the poor? Table 2.3, derived from data prepared for the U.S. House of Representatives, Committee on Ways and Means (1987), by the CBO, presents such a decomposition. Between 1979 and 1985, the earliest and latest years for which comparable data are available, poverty, measured after the receipt of all cash and in-kind transfers for food and housing and after the payment of federal income and payroll taxes, increased from 6.28 to 10.27 percent for married-couple families with related children, and from 30.1 to 39.6 percent for single-parent families with related children.

If one proceeds sequentially from market income to this income concept by adding social insurance income, then welfare income, and then subtracting taxes, one can apportion the total percentage-point change in poverty into the components shown.[9] Four points stand out. First,

Table 2.3. Sources of increase in poverty among non-aged persons living in families with related children, 1979–1985

	Married-couple families (1)	Families with unmarried head (2)
Poverty rate, after receipt of cash transfers, plus noncash transfers for food and housing, less federal income and payroll taxes		
1979	6.28%	30.1%
1985	10.27	39.6
Decomposition of percentage point change in poverty[a]		
Market income changes	70.43%	7.37%
Social insurance program changes	−1.25	8.42
Welfare program changes	4.01	74.74
Federal tax changes	26.82	9.47
Total change	100.00	100.00

Source: U.S. House of Representatives, Committee on Ways and Means (1987), pp. 641–645.

Note: A negative sign means that more persons were taken out of poverty by this source in 1985 than in 1979; a positive sign means that fewer persons were taken out of poverty by this source. For tax changes, a positive sign means that more persons were made poor by the payment of taxes in the later year than in the earlier year.

a. The poverty rate increased by 3.99 percentage points for married-couple families and 9.5 percentage points for families with an unmarried head.

changes in market incomes were the major factor for persons living in married-couple families, accounting for about 70 percent of the increase. Market-income changes accounted for only about 7 percent of the increase for single-parent families. Second, changes in the antipoverty effects of welfare programs had a relatively small impact on married-couple families, but accounted for almost 75 percent of the increased poverty among single-parent families. Third, changes in federal taxes accounted for about 10 percent of the poverty increase among single-parent families, but for over 25 percent of the increase for married-couple families. These differences between married-couple and single-parent families reflect the facts that the former are more likely to be working poor and not receiving welfare, while the latter are more likely to be nonworking welfare recipients.[10] Fourth, changes in social insurance programs reduced poverty slightly for married-couple families and accounted for about 8 percent of the increase for families with an unmarried head.

One reason that the poverty rate for *all* children is high is because the rate for children living in single-parent families is so high.[11] But there are also important differences by race and ethnicity. Figure 2.3 shows that child poverty rates in 1985 were almost 40 percent for white, non-Hispanic children and more than 60 percent for black, non-Hispanic and Hispanic children living only with their mothers. Poverty rates for minority children living with both parents were much lower than these rates, but much higher than those for white children in similar families.

Further details on poverty and welfare receipt among children in one- and two-parent families are shown in Table 2.4. Children are classified in the four mutually exclusive and exhaustive categories shown in each of the first four columns. Column 1 includes children who were not poor judging by their parents' market incomes. Column 2 includes those children who were pretransfer poor but received enough in government transfers (cash transfers plus Food Stamps plus energy assistance) to escape poverty. The children in column 3 received government assistance, but not enough to escape poverty, while those in column 4 received no transfers at all.

The sum of columns 3 and 4 represents children who remained poor and are the target group for welfare reform and other expanded antipoverty policies. Reforms focused on welfare recipients offer no help to the pretransfer poor children in column 4—about one-third of pretransfer poor children in two-parent families and about one-seventh in female-

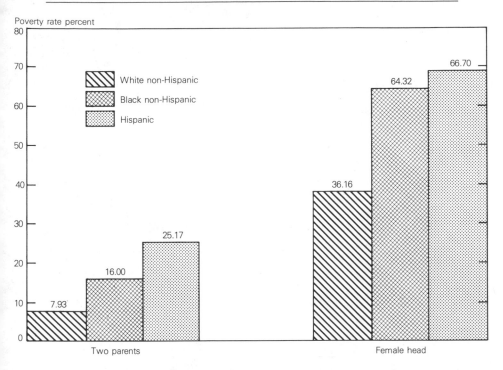

Poverty rate percent

Fig. 2.3. Child poverty rates, 1985

headed families. There are also large differences by race and ethnicity (data not shown). About a quarter of all white and Hispanic pretransfer poor children, and about an eighth of poor black children received no transfers.

Consider first children living with two parents who were not classified as poor (column 1). Their parents worked much of the year: the fathers averaged almost 48 weeks; the mothers, 28 weeks. Fewer than 5 percent received welfare and about 14 percent received nonwelfare transfers. The parents most like this group are those who were pretransfer poor but received no transfers (column 4). Together, both parents worked 55 weeks on average, but at low wages, and fell through all safety nets. Moreover, their poverty gap was almost $5,000 (see the Appendix for a definition of the poverty gap). The extension of AFDC benefits to two-parent families would offer them some help. Since they are already working, they will not be affected by current "workfare" proposals targeted on nonworking recipients. The best way to aid them without taking

Table 2.4. Poverty and income transfer receipt among children, 1985[a]

| | Not pretransfer poor (1) | Pretransfer poor[b] | | | All children, by category (5) |
		Not post-transfer poor (taken out by transfers) (2)	Received transfers, but not enough to escape poverty (3)	Received no transfers (4)	
Two-parent families					
% of (two-parent) children	86.33	2.89	6.34	4.44	100.00
Weeks worked by head	47.85	22.07	21.79	40.45	45.13
Weeks worked by spouse	28.14	11.50	8.08	14.69	25.79
Mean transfers	$644	$8,472	$4,911	0	$1,112
Mean poverty gap[c]	0	0	$4,246	$4,831	$484
% receiving welfare transfers[d]	4.69	60.84	87.34	0	11.35
% receiving nonwelfare tranfers[e]	14.07	71.51	37.95	0	16.62
Female-headed families					
% of (single-mother) children	40.22	7.76	43.65	8.36	100.00
Weeks worked by head	45.55	16.25	9.04	26.01	25.70
Mean transfers	$1,156	$8,727	$5,448	0	$3,521
Mean poverty gap[c]	0	0	$4,007	$5,229	$2,187
% receiving welfare tranfers[d]	14.24	69.54	94.65	0	52.45
% receiving nonwelfare transfers[e]	20.01	58.97	18.64	0	20.76

All children

% of all children	76.28	4.04	14.26	5.42	100.00
% of all pretransfer poor children	0	17.03	60.12	22.85	100.00

Source: Computations from March 1986 Current Population Survey computer tapes.

a. About 3 percent of all children (1.89 million) lived in single-parent families headed by males; they are excluded from this table. Of the remaining children, 48.55 million lived with two parents, and 13.38 million lived in female-headed families.

b. Pretransfer income is determined by subtracting government cash transfers from a family's money income.

c. The poverty gap is the dollar amount needed to bring a poor family up to the poverty line.

d. Includes food stamps, energy assistance, AFDC, SSI, and general assistance.

e. Includes social security, railroad retirement, unemployment insurance, workers' compensation, government employee pensions, and veterans' pensions and compensation.

them through the welfare system would be with some combination of wage subsidies, expanded tax relief, and subsidized medical insurance (Lerman, 1987).

Now consider pretransfer poor children living with two parents who received transfers (columns 2 and 3). Those who escaped poverty (column 2) lived in households where the father worked about 20 weeks and the mother about 10 weeks and most received *both* welfare and nonwelfare transfers. Transfers totaled about $8,500.

Because the labor force attachment of their parents and their transfer benefits were low, many children remained poor (column 3) despite almost universal welfare recipiency and receipt of substantial nonwelfare transfers.[12] Total transfers for these families averaged about $5,000, leaving a poverty gap of about $4,000. If workfare or employment and training programs could increase their wages or weeks of work and continue to provide some form of income supplement, they could reduce poverty for this group.

The middle panel of Table 2.4 presents the same information for children living in female-headed families. These children comprised 21 percent of all children but 55 percent of all poor children. Compared to children in two-parent families, a greater percentage were pretransfer poor. And a smaller percentage of those who received transfers escaped poverty. Their mothers worked few weeks and were much less likely to receive nonwelfare transfers than were two-parent families.

The large group in column 3, 43.65 percent of all children in female-headed families, received transfers but remained poor and lived with mothers who worked less than 10 weeks per year. They will be most affected by welfare reforms directed toward long-term AFDC recipients. However, if those reforms are to reduce poverty, they must do more than replace welfare transfers with an equivalent amount of earnings. At a minimum, this means that workfare programs should not prevent a recipient from earning more than her current AFDC benefit. In fact, at a wage of $4.00 per hour, a single parent who works for three-quarters of the year will earn only $6,000. Since this will terminate AFDC benefits under current rules in most states, the woman will need expanded child-support payments, wage subsidies, and tax relief if she is to avoid poverty.

To sum up, the current system of welfare and nonwelfare transfers provides some aid to more than three-quarters of all pretransfer poor children (last row of Table 2.4, the sum of columns 2 and 3). But in 1985 only about one-sixth of them escaped poverty. Another 60 percent of the pretransfer received some aid, but not enough to escape. The fifth of all children who remained poor (next to last row, columns 3 and 4) were about $4,000–$5,000 below the poverty line, indicating that current welfare reforms alone cannot significantly reduce their numbers.[13]

Persistent Poverty and Welfare Receipt

Current welfare (AFDC) reforms neglect most of the 33.06 million people who were classified as poor by the official definition in 1985, because most of them did not receive AFDC. However, a focus on this aid program does target the most disadvantaged group—black children, particularly those living in female-headed familes, who not only have very high probabilities of being poor and of receiving welfare in a given year, but have even higher probabilities than others of being poor and of receiving welfare over periods as long as fifteen years.

The Census Bureau data presented in the tables provided a "snapshot" of those who were poor in any given year. However, some persons who were poor last year will experience only brief episodes of poverty. To the extent that their poverty is transitory and self-correcting, it may be of limited policy concern (unnecessary, for example, for a person who was poor last year when she was a full-time student, but was not poor this year after she graduated and got a job).

The data from the Michigan Panel Study of Income Dynamics (PSID) now allow one to follow the same individuals over periods as long as fifteen years and thus to identify those who were persistently poor and those who were persistent welfare recipients. Persistence is a subjective concept, and there is no consensus as to how it should best be defined. For example, Adams and Duncan (1987) find that 35 percent of urban residents who were poor in 1979 were poor in at least eight of the ten years they examined. However, if they defined persistence for these same people on the basis of their average annual income over the same ten-year period, 63 percent were found to be persistently poor.[14]

Table 2.5 contrasts annual measures of poverty and welfare receipt with estimates of persistent poverty and persistent welfare receipt for all persons, all children, and black children. The estimates of persistence are derived from many recent studies, all using the PSID data but differing in the time period covered (some use ten years of data; others, fifteen),

Table 2.5. Poverty and welfare receipt: 1985 levels and estimates of persistence

	All persons (1)	All children (2)	Black children (3)
Persons (millions)			
Population totals[a]	236.75	62.02	9.41
Official poor[a]	33.06	12.48	4.06
Prewelfare poor[b]	35.17	13.02	4.23
AFDC recipients[c]	10.90	7.23	3.25
Persistently poor	11.57[d]–20.83[d]	2.98[e]–4.71[f]	2.72[e]–3.20[f]
Persistent AFDC recipients	5.92[g]	2.98[h]–4.05[i]	1.96[h]–2.54[i]
Rates (percentages)			
Official poverty rate	14.0	20.1	43.2
Persistent poverty as a percentage of official poverty	35.0[d]–63.0[d]	23.9[e]–37.7[f]	67.0[e]–78.8[f]
Persistent poverty as a percentage of population	4.9[d]–8.8[d]	4.8[e]–7.6[f]	28.9[e]–34.0[f]
Percentage of prewelfare poor receiving welfare	31.0	55.5	76.8
Percentage of persistently poor receiving welfare in a given year[j]	57.0	69.6	n.a.
Percentage of official poor who are persistent welfare recipients	17.9[g]	23.9[h]–32.5[i]	48.3[h]–62.6[i]
Percentage of population that is persistently welfare dependent	2.5[g]	4.8[h]–6.5[i]	20.8[h]–27.0[i]

a. Total U.S. population and official poverty count are from U.S. Bureau of the Census (1987b).

b. Estimates of persons who would have been poor in the absence of cash welfare benefits are based on computations from a March 1986 CPS computer tape.

c. Average monthly numbers of AFDC recipients in fiscal years 1985 and 1986 are from U.S. House of Representatives, Committee on Ways and Means (1987), p. 429.

d. Adams and Duncan (1987) report that 35 percent of urban residents who were poor in 1979 were poor in 8 of the 10 years between 1974 and 1983; 63 percent were poor "on average," meaning that their 10-year average income was below the 10-year average poverty line.

e. Duncan and Rodgers (1987) find that 4.8 percent of all children and 28.9 percent of black children who were less than 4 years old in 1968 were poor for at least 10 of the 15 years between 1968 and 1982.

f. Ellwood (1987) finds that 7.6 percent of all children and 34 percent of black children born between 1967 and 1972 were pretransfer poor for at least 7 of the 10 years between 1972 and 1982.

g. Duncan et al. (1984), p. 75, report that 8.1 percent of persons received cash welfare or Food Stamps in 1978, and that 4.4 percent of persons had received welfare for 8 or more years between 1969 and 1978. This ratio (4.4/8.1 = .54) was multiplied by the number of AFDC recipients under "All persons."

h. Hill (1983) finds, among children between the ages of 1 and 6 in 1970, that 4.8 percent of all children and 20.8 percent of black children were dependent on cash welfare or food stamps (i.e., welfare income was at least one-half of the total annual income of their parents) for at least 6 of the 10 years between 1970 and 1979.

i. Ellwood (1986) reports that 56.0 percent of current AFDC recipients have expected welfare careers of 10 or more years. Because his reported spell-lengths for blacks exceed those of whites, I estimate the corresponding percentage for blacks to be 78.0 percent.

j. Adams and Duncan (1987) find that these percentages of the persistently poor received AFDC or general assistance in a single year (1979).

their definition of persistence (for instance, six out of ten years; eight of ten years; ten of fifteen years), and in the population examined. Details as to how I derived the numbers in Table 2.5 are provided in the notes to the table. When two high-quality studies provided different estimates (as in rows 5 and 6), I have listed a range rather than a point estimate.[15]

For each of the rates shown in rows 7 through 13, the poverty situation of black children is much more severe than that of white children or all persons. Moreover, this deficiency increases under persistent as opposed to annual measures. For example, black children were about twice as likely as all children to be poor in 1985 under the official definition (43.2 versus 20.1 percent in row 7). But poverty among black children is much more likely to be persistent (row 8): about one-third of all poor children, but more than two-thirds of poor black children, were persistently poor. As a result of high poverty rates and high rates of persistence, they were about five times as likely to be persistently poor (row 9) as all persons or all children.

Large differentials also appear in terms of welfare receipt. Among those who were poor on the basis of their prewelfare income, about three-quarters of black children, one-half of white children, and one-third of all persons received welfare in 1985 (row 10). An even greater percentage of the persistently poor received welfare during a given year (row 11)—almost 60 percent of all persons and almost 70 percent of all children.

A policy that is targeted on long-term AFDC recipients—about one-sixth of all of the poor—has the potential to aid about one-quarter to one-third of all poor children and about one-half to about two-thirds of poor black children (row 12). It is shocking that two decades after declaration of the War on Poverty, in the midst of a robust economic recovery, between one-fifth and one-quarter of all black children were persistently dependent on welfare (row 13), and almost one-third (row 9) were persistently poor. While current welfare reforms will disproportionately aid these children, the amount of increased aid being considered cannot possibly deal with the grave disadvantages they will incur as they pass through childhood.

Some Antipoverty Reforms

Although current welfare reform proposals will aid only a minority of the poor, most of them would, if implemented, represent an improvement over the current situation. I would caution that the consensus about getting able-bodied welfare recipients to work more than they now do does not resolve the question of how much they should be allowed to work. Under some workfare programs, recipients can work only until they have earned an amount equal to their welfare benefit. In this case welfare dependency declines, but poverty does not. Only if the program allows the recipient to work full time can workfare become a work-opportunity program with the potential for alleviating poverty.

Let me now turn to some other antipoverty reforms directed at families with children that could aid all of the poor, avoid the expansion of welfare for the able-bodied, and in some cases be implemented with minor budgetary consequences (Lerman, 1987, discusses a similar range of proposals). They would provide increased spending through refundable tax credits and child-support payments.

These proposals could be financed in part through higher taxes on the general population. Tax policy has recently shifted in this direction by eliminating some of the special federal income tax provisions that disproportionately aided the non-poor elderly. These included the repeal of the double personal exemption for the elderly and the taxation of one-half of social security benefits (employer share) for those with higher incomes. A further move would be to tax employer-provided health insurance and the implicit subsidy in Medicare in the same way that social security is being taxed.[16]

The Tax Reform Act of 1986 has made an important step in the direction of aiding poor children by removing most of their families from the income tax rolls by expanding the earned income tax credit, the standard deduction, and the personal exemption and indexing them to the cost of living. Yet these changes will only partially offset the declining transfer benefits and stagnant family incomes that have characterized the period since 1973. Congress has also begun to change the Medicaid program so that poor children can be covered even if their parents are not eligible for the AFDC program or do not participate in it.

Two additional tax reforms would aid all of the poor. I advocate replacing the $2,000 personal exemption with a per capita refundable credit of $560 (what it is worth to taxpayers in the 28 percent bracket). This would be equal to an exemption of about $3,700 for taxpayers in the lowest tax bracket. But because of refundability, it would greatly aid poor and near-poor taxpayers. It would also help offset much of the social security tax burden of the working poor. A refundable per capita credit targets foregone revenue on those with lower incomes better than would a higher personal exemption that would forego the same amount of revenue. A less ambitious version would begin by replacing the personal exemption only for children. The refundable tax credit would then function like the children's allowances provided by many Western European countries.

An even more ambitious proposal would raise the value of the per capita refundable credit, and in return terminate both the personal exemption and the Food Stamp program.[17] The rationale is that such credits can effectively target the poor, lower their marginal tax rate, and avoid the stigmatization of recipients and the higher administrative costs of welfare programs. For example, a family of four with no other income is currently eligible for about $3,500 per year in Food Stamps and faces a net benefit reduction rate (marginal tax rate) in that program of 24 percent. With a refundable credit of $875 per person, the family head with no other income would be equally well off as today, and the only marginal tax rate she might face would come from the payroll tax, not the sum of the payroll tax and Food Stamp rate. Of course, since the current personal exemption is not refundable, and many poor and near-poor families do not participate in the Food Stamp program, such a change would require substantial additional revenues.[18]

The lower marginal tax rates in the reformed income tax, however, provide a more efficient mechanism for raising revenue to aid low-income families than did the former, higher rates. The lower rates reduce the work disincentive effects of broadening the tax base. Assume, for example, that these refundable credits will be financed by taxing the employers' contribution for health insurance. With only three tax brackets, a smaller percentage of the population will be shifted into a higher marginal tax bracket by this base-broadening than would have been the case under the pre-1986 rate structure.[19]

A second tax reform on behalf of poor children would make the child-care tax credit refundable. The current nonrefundable credit allows two-earner couples and working single parents to partially offset work-related child-care costs. Only a very small percentage of poor families make use of the nonrefundable credit. On the other hand, higher-income taxpayers receive credits of up to $960 if they have more than one child and if they spend at least $4,800 on care.

The credit begins at 30 percent of expenses for families with incomes below $10,000. Consider the case of a single mother of one child who works part time, earns $5.00 per hour for 1,500 hours per year, and spends $1.50 per hour, or $2,250, to keep her child in day care while she works. If this is her only income, she will not have an income tax liability (indeed, the expanded earned income tax credit will offset a portion of her social security taxes). Her potential child-care credit—$675, or 30 percent of $2,250—is thus of no value to her because it is not refundable. Refunding this credit would not only raise her net income, but would also make welfare recipiency less attractive.

Another antipoverty strategy, the Wisconsin Child Support Assurance System or the system proposed by Lerman (Chapter 8), would target all children in single-parent families and would reduce both poverty and welfare dependency through increased parental support. Uniform child-support awards would be financed by a percentage-of-income tax on the absent parent. If this amount is less than a fixed minimum level because the absent parent's income is too low, the support payment would be supplemented up to the minimum by government funds.

These tax-based and child-support reforms together with the workfare proposals for employable welfare recipients (discussed elsewhere in this volume) would have their greatest impacts on those able to work. After these reforms had been implemented, one might consider a long-standing goal of the last two decades of welfare reform—providing a national minimum welfare benefit. For 1986, the Congressional Budget Office (U.S. House of Representatives, Committee on Ways and Means, 1985) estimated the effect on the incidence of poverty, on the poverty gap, and on the federal budget of establishing a national minimum for AFDC plus Food Stamps at 65 percent of the poverty lines. For a family of four, this would have meant $7,638 per year, requiring an AFDC benefit of $467 per month. In January 1987, the median state's AFDC benefit for a family of four was $415.

Under this simulated plan, benefits would be raised for about 60 percent of existing AFDC families and the welfare rolls would increase by about 5 percent. The cost to the federal government of the plan would have been about $3.5 billion, or 40 percent of federal AFDC benefit payments, but less than 2 percent of social security benefits. If these other reforms were implemented first and succeeded in reducing welfare rolls, then the costs of subsequently adopting a national minimum would obviously be lower.

A refocused antipoverty effort is the only meaningful way to reduce poverty and welfare dependency for the diverse demographic groups with very high rates. The welfare and nonwelfare reforms suggested here and in the other chapters provide a reasonable beginning for such an effort, even in a period of severe budgetary restrictions.

Appendix: The Measurement of Poverty

The federal government's official measure of poverty provides a set of income cutoffs adjusted for household size, the age of the head of the household, and the number of children under age eighteen. (Until 1981, the measure took into account the sex of the head and whether the household lived on a farm.) The cutoffs provide an absolute measure of poverty that specifies in dollar terms minimally decent levels of consumption. For 1985, the lines ranged from $5,156 for a single elderly person to $22,083 for a household of nine or more persons. The threshold for a family of four was $10,989.

The official income concept—current money income received during the calendar year—is defined as the sum of money from wages and salaries, net income from self-employment, social security income and cash transfers from other government programs, property income (such as interest, dividends, net rental income), and other forms of cash income (such as private pensions, alimony). Current money income does not include capital gains, imputed rents, or government or private benefits in-kind (such as Food Stamps, Medicare benefits, employer-provided health insurance) nor does it subtract taxes, although all of these affect a household's level of consumption.

The official poverty cutoffs (column 1, Table A.2.1) are updated yearly by an amount corresponding to the change in the CPI (column 4) so that they represent the same purchasing power each year. According to this absolute standard, poverty will be eliminated when the incomes of all households exceed the poverty lines, regardless of what is happening to average household income.

There have been numerous discussions over the past two decades as to the appropriateness of the official poverty thresholds and income concept. Despite these controversies, the official measure of poverty has become an important social indicator. According to Tobin (1969), "Adoption of a specific quantitative measure, however arbitrary and debatable,

Table A2.1. Poverty line compared to median family income, selected years, 1959–1986

Year	Poverty line for a nonfarm family of four[a] (1)	Median family income[b] (2)	Ratio of poverty line to median family income (3)	Consumer price index (1967 = 100) (4)	CPI-X1 (1967 = 100) (5)
1959	$ 2,973	$ 5,417	.55	87.3	87.3
1965	3,223	6,957	.46	94.5	94.5
1968	3,553	8,632	.41	104.2	103.7
1973	4,540	12,051	.38	133.1	129.7
1979	7,412	19,587	.38	217.7	203.6
1985	10,989	27,735	.40	322.7	293.1
1986	11,203	29,458	.38	328.4	298.3

Source: U.S. Bureau of the Census, CPS, P-60, various issues.
a. Current dollars; the farm/nonfarm distinction was eliminated in 1981.
b. Current dollars; unrelated individuals are not included in this median.

will have durable and far-reaching political consequences. Administrations will be judged by their success or failure in reducing the officially measured prevalence of poverty. So long as any family is found below the official poverty line, no politician will be able to claim victory in the war on poverty or ignore the repeated solemn acknowledgments of society's obligation to its poorest members" (p. 83).

Income poverty is a complex concept, and different definitions of poverty thresholds and income are appropriate for different purposes. An absolute perspective, such as the official measure, focuses on those with incomes that fall short of a minimum (fixed) level of economic resources. On the other hand, a relative definition draws attention to the degree of inequality at the lower end of the income distribution. Those whose incomes fall well below the prevailing average in their society are regarded as poor, no matter what their absolute incomes may be. A relative poverty threshold, therefore, changes at about the same rate as average income.

Columns 2 and 3 suggest how the official poverty line would vary if it were to be adjusted for changes in median family income rather than consumer prices. In 1965, the official line for a four-person family was 46 percent of the median. In 1986, 46 percent of the median would have meant a poverty line of $13,551 for a family of four rather than $11,203.

Conversely, problems with using the CPI to adjust the official poverty lines in periods of rising housing prices and mortgage rates during the 1970s suggest that the lines would now be lower if they had been "more appropriately" adjusted for these price changes. Until 1981, the CPI (column 4) reflected the costs of home ownership in such a way that changes in the housing costs of the poor were overstated. The CPI-XI series (column 5) shows the price changes that would have been used to update the poverty line if the post-1981 CPI had been in effect since 1965. (The CPI-XI incorporates estimates of the cost of renting, rather than owning, housing.) Multiplying the official line by the ratio of the column 5 index to the column 4 index yields a 1986 absolute poverty line of $10,176.

Table A.2.2 and Figure A.2.1 show the poverty trend for all persons according to the official measure, and as seen under two alternative measures for the period after 1967. Because the CPI-XI rose less than the CPI, the CPI-XI poverty lines and poverty rates (column 2) are below the official rates (column 1) for all years after 1967. Similarly, because the relative poverty line is defined as a constant percentage of median family income while the official line falls as a percentage of the median, the official rates are below the relative rates (column 3). The official line is roughly midway between these two alternative lines, and the trends and turning points in all three series are similar. As a result, I conclude that the official series is an acceptable one. The large differentials in poverty rates by demographic groups, discussed in the text, would not be affected by the adoption of either of these alternative poverty lines.

The U.S. Department of Commerce, Bureau of the Census (1987a) now publishes several series for the 1979–1986 period on poverty rates

Table A2.2. Trends in poverty among all persons, selected years, 1967–1985

Year	Official measure (1)	Official measure with CPI-X1 adjustment (2)	Relative measure[a] (3)
1967	14.3%	14.3%	n.a.
1972	11.9	11.4	15.7%
1979	11.6	10.5	15.7
1982	15.0	13.2	17.8
1985	14.0	12.3	18.0

a. Defined as 44 percent of the ratio of family income to poverty line in each year; see Plotnick and Skidmore (1975) for details.

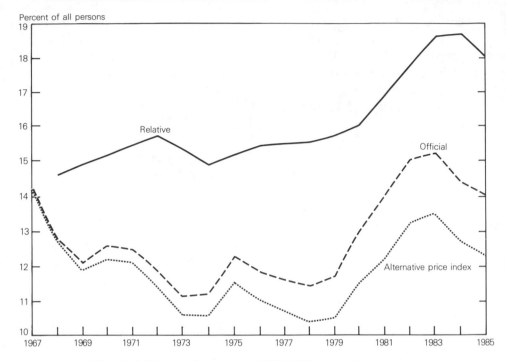

Fig. A2.1. The trend in poverty, 1967–1985, alternative measures

that are adjusted to include the value of public in-kind transfers. When the official definition of poverty was developed in the early 1960s, the poor received few noncash transfers, so the official measure's comparison of cash income to the poverty line provided a fairly accurate picture of a family's situation. However, noncash transfers have increased rapidly in recent years. They accounted for only about 12 percent of public assistance spending in 1966, but 70 percent by 1983. Clearly, some adjustment is needed to the official measure to account for the increased consumption made possible by the growth in these benefits.

By definition, poverty rates that are adjusted to reflect the value of noncash benefits must be lower than the official (money income) rates. The data in column 3 of Table A.2.3 show how poverty rates in 1986 are lowered by taking into account the market value of food, housing, and medical benefits for noninstitutionalized persons. The market-value method of adjustment—what it would cost to buy the services provided—yields lower poverty rates than does the "recipient-value" approach—

Table A2.3. Alternative measures of the incidence of poverty, 1967 and 1986

Persons living in poverty	Official measure, 1967 (1)	Official measure, 1986 (2)	Money income plus in-kind transfers at market value, 1986[a] (3)
All persons	14.2%	13.6%	9.0%
Persons with white household head	11.0	11.0	9.4
Persons with black household head	39.3	31.1	19.8
Persons with Hispanic household head	n.a.	27.3	18.7
Persons with female household head, no husband present	40.6	34.2	23.5
Elderly (65 and over)	29.5	12.4	3.0
Children	17.0	19.8	13.8

Sources: For 1986, U.S. Bureau of the Census (1987a). For 1967, U.S. Bureau of the Census, *Money Income and Poverty Status of Families and Persons in the United States: 1982,* P-60, no. 140 (Washington, D.C.: U.S. Government Printing Office, 1983).

a. In-kind transfers for food, housing, and medical benefits for noninstitutionalized persons.

how much cash the recipients would be willing to pay for such services given their income. Although the recipient-value approach is favored by many economists, the market-value estimates still reinforce the discussion in the text. First, adjusted poverty in 1986 (column 3) is lower than in 1967 when the amount of noncash transfers was relatively small (column 1), primarily because of the increased antipoverty effectiveness of government transfers. Second, poverty rates for minorities, children, and persons living in female-headed families remain well-above the aggregate rate.

The text reports a variety of poverty measures. A matrix clarifying the differences among the measures is presented in Table A.2.4. The official income measure lies somewhere between pretransfer income (I) and post-transfer, post-tax income (II) in the first row. Census data about money income do not distinguish between income derived from market and private transfer sources (such as wages, dividends, alimony) and income derived from government sources (such as Social Security, public assistance income). As such, the official measure fails to separate the private economy's antipoverty performance from the performance of government cash transfer programs. Households that do not receive enough money income from private sources to raise them over the poverty lines constitute the pretransfer poor (a more exact title would be pregovernment-transfer poor). The relative poverty definition shown in Table A.2.2 falls between the columns marked III and IV in Table A.2.4.

The valuation of in-kind transfers does move the Census Bureau closer to the concept of post-transfer, post-tax income. To provide this preferred measure would have required the Census Bureau to add, in addition to in-kind government transfers the poor received, the in-kind private transfers (such as employer-provided fringe benefits) they received, and to subtract the direct taxes paid. The U.S. House of Representatives, Committee on Ways and Means (1987) has moved in this direction by publishing a post-1979 series which subtracts federal income and payroll taxes, as reported in Table 2.3.

One additional measurement issue should be noted. The incidence of poverty reveals the percentage of persons whose incomes fall below the poverty threshold, but does not distinguish the degree of poverty. The "poverty gap," which measures the total amount of income required to bring every poor person up to the poverty threshold, does distinguish between poor persons who are very close to the borderline and those who are farther away from the thresholds. Table A.2.5 shows the pretransfer (column 1) and post-transfer (column 3) poverty gaps in billions of constant 1985 dollars for selected years between 1967 and 1985. Cash transfers received by the pretransfer poor and reported in the CPS (Current Population Survey) are shown in column 2. The fourth column shows the percentage reduction in the poverty gap due to these cash transfers.

Between 1967 and 1974, total cash transfers to the pretransfer poor grew much faster than the pretransfer poverty gap, so the antipoverty effectiveness of transfers increased and the post-transfer gap declined. Between 1974 and 1985, the pretransfer gap grew faster than did trans-

Table A2.4. Matrix of alternative poverty definitions

Type of poverty threshold	Income measure	
	Pretransfer poverty	Posttransfer-posttax income
Absolute	I	II
Relative	III	IV

Table A2.5. Poverty gap before and after cash transfers, selected years, 1967–1985

Year	Pretransfer poverty gap[a]	Cash transfers received by pretransfer poor households[a]	Posttransfer poverty gap[a]	Percentage reduction in poverty gap due to cash transfers
1967	$ 75.7	$ 56.4	$34.1	55.0%
1974	96.2	124.9	31.0	67.8
1979	102.9	118.5	34.3	66.7
1982	126.1	131.6	48.9	61.2
1985	123.2	134.1	47.8	61.2

Source: Computations from various March Current Population Survey computer tapes.
a. Billions of constant 1985 dollars.

fers. As a result, the antipoverty impact of transfers declined and the post-transfer gap increased in real terms.

The 1985 pretransfer poverty gap of $123.2 billion means that the pretransfer income of the typical poor household was about $4,700 below its poverty line; the post-transfer gap of $47.8 billion means that the post-transfer poor were about $3,500 below the line (for a more detailed discussion of the poverty gap, see Weinberg, 1987). The median gap in 1985 for unrelated individuals who account for about half of all poor households was about $2,400; it was about $4,300 for families of two or more persons.

Poverty, Joblessness, and the Social Transformation of the Inner City

Loïc J. D. Wacquant and William Julius Wilson

The conspicuous problems of inner-city poverty and welfare cannot be understood, and therefore successfully tackled, in and of themselves: they do not emerge, develop and eventually dissolve in a social vacuum. Rather, they are the outcome of the historical interplay of forces and struggles that cut across the field of politics and public policy, the economic field, and the field of class and race relations.[1]

Nonetheless, the public debate on welfare tends to pay scant attention to the basic societal processes that produce and sustain poverty in the first place.[2] As a result, the malady is often ill-identified and the cure prescribed ends up falsely putting the blame on the victims (the poor) or on the programs of assistance designed to help them (welfare).[3] The underlying causes for the emergence and ongoing crystallization of a black underclass, for instance, have typically been obscured by an excessive concern for the alleged individual deficiencies—behavioral, moral or cultural—of those who compose it, or worse yet, unfounded claims that such an underclass is one of the "counterintuitive" effects of welfare programs.

In this chapter, the *linkages between welfare and societal organization* are explored by unraveling recent social changes in the inner-city neighborhoods of the country's largest urban centers.[4] In order to relate public aid to transformations in the social structure and political economy of these areas, we first survey the demographic and racial correlates of the rise of welfare among inner-city residents. We then document the adverse impact of deindustrialization and of the shifts in the labor market on the economic opportunities of the urban poor. Drawing on a detailed examination of Chicago, we show how the class and institutional transformations undergone by central city ghettos in recent decades have further exacerbated the effects of the broader economic changes. In conclusion, we sketch out the implications of this analysis for the current public policy debate, arguing that its terms be broadened to include social structural factors and that the integration of economic and social policies be considered seriously.

Welfare, Joblessness and the Growing Concentration of Poverty, 1970–1980

The structure of poverty has undergone significant changes in recent years (see Wilson et al., 1988). Poverty has become at once more urban, more concentrated, and more deeply rooted in big cities, particularly in older industrial centers with vast, highly segregated black and Hispanic populations.[5] Accordingly, the number of recipients of public assistance in these metropolises has soared. Today, welfare seems a fact of life in many poor neighborhoods of urban America. But increased welfare dependency is only a surface manifestation of deeper social changes.

The nature and magnitude of these changes can perhaps best be captured by tracing the demographic evolution of the ten largest central cities from 1970 to 1980.[6] These metropolises alone comprised over half of the poor living in the 50 largest cities of the country in 1980, and over one third of all central-city poor over this decade.

One remarkable change is that although the total population of these ten cities dropped by 7 percent (from 21.8 to 20.2 million), owing to the exodus of more than 4 million whites, there was a *marked increase, both relative and absolute, in their poverty population.* The number of poor residents grew by 19 percent, from 3.1 to 3.8 million, while the overall poverty rate jumped from 14.6 to 18.7 percent. This increase was due entirely to the growth of poverty among minorities. Poor blacks and Hispanics reached 29 percent by 1980, compared to 11 percent of whites, while the national official poverty rate stagnated in the 11–13 percent range throughout this period (U.S. Bureau of Census, 1986a). Now, it is important to disaggregate these data and to look at individual cities, for this reveals recurrent contrasts between the old, waning, industrial centers of the Midwest and Northeast and the newer, booming metropolises of the South and West.[7]

While Los Angeles, Dallas, and Houston recorded slight to moderate population gains from 1970 to 1980, due to increases in minority residents that more than offset a small outmigration of whites, Rustbelt cities all suffered demographic decline: Indianapolis lost 6 percent of its population, New York City and Chicago 9 percent, Philadelphia and Baltimore dropped 14 percent, and Detroit and Cleveland between one fourth and one fifth. In these cities whites moved out en masse, as can be seen in column 2 of Table 3.1, with Chicago and Cleveland losing one third of their white residents and Detroit a full one half. Only Philadelphia and Cleveland saw their black population slip, by 2 percent and 13 percent respectively, and Baltimore was the only large city where the Latino population did not rise. Everywhere else, black and Hispanic residents multiplied. These large cities are thus undergoing a process of *rapid racial polarization:* whereas whites made up 71 percent of their aggregate population in 1970, by 1980 this figure had dropped to 58 percent.[8]

In spite of this depopulation, the number of poor rose rapidly everywhere, with the exception of Cleveland[9]; by 30 percent in Los Angeles, 24 percent in Chicago, 20 percent in New York City, 16 percent in Philadelphia, Detroit, and Houston, 11 percent in Dallas and Indianapolis, and 7 percent in Baltimore. The only cities that did not experience an increase in the rate of poverty were Dallas (where it remained constant at 14 percent) and Houston (where it dipped slightly to 13 percent). In all Rustbelt cities except Indianapolis[10] poverty rates rose substantially (by a uniform 5 percentage points), to hover around 20–23 percent in 1980.

Growth of poverty is not the whole story, however. For there was an even *sharper increase in the population, both poor and nonpoor, living in poverty areas and especially in extreme poverty areas* in these ten cities.[11] The number of residents living in poverty tracts rose by 34 percent overall and those in extreme poverty tracts more than doubled (from .9 to 2.1 million). Poverty areas naturally include both poor and nonpoor individuals; it is therefore worth noting that the increase in the poor population of these areas was even more pronounced, due exclusively to changes among blacks and Hispanics. This growth was particularly acute in five of the seven Rustbelt cities, as indicated in columns 4 and 5 of Table 3.1. In New York City, for example, the poor population residing in extreme poverty areas grew by a whopping 269 percent; in Chicago and Detroit by 162 percent and 117 percent; in Indianapolis by 150 percent, and in Philadelphia by 128 percent. By contrast, the number of poor living in the poorest neighborhoods of Los Angeles and Houston

Table 3.1. Changes in population, poverty, poverty concentration, and welfare receipt in the ten largest cities, 1970–1980 (in percentages)

City	Total population	White population	Poor population	Population in poverty areas[a]	Population in extreme poverty areas[b]	% of blacks living in extreme poverty areas[b] 1970	% of blacks living in extreme poverty areas[b] 1980	% of families receiving public assistance 1970	% of families receiving public assistance 1980	# of families on welfare	# of families on welfare in poverty areas[a]
New York City	−9	−29	+20	+53	+269	15	45	9.7	16.2	+44	+62
Chicago	−9	−32	+24	+62	+162	24	47	7.5	17.0	+95	+120
Philadelphia	−14	−23	+16	+56	+128	25	39	8.6	19.0	+93	+132
Detroit	−21	−51	+16	+50	+117	13	22	8.3	23.4	+119	+176
Baltimore	−14	−29	+7	+30	+33	38	42	9.7	21.0	+90	+106
Cleveland	−24	−33	−3	+31	+23	35	43	8.5	18.0	+53	+104
Indianapolis	−6	−11	+11	+38	+150	8	16	2.9	7.8	+161	+188
Los Angeles	+5	−16	+31	+75	+17	20	19	9.9	12.1	+23	+60
Houston	+29	+8	+16	−14	+18	17	16	3.9	5.2	+74	+52
Dallas	+7	−12	+11	+4	−13	33	28	4.5	6.0	+39	+43
Total	−7	−25	+19	+48	+138	22	38	8.9	15.0	+62	+88

a. Poverty areas are census tracts in which 20 percent or more of the population is poor.
b. Extreme poverty areas are census tracts in which 40 percent or more of the population is poor.

increased by only 17 percent, and decreased in Dallas by some 13 percent.

The differential rise of poverty across areas produced an *increasing concentration of the (minority) poor in the poorest sections of these cities.* In this decade, the number of poor residents found in extreme poverty tracts grew by 138 percent (from 428,000 to just over one million) as indicated in Table 3.2. This growing concentration of the poor in extreme poverty areas is almost entirely a minority phenomenon. As columns 6 and 7 of Table 3.1 show, the proportion of poor blacks living in extremely poor neighborhoods increased substantially in all seven Rustbelt cities: it doubled in Chicago (from 24 to 47 percent) and tripled in New York City (from 15 to 45 percent); it climbed from 35 to 43 percent in Cleveland, from 38 to 42 percent in Baltimore, from 25 to 39 percent in Philadelphia, from 13 to 22 percent in Detroit, and from 8 to 16 percent in Indianapolis. In the same period the concentration of poor blacks remained unchanged in Los Angeles and Houston and even decreased slightly in Dallas. Poor Hispanics were also disproportionately concentrated in extreme poverty areas, but this was more true of Puerto Ricans in Rustbelt cities than of Latinos of Mexican origin clustered in the Sunbelt. In Los Angeles, Dallas, and Houston, the three cities with the largest proportions of Mexicans, the number of Hispanics dwelling in extreme pov-

Table 3.2. Growing concentration of poverty by race in the ten largest central cities, 1970–1980 (as measured by the number and percentage of residents living in tracts with poverty rates of 40% and more)

	1970		1980	
	n	*%*	*n*	*%*
Total population	918	4.2	2,048	10.2
Whites	233	1.5	336	2.9
Black	676	11.5	1,378	21.8
Hispanics	173	7.5	516	16.5
Poor population	428	13.5	1,016	26.9
Whites	110	6.7	144	10.9
Blacks	322	21.9	688	37.6
Hispanics	76	14.5	272	29.8

Source: U.S. Bureau of the Census (1973, 1985).
Note: Number *n* in thousands.

erty tracts ranged from 5 percent to 7 percent; the figure for both Chicago and Detroit was 13 percent. By contrast, in the three cities with large numbers of Puerto Ricans, the proportion of Hispanic residents in depressed areas was typically high: 57 percent in Philadelphia, 45 percent in New York City, and 30 percent in Baltimore.[12]

A clear majority of the roughly 1.5 million poor whites in the ten largest central cities in the United States lived in nonpoor areas throughout the decade of the 1970s (65 percent in 1970, 57 percent in 1980) and only a very small fraction of them lived in extremely poor areas.[13] In sharp contrast, only 1 poor black in 6 and 1 poor Hispanic in 5 resided in a nonpoor neighborhood by 1980. Indeed, most poor blacks in these metropolises lived in tracts with poverty rates exceeding 30 percent— almost two thirds did so in 1980, up from one half only ten years before. Moreover, if one makes a distinction between Hispanic whites and non-Hispanic whites, as allowed by the 1980 census reports, it turns out that a full two-thirds of all poor non-Hispanic whites lived in nonpoor areas in 1980, with a mere 6 percent residing in extreme poverty areas. Poor blacks are thus six times more likely to live in severely depressed neighborhoods than are poor non-Hispanic whites. This fact is crucial for understanding the formation of a black ghetto underclass.

Changes in the incidence and concentration of poverty were *closely related to changes in joblessness*. Thus while the unemployment rate for blacks increased nationwide from 6.3 percent in 1970 to 12.3 percent in 1980, in the poverty areas of Rustbelt central cities the situation was somewhat worse to start with, and it deteriorated at a more rapid pace. In Detroit, for instance, the unemployment rate for blacks living in poor tracts was already 10 percent in 1970 and shot up to 31 percent in 1980. In Philadelphia, the corresponding figures were 9 percent and 20.5 percent; in Chicago, 8.5 percent and 20.8 percent; in Cleveland, 10 and 18 percent; in Indianapolis, 12 and 22 percent; in Baltimore, 7 and 19 percent; in New York City, 6 and 15 percent. Once again, Sunbelt cities looked quite different: in Houston, black unemployment increased, but rates were significantly lower than either the national average or Rustbelt cities figures (from 3.7 percent to 8 percent); in Dallas, unemployment among black males residing in poverty areas actually dropped from 4.6 percent to 2.1 percent. In Los Angeles, levels were high but the increase was comparatively slight (from 12 to 15 percent).

Because official unemployment rates do not take into account those who have given up on the job search, employment rates[14] are a better measure of the state of the labor market; they tell more accurately the worsening economic situation of inner-city blacks. For whereas national employment rates among white males sixteen years and older stayed around 70 percent throughout this decade, that of their black counterparts dropped from 63 percent to 56 percent. In the poverty areas of the Rustbelt cities, moreover, employment rates dropped to considerably lower levels. In Philadelphia, less than half (46 percent) of all black males living in poor tracts were employed in 1980, down from 61 percent only ten years before. In the poverty areas of Detroit, a staggering 60 percent of all black males did not hold a job by 1980 (up from 39 percent in 1970). In the poor neighborhoods of Chicago, the black male employment rate fell from 62 percent to a mere 48 percent. And barely half of all black males living in New York's and Baltimore's poverty areas had gainful employment in 1980, a 20-point drop in a decade. Nothing of the sort happened in our Southern central cities: a full two-thirds of the black residents of the poverty areas of Dallas and Houston were employed in 1980 (down from three-fourths in 1970).

Given these general trends in poverty and unemployment, it should come as no surprise that, contrary to the national trend (the proportion of families receiving welfare payments stagnated at roughly 5 percent in urban America), public assistance receipt expanded noticeably in central-city areas over this decade (see Table 3.3).[15] While the total number of families in these ten cities decreased by 4 percent, the number of families on public assistance grew by 62 percent, from 466,000 (8.4 percent of all families) in 1970 to 754,000 (15 percent) in 1980, due almost entirely to increases among blacks and Hispanics. Moreover, 84 percent of this growth in the number of assisted families occurred in poverty areas. As of 1980, one of every three black or Latino families dwelling in a poverty area of these cities was on welfare (compared to a national figure of 23 percent for all black Americans).

The proportion of families on welfare who lived in poverty areas went up noticeably for both blacks and Hispanics in the 1970s, whereas it remained constant among whites.[16] The net result was that, in 1980, white families composed only 18 percent of those receiving public assistance in poor neighborhoods, down from 31 percent in the previous decade. Among welfare recipients, then, we find once again a sharp contrast between a white population residing primarily in nonpoor areas (60 percent) and a black and Hispanic component heavily concentrated in poor tracts (82 percent and 76 percent respectively). The percentage

Table 3.3. Families receiving public assistance, by race, in the ten largest central cities, 1970–1980.

	All tracts		Tracts with 20% or more poor		Percent of families on aid living in poverty areas	
	1970	1980	1970	1980	1970	1980
Total						
n	466	754	275	518	59.1	68.7
%	84.0	15.0	21.8	29.7	—	—
Whites						
n	214	235	84	94	39.3	39.9
%	5.3	7.8	18.2	19.5	—	—
Blacks						
n	251	411	191	337	75.8	82.4
%	18.5	27.2	24.5	34.8	—	—
Hispanics						
n	96	172	96	130	69.5	76.0
%	17.8	23.6	26.7	31.3	—	—

Source: U.S. Bureau of Census (1973, 1985).
Note: Number *n* in thousands.

of all families which both resided in poverty areas and received income from means-tested programs exhibits the same pattern: stable among whites where it represented a tiny minority (from 2 to 3 percent); on the rise among Hispanics (from 12 to 18 percent) and among blacks, among whom one of every four families was on welfare in a poverty area by 1980 (up from 14 percent ten years earlier).

City differences in rates of public assistance closely parallel those for poverty and unemployment, in spite of marked differences in rules of welfare eligibility and levels of support across states (see columns 8 and 9 of Table 3.1). Indeed, the three cities (Dallas, Houston, and Indianapolis) with the lowest levels of poverty, poverty concentration, and joblessness in 1970 also had the lowest rates of public assistance (less than 4.5 percent of all families). All the other cities had rates around 8 to 10 percent at that time. Over the ensuing ten years, the incidence of welfare receipt increased by about 6 to 12 percentage points in Rustbelt cities (reaching 23 percent in Detroit, 21 percent in Baltimore, and about

18 percent in New York City, Chicago, and Cleveland), while they rose by less than 2 percentage points in Los Angeles, Houston, and Dallas.

In summary, in the ten-year period from 1970 to 1980,[17] and despite depopulation caused by the massive suburban flight of whites, the ten largest central cities of the country suffered an absolute and relative increase in poverty, accompanied by an even speedier growth in the population living in poor and extremely poor areas. For the most part, these trends applied to blacks and Hispanics, who have become increasingly concentrated in the most depressed neighborhoods of these cities. These demographic trends closely followed gross trends in unemployment, especially among blacks; the growth of unemployment and poverty, in turn, fueled the rapid expansion of welfare. Public assistance rose among blacks and Hispanics in all cities, but did so at a faster pace in their poverty areas. And on all indicators, the older industrial centers of the Rustbelt (particularly Chicago, Detroit, New York City, Philadelphia, and Baltimore) fared considerably worse than the cities of the West and South.

Although more research is needed to compare a larger set of cities and more closely examine the effects of their racial and industrial composition on poverty and welfare, this preliminary review suggests that massive and growing concentration of extreme poverty is a problem that plagues not a few specific urban areas, but metropolises that typically combine a large black population confined in highly segregated ghettos with an aging industrial structure, and which therefore suffered important employment losses in recent years.[18]

Deindustrialization and the Declining Employment Base of Rustbelt Central Cities

The rise and fate of the underclass—and hence the efficacy and need for welfare—are inextricably connected to the structure and performance of the American economy. At the macro level, poverty rates closely follow fluctuations in economic activity. Econometric research has established, for instance, that when unemployment goes up by one percentage point, the national poverty rate rises by 1.1 percent (whereas a one point increase in inflation is accompanied by only a 0.15 percent increase in poverty) (see Blank and Blinder, 1986; and Blinder and Esaki, 1978).[19] Also, as the level of wages rises (after adjusting for inflation), poverty rates descend. When real wages stagnate or go down, as they have in recent years, the proportion of Americans in poverty, particularly among minorities, goes up. This connection could have been better understood by paying due notice to the continued weakening of the American economy. In the seventies, recessions occurred every few years and each cycle of boom and bust created higher levels of unemployment, forcing down wages in a stepwise fashion. Joblessness and diminishing real wages combined to increase poverty and related problems such as family breakup, welfare receipt, and crime.[20]

More than by conjunctional fluctuations, the minority residents of large industrial metropolises have been especially hurt by the accelerating *structural economic changes* of the past three decades. The shift to service-producing industries, together with the relocation of plants abroad or to cheaper labor sites nationally (in the suburbs and in the South, where unions are weak and employers find themselves in a buyer's market), has led to enormous declines in entry-level blue-collar jobs, particularly in the older central cities of the Middle-Atlantic and Midwestern regions. Because of the disproportionate concentration of blacks in these goods-producing industries, particularly heavy manufacturing, such massive job cutbacks have disproportionately affected central-city blacks, and the poor in particular (see Levy, 1987).[21]

Indeed, from 1958 to 1982, according to data from the censuses of manufactures, the number of factories located in the Rustbelt cities plummeted, falling by one half or more in New York, Chicago, Philadelphia, and Detroit, and by 40 percent in Cleveland and Baltimore. By contrast, in the central cities outside the Northeast and Midwest the number of manufacturing establishments typically rose—by 6 percent in Los Angeles, by more than half in Dallas, and by 115 percent in Houston. In the period from 1967 to 1982 alone, New York City lost 39 percent of its 11,300 factories and Chicago 38 percent of 8,455. Forty-three percent of Philadelphia's plants disappeared, and Detroit, which was hit hardest of all, lost more than 1,400, or nearly half, of its plants.

The impact of deindustrialization and plant relocation on the employment opportunities of inner-city residents have been nothing short of dramatic. In the last thirty-five years, Rustbelt central cities lost close to half of their total manufacturing employment and upwards of six-tenths of their production workers in this sector alone. Nationwide, the number of employees holding production jobs in manufacturing, that is, blue-collar workers up to and including foremen, increased by 6 percent in the years from 1958 to 1982 (from 11.6 to 12.4 million, with a peak of 13.7 million in 1977). But, as Figure 3.1 testifies, such jobs declined by more than one-half in New York City (from 670,000 to 311,000) and Chicago (from 390,000 to a meager 172,000), by 61 percent in Philadelphia (from 208,000 to 81,000) and Detroit (from 145,000 to 59,000), and by 54

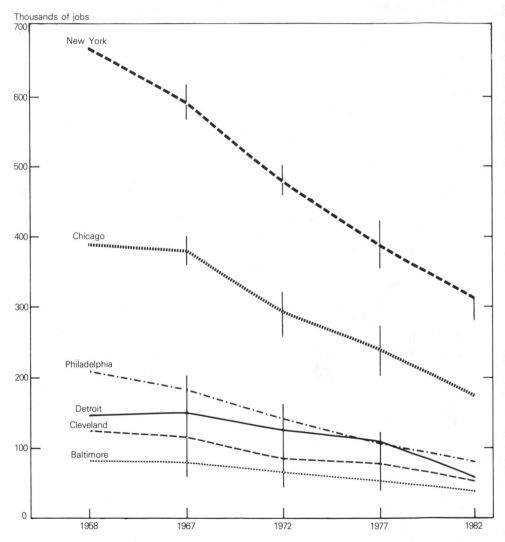

Fig. 3.1. The decline of production jobs in the manufacturing sector of Rustbelt cities, 1958–82

percent in Cleveland and Baltimore. And the sharpest cuts in production employment in all six of these cities occurred after 1967. In fact, looking again at the 1967–1982 period, it can be seen that New York, Baltimore, and Cleveland lost half of their manufacturing blue-collar workers; Chicago and Philadelphia a full 55 percent; while Detroit lost a staggering 61 percent. This is in sharp contrast to Los Angeles, Dallas, and Houston, where blue-collar employment in the manufacturing sector increased, by 3, 21, and 109 percent respectively.

The economic predicament of inner-city residents can be better ascertained by tabulating together changes in the principal economic sectors, namely, manufacturing, retail trade, wholesale trade, and services. Table 3.4 reports these data for each of the ten largest cities in the country.[22] The first column tallies the losses in total manufacturing employment (including jobs other than production) experienced by Rustbelt cities and the gains in Sunbelt cities from 1967 to 1982. The middle columns show how retail and wholesale trade aggravated this divergence: employment in both of these sectors decreased substantially in all Rustbelt cities[23] but increased in Los Angeles, Dallas, and Houston. More interestingly, the fourth and fifth columns of Table 3.4 reveal that the growth of services, observed in all cities, fell far short of providing adequate replacement for the losses incurred in the other economic sectors in the Rustbelt.

Table 3.4. Employment losses and gains, by economic sector, in the ten largest central cities, 1963–1982 (in thousands of jobs)

City	Manufacturing	Retail trade	Wholesale trade	Selected services	Balance
New York	− 366	− 85	− 60	+ 118	− 393
Chicago	− 269	− 64	− 47	+ 57	− 323
Philadelphia	− 139	− 22	− 22	+ 12	− 171
Detroit	− 103	− 34	− 26	+ 9	− 154
Baltimore	− 48	− 15	− 9	− 15	− 87
Cleveland	− 79	− 17	− 9	+ 7	− 98
Indianapolis	− 10	+ 4	+ 1	+ 9	+ 4
Los Angeles	+ 18	+ 45	+ 14	+ 135	+ 212
Dallas	+ 8	+ 38	+ 21	+ 55	+ 122
Houston	+ 76	+ 100	+ 62	+ 133	+ 371

Note: Trends in Indianapolis are not strictly comparable because of the incorporation of Marion county into the city after 1970.

Indeed, in the urban centers of the industrial Midwest and Northeast, the gains in service employment came only to a fraction of the cutbacks in manufacturing production jobs alone. For instance, the 118,000 jobs gained in selected services in New York City from 1963 to 1982 represented less than 42 percent of those lost from 1967 to 1982 in blue-collar manufacturing employment alone; in Chicago, service employment increased by 46 percent, but this expansion amounted to but one fourth of the job decline in manufacturing production; in Philadelphia and Cleveland, the ratio was 1 for 9, in Detroit 1 for 10. The final result is that whereas overall employment increased noticeably in the cities of the Sunbelt, Rustbelt cities recorded a net loss of literally hundreds of thousands of jobs that far outstripped the decrease of their population.

In short, contrary to what is often believed, *the growth of service jobs in Rustbelt central cities has been moderate and has fallen far short of compensating for the staggering decline of manufacturing jobs.* And when one takes into account nonproduction manufacturing employment (retail and wholesale trade positions), the employment opportunities available to the growing population of the urban poor are even more limited.

It must be emphasized further that this metamorphosis of the employment base of the inner city entails much more than a simple, if drastic, reduction of the volume of job openings: it also means a switch to quite different kinds of job prospects. It is well known that service jobs which are not part of the knowledge-intensive service sectors (that is, those that are normally more accessible to the inner-city poor) are considerably less secure, provide far fewer benefits, and offer much lower pay than does traditional unionized, blue-collar work. A recent study by the Congressional Office of Technology Assessment found that of the 11.5 million workers who lost jobs because of plant shutdowns or relocations between 1979 and 1984, only 60 percent found new jobs, and of these, about half had taken pay cuts, often severe.[24] Another study by Bluestone and Harrison has probed the proliferation of low-wage employment and linked it directly to the loss of jobs in the manufacturing sector, the continued expansion of services, and the attendant reorganization of work toward more part-time schedules. This research also established that deindustrialization has triggered "an enormous downward wage mobility" that has disproportionately affected younger workers in the predominantly industrial states of the Midwest (Bluestone and Harrison, 1987). In the cities of the Rustbelt, then, the dwindling supply of employment has "magnified the competition for jobs among the urban black underclass, further diminishing chances for economic advancement" (Lichter, 1988).[25] Most jobs that are now within reach of the urban poor (in terms of education, geographic location, skills, and so forth) also provide substantially lower monetary and welfare returns than was the case in previous decades. This, in turn, is part of a national trend toward increased income inequality among economic sectors and families, indeed, a general movement of class divergence that affects the entire American social structure.[26]

For all these reasons, any public policy designed to alleviate poverty and reduce welfare dependency in America's large cities ought to take into account the consequences of these basic economic mutations. It bears stressing, at this juncture, that the relation between shifts in the economy and the rise of welfare receipt is never one-to-one and direct. It is mediated, among other factors, by local social structures and their institutional functioning. In this regard, recent transformations in the economy have not merely depleted the employment pool of poor central-city residents, generated extremely high levels of joblessness in Rustbelt cities, and contributed to the growing concentration of the poor; these broad economic shifts have also triggered wide-ranging, ramifying changes in the social life of the ghetto that go hand in hand with, and indeed further accelerate, the growth of public assistance.

Chicago's Inner City: From Institutional Ghetto to Physical Ghetto

The extent to which conditions in the inner city have deteriorated and the ways in which such deterioration fuels the expansion of welfare can best be ascertained by probing the transformations of the social and economic fabric of these decaying urban areas. Because of the long-standing importance of smokestack industries in its economy, together with its extreme levels of racial segregation and trends in the concentration of poverty that parallel those of other Rustbelt metropolises, the city of Chicago offers a particularly favorable terrain for unraveling these changes.

Table 3.5 offers a synoptic overview of the spectacular rise of social dislocations in Chicago's inner city. In a period of only ten years, conditions worsened dramatically in the black communities of the South and West Sides, increasing the schism between poor black neighborhoods

Table 3.5. Selected social and demographic characteristics of Chicago's ten poorest inner-city neighborhoods, 1970–1980

	% of families below poverty level		% of families headed by a female		% of adults (aged 16 or over) not in labor force		% of population on AFDC-GA		% change, 1970–1980		
									Population	Net migration	Number of AFDC-GA recipients
	1970	1980	1970	1980	1970	1980	1970	1980			
South Side											
Near South Side	37.2	42.7	41.0	76.0	55.2	62.4	22.4	72.8	−17.4	−28.0	+168.6
Douglas	31.1	42.6	43.0	70.0	48.9	57.0	24.3	36.6	−13.5	−33.0	+30.6
Oakland	44.4	60.9	48.0	79.0	64.3	76.0	38.4	60.5	−8.4	−25.6	+44.1
Grand Boulevard	37.4	51.4	40.0	76.0	58.2	74.5	30.4	45.6	−32.9	−37.6	+0.7
Washington Park	28.2	43.2	35.0	70.0	52.0	67.1	23.2	48.2	−30.6	−35.7	+50.5
Englewood	24.3	35.8	30.0	57.0	47.7	61.9	21.8	41.4	−34.2	−46.2	+25.0
West Side											
Near West Side	34.7	48.9	37.0	66.0	44.6	64.8	26.9	44.4	−27.2	−37.9	+20.1
East Garfield Park	32.4	40.3	34.0	61.0	51.9	67.2	32.5	42.7	−39.5	−53.8	−20.6
West Garfield Park	24.5	37.2	29.0	58.0	47.7	58.4	24.6	40.4	−30.1	−46.7	+14.8
North Lawndale	30.0	39.9	33.0	61.0	56.0	62.2	32.2	40.6	−35.1	−50.1	−18.0
Chicago	12.2	16.8	29.7	27.0	41.5	44.8	8.5	16.9	−10.8	−17.3	+78.1

Sources: Chicago Fact Book Consortium (1984), City of Chicago (1973), and Chicago Area Geographic Information Study (no date).

and the rest of the city (not to mention its suburbs). In 1970, the citywide percentage of families living under the poverty line in Chicago was around 12 percent; in the ghetto, these rates were already in the twenties and thirties for most neighborhoods. A decade later, the city's poverty rate had risen by less than 5 percent, but shot up an average of 12 percentage points in its poorest sections. In eight of the ten community areas that make up the historic core of the Black Belt, upwards of four families in ten were mired in poverty. Accompanying this rise of poverty was a proliferation of single-parent families: on the South Side, more than 70 percent of all households were headed by women in 1980, compared to a level of about 40 percent ten years earlier and to a citywide figure of less than 27 percent in 1980. Even more spectacular was the growth and spread of public aid receipt. Despite heavy population losses due to voluminous outmigration (from one third to one half of the residents of these areas deserted them in those ten years), the number of recipients of AFDC and general assistance increased throughout the ghetto to reach unprecedented levels.

As can be seen in Figure 3.2, public assistance receipt in Chicago both rose and expanded rapidly over this decade, radiating outward from the poorest ghetto neighborhoods of the city. In 1970, four community areas had rates of welfare receipt of about one third,[27] and in the poorest of all, Oakland, 41.5 percent of the total population was on welfare; only 14 of the 77 community areas had rates exceeding one in five. Ten years later, 28 did, including seven which topped the 50 percent mark. In Grand Boulevard, Oakland, and the Near South Side, respectively 61 percent, 71 percent, and 84 percent of the population were on one public assistance program or another in 1980.[28] Not surprisingly, the neighborhoods hit hardest by unemployment and poverty, that is, the ghetto communities of the South Side and West Side, were those where welfare receipt rates grew most rapidly.

The juxtaposition of Figure 3.3, which captures changes in unemployment by community area, with Figure 3.2 evidences a clear geographical pattern in the growth and extension of public assistance that correlates tightly with the increase and spread of joblessness.[29] In fact, each map is nearly a reproduction of the other. Together, they show how economic hardship and social dislocations have cumulated in the same areas of concentrated poverty.

It is well established in the sociological literature that economic hardships adversely impact the formation and stability of families. Research

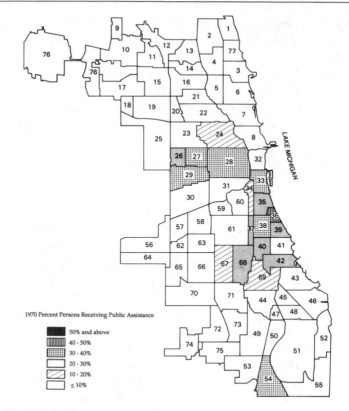

Fig. 3.2. Public assistance in Chicago by community area, 1970–1980

has consistently demonstrated, for example, a direct relation between the timing of marriage and economic conditions: the more encouraging the latter, the earlier young people tend to marry. Once married, the higher the income of the couple, the lower their chance of divorce, and so on. In this connection, the weak employment status of a large and growing number of black males has been hypothesized as the main reason for the fact that blacks marry considerably later than whites and have much lower rates of remarriage, each of these phenomena being closely associated with the high incidence of out-of-wedlock births and female-headed households that has gripped the ghetto in recent years. Indeed, black women generally, but especially young black females residing in large cities, are facing a shrinking pool of "marriageable" (that is, economically secure) men.[30] And this problem is particularly acute in the

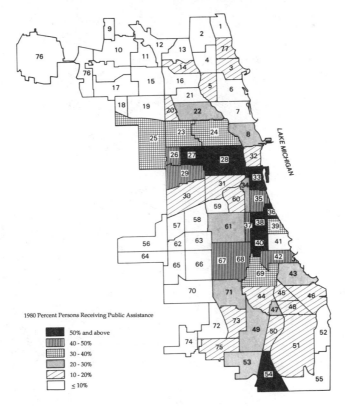

Fig. 3.2. (continued)

ghetto areas of the inner city. For example, in Oakland, Grand Boulevard, and Washington Park, three areas which compose the heart of Chicago's black ghetto, the aggregate ratio of employed males over adult females has decreased sharply and continuously since 1950 (see Figure 3.4). At that time, there were between six and seven employed males for every ten adult women in these neighborhoods, a ratio close to the citywide figure of 73 percent.[31] Thirty years later, this proportion had dropped to 56 percent in Chicago, but plummeted to 24 percent in Grand Boulevard, 29 percent in Washington Park, and a mere 19 percent in Oakland. No other group in urban America has experienced such a rapid and near-total depletion of the pool of marriageable men.

This argument involves no presumption that the marriage rate will rise automatically once a sufficient number of employed males are present

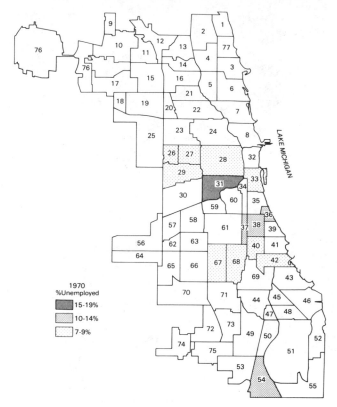

Fig. 3.3. Unemployment in Chicago by community area, 1970–1980

in a neighborhood, for clearly a host of other factors are involved in the process of family formation, such as the cultural meaning of marriage, the balance of power between genders, the cultural acceptability of cross-racial or live-in unions, the age considered proper for mating, together with the differential age composition of gender groups, and so on. But, other things being equal, a minimal pool of securely employed males is a necessary, if not a sufficient, condition for the smooth functioning of a stable marriage market;[32] it is hard to deny that a large demographic deficit of such partners, as evidenced by Figure 3.4, places severe structural constraints on marriage processes, irrespective of the cultural idiom of the population in question. As Blau (1987) aptly puts it, "whether our choices are fully determined by our constitution, background, and experiences or whether we are entirely free to marry anyone who is willing

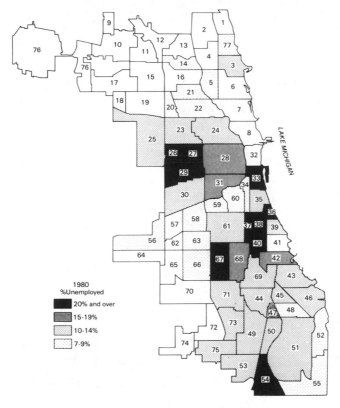

Fig. 3.3. (continued)

to marry us, we cannot marry Eskimos if there are none around."[33] When aggregate ratios of women (of all ages) per employed men drop to such lows as one for seven, it seems warranted to conclude that joblessness hinders family formation in the inner city.

The sharp drop in the pool of "marriageable" men is a reflection of a cumulation of economic and social dislocations that have fundamentally altered the social fabric of inner-city communities. Today's ghetto neighborhoods are not only very different from other urban neighborhoods: they are also quite different from what they were twenty or thirty years ago. The evolution of the class structure of the ghetto testifies to an increasing segregation of the most deprived segments of the black community. This is most clearly seen in the skyrocketing rates of labor market exclusion. The number of working adults in the inner-city neighborhoods

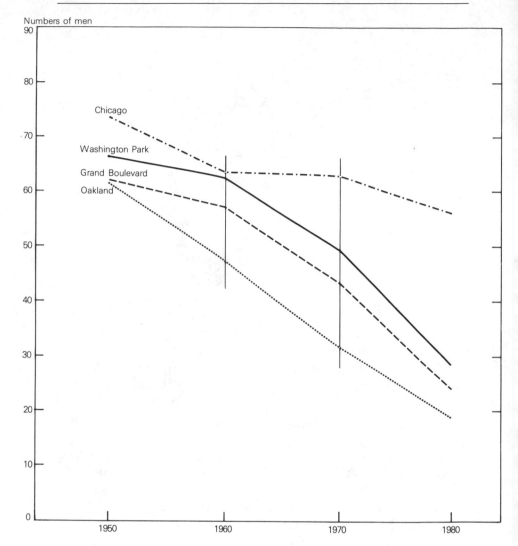

Fig. 3.4. Employed men per 100 women in Chicago and three inner-city communities in Chicago

of the South Side dropped by 50 percent in the decade from 1970 to 1980 alone. Whereas a majority of adults residing in Oakland, Grand Boulevard, and Washington Park were gainfully employed in 1950, by 1970, 57 percent of them did not hold a job, and in 1980 that figure had risen to a staggering 73 percent. By comparison, the employment rate for the city as a whole remained above 55 percent throughout this thirty-year period. As might be expected, the most severe losses occurred among blue-collar workers. In 1950, more than 35,800 residents of these three communities were laborers and operatives, and a full 6,600 were foremen and craftsmen. By 1980, these occupations added up to fewer than 6,200, a drop of more than 85 percent. The number of managers, professional, and technical staff living in these areas also dropped, from 5,270 in 1950 to 2,225 in 1980; the number of clerical and sales employees, from 10,300 to 5,200. These middle-class occupations represented at most 10 percent of the adult population of these ghetto neighborhoods at any time; by contrast, their proportion more than doubled among black adults in the entire city over that period to exceed 17 percent by 1980.

The fate of the black community of North Lawndale on the city's West Side vividly exemplifies the cumulative process of social and economic dislocation that has swept through Chicago's inner city.[34] After a quarter-century of uninterrupted deterioration, North Lawndale resembles a war zone. Nearly half of its housing stock has disappeared since 1960; what remains is, in most cases, run-down and dilapidated. A recent survey of the area found that only 8 percent of its buildings were in good to excellent condition, with 10 percent on the verge of collapse and another 40 percent in need of major rehabilitation. The physical decay of the neighborhood is matched only by its social deterioration. Levels of crime in North Lawndale have reached astronomical proportions: in 1985, its murder rate was twice that of the city and six times the national figure. Police contacts with juveniles, for instance, were 20 times more frequent there than in the white neighborhoods on the North side of town, with 5 percent of all youths referred to court in the year 1980 alone. While infant mortality has dropped both nationwide and in Chicago, it has continued to climb in North Lawndale. In 1985 it peaked at 28 deaths per 1,000 live births, almost three times the national figure. According to recent counts, a full 70 percent of all babies born in this community are born out of wedlock. And half of all births are currently to mothers twenty-one years or younger, with one in seven to girls aged less than seventeen. The proportion of households headed by women doubled in the last decade, reaching 61 percent or twice the city average in 1980. At the same time, the percentage of those receiving welfare assistance, including Food Stamps and no-grants medical assistance, rose from one third to one half of the entire population.

This staggering explosion of social woes is closely related to a string of plant and store shutdowns that have gradually turned North Lawndale from a lively industrial and commercial hub into one of the most destitute ghetto communities of the city. Chicago still had more than 8,000 factories in 1970; by 1982, this figure was down to 5,200, a net loss of more than 35 percent. Because North Lawndale, like many inner-city neighborhoods across the country, depended heavily on smokestack industries for low-skilled jobs and steady income, it has shouldered more than its share of the costs of this deindustrialization. In its good days, the economy of this West Side community was anchored by two huge factories, the famous Hawthorne plant of Western Electric with over 43,000 jobs, and a Harvester plant employing some 14,000 workers; the world head-quarters of Sears, Roebuck and Company was also located in its midst, bringing another 10,000 jobs. Lorean Evans, a resident of North Lawndale and head of a local economic development group, recalls how the whole area was "just a conglomerate of stores then. We had an auto center and banks, a York's department store, a Woolworth's. We had all kinds of specialty shops" (*Chicago Tribune*, 1985). There were, among others, a Zenith and a Sunbeam factory, a Copenhagen snuff plant, an Alden's catalogue store, a Dell Farm food market and a post office bulk station. But things changed quickly: Harvester closed its gates at the end of the sixties and is now a vacant lot. Zenith, Sunbeam, and Alden, too, shut down their facilities. Sears moved most of its offices to the downtown Loop in 1973, leaving behind only its catalogue distribution center, with a work force of 3,000, until last year, when it was moved out of the state of Illinois. The Hawthorne factory gradually phased out its oper-ations and finally closed down in 1984. As the big plants went, so did the smaller stores, the banks, and countless other businesses dependent for their sales on the wages paid by large employers. To make matters worse, scores of stores were forced out of business or pushed out of the neighborhood by insurance companies in the wake of the 1968 riots that swept through Chicago's West Side after the assassination of Martin Luther King. Tens of others were burned or simply abandoned. It has been estimated that the community lost 75 percent of its business estab-lishments from 1960 to 1970 alone. Today North Lawndale has 48 state lottery agents, 50 currency exchanges, and 99 licensed bars and liquor stores, but only one bank and one supermarket for a population of some 50,000.

During the decades since the fifties, the easing of racial strictures on housing and the rapid improvement of economic opportunities for educated blacks in the corporate and public sectors, spurred by the civil rights movement and affirmative action legislation, led many black middle-class and stable working-class families to leave the ghetto (Wilson, 1980 and 1987). From 1970 to 1980, the number of poor families in North Lawndale decreased by one tenth, but the number of nonpoor families dropped by more than a third. The heavy bleeding of industrial jobs—the number of North Lawndale residents employed in manufacturing and construction declined by two thirds, from 15,200 in 1960 to less than 5,200 twenty years later—combined with the accelerating exodus of working families to produce a quadrupling of the official unemployment rate and an even sharper drop in employment rates. In 1980, a large majority of all adults (62 percent) living in North Lawndale did not hold a job, compared to only four in ten in 1950, when the neighborhood enjoyed the same employment ratio as the rest of the city. These job losses resulted in a sharp drop in the median family income from 74 percent of the city average in 1960 to less than half in 1980. By then, 7 of the 27 census tracts that comprise North Lawndale had poverty rates in excess of 50 percent, while the overall poverty rate peaked at 43 percent, up from 30 percent only ten years before.

Needless to say, the heavy loss of entry-level jobs in industrial plants across the city and the accompanying outmigration of middle-class and stable working-class families were not the only factors involved in the growing social dislocations of Chicago's inner city. The "urban renewal" policy of the last thirty years contributed very directly to entrenching the underclass by concentrating massive public housing projects in the most segregated and poorest neighborhoods of the city (see Hirsch, 1983). Moreover, inner-city schools have declined along with the other institutions of the ghetto. Far from offering an avenue of upward mobility, or even of integration into the working class, let alone into the middle class, the public education system now serves to further solidify the social and economic isolation of the underclass. Of the 39,500 students who enrolled in the ninth grade of Chicago's public schools in 1980 and should have graduated in the spring of 1984, only 18,500 (or 47 percent) did so, and a mere 6,000 (15 percent) of them were capable of reading at or above the national twelfth-grade average. And educational failure was even more likely for those black and Hispanic students who attended nonselective segregated public high schools (as opposed to integrated or selective academic schools) and who represented two thirds of the original class of 1984. Of their cohort of 25,500 ninth-graders, a full

15,900 (63 percent) never finished their secondary schooling. Of the 9,600 who did graduate, 4,000 read at or below the junior level and a meager 1,900 or 7.6 percent read at or above the national average (Designs for Change, 1985). In the early 1980s, then, the probability that a youngster living in Chicago's inner city will successfully complete his or her high school education is of the order of 1 in 14, compared to a national chance of more than 1 in 3 (and 6 in 10 in selective academic high schools of the Chicago area).

Looking beyond high school, the fate of those privileged few who did graduate from inner-city high schools proves no brighter. Of the 16,000 graduates tracked by a recent study, only 31 percent held jobs and 32 percent were reported as unemployed.[35] The paucity of school resources, the grossly skewed class and racial composition of its public,[36] the severely limited chances of mobility it affords and the absence of a perceptible connection between educational and occupational success, all add up to make the school a mechanism of exclusion for the children of Chicago's ghetto residents. As a former superintendent puts it, inner-city public schools have become "reserves for the poor."[37]

Changes in North Lawndale typify the social transformation of inner-city neighborhoods in Chicago. They reveal a shift from what we may, in ideal-typical terms, describe as an "institutional ghetto," largely duplicating the activities and organizational texture of the larger society, to a physical ghetto incapable of offering even the most basic resources, services, and opportunities.[38] Our analysis of the increasing concentration of poverty, joblessness, and welfare receipt in other Rustbelt central cities, as well as of the bleeding of industrial jobs on which the urban poor have traditionally relied most, suggests that this bleak picture of Chicago's inner city is not unique. It indicates, rather, not only that life-conditions have dramatically worsened in the ghettos of the country's large metropolises, but also that these racial enclaves now harbor unprecedented concentrations of the most underprivileged segments of the urban poor.

Effects of the Social and Institutional Transformation of the Inner City

Increased joblessness, poverty, and receipt of welfare do not simply result mechanically from having large numbers of poor together in the same areas. They signal, rather, a *transformation of the social and institutional structure of the inner city* which, given the profound economic changes discussed above, puts their residents in a radically more constraining situation than their counterparts of earlier times or the poor of other neighborhoods.[39]

First, in extreme poverty areas, the steady exodus of working- and middle-class families has removed an important "social buffer" that used to deflect the full impact of unemployment, thus leaving the ghetto poor more vulnerable to the kind of prolonged and increasing joblessness that has plagued inner-city communities in the 1970s and early 1980s as a result of uneven economic growth and periodic recessions (Wilson, 1987). The absence of stable working families makes it considerably more difficult to sustain basic institutions in the inner city, for it cuts deep into their membership and saps their base of support: banks, stores, professional services, and restaurants lose their best and most regular patrons; churches see their audience dwindle and their resources shrink; recreational facilities, block clubs, community groups, and other informal organizations also fail to retain their most likely users.[40] The decline of these organizations, in turn, weakens means of formal and informal social control and contributes to increasing levels of crime and street violence, which helps accelerate the deterioration of the neighborhood.

Second, as we have seen, the concentration of poverty significantly impacts on the schools and educational processes. More specifically, with the lowering of the class composition of the student body and of the volume of "cultural capital" (Bourdieu, 1979) that children bring in from outside the school, chances of academic success are significantly reduced. The concentration of low-achieving students itself undermines teachers' morale and discipline. It also weakens the perception of a meaningful relation between education and work and thus decreases academic aspirations. The neighborhood in which the school is located is also less supportive of education and less demanding with regard to educational achievement.[41] All of this makes it exceedingly difficult for the school to compete with other available sources of income and status, including nonconventional and illegal ones.

Third and most important, the class transformation of the inner city drastically cuts off employment channels. For one thing, there are fewer local businesses, service establishments, and stores around that can offer jobs—not only full-time positions on which a wage-earner might be able to raise a family, but also the kind of part-time jobs that are crucial to initiate youths into the world of work. Illegal activities such as drug dealing or fencing stolen goods are often the only readily available means by which teenagers from these communities can get the income they and their families need. As a result, many inner-city adolescents routinely become involved with crime rather than work at an early age. More crucially, though, inner-city residents become *isolated from the job networks* that permeate other neighborhoods. They lack the kind of informal contacts with employers or workers that are decisive in obtaining employment: with fewer kin, friends, or acquaintances holding jobs or in a position to influence hiring, they are less likely to learn about openings, to be recommended for, and to retain such jobs as might become available.[42] A recent series of interviews with black residents of Chicago's inner city has shown that such contacts are indeed held to be decisive in the job hunt: when asked "what it takes to find a good job in Chicago today," a majority of respondents spontaneously mentioned "connections" as the most critical factor.

Fourth, as the structure of opportunity is distorted by the class transformation of the inner city, the social perception of this structure is also altered. When the objective probability of achieving a socially rewarding and stable life, symbolized by the presence of working- and middle-class families, decreases abruptly, conventional aspirations make much less sense and prove more difficult to sustain, and individuals are more likely to try to adjust to a condition that appears unchangeable and inevitable. This triggers a circular process that feeds back onto itself, whereby subjective expectations and hopes act to reinforce the objective mechanisms that limit prospects and avenues for mobility. In a neighborhood plagued by uninterrupted material and social decay and massive exclusion from the productive sphere of society, where stable employment opportunities are objectively minimal and where chances of economic self-sufficiency are simply not a reality for a large majority of the residents, it should not be surprising that many find it difficult to maintain a solid commitment to the labor force and belief in the economic promises of middle-class America. The experience of long and repeated spells of unemployment, or a succession of low-paying, dead-end jobs that cannot generate sufficient income to support a family are hardly conducive to a strong attachment to the labor market. As the German sociologist Claus Offe has remarked, "to the extent that the experience (or the anticipation) of unemployment, or involuntary retirement from worklife, increases, the more the effect of moral stigmatization and self-stigmatization generated by unemployment wears off because, beyond a certain threshold (and *especially if unemployment is concentrated* in certain regions and industries), it can no longer be accounted for plausibly in terms of individual failure or guilt" (Offe, 1985; emphasis added).

Thus it is the local social setting and its associated structure of opportunities which explain the behavior, aspirations, and hopes of inner-city residents. Far from arising from a self-reproducing culture of poverty, their disposition toward the future, which is characterized by what may appear (from the middle-class standpoint of someone whose life is objectively ordered and regular) as a certain lack of rational planning and personal ambition, is an expression of their objective future.[43] And it is in this new structural context that the tangle of disruptions associated with poverty must be placed in order to be fully comprehended. The expansion of inner-city welfare, then, is not an autonomous force that generates other social problems, but a response to the complex interaction of economic and social forces that have severely reduced the opportunity prospects and resources of poor inner-city dwellers and led to their increasing social isolation. The implications of our analysis for social policy in general, and the current welfare reform discussion in particular, is the subject of our concluding section.

The Economy, the Underclass, and the Limited Vision of Welfare Reform

The *growth of welfare in large inner cities is but a surface manifestation of deeper social-structural and economic changes,* including deindustrialization, skyrocketing rates of joblessness, the increasing concentration of poverty, and racial polarization. Let us stress here that these sharp increases in public assistance and associated dislocations took place during the very period when both the eligibility requirements for public aid became tighter and the real dollar value of the basic welfare package (AFDC plus food stamps) went down (by 22 percent between 1972 and 1984; see Danziger and Gottschalk, 1985). Therefore they can hardly be attributed to the greater generosity of the welfare state. Disaggregating these data allowed us to show that the problems of rising poverty, joblessness and welfare dependency since 1970 have essentially struck the Rustbelt cities of New York City, Chicago, Philadelphia, Detroit, Cleveland, Indianapolis and Baltimore. Underlying these trends were sharp differences in the fate of the employment infrastructure of Sunbelt and Rustbelt metropolises. Whereas the pool of jobs increased steadily in all major economic sectors in the South and West from the late fifties to the early eighties, employment in manufacturing, retail trade, and wholesale trade declined dramatically in all of the Rustbelt centers. Indeed, the expansion of services in these central cities compensated for only a small portion of the losses caused by massive deindustrialization, so that by the end of this period they had incurred a net deficit of hundreds of thousands of the jobs generally most accessible to poor central-city residents.

These differences between older industrial centers situated in declining economic regions and the newer, growing, metropolises of the economically expanding Sunbelt[44] demonstrate the importance of relating the evolution of public assistance to basic trends in the broader society and economy. In addition, as our account of the deterioration of Chicago's ghetto over recent decades testifies, the movement of these broader structures has had wide-ranging repercussions in the social fabric of inner-city communities, transformations which further exacerbated the impact of basic economic dislocations. The result is that the poor living in today's large urban ghettos are more concentrated and socially isolated than ever before. It is the complex articulation of all these factors—shifts in industrial base and the accompanying recomposition of labor markets, together with demographic and racial changes, poverty concentration, and the local social structure—that constitutes the matrix of forces out of which welfare receipt evolves.

What implications does this analysis have for the current debate on welfare? In recent years, a liberal-conservative consensus on the question of welfare reform has emerged around the notions that (1) public assistance should be based on reciprocal responsibilities whereby society is obligated to provide assistance to welfare recipients, who in turn are obligated to society to behave in socially approved ways; and (2) able-bodied adult recipients should be required to prepare themselves for employment, to search for work, and to accept jobs when they are offered.[45] Both of these themes were emphasized in the major welfare reform reports released in 1986 and 1987,[46] and figure prominently in the House and Senate versions of the welfare reform legislation currently under discussion.

These two points of agreement are predicated on the implicit assumption that it is not the availability of (decent) jobs, but the willingness to work that is the obstacle to be vanquished on the road to self-sufficiency; that a "welfare ethos" has emerged which encourages recipients of public assistance to shirk their social obligations as citizens to work, to be educated, to form and maintain families, and to obey the law. In other words, *it is the moral fabric of individuals, not the social and economic structure of society, that is taken to be the root of the problem.* This assumption is, in our opinion, both *unwarranted and untenable.* To date, no rigorous research can support such a view. Indeed, the basic timing and spatial patterning of mounting social dislocations and welfare receipt in recent years belie it. In many ways, this transformation of a societal problem into a question of individual attributes and incentives is little more than a modernized version of the sort of conventional attacks that have been launched against welfare programs since their inception by proponents of a market society.[47]

Because those involved in the formulation of new welfare policy often share this individualistic and moralistic vision, they have paid too little attention to the broader economic and social-structural factors that are responsible for the crystallization of a large underclass and persistent welfare dependency. Except for the New York State Task Force (1986) report on welfare reform, submitted to Governor Cuomo, most calls for changes in the welfare system fail to consider the problems associated with the loss of jobs due to structural shifts in the economy and the periodic recessions that accompany them. These problems, ranging from family breakup and marriage delay to the deterioration of inner-city neighborhoods, are prime sources of continued welfare need.

If the structural forces that affect public asssistance are not recognized, proposed programs for welfare reform will have minimal impact, should they be adopted. For example, an employment-oriented welfare program that is not part of a broad framework including some macro-management of the economy remains at the mercy of its vagaries. As Robert Reischauer has pointed out, "in recessionary periods, when jobs are scarce throughout the nation, a credible emphasis on work will be difficult to maintain. Unskilled welfare recipients will realize that they stand little chance of competing successfully against experienced unemployed workers for the few positions available. In regions of the country where the economy is chronically weak, this dilemma will be a persistent problem. Evidence from one such area, West Virginia, suggests that work-welfare programs can do little to increase the employment or earnings of welfare recipients if the local economy is not growing. A public sector job of last resort may be the only alternative in such cases" (Reischauer, 1987b).

Our analysis thus leads us to strongly favor the nonwelfare approach to welfare reform, that is, to move beyond workfare programs in favor of a comprehensive package of policies anchored in *economic measures designed to attack the structural roots of the problem, rather than treat its more apparent symptoms at the level of individuals.* A program that combines progressive welfare reform with a policy to create jobs and universal provision of child and health care would be far more effective in the long run in lifting people out of poverty and off the welfare rolls. But given the seriousness of the problems of poverty concentration and social dislocations in the inner city, we also find it imperative to change the current tax laws in order to obtain the financial means necessary to launch comprehensive reforms in the areas of education, training and retraining, and child support assurance, and to expand the earned-income tax credit. Key to the success of such programs is their universal character, which will require putting an end to the categorization and balkanization of welfare in American political life. The debilitating bifurcation of welfare and social insurance policies is arguably the single greatest political impediment to a successful attack on poverty in this country.

The current poverty situation in the inner city calls for a comprehensive, social-democratic agenda of reform. We cannot discuss here such a program in detail.[48] But the first and foremost item on this agenda would surely be full employment. There are several bills before Congress now that address issues of employment and that would do far more to enhance the lives of the poor than any of the current proposals of welfare reform. One of these bills, the Quality of Life Action Act (authored by Congressman Charles Hayes of Illinois and introduced on March 4, 1987), establishes a program for carrying out the Employment Act of 1946 and the Humphrey-Hawkins Full Employment and Balanced Growth Act of 1978, two laws which have never been implemented. Another bill, the Economic Bill of Rights (introduced on July 1, 1987, by Congressman Hayes along with Augustus F. Hawkins of California), outlines legislation patterned after President Franklin Roosevelt's original Bill of Economic Rights set forth in 1944. It affirms the commitment of the federal government to assure the eight basic rights originally introduced by President Roosevelt over forty years ago: (1) the right to useful paid employment; (2) the right to earn enough to provide an adequate living; (3) the right of every farmer to raise and sell agricultural products at a return which will provide a decent family living; (4) the right of every business, large and small, to trade in an atmosphere of freedom from unfair competition and domination by monopolies at home and abroad; (5) the right of every family to a decent home; (6) the right to adequate medical care and the opportunity to achieve and enjoy good health; (7) the right to adequate protection from the economic fears of old age, sickness, accident, and unemployment, and (8) the right to a good education. Items 1 and 2 and 5 through 8 would seem especially relevant to the present welfare debate. A less ambitious but no less important employment bill, the Guaranteed Job Opportunity Act, was recently introduced by Senator Paul Simon. This bill would establish a program of project-oriented jobs, modeled on the Works Progress Administration (WPA), that would guarantee job opportunities to every American citizen unable to find employment in the private sector.

Odd as it may seem, another chief concern of welfare reform should be the need to raise the minimum wage. It is not enough to require of a welfare recipient to be employed when such jobs as he or she may find do not pay enough to support a family. Today, upwards of 9 million Americans work and still officially live in poverty.[49] The current minimum wage, after adjusting for inflation, is over 20 percent below its average of the 1970s and a third less than its peak of 1968. A full-time, year-round, minimum-wage worker earns about $6,968 in a year, coming 20 percent short of the poverty line for a family of three and 38 percent below for a family of four (compared to 120 percent in 1968).[50] In 1985 about 7.5 million worked at the minimum wage, more than two thirds of them adults and three of every ten heads of households. Raising the minimum wage would appreciably improve the situation of the working poor.

The fact that the effects of welfare reform alone are likely to be extremely limited is another justification for going beyond it.[51] There are, officially, over 32 million poor today in the United States (most of them children and women) and only one third of them receive public assistance: those not on the welfare rolls should not be forgotten. Universal programs provide the only means of including them among the beneficiaries of social spending. Furthermore, such social insurance programs have historically proved considerably more effective in fighting poverty than have means-tested programs (Burtless, 1986).

To conclude, welfare cannot be divorced from the diverse and profound changes that are reshaping the American social structure and the country's political economy. It is these underlying structural changes, and not the expansion of welfare programs or the mysterious ascendancy of a "culture of poverty," that are the moving force behind the growing social woes of large American cities and associated increases in public aid receipt. Policy responses must therefore aim not at ameliorating the assumed individual traits of the poor, but at checking the structural mechanisms that produce them. As we contemplate the political obstacles that stand in the way of devising and implementing a comprehensive program that would integrate economic, social, and tax policy to attack the roots of poverty not only in the inner city but in the larger society as well, we consider that the first essential step is to break out of the narrow vision of the current welfare debate and to change its terms in order to *bring the society and the economy back to center stage.*

FOUR

The Effect of Reform on Employment, Earnings, and Income

Gary Burtless

Over the past two decades a great deal has been written about the defects of the American welfare system. Public assistance programs for able-bodied adults are said to discourage work and encourage illegitimacy and divorce. They provide too little income to sustain a life of dignity but too few incentives to encourage or compel recipients to end their dependency. Unhappiness with welfare has led three of the last four presidents to propose major reforms in the basic design or administration of the main cash program, AFDC. None of these reform packages has been enacted into law, although Congress has several times made modest changes in the program. Within the past two years, dissatisfaction with the current system has once again stimulated calls for reform, from both the Reagan Administration and the Congress. In addition, a number of study commissions have recently concluded that significant reform is needed. Partly in response to their proposals, Congress passed a modest reform package in late 1988.

Virtually all recent reform proposals share a few common goals. A central goal is to reduce long-term dependency by raising employment and earnings levels among single mothers who would otherwise receive welfare. Most reformers also wish to raise the well-being of single mothers and their children, at least eventually, by ensuring that net earnings gains among the mothers more than offset any temporary losses in welfare benefits that may result from reform. Quite a number of reformers expect (or at least hope) that their suggested reforms will ultimately reduce government outlays on the dependent, working-age poor. Even if outlays must temporarily rise in order to pay for added education, training, or support services, it is hoped that these investments will someday pay for themselves in the form of lower public assistance benefits to the able-bodied poor.

This chapter will examine the potential effects of the proposed welfare reforms, especially of those involving changes in recipients' financial incentives to work and in the employment, education, and training options available under the federal-state welfare program. Two distinct types of reform have been proposed. The first calls for enrichment of the traditional employment and training options available to welfare recipients. The second requires recipients to participate in specific employment and training programs (for example, mandatory workfare or compulsory job search programs). The first type of reform is typically advocated by political liberals; the second, by conservatives.

Another reform that is frequently mentioned is strengthened enforcement of the child-support obligations of absent fathers—an idea that can have potentially far-reaching effects on the work effort and incomes of single mothers. However, I will not discuss child-support proposals here, for they are the topic of another chapter.

A major part of this essay is devoted to describing the evidence accumulated over the past decade about the effectiveness of alternative strategies for welfare reform. Like other authors who have recently surveyed this material, I conclude that none of the recent reform proposals is likely to have more than a small impact, in the short run, on employment and earnings among single mothers. The work behavior of low-income single mothers appears to be quite impervious to fairly wide swings in welfare policy and administrative practice. Statistical evidence and historical experience confirm that it is very difficult to raise substantially the earnings of disadvantaged single parents.

This does not imply that the effort to do so is futile: quite the contrary. The data indicate overwhelmingly that employment and training programs for dependent single mothers can raise their earnings and can do so in a cost-effective way. But the evidence is also quite convincing in demonstrating that the earnings gains achieved in these programs are not enough by themselves to raise many single mothers out of poverty and intermittent dependency. If the fundamental goal of reform is to reduce poverty among single mothers, advocates of reform are likely to be disappointed by the magnitude of responses discussed here.

I should add, however, that the examination of the short-term impacts that follows does not really resolve the critical issues that form the crux of the current debate about welfare. For one thing, the long-term effects of most policy reforms are only poorly understood if they are understood at all. A short-term spurt in earnings, for example, may eventually become a very large gain in earnings, or it may disappear altogether. Reforms that raise the earnings and reduce the dependency of welfare mothers today may have even larger effects on the earnings and dependency of their children, or they may not affect the children at all. Policies that discourage single mothers from becoming dependent may encourage them to marry or remain married, or they may simply increase poverty in one-parent households.

Even if our knowledge about the long-term effects of policy were perfect, such knowledge would not necessarily resolve the conflicts among policy advocates who hold fundamentally different views about the proper objective of welfare policy. Some people are interested in reducing poverty in a cost-effective way, while others wish to improve child welfare while maintaining or enhancing the dignity of single mothers. Some place greatest emphasis on reducing poverty; others, on reducing welfare dependency. Depending on their goals and their social and moral values, two would-be reformers could advocate different policies even when they agree completely on the short- and long-run consequences of alternative policies.

The remainder of this chapter is organized as follows. The next section describes the major employment and training options that are available to raise earnings among AFDC recipients. This section presents a brief survey of empirical evidence on the effectiveness of different reform options. It concludes with a synthesis of the policy implications of this evidence. In the third section I discuss possible reforms in the benefit formula of AFDC, with emphasis on reforms that are believed to encourage work. That section also considers the potential effects of an earnings or wage-rate subsidy, such as the existing Earned Income Tax Credit (EITC). Several recent reform proposals involve liberalization of the EITC or introduction of a generous wage subsidy to supplement earnings or encourage additional work among low-income families with children. The chapter ends with a brief discussion of policy conclusions.

Employment and Training

When Aid to Dependent Children (ADC) was established under the Social Security Act in 1935, one of its main goals was to enable widows and other single mothers to care for their children without being compelled to seek or hold a job. A mother's principal role was seen as that of a caregiver and homemaker, not that of a breadwinner. The Committee on Economic Security, whose recommendations were followed by President Franklin D. Roosevelt and Congress in establishing Social Security, wrote of "aid to release from the wage-earning role the person whose natural function is to give her children the physical and affectionate guardianship necessary not alone to keep them from falling into social misfortune, but more affirmatively to rear them into citizens capable of contributing to society" (see U.S. Congressional Budget Office, 1987, p. 7).

By the mid-1960s this view had significantly changed. Many beneficiaries of ADC—and its successor program AFDC—were no longer widows and orphans, as had been the case in the Depression. A growing fraction of recipients were mothers who had never been married or who had been divorced or deserted by husbands who failed to provide financial support to their children. The dependency of these mothers and their children was seen as at least partly due to the incentives embodied in AFDC itself. By providing a dependable source of income when a male breadwinner was absent, the program discouraged never-married mothers from seeking to marry and encouraged dissolution of marriages when the father's income was low or erratic. It is not certain whether these incentives are an important explanation for rising illegitimacy and divorce rates, but a causal relationship has been widely assumed in public discussions.

Work incentives in AFDC became more popular because of a broad change in social attitudes toward work among mothers. Because work was increasingly common among married mothers, including mothers with very young children, there seemed little reason to excuse single women from the obligation to work solely because they were responsible for rearing children.

The new attitude toward work among AFDC recipients was reflected in the establishment of the WIN program in 1967. The WIN legislation changed two aspects of the AFDC program. First, it altered the benefit formula in a way that was thought to encourage work among recipients. This financial incentive to work will be discussed in greater detail below. Second, the legislation established a counseling and training program to enable recipients with older children to seek and retain jobs. Over the next decade the amount of resources devoted to the counseling and training program gradually rose. Local welfare officials were required to refer certain adult recipients to the program. Typically, adult women were to be excused from registering only if they were already receiving schooling, were disabled, or were responsible for children under age six. As a practical matter, however, many women referred to WIN counseling and employment programs were not given much help in obtaining work or training. The level of resources available to assist mandatory partic-ipants in WIN was simply too low. In many jurisdictions, participation in WIN activities, such as counseling, training, work experience, or job search, was largely voluntary among women who were required to reg-ister in the program.

The OBRA legislation of 1981 authorized states to experiment with tougher work and training obligations than those previously permitted under WIN. For example, states were permitted to require a mother to register for work or training when her youngest child was three rather than six years old. States were also given the authority to institute com-munity work experience (or "workfare") programs in which able-bodied AFDC recipients could be required to perform short-term, unpaid com-munity service in exchange for their welfare grants. Although such pro-grams had been tried before, previous attempts had typically been modest and short-lived.

At the same time that Congress and the administration authorized novel work and training programs for AFDC recipients, they significantly cut federal funding of such efforts under the WIN program. In 1986, for example, federal spending on WIN was about $200 million, or only about one-third the level in 1979 (U.S. Congressional Budget Office, 1987). Moreover, federal support of other employment programs also waned. In 1980, federal outlays on employment and training services in the ETA amounted to $9.3 billion. By 1986 these outlays had been reduced to just $3.7 billion.[1] Some of this spending is targeted on AFDC recipients. As the federal government has given states greater flexibility in imposing work and training obligations on welfare recipients, it has substantially reduced the level of federal funding to support work and training efforts at the local level.

Work and Training Options

Much of the current discussion of employment and training among AFDC recipients focuses on what specific programs should be offered and which recipients, if any, should be obligated to participate. The potential programs range from the very cheap, such as loosely monitored job search efforts, to the very expensive, such as formal education and training lasting up to a year. There is an equally wide range in proposals regarding the fraction of the AFDC caseload that should be subject to mandatory participation in work and training programs. While many liberals would excuse mothers with young children or women who appear to be short-term recipients, some conservatives would require some form of participation on the part of virtually every mother free of physical or mental handicap.

Over the past decade analysts have sought to determine the effectiveness of alternative employment and training strategies. Much of this research is pertinent to the current debate about work and training requirements in AFDC. Some is relevant to assessing the efficacy of cheap and simple (as opposed to expensive or elaborate) forms of assistance. Within the past couple of years the MDRC has obtained reliable evidence about the effects of imposing certain kinds of work and training obligations on welfare recipients. Although these results cannot be used to predict the exact consequences of a specified course of reform, they can be used to evaluate the relative effectiveness of several broad strategies.

Here I will consider enriched work and training programs and mandatory programs. Although the obligatory programs might seem more relevant to current discussions of welfare reform at the federal level, at the state level the terms of debate are somewhat different. Two large states—California and Massachusetts—have enacted programs that direct significant new resources to work and training efforts. One limitation of much of the evidence discussed below is that it is based on programs aimed at only a fraction of welfare recipients. Virtually all programs tried in the recent past have been targeted on men and women who are mandatory participants in the WIN program or who are voluntary participants in that program. Few studies have examined the impact of programs that significantly broaden the definition of the population required to participate in WIN. At the end of this section I will consider the policy implications of this limitation.

Basic Forms of Employment and Training Service

Manpower agencies, whether funded under the Work Incentive program or some other auspices, offer only a few basic types of services. One of the most common forms is classroom training, that is, vocational or occupational training, and basic or remedial education delivered in a classroom setting. This kind of training can last from a few weeks to several months. When the target population consists of low-income workers, classroom training rarely lasts as long as a year. This is not because long-term training has been found to be unhelpful, but because manpower agencies can seldom afford expensive training courses.

Another common type of assistance is employment counseling and job placement assistance. This type of help can be more or less expensive depending upon the level of effort that counselors devote to assessing a client's job readiness and then searching for an optimal job or training position. OJT is a form of assistance in which clients receive publicly subsidized job training at the work site of a private employer. If the training turns out to be successful, the client is often kept on as a permanent, unsubsidized employee of the firm. OJT, while apparently quite effective, is less common than classroom training or employment counseling because training slots are difficult to arrange among private employers.

One of the most controversial forms of manpower aid is work experience. This broad term covers at least three distinct types of programs. One program, PSE, is paid work experience in a public or nonprofit agency. Ordinary work experience programs, such as those once run under CETA, provide unpaid work experience clearly aimed at enhancing a client's employability. Community work experience programs, such as those authorized under OBRA, provide unpaid public jobs (with no necessary training component) to Food Stamp or public assistance recipients. Participation in such programs may be a prerequisite for continued receipt of transfers. Public service employment has historically been the most expensive form of manpower assistance; community work experience or workfare is one of the cheapest.

An even cheaper form of aid is job-search assistance. In a typical job-search assistance program, several days will be devoted to teaching clients how to obtain job leads and apply for work. Clients are then expected to engage in active job search for up to eight weeks, making frequent calls or visits to potential employers and otherwise struggling to land a job. This form of aid is inexpensive because it is the client, rather than a job placement officer, who is obligated to exert the greatest effort to find a job. The main cost to the manpower agency is providing the initial training or orientation and monitoring the search efforts of clients. Zealous monitoring has been shown to have positive effects both on the effort devoted to the search and the speed of finding a job.

WIN Services

One of the most comprehensive examinations of WIN was performed by Ketron, Inc. (1980) based on interviews with 4,000 people who entered the program between January 1974 and July 1975. These participants were selected from among program entrants in 78 nationally representative sites. In order to determine the effects of WIN services on participant behavior, Ketron also interviewed 5,000 individuals who were eligible for WIN services but who did not participate in the program.

Ketron then formed its estimate of the program's effect by comparing outcome variables, such as earnings and welfare benefit levels, in the participant group with values of the same outcome variables observed in the nonparticipant comparison group. Statistical adjustments were made to reflect observable differences between the two groups, such as differences in average age, education, or previous employment. This form of analysis is frequently referred to as a nonexperimental comparison-group design, because the estimates of program effect are obtained using a comparison group that is not experimentally selected. In this case the comparison group consisted of individuals who were eligible to participate in WIN but who for some reason chose not to.

It seems likely that the choice not to participate in WIN made this comparison group quite different from the group that chose to participate, not only in measurable ways—such as age and education—but also in unmeasurable ways—such as intelligence and ambition. The two groups therefore differ from one another not just because only one of them has received WIN services, but additionally because one group may have greater average levels of intelligence and ambition than the other. Unfortunately, since these factors cannot be measured, they cannot be controlled for in the analysis. The statistically adjusted difference between outcome variables in the treatment group and the nonexperimental comparison group may thus provide a misleading estimate of the effect that is solely due to the program. The difference may reflect an unknown amount of selection differences between the two groups.

Given this limitation in Ketron's methodology, the estimates nonetheless provide some helpful information in assessing manpower programs targeted on welfare recipients. First, the findings reflect the effects of a program on the portion of the current caseload that is most likely to participate in employment and training programs. They also reflect the average response to the type of manpower program that officials were actually administering in the mid-1970s. Other programs that have been evaluated using more reliable estimation methods are unlikely to be implemented any time soon. Finally, Ketron collected data from an unusually long follow-up period—three years.

Ketron found WIN services to be reasonably effective in raising the earnings of female participants. The average impact of services was to raise earnings by $570 in the first postprogram year, by $520 in the second postprogram year, and by $340 in the third postprogram year.[2] Interestingly, however, the average effects were very unequal for women who reported previous employment and those who reported no previous occupation. Women in the second group enjoyed earnings gains of $920 to $980 in each of the first two years, whereas women with previous employment experienced gains of only $260 to $360. In the third follow-up year, earnings gains among women with no previous occupation were $750; earnings gains among women with a previous occupation were only $90.

The relative gains in these two groups reflect a pattern that has been found in several employment and training programs targeted on low-income women. Larger gains are frequently enjoyed by women who are the most dependent and least employable, as measured either by prior welfare receipt or previous employment experience. Smaller gains are experienced by women who have only recently become dependent or unemployed.

Two other aspects of the Ketron study are worth mentioning. First, although the analysts concluded that the program significantly raised earnings among participants, they did not find that it reduced welfare payments. In fact, welfare benefits may have risen in the WIN participant group relative to those received by the nonparticipant group. Second, Ketron analysts also attempted to measure the effects of alternative program services. These estimates are probably subject to much greater bias due to self-selection than the estimates of overall program effect, so they should be viewed with skepticism. The largest gains in earnings were reported for women who received on-the-job training, where the earnings gains were $1,800 in the year after program participation and nearly $1,200 in the third year.[3] WIN classroom training was less beneficial, leading to earnings gains of approximately $800 per year over the follow-up period. Work experience, which was initially restricted to thirteen weeks, was approximately as effective as classroom training. First-year earnings gains were estimated to be $1,000, rising to approximately $1,400 by the third postprogram year. Ketron found virtually no effect of WIN job placement assistance, presumably because so few placement assistance services were actually delivered to participants in this program component.

Mead (1987) has used state-level WIN administrative data to assess the effectiveness of alternative job placement strategies on WIN performance. States differ in the mix of services they offer to participants, the composition of their caseloads, and the generosity of their benefit formulas. Mead concludes that a primary determinant of their relative success in pushing clients into jobs is the share of welfare clients they compel to participate in the program. If a high fraction of recipients is expected and obligated to participate, the fraction of recipients entering employment will be high. If few recipients are expected to work and compelled to participate, the number of job placements will also be low.

Some of the more interesting studies of the WIN program came from the Louisville WIN Labs. The WIN Labs were conducted using random assignment. Under this procedure, people who are eligible to receive or who apply to receive program services are randomly assigned to a treatment group, which is eligible to receive the program service, or to a control group, which is ineligible to receive the service but which may nonetheless be permitted to receive some other set of nonexperimental services. Because assignment to the two groups is determined by chance alone, the analyst is assured that the groups differ only with respect to their eligibility to receive services. There are no systematic unmeasured differences between the two groups, so the estimate of program impact is not subject to the selection bias which can potentially affect nonexperimental comparison-group estimators. The random assignment procedure permits an analyst simply and reliably to measure the impact of the service on client behavior by comparing average outcomes in the treatment group with those in the control group.

The Louisville WIN Labs provide evidence about the effectiveness of two particular forms of job search assistance. In the first experiment, conducted in 1978 and 1979, WIN clients were assigned to participate in three days of group instruction in job search techniques, followed by six weeks of closely monitored individual job search. The second experiment, conducted between October 1980 and May 1981, tested a more expensive group-oriented program of job finding. After a one-week orientation in job-finding techniques, WIN clients were assigned to small groups in which they conducted intensive job searches under the close supervision of a program counselor.

In comparison to the ordinary mix of WIN services available to the control group, the experimental treatments were more successful in raising employment and earnings. During the first fifteen-month follow-up period in the first Louisville experiment, 64 percent of clients in the treatment group held jobs in comparison to 59 percent among controls. The increase in earnings amounted to approximately $400 per year measured in 1985 dollars. The increase in employment and earnings resulted in a 3-percent decline in welfare benefits in the first follow-up period. Surprisingly, the analysts found no decline in the earnings or welfare effects during a subsequent nine-month follow-up period.

The second WIN Lab achieved even greater gains in client employment and earnings, but the follow-up period was restricted to only six months. As in the earlier experiment, analysts could find evidence of only small reductions in welfare benefits and dependency. Moreover, there was a rapid decline in the amount of welfare savings over time (see Grossman et al., 1985). One point worth emphasizing is that the services provided in the two Louisville experiments were relatively inexpensive. The cost of the individually oriented job search program, for example, was less than $200 per person enrolled. Given these very low program costs, large gains in earnings or reductions in welfare dependency are not needed in order to make the program appear worthwhile. The program can be extremely cost-effective and yet have only a small impact on clients' employment and welfare benefits.

CETA

In addition to directly providing employment and counseling services to AFDC recipients, the WIN program also refers large numbers of its clients to outside agencies for manpower assistance. Many welfare recipients obtain services provided by local agencies funded under the federal JTPA. Since the JTPA program was established in 1982, about one-fifth of trainees funded under Title II-A of the act have been from families receiving AFDC benefits.[4] During 1984 about 120,000 AFDC recipients were participants in programs funded under Title II-A. Unfortunately, we have almost no information about the effectiveness of JTPA-funded services since the primary evaluation of the program has only recently begun.

It is likely, however, that the manpower assistance provided under JTPA is broadly similar to that provided under its predecessor, CETA. Many of the local agencies which now run JTPA programs are identical to the ones which earlier ran CETA programs. Most of the services they deliver are identical or very similar to those they delivered under CETA. Unlike JTPA, CETA has been the subject of numerous evaluations.

Most of the manpower services provided to AFDC recipients under CETA and JTPA went to volunteers from the AFDC caseload. Participation in CETA or JTPA-sponsored programs was rarely required of AFDC recipients as a condition for continued receipt of welfare benefits. Hence the average impact of CETA or JTPA programs on AFDC recipients must be interpreted as the program impact on a self-selected group of volunteers. There is no assurance that the same average impact would be observed if a similar mix of services were offered to a larger group of welfare recipients who were obligated to participate in CETA or a similar manpower program. The average effect of mandatory participation would probably be smaller than that of voluntary participation, for it is likely that welfare recipients would volunteer for the program only when they expect to gain from it. Nonvolunteers probably have less optimistic expectations about the potential benefits of participation. If these expectations are valid, the participation of nonvolunteers in a work or training program would reduce its average effectiveness.

Barnow (1987) has ably summarized the evaluation studies of CETA. Like Ketron's (1980) analysis of WIN, the CETA evaluation studies relied on a nonexperimental, comparison-group design to measure the effects of the CETA program on participant earnings. The data for all the studies were collected from CETA participants enrolled in the middle to late 1970s. Each evaluation used a somewhat different procedure to adjust for the differences between program participants and comparison-group nonparticipants. Unfortunately, these analytical differences yielded substantial differences in estimated effects, even where analysts were measuring earnings impacts for identical populations. This lack of consistency suggests that the findings cannot be used to assess the precise impact of CETA programs on participant earnings.

Nonetheless, a few consistent patterns of response did emerge in all or most of the evaluations. All of the evaluations concluded that women benefited more than men from participation in CETA, or were harmed less by their participation. Usually the earnings gains among women were far higher than those among men (or the earnings losses were far smaller). The average impact of CETA services was consistently positive for adult women, although one of the evaluations concluded that the overall effect was very small (an earnings gain of less than $20 per year). Among components of the CETA program, public service employment (or paid work experience) was consistently found to have a large and beneficial impact on the postprogram earnings of adult women. Of course, public service employment was by far the most costly component as well. There was less agreement about the relative effectiveness of other services—unpaid work experience, classroom and on-the-job training, and multiple program activities—but they were generally found to be beneficial for adult women.

Eight of the evaluations described by Barnow (1987) studied the overall impact of CETA on one or more groups of adult women. They provided an estimate of the average effect of combined CETA services during a calendar year beginning six to thirty months after a participant's enrollment in the program. Measured in 1985 dollars, the estimated earnings gains ranged from a low of $20 per year in one study to a high of $1,350 per year in another. Ignoring the lowest and highest estimates of earnings gains, the range of estimates was from $650 to $1,200 per year. The one study that specifically examined earnings gains among female welfare recipients found gains in the upper part of this range. Of course, it is uncertain whether these earnings gains are permanent. They could diminish over time, or they could grow.

Experimental Enrichment Programs

I will consider the impacts of three experimental employment and training programs aimed at welfare recipients and other low-income breadwinners: the EOPP, the Supported Work Demonstration, and the AFDC Homemaker-Home Health Aide Demonstrations.

The Employment Opportunity Pilot Project. EOPP was originally established to test the feasibility and effectiveness of offering a saturation public service jobs program. Low-income breadwinners who headed families with children were to be guaranteed public service jobs if they could not find private jobs after a six- to eight-week period of directed, intensive job search. If this original goal had been realized, it is doubtful whether the findings of the EOPP demonstrations would have much interest today. PSE programs have been substantially eliminated in the 1980s, and only a few policy makers hope or expect that new ones will be developed any time soon.

The EOPP program as actually implemented, however, was quite different from the one originally intended. In most of the participating sites, the main emphasis of the program was on offering intensive job search assistance and support services, such as child care and transportation aid. Services were delivered primarily to single mothers on AFDC, although other poor single mothers and some male heads of household were also enrolled. Enrollees in the program who were unsuccessful in finding unsubsidized jobs after supervised search were offered a training position or a subsidized public service job. Very few participants ended up in PSE jobs, however.

The most interesting aspect of EOPP is that it enabled welfare administrators to offer manpower services to a high percentage of AFDC recipients who were registered in WIN. Because the WIN program is not well funded and the number of CETA or JTPA training positions is small, many registrants in WIN are not assigned to any specific program activity. Although they are registered, they are obligated to do little to become employed or employable. EOPP changed this situation in the 15 demonstration sites, where WIN counselors were in a position to require registrants to enroll in a specific employment-related activity, usually the EOPP job search program.

In the ten EOPP sites analyzed by Mathematica, one-third of mandatory WIN registrants were enrolled in the EOPP program (Mathematica Policy Research, 1983). Because of limitations in the evaluation of EOPP, it is not clear whether this level of enrollment represents an equivalent increase in the fraction of WIN registrants who were required to participate in an employment-seeking activity. Mathematica nevertheless concluded that the EOPP services had a measurable and fairly sizable impact on the employment status of low-income single mothers residing in EOPP sites. Employment rates among these women rose by 3 to 4 percentage points (or 8 to 11 percent) in comparison to the rates that would have prevailed in the absence of the treatment.[5] Among single women enrolled in the program, the employment gains may have been 12 to 16 percentage points (or 60 to 80 percent), although this figure is highly uncertain because of the estimation methodology on which the analysts were forced to rely. Earnings gains among low-income single women were also impressive. Mathematica estimated, for example, that the unsubsidized earnings of low-income single women within the EOPP sites rose by nearly $300 per year—or 9 percent—in the first two years after program enrollment. Since only about one single women out of every five who were eligible enrolled in EOPP, the effect of the program per enrollee was five times larger, or approximately $1,500 per year.[6]

Mathematica found no evidence, however, that welfare dependency rates among single women were reduced in the EOPP sites. In fact, the evaluation report suggests that average AFDC benefits probably rose slightly. This result appears astonishing in light of the fact that over two-thirds of the unmarried women participating in EOPP were also recipients of AFDC benefits. Mathematica suggests that the earnings gains experienced by EOPP participants may have been too small to affect their eligibility. It is also conceivable that earnings gains were concentrated among women who would have left welfare even without the assistance provided by EOPP. A simpler explanation may be that the services delivered under EOPP—such as child care, transportation aid, and job training—were attractive to recipients and potential recipients of AFDC. By making participation in welfare more desirable or less onerous, EOPP may actually have increased the rate of entry or reduced the rate of exit from AFDC for some kinds of welfare recipients, including those recipients who found jobs through the EOPP program.

Supported Work. The National Supported Work Demonstration tested an ambitious and expensive form of paid work experience. The experimental treatment offered up to twelve months of carefully tailored work experience to participants drawn from four hard-to-employ target groups. Although the high cost of the program makes its relevance somewhat questionable today, the findings from the demonstration were important in establishing the potential effects of making large investments in training the extremely disadvantaged.

For present purposes the most interesting results pertain to AFDC recipients who were enrolled in the program. These recipients were dependent on welfare at the time of their enrollment, having received AFDC benefits in at least thirty of the prior thirty-six months. None had recent work experience. Despite the extreme disadvantage of the target population, the Supported Work treatment induced large gains in unsubsidized employment and earnings. During the period from the nineteenth through the twenty-seventh month after enrollment, the employment rate of enrollees was 8.5 percentage points above that in the randomly assigned control group (49 percent versus 40.5 percent). Earnings in the treatment group were 46 percent greater than those in the control group (MDRC, 1980). Measured in 1985 dollars, the annual rate of gain in earnings was $1,500.

These earnings gains must be assessed against the direct administrative costs of the program (approximately $10,000 per participant, measured in 1985 dollars), which were far higher than those in most manpower training programs. Nevertheless, MDRC concluded that the long-run social benefits of the program outweighed the social costs. From the perspective of taxpayers the program was beneficial, too, primarily because of substantial reductions in AFDC and Food Stamp outlays ($1,300 per woman enrolled) and the value of the services delivered by subsidized trainees. During the period from the nineteenth through the twenty-seventh months after enrollment, these benefit payments were nearly 23 percent below the level observed in the control group. While these reductions in transfer payments are beneficial to taxpayers, they represent a very large percentage of the earnings gains enjoyed by participants. Clearly, the net income gains to Supported Work participants were far smaller than the gains in gross earnings.

AFDC Homemaker-Home Health Aide Demonstrations. These demonstrations were authorized by Congress to give training and subsidized employment to AFDC recipients, who in turn were expected to provide health care services in the homes of functionally impaired clients. Sponsors of the demonstrations wished simultaneously to raise AFDC recipients' earnings by placing them in subsidized and unsubsidized jobs, and reduce government health-care costs by keeping the needy elderly and disabled out of nursing homes. While the demonstrations were notably unsuccessful in achieving the latter goal, they were more successful in accomplishing the former.

In the seven demonstration sites, administrators enrolled volunteers from the AFDC caseload into a four- to eight-week course to train participants to provide home health care and homemaker services to functionally impaired elderly and disabled clients. The training was followed by up to a year of subsidized employment as a homemaker-home health aide. During this year of employment the trainees continued to receive Medicaid coverage and work-related support services. AFDC aides were paid the same wage as regular homemaker aides. The treatment, which was analogous in many ways to Supported Work, was evaluated using a rigorous experimental design. Applicants to the program were randomly assigned to either treatment or control status. Applicants assigned to the latter group continued to be eligible for other WIN services that were locally available. The findings, like those of the Supported Work study, are of interest because they show the potential effects of a very expensive intervention. (Subsidized wages and training and administrative costs totaled slightly more than $10,000 per enrollee.)

The findings suggest that expensive interventions can be a cost-effective way of raising welfare recipients' employment and earnings. Not surprisingly, the overall level of earnings—including subsidized and unsubsidized wages—was substantially higher in the treatment group than in the control group. During the first year and a half after enrollment the entire difference between the two groups was attributable to subsidized wages paid to demonstration home health care aides. However, employment and earnings gains in the treatment group persisted in most sites after the subsidized jobs ended. Significant gains in subsequent unsubsidized employment were registered in four of the seven sites; gains in unsubsidized earnings were observed in five of the seven sites. During the second postprogram year, average earnings gains across the seven sites amounted to $1,100 per year. In various sites the annual gain ranged from a low of $130 to a high of $1,930 (Enns et al., 1986).

In addition to these improvements in employment and earnings, the Abt analysts found a marked postprogram decline in AFDC and Food Stamp payments in four of the sites (Bell, 1986). In one of the other sites, however, a gain in postprogram earnings was not matched by a drop in AFDC and Food Stamp benefits. This discrepancy is consistent with a body of evidence suggesting that it is sometimes easier to raise trainee earnings than it is to reduce trainee welfare benefits. For reasons that are not fully understood, earnings gains in the treatment group did not necessarily cause welfare benefits to fall.

Mandatory Employment and Training Programs

The programs discussed above were predominantly voluntary. Except in the case of the basic WIN program, few welfare recipients were obligated to participate in any of the treatments described. Even in the case of WIN, it is doubtful that a large fraction of AFDC recipients is required to do much more than register in the program in many states. AFDC recipients are rarely obligated to undertake a specific course of activity in order to become employed or employable.

The OBRA legislation passed in 1981 encouraged states to enforce a work-related obligation on a higher proportion of AFDC recipients. States were given the authority to establish demonstration programs to test the effectiveness of imposing work-related requirements. They were also authorized to impose registration requirements or work obligations on single mothers whose youngest child was three or older. (Under the previous federal standard, mothers could be exempt if their youngest child was less than six years old.) The response of the states to recent federal legislation has been described in U.S. Government Accounting Office (1987), Nightingale and Burbridge (1987), and U.S. Congressional Budget Office (1987). MDRC, in cooperation with eleven states, conducted comprehensive evaluations of a variety of state work-welfare initiatives and produced the most interesting reports. In eight of the states, program administrators were persuaded to make random assignments of eligible clients to treatment and control groups. This method yields highly reliable estimates of program effectiveness.

In the next few pages I will describe findings from six of the eleven MDRC demonstrations: in Arkansas, Illinois, Maryland, San Diego, Virginia, and West Virginia. The range of programs tested was quite broad. All of the demonstrations tested work-related programs aimed at AFDC recipients. Three sites also enrolled participants in the AFDC-U program, which provides cash assistance to two-parent families where the main breadwinner is unemployed. I will emphasize results for the AFDC recipients.

Five of the six demonstrations (all but the one in Maryland) tested an unpaid community work experience program. In four sites job assignments occurred only after welfare recipients participated in several weeks of supervised or unsupervised job search. If clients were unsuccessful in finding an unsubsidized job while enrolled in the job search program, they were expected to perform unpaid community service in a public or nonprofit agency. In theory, participants in the program were supposed to work a specified number of hours each month, often computed as the monthly welfare grant divided by the minimum wage rate. In four of the five demonstrations with an unpaid work component, the work requirement was limited to a specified period, usually thirteen weeks. In the West Virginia demonstration the work obligation could last indefinitely.

Four demonstrations examined the effects of job search assistance programs, either alone or in combination with community work experience programs. The demonstrations in San Diego and Cook County,

Illinois, tested two models—job search assistance alone and job search assistance combined with a community work obligation. The demonstration in Baltimore, Maryland, was unique in offering a flexible and relatively expensive package of services aimed at raising the long-term employability of participants. This package did not include an unpaid work obligation, but it did provide job search assistance, access to classroom training, and reasonably generous supportive assistance, such as child care and transportation aid. While participation in the Baltimore program was obligatory for the WIN mandatory clients who were assigned to the experimental plan, the program did not include an obligatory sequence of activities through which participants were expected to pass.

Although the demonstrations were similar in their goal of requiring participants to engage in some work-related activity, they were quite varied in the approach taken to accomplish this goal. In West Virginia, unpaid work was the primary mechanism used to push AFDC recipients into the labor market.

The Baltimore demonstration relied mainly on training and job search assistance. The other four placed greatest emphasis on job search training and individual or group-oriented job search programs. While each of these four demonstrations implemented a community work experience program, participation in work experience was comparatively rare. Only 3 percent of clients enrolled in the Arkansas program did community work; approximately 7 percent participated in workfare in Illinois; 10 percent in Virginia; and 20 percent in San Diego.

The demonstrations varied in the extent to which they penalized clients who did not comply with program rules. For example, in the Cook County demonstration 15 percent of experimental participants were sanctioned for noncompliance with rules, while in Baltimore sanctioning was rare.

The demonstrations also differed markedly in the cost of the services they delivered. The Illinois program was the least expensive ($125 to $140 per enrollee), principally because its job search component relied almost entirely on the unaided efforts of clients themselves and because few participants were actually assigned to a work experience job. Much of the administrative cost in Illinois was associated with monitoring the compliance of participants to the job search obligation. Little money was spent in providing support or services. The Baltimore program was by far the most expensive, with support, training, and administrative costs of about $1,000 per person enrolled. The San Diego demonstration appears to have conducted the most carefully monitored and elaborate job search program, with costs running around $540 to $610 per person enrolled. The experience in these demonstrations suggests that a work-related obligation can be imposed at little cost or at high cost, depending upon the level of training or support services offered. A program can be quite inexpensive if it merely requires welfare recipients to attend orientation meetings and then to prove that they have engaged in systematic job search. The program can cost substantially more if it provides training and support services to ensure that the search efforts are worthwhile.

Given the important differences among the demonstrations, it is hardly surprising that they failed to produce uniform results.[7] MDRC found evidence of earnings impacts on AFDC recipients in four of the six demonstrations. There was little or no detectable effect on earnings in Illinois and West Virginia. The largest short-run impact on AFDC earnings was found in the San Diego program that combined job search assistance with a work obligation. From the second through the sixth calendar quarters after participants' enrollment, this program raised the treatment group's earnings by 23 percent (or $560 per year) above the level observed in the control group. During the brief follow-up periods available for the Virginia and Arkansas demonstrations, earnings rose at rates of approximately $110 and $150 per year, respectively. Earnings gains in Maryland were about $250 per year during the third through the fifth quarters following enrollment, although longer term follow-up data suggest that these earnings impacts were still growing.

MDRC also measured the impact of the demonstrations on welfare benefits and dependency. Again, the largest effect occurred in San Diego, where AFDC benefits in the job search-work experience program fell by $200 per year, or 8 percent of average benefits in the control group. The San Diego program that offered only job search assistance without any community work had less success in raising participant earnings and reducing welfare benefits. Hence the evidence, though weak, tells us that the combined program was somewhat more effective than the job search program by itself. The combined job search-work experience requirements in Arkansas and Virginia caused smaller welfare savings— $120 per year and $80 per year, respectively.

The smallest welfare reductions occurred in Illinois, Maryland, and West Virginia, where benefit reductions amounted to 3 percent or less. While the small effects in Illinois and West Virginia are consistent with the finding that earnings were almost unaffected by the program, it is more difficult to explain the small impact of the program in Maryland. The Baltimore program succeeded in significantly raising earnings among AFDC recipients, but had very little if any impact on benefits and dependency. The explanation may be that the program helped raise the earnings of women who would have left welfare even without the assistance provided through the program. Alternatively, the support and training services offered by the demonstration may have made continued dependency more attractive (or less costly) for a small fraction of welfare recipients, thus prolonging their stays on welfare.

The work-welfare demonstrations appear to offer a few major lessons for policy. First, welfare administrators can substantially raise the fraction of AFDC recipients who are subject to work-related requirements, and can do so with programs that need not cost much money. Three of the six demonstrations—those in Arkansas, Illinois, and West Virginia—cost less than $300 per client enrolled. Even these inexpensive programs were successful in imposing a work-related obligation on many more clients than had faced such obligations in the past. Even though two of these inexpensive programs failed to raise participants' earnings, all three probably achieved at least small reductions in welfare payments. These savings presumably occurred because the perceived cost of receiving welfare had been raised.

Second, more intensive provision of services to AFDC clients can produce larger gains in their subsequent employment and earnings. Of the programs considered here, the demonstrations in Baltimore and San Diego were the most costly and elaborate and produced the largest gains in earnings. Illinois and West Virginia provided fewer and far less expensive services. Their programs also had the smallest impact on paid employment and earnings.

Third, even the largest gains in the most successful mandatory programs turned out comparatively small. To be sure, the earnings gains were sometimes large in relation to average earnings reported in the control group. The earnings gain in Arkansas, for example, represented a 36 percent improvement over average earnings in the control group. But these large proportional gains do not represent major improvements in an average participant's standard of living. The largest average earnings gain, in the San Diego demonstration, was about $560 per year, or less than 7 percent of the poverty-line income for a family consisting of one adult and two children.

Fourth, in most cases the earnings gains achieved in the program were partly or wholly offset by reductions in public transfer benefits. While this is surely the goal of reformers who wish to reduce public dependency and represents a net gain to taxpayers, it reduces or eliminates the gain in living standards that families can expect from participating in the programs. In San Diego, the short-term loss in welfare benefits was approximately 35 percent of the short-term gain in earnings. In Arkansas and Virginia, benefit reductions offset about 80 percent of short-term earnings gains. In both Illinois and West Virginia, where earnings gains were absent, participants probably suffered a net loss in their standard of living because their welfare grants fell slightly. Even if all of the earnings gains caused by the programs were retained by participants, the net effect of the programs on participant well-being would be small. But because earnings gains must be shared with taxpayers through benefit reductions in transfer programs, the effects on participant well-being are even smaller. Of course, if the earnings gains produced by the program tend to grow over time, the gains in participant well-being would grow as well.

Finally, MDRC's analysis showed that most of the tested programs—whether expensive or cheap—were cost-effective. Within a relatively brief period, the direct and indirect costs of the program were offset by social benefits in the form of higher participant earnings or services produced in the community work experience programs.

Subgroup Impacts. Several recent reform proposals have included provisions encouraging state or local authorities to concentrate on serving certain classes of welfare recipients, such as long-term recipients or recipients without recent work experience. This strategy would be advantageous if there were clear evidence that such groups benefited disproportionately from work and training programs, or if welfare benefits were unduly concentrated on these groups. While it is known that certain types of AFDC participants are more likely to become long-term recipients of welfare, it is less clear that employment and training programs have predictable patterns of effects on different categories of participants.[8]

Two studies have recently examined the relative effectiveness of employment and training programs for different classes of welfare participants. Grossman and others (1985), of MPR, examined the subgroup impacts of the Supported Work, EOPP, and WIN programs and the Louisville WIN Labs. Friedlander and Long (1987), of MDRC, evaluated the impacts of three of the recent Work/Welfare Initiative experiments. Whereas Friedlander and Long believed they found a fairly clear pattern of effects, Grossman and coauthors detected no strong pattern of effects in the several programs they examined.

Under Friedlander and Long's interpretation, the women in the Work/ Welfare experiments with less work experience and greater welfare dependence experienced greater earnings gains than women with more work experience and less previous dependence. Although this pattern of findings might suggest that employment and training programs should be targeted on welfare recipients with lengthy previous spells of dependency and limited work experience, the implications of the study for resource allocation are in fact quite ambiguous.

First, the Work/Welfare experiments probably induced employment and earnings gains even among women with fairly extensive previous work experience. Second, the largest gains in employment and earnings were observed among women with moderate spells of previous dependence on welfare rather than among women with the longest spells of dependence. Perhaps the women with the greatest dependency would have benefited from more intensive services than those provided in the Work/Welfare experiments. Finally, the largest reductions in welfare benefits and welfare dependency were registered among women with no previous spells of dependency, even though these women did not appear to enjoy earnings gains from their participation in the Work/Welfare program. The program may have deterred some of these women from participating in AFDC, even though it did not help them find jobs any faster than they might have done otherwise.

In analyzing the impact of Supported Work, EOPP, and WIN, the MPR analysts distinguished between inexpensive job search programs and more expensive training and work experience programs. The job search programs appeared to be more successful in raising the earnings of women with high AFDC grants than in improving earnings among women with low grants. But no other strong patterns of impact emerged from the analysis of job search programs. The more expensive work and training programs caused larger earnings gains than the job search programs, as noted above. In addition, MPR found that women enrolled in these programs who had no recent work experience tended to benefit more than women with more extensive work experience.

The findings from the MDRC and MPR studies, while suggestive, lead to few definitive lessons for policy making. One tentative conclusion is that inexpensive programs, such as structured job search, should be made available to nearly all AFDC participants, but that more expensive interventions, such as subsidized work or classroom training, should be reserved for recipients who have little work experience and have been dependent longer than a year or two. The statistical basis for this conclusion is not terribly strong, however.

Summary

This brief survey indicates that employment and training programs for welfare recipients can have a measurable impact on earnings. Several of the programs—CETA, EOPP, Supported Work, and the AFDC Home Health Aide Demonstration—apparently caused fairly sizable gains in employment and earnings among participating women. Before considering the implications of this finding for welfare policy, it is worthwhile reflecting on some of the uncertainty that surrounds it.

First, it is uncertain whether the earnings gains measured in employment and training programs will persist. Virtually all program evaluations are based upon a short follow-up period. In several evaluations, the analysts lacked information for the second year following training. When performing cost-benefit analyses of training programs we are therefore forced to rely on unreliable projections of the earnings gains that can be expected in the period after the follow-up data end.

In many cases there are good reasons to expect that gains from a particular treatment will gradually disappear over time. For example, it seems unlikely that a short-duration job search assistance program will raise a participant's earnings as much five years after participation as it does in the first year after participation. The program probably speeds up job finding among its current clients, but the short-term earnings gains from speedy job finding cannot persist indefinitely. Other forms of manpower assistance, however, could raise earnings by an amount that grows over time. Completion of college typically gives workers a long-term earnings advantage over high school graduates. None of the programs considered here gave participants training comparable to a college education, but a few of them provided training that might have affected participants' occupational choice. If the training could change a participant's occupation it could also change her lifetime earnings. Given the limits on follow-up earnings data, it is impossible to decide whether past training programs caused a brief spurt in earnings or a permanent gain.

A second type of uncertainty involves the effects of work and training programs on nonparticipants, many of whom may be hurt by job displacement. If a program trains 100 welfare recipients to be skilled haberdashers and then succeeds in placing them in men's shops, it will reduce the number of haberdashery vacancies by 100. This will make life more difficult for nonparticipants who had aspired to a career in haberdashery. Some may lose their jobs; others may fail to find them. If some of these people are forced to apply for welfare, the effects of the training program on public dependency are less than we would infer just by examining the receipt of welfare benefits among the 100 trainees. To the extent that earnings gains among trainees are offset by earnings losses among nontrainees, the social benefits of the training program will be less than the gains to participants. If most of the earnings losses are concentrated among people who are just as disadvantaged as the trainees, the training program may not even yield an improvement in the income distribution.

The general population can be affected in another way as well. In many cases the purpose of a work or training program is to deter potential welfare recipients from applying for benefits. If the program attains this goal, the effects would not be detectable simply by observing the behavior of welfare recipients. Moreover, this impact on potential welfare applicants may take several years to develop, as details of the work or training obligation become publicly known.

It is thus unlikely that the full impact on nonparticipants will ever become known from a short-term work or training demonstration. Potential welfare applicants may also be induced to apply for benefits if the associated work or training program is attractive enough. Even if the program were effective in training and placing welfare recipients in unsubsidized jobs, it might fail to reduce the size of the AFDC caseload. Enough new applicants could be attracted to AFDC to offset the loss of recipients who are cycled into employment. The microeconomic experiments conducted by MDRC cannot shed any light on this question.

Finally, the available evidence provides no guidance on the effects of work and training programs on participants' and nonparticipants' work ethic. From an economist's standpoint, a person with a powerful work ethic is someone who would choose to work long hours whether or not the reward for doing so was especially large. A zealously applied work and training obligation could conceivably affect welfare recipients' taste for work in the long run. No evidence for such an effect has yet emerged, though many critics of the WIN program would argue that no work obligation has ever been enforced on welfare recipients. In the short run, attempts to increase the work ethic of welfare recipients through work obligations will have little effect. If the obligations are made onerous enough welfare dependency may drop, not because work has become more attractive, but because welfare receipt has been made less attractive. In the long run, however, it is conceivable that such obligations would affect social values and hence the preferences of low-income single mothers.

An important question, only lightly touched upon earlier, is how the benefits from the manpower programs are divided between participants and taxpayers. Some who propose work obligations or training opportunities naively assume that the benefits of such programs are extensive enough to satisfy everyone—welfare recipients as well as taxpayers. The evidence does not support this idea.

The largest gains in participant earnings were typically observed in the most expensive programs—CETA, Supported Work, and the Home Health Aide Demonstrations.[9] The initial investment of taxpayers in these programs was large, so large benefits were needed just to recoup the program costs. Careful benefit-cost studies of Supported Work and the Health Aide Demonstrations suggest that the benefits were indeed large enough to offset taxpayer investments, at least in the long run, in many of the demonstration sites. The eventual gain to taxpayers in the Supported Work study was found to be large as a result of the decline in public transfer payments to the participants (Kemper, Long, and Thornton, 1981). In three of the seven Home Health Aide Demonstrations, taxpayers received net benefits from the program (Orr, 1986). However, the MDRC and Abt calculations depend on the assumption that generous training programs do not attract additional applicants to the AFDC program. If this assumption is wrong, the cost of the program to taxpayers could be understated.

If the taxpayers' share of the gain from manpower programs is large, then the potential trainee's advantage is commensurately small. This has two implications for the design and implementation of work programs in welfare. First, if the net benefit to trainees is small, participation in the program will have to be coerced. Few people will volunteer to devote time and effort to a program that offers limited rewards, except to taxpayers. Second, the impact of the program on the well-being of participating single mothers will be limited. If policy makers wish to improve substantially the financial health of participating families, they must permit them to retain a hefty share of the earnings gains produced by the program. This reduces the likelihood that the program will offer much payoff to taxpayers.

It should last be noted that the work and training programs discussed above were targeted on AFDC recipients who were registered in WIN. Several of the programs, such as CETA and Supported Work, enrolled only volunteers from this population. Hence the findings from these studies are not necessarily indicative of the effects of programs targeted on the entire welfare caseload. Only one-third of AFDC recipients were voluntary or mandatory WIN registrants in 1985 (U.S. Congressional Budget Office, 1987). A work or training program that has a large impact on this portion of the caseload may have only negligible effects on the remaining two-thirds.

Financial Incentives to Work

Grant Levels and Benefit Reduction Rates

Although the AFDC benefit formula is not currently a major topic of debate, at least on the federal level, the effects of the formula on work behavior have been a source of continuing controversy for most of the past two decades. Analysts and policy makers have been concerned with the basic grant level, which determines the cash income available to an eligible family with no other resources, and the treatment of earned income in computing a family's benefit.

These two aspects of the payment formula have been subject to ceaseless tinkering over the last twenty years, with little apparent effect on the work behavior of single mothers. At the state level, governors and legislatures have permitted the real value of the basic AFDC grant to fall by nearly one-quarter since 1969, from $575 per month in 1969 to $442 per month in 1985.[10] At both federal and state levels, authorities have repeatedly changed their treatment of earned income, through legislation and changes in administrative practice.

Until 1967 a family's AFDC benefits were nominally subject to a dollar-for-dollar reduction whenever there was a rise in its reported net earnings. Wage earners were rarely faced with a 100-percent marginal benefit reduction rate, however, because caseworkers exercised wide discretion in determining the level of a client's countable earnings. Subtractions from gross earnings were made for taxes, child-care expenses, and all other expenses "reasonably attributable" to working. In 1967 Congress passed legislation requiring states to permit a deduction of $30 per month plus one-third of gross monthly earnings (that is, earnings before subtraction of work-related expenses), in addition to deducting work-related expenses. The remaining amount of net earnings was to be subtracted from the family's basic grant level in determining its monthly AFDC payment. (The $30 and one-third adjustment was only applied in computing benefits for a family which was already eligible; the adjustment could not be applied in determining a family's original eligibility.) The theory behind this tax rate reduction was that it would create a financial incentive for many current recipients to work, spurring them to accept jobs and thus become less dependent on welfare. The reform succeeded in cutting the effective tax on recipients' earnings by nearly half, but its net impact on employment patterns among low-income women is far less clear (see Moffitt, 1987). Arguably, work effort among poor single mothers may even have fallen as a result of the tax rate reduction (see Levy, 1979).

In the decade of the 1970s effective tax rates on recipients' earnings gradually rose, as state AFDC administrators clamped down on the definition of allowable work-related expenses. By 1979 the effective benefit reduction rate was approaching its level in 1967, the year before the $30 and one-third disregard had become effective (Fraker, Moffitt, and Wolf, 1985).

In 1981 Congress modified the disregard as well as the treatment of work-related expenses. To reflect a client's work-related expenses, caseworkers were permitted to deduct the first $75 of a full-time worker's monthly earnings and up to $160 per month to cover the actual cost of care for each AFDC child in the household. The 1981 legislation thus removed much of the latitude states had previously enjoyed in determining work expenses. After work-related expenses were subtracted, $30 plus one-third of remaining earned income not already disregarded could be deducted from net monthly earnings.[11] However, this $30 and one-third exemption was limited to just four months. In the fifth month of a recipient's job, the exemption ceased and net-of-work-expense earnings became subject to a 100-percent benefit reduction. Furthermore, the 1981 OBRA legislation placed a cap on allowable gross family income—nonwage income plus gross wages—equal to 150 percent of the state's standard of need. This cap is low enough so that for practical purposes many adult recipients were precluded from receiving welfare while holding a job. The OBRA reforms undoubtedly had an impact on the effective tax rate faced by welfare recipients. According to estimates by Fraker, Moffitt, and Wolf (1985), the effective benefit reduction rate in AFDC rose from 24 percent in 1981 to 70 percent in 1982, when the 1981 legislation became effective.

In 1984 Congress liberalized the treatment of earned income in AFDC. It raised the gross income limit for welfare eligibility from 150 percent to 185 percent of the state's standard of need. It required states to continue a $30 earned income disregard for an additional eight months beyond the expiration of the $30 and one-third disregard. And it extended the $75 work-expense deduction to all recipients who work, rather than only to those who work full time.

As this brief survey demonstrates, basic benefit levels have been reduced and benefit reduction rates cut sharply and then raised sharply over the past two decades. While these changes in policy have affected the size and composition of the population eligible to receive AFDC, there is remarkably little evidence they have measurably affected the work habits of single mothers, about half of whom receive AFDC benefits.[12] Changes in the basic benefit level and benefit reduction rate clearly affect the size of the eligible population. If the basic benefit level is raised while the benefit reduction rate remains unchanged, the income cutoff point for eligibility will rise. More single mothers with higher average levels of earnings will be eligible to receive benefits. If the benefit reduction rate is raised while the basic benefit level is left unchanged, the income cutoff point for eligibility will decline. Fewer single mothers with lower average levels of earnings will be eligible to receive benefits.

In fact, changes in the composition of the welfare caseload have generally followed the predictions of this simple model. There was a jump in the average level of earnings of AFDC recipients immediately after the $30 and one-third disregard was enacted. Between 1967 and 1969–1975, average real earnings of AFDC recipients rose by about 45 percent, from $63 a month to $93 a month (Moffitt, 1987, Table 4). Average earnings gradually declined over the 1970s as basic benefit levels fell and effective benefit reduction rates rose. After implementation of the OBRA legislation in 1982, there was a sharp drop in the fraction of AFDC recipients with earnings. The size of the AFDC caseload has also been affected by federal and state reforms. After surging in the late 1960s and early 1970s for reasons that had little to do with changes in the formula, the caseload has stabilized although the number of single women with children continues to rise. The fall in the income eligibility limit simply implies that a smaller fraction of single mothers is eligible to receive benefits.

Despite changes in the AFDC benefit formula and in the treatment of recipient earnings, the work behavior of single mothers has remained remarkably constant over the past twenty years. As documented by Moffitt (1987), employment rates among single mothers with children under age eighteen have fluctuated within a few percentage points of 52 percent since 1968. In 1968 the fraction employed was 52 percent; in 1985 it was 53 percent. The proportion of working single mothers who were on full-time schedules was 71 percent in 1968 and 72 percent in 1985. Average paid hours per week among single mothers, including nonworking mothers, have also held fairly steady, hovering around 19 hours since 1968. If living standards have deteriorated among these women, it is not because work effort has lagged, nor is it because changes in the AFDC benefit formula have induced large swings in employment or earnings.

According to Danziger and others (1981) and Moffitt (1987), the evidence shows unequivocally that work hours among AFDC recipients are reduced by the program, though the exact magnitude of the reduction is uncertain. Yet even the largest estimate of effect does not suggest that hours and earnings of single mothers would be dramatically raised by changes in the program, including its complete elimination. As noted by Moffitt (1987, p. 17), AFDC recipients work approximately nine hours per week on average. Even if we accept the highest estimate of the impact of AFDC—a 50 percent reduction in work effort by recipients—the potential earnings gains from eliminating AFDC do not appear impressive. If the average wage of AFDC recipients is $4.00 per hour, a doubling of their hours would raise average earnings among recipients by less than $2,000 per year. This would raise average earnings among all single mothers by about $800 per year. While these gains are far from trivial, they are too small to lift very many single-parent families out of poverty, particularly in a world in which AFDC benefits are no longer available. Also recall that this projection is based upon the highest estimate of AFDC's impact. Most estimates imply a much smaller work effort response.

Few people have seriously suggested the elimination of welfare, however. Most reform proposals have been considerably more modest and have been aimed at making work more attractive or welfare less attractive on the margin. The best evidence about financial work incentives suggests that only one of them—a simple reduction in the basic benefit amount—will unambiguously increase work effort among both recipients and non-recipients. Manipulation of the benefit reduction rate has an ambiguous effect on the work effort of single mothers, and in any event is unlikely to have a large overall impact one way or the other.

A reduction in the basic benefit level encourages work for an obvious reason. Those who receive payments will have less total income, so the necessity for additional earned income rises. A single mother whose nonwelfare income is just below the initial cutoff level for welfare eligibility will find that she loses her benefits altogether, because a reduction in the basic benefit level leads to a proportional reduction in the income eligibility limit. Hence fewer single mothers will receive benefits and be subject to their disincentive effects.

The response to a change in the benefit reduction rate is more complicated, as Congress learned after 1967 and again after 1981. The response that many policy analysts emphasized is that of single mothers who would be welfare recipients both before and after the reform. When the benefit reduction rate is lowered, initial recipients get to keep more of their work earnings, so this kind of reform is widely interpreted as a work incentive. Yet a lowered benefit reduction rate also increases the size of the eligible population, for it raises the income cutoff point for program eligibility. The single mothers who become newly eligible for benefits are faced with two disincentives to work. First, because they are now eligible to receive more nonwage income, earned income is less necessary. Second, because their earnings are now subject to the program's benefit reduction rate, work is less rewarding. (Even after Congress lowered the benefit reduction rate from 100 percent to 67 percent in 1967, the tax rate faced by someone receiving AFDC benefits was far above that faced by someone not on welfare.)

It is unclear whether the work reductions among new recipients will offset the work increases among women who were original recipients. Levy (1979) and Burtless (1987) have argued that a tax rate reduction will on balance constitute a work disincentive for single mothers, while Moffitt (1985) argues that it would constitute a slight incentive. All of us agree, however, that the magnitude of the overall change in work behavior is small, since work increases among initial recipients are partially or wholly offset by work reductions among new recipients.

I wish to emphasize here that my conclusions pertain to short-run measurable responses to changes in policy. It is conceivable, as some conservatives argue, that the long-term effects of policy changes would be much larger. For example, if current benefit levels were cut in half, the work behavior of single women within the next five or ten years might change only slightly. But in the long run the impacts could snowball as they begin to affect social mores and attitudes toward work and dependency. Because women and children receiving welfare would lead much more degraded lives, nonrecipients might be more inclined to regard dependency as a condition to be avoided. They might either undertake active measures to avoid dependency, such as attending school or diligently seeking work, or they might avoid behaviors, such as promiscuity or malingering, that can lead to dependency.

Although such expectations are logical, it is unknown how large the positive effects will be or when they will occur. If they turn out to be sizable, the dual problems of poverty and dependency among single mothers will recede. If instead these societal effects are trivial, a large number of children will grow up in circumstances that are even more dreadful than those faced by poor children today. Given this uncertainty, I find it unsurprising that only a handful of people have publicly called for the elimination or drastic cutback of public assistance programs. Reforms on a smaller scale are unlikely to produce major changes in the work behavior of single mothers, as demonstrated by two decades of ceaseless reform.

Wage and Earnings Subsidies. An alternative mechanism to supplement the earnings of the poor and, at the same time, to encourage them to work is to offer earnings or wage-rate subsidies. A worker eligible for this type of subsidy receives an income supplement that grows rather than declines as hours of work rise. An earnings subsidy payment is calculated as a specified percentage of the worker's annual wages, though the level of earnings on which a subsidy can be paid is usually limited, for example, to an amount below $8,000 a year. A wage-rate subsidy is a supplement to the worker's hourly wage. It might be calculated as a flat percentage of the difference between the worker's wage rate and a target wage of, say, $5.00 per hour. If the worker's wage were $4.00 an hour and the government subsidy amounted to 50 percent of the difference between the wage and $5.00 an hour, the subsidy would be equal to 50 cents per hour of work.

The two types of subsidies share the same general goal, but differ in important ways. An earnings subsidy must obviously be limited in some way, otherwise the highly paid would receive larger subsidies than the poorly paid. If the subsidy rate is 10 percent and the maximum subsidy payment is $600 per year, it is obvious that annual wages above $6,000 would not be eligible for subsidization. This implies that an earnings subsidy will only provide an inducement to work extra hours for those with very low levels of work effort. People whose wages are already above $6,000 are made better off, but their reward for working longer hours is unchanged. By contrast, a wage-rate subsidy can raise the reward for work, irrespective of the worker's initial level of effort. For a worker whose wage is low enough to qualify for a subsidy, the fiftieth hour of work per week is as generously subsidized as the first.

Unfortunately, the information requirements of a wage-rate subsidy make it more difficult to administer than an earnings subsidy. To calculate a wage subsidy, the government must know the worker's wage rate and his or her level of hours. An earnings subsidy can be computed simply by knowing the level of earnings, a number which is already reported to the tax authorities and the Social Security Administration.[13] These administrative differences between the two subsidies clearly favor earnings subsidies, even though the work incentive effects of a wage subsidy appear more promising.

The EITC represents a fairly straightforward, though modest, earnings subsidy plan. First enacted in 1975, the credit subsidizes the earnings of single or married workers who have financial responsibility for children and who have modest earnings and taxable incomes. In 1987 the credit was equal to 14 percent of the first $5,714 of earnings, including self-employment earnings. The maximum credit is thus $800. For each dollar by which a family's gross income exceeded $6,500, the credit was reduced by 10 cents, implying that the credit was phased out when income reached $14,500 a year. In 1988, the phase-out range of income began at $9,000 per year and declined to zero at $17,000 per year. The House Ways and Means Committee estimates that the total value of the credit to low-income families will jump to $6 billion in 1988, from about $4 billion in 1987 (U.S. House of Representatives, Committee on Ways and Means, 1987).

A number of people have suggested that the tax credit be liberalized in order to increase its value to large families. Robert Reischauer, for example, has recommended that the current subsidy rate in the program be tied to the number of children in the family (Reischauer, 1987). He has suggested that the current rate of 14 percent be maintained for families with one child, but raised by 4 percentage points for each additional child. This reform would add about $250 per child to the maximum annual credit that could be received by each family.

Earnings and wage rate subsidies can both provide an incentive for additional work to people with low hours and low wages. This contrasts with a public assistance program, in which clients receive lower payments as their earnings rise. Clearly, however, earnings and wage subsidies cannot fulfill the basic role of income maintenance that is performed by public assistance. The subsidies provide no support or only limited support to those families without a full-time breadwinner, notably, many families headed by a single mother. A substantial liberalization of the EITC credit would provide no help to the 47 percent of single mothers who do not work and only limited aid to the 15 percent who work on a part-time schedule. Hence earnings and wage subsidies are properly regarded as a source of income supplementation for working poor and near-poor families, most of which contain two parents.

Although many advocates of earnings and wage subsidies emphasize their work incentive effects, these effects are impressive only in comparison to those in most other income maintenance programs. Subsidy programs do not necessarily raise earnings among subsidy recipients, and at least two studies suggest that earnings would actually decline if a wage subsidy were established. The intuition behind this hypothesis is simple. A wage rate subsidy raises the reward for working and hence should make work more attractive on the margin. But for someone already at work when the program is implemented, the subsidy causes his or her net income to rise and so should make work less necessary. Some people will consequently raise their work effort and others will reduce it. On balance, Rea (1974) and Betson and Bishop (1982) have concluded that work and earnings reductions would slightly outweigh work and earnings increases, at least within the context of the specific wage rate subsidies they considered.

The overall work incentive effects of an earnings subsidy, such as the EITC, are probably even worse than those of a wage subsidy. Recall that a wage subsidy raises the reward for work among all low-wage workers. An earnings subsidy raises the reward for work only in the case of workers who earn less than the level of earnings at which the subsidy is capped. In the EITC, this earnings level was $5,714 in 1987. Workers earning between $5,714 and $6,500 received no extra reward for working more hours. Because their net incomes have been raised $800 by the program, some of them may actually work slightly less than they would without the credit. Workers earning between $6,500 and $14,500 face two work disincentives from the credit. Their net income is higher than it otherwise would be, and their after-tax wage is lower. Even if the combined effects of these disincentives are small per person affected, many wage earners fall in the relevant income range. On balance, the EITC probably reduces aggregate work effort among affected people earning less than $14,500 a year. While the reduction is likely to be small, it offsets to some degree the direct redistributive impact of the subsidy payments.

Assuming that both wage rate subsidies and earnings subsidies slightly reduce participant earnings, how should these policy options be viewed in the current debate over welfare reform? The overwhelming majority of families receiving AFDC are headed by a single mother. An earnings or wage-rate subsidy would improve the well-being of single mothers who currently earn enough to place them just above the eligibility limits for welfare. At the same time, it would reduce the level of hours of work required in order for a single mother to rise above the welfare eligibility line. Thus it would improve the condition of families who are not now entitled to welfare, and it would reduce the number of families receiving AFDC benefits. Finally, it would make work more attractive to single mothers who do not work at all. This is the group of mothers for whom an earnings or wage rate subsidy provides an unambiguous incentive to work.

The major argument for this type of subsidy is that it raises the well-being of participating families without causing major reductions in their own self-support. Many taxpayers may approve of the distributional consequences of the subsidy because it provides the largest rewards to beneficiaries who do the most to support themselves. But taxpayers whose greatest interest is their own pocketbook will be no more pleased by wage and earnings subsidies than they are by other forms of redistribution, because subsidies will not save taxpayer dollars either in the short run or the long run.

Policy Implications

The evidence surveyed above suggests unequivocally that welfare reform can affect the work behavior and standard of living of families receiving public assistance. It also implies, however, that the short-term effect on labor supply behavior is likely to be quite modest. Within the range of policies that have been attempted in the recent past—and are likely to be tried in the near future—no single policy reform or set of reforms has the potential to raise earnings by enough to put a sizable dent in poverty rates among single-parent families with children.

Programs that have had the largest effects on participant earnings are

CETA, public service employment programs, Supported Work, and the AFDC Homemaker-Home Health Aide projects. These programs may have raised the earnings of participants by as much as $1,100 to $1,500 per year during the period immediately after completion of training. Even if all of these gains had been reflected in higher net family incomes among participants, many poor families would be left with incomes well below the poverty line. According to the income statistics reported by Sheldon Danziger in Chapter 2, the average poverty gap among poor families with children is about $4,300, or approximately three times the level of earnings gains registered in the most successful employment and training programs.

It is, of course, highly unlikely that the earnings gains reported in the most successful past programs would be produced by any reform proposal that could be enacted any time soon. Nor is it likely that the earnings gains produced by such a reform would be fully reflected in higher incomes among participating families.

First, nearly all of the most successful programs have been quite expensive, costing about $10,000 per participant. While it is possible to conceive of a reform that might cost this much, it is hard to believe that this level of resources would be invested in very many welfare mothers. Current budgetary constraints, both at the federal and state levels, make a costly, extensive program quite unlikely. If fewer mothers were served, the overall effect on single-parent families would be commensurately reduced. It is more plausible to expect that reform will involve small-scale investments, but spread across a large number of participants. Job search assistance and unpaid work programs are substantially cheaper than public service employment or Supported Work, but they are also much less effective in raising participant earnings.

Second, the most successful programs have typically served volunteers from the AFDC population.[14] Programs that compel participation on the part of all welfare recipients are likely to produce smaller earnings gains per person served. After all, an important reason that women fail to volunteer for employment and training programs is that they believe the programs will not be beneficial.

Finally, women who benefit from participating in work-related programs will not be allowed to keep all of the benefits arising out of their participation. Unless current tax and transfer programs are radically altered, some of the earnings gains must be shared with taxpayers. AFDC, Food Stamp, and Medicaid benefits received by these women will fall, and tax payments will rise. As noted above, most of the earnings gains produced by the Supported Work program were not retained by trainees, but were instead passed on to taxpayers in the form of reduced expenditures on AFDC and Food Stamps.

While I have emphasized that the overall behavioral effects of likely reforms will be small, some employment and training reforms do appear to be highly cost-effective. That is, the earnings gains produced by the programs are larger than the taxpayer investments that are required in order to obtain them. Even relatively modest investments, such as structured job search programs or short-term classroom training, appear to be quite effective by this criterion.

An important issue for policy makers is to decide how these modest earnings gains will be divided up among welfare recipients and taxpayers. High marginal tax rates in AFDC, small investments in support services such as child care, and stringent eligibility limits on Medicaid will ensure that most benefits of reform will be passed on to taxpayers. Low marginal tax rates, generous support services and earnings subsidies, and liberalized eligibility for Medicaid or other health insurance would give a larger share of the benefits to current welfare recipients.

If policy makers attempt to give the benefits of reform primarily to taxpayers, they must compel participation among welfare recipients, for example, by making AFDC or Food Stamp benefits contingent upon participation in a work or training program. Such a work or training program can directly raise the earnings and lower the assistance payments of participating women. Moreover, by making public assistance less attractive, a mandatory program can reduce participation in public assistance among women who would otherwise be eligible to receive benefits. Note that the combined effect of this type of mandatory work and training program may be to reduce public dependency and to raise poverty rates among single-parent families. This combined effect is also present when policy makers raise the effective tax rate on earned income in AFDC; public dependency falls, but poverty among single-parent families rises.

Conversely, if policy makers confer most benefits of reform on welfare recipients, there will be much less difficulty in obtaining the voluntary cooperation of low-income single mothers. For example, a work and training program with good child care could be attractive to a large fraction of new welfare recipients. Indeed, this type of program might be so attractive that it could increase the participation rate of single mothers in AFDC. The program could raise public dependency (or fail to reduce dependency) even as it increased participants' earnings.

In the final analysis, the decision of policy makers to adopt or reject a particular set of reforms will not hinge on the exact behavioral consequences of reform, even if these were known with certainty. Virtually all participants in the welfare reform debate agree on the desirability of reducing poverty among single-parent families. And most—though not all—also agree on the desirability of raising the earnings of single mothers. But there is little agreement on how to accomplish these two objectives.

Much of the disagreement revolves around deeply held social and moral values. Some participants in the reform debate believe that welfare recipients ought to assume ultimate responsibility for improving their own lives and those of their children. The immediate goal of reform must be to spur recipients to become less dependent on state-provided benefits and more reliant on their own ability to provide earned income to their families. Others believe that the living standards of poor children are woefully inadequate and must be improved in the near future, regardless of the consequences on the work behavior of their parents. Social scientific evidence and historical experience suggest no miraculous program or set of programs can reconcile these deeply divergent views. And if such a program existed, elaborate social scientific inquiry would probably not be needed to discover it.

It seems indisputable that significant policy reform—inside and outside the welfare system—is needed if low-income single mothers and their children are to be brought within hailing distance of the American mainstream. Mandatory work and training programs and earnings subsidy schemes are two feasible reforms for improving the well-being of single mothers while at the same time encouraging their participation in the work force. Though these kinds of programs, if effective, are likely to cost taxpayers a good deal of money, the money is well spent in my view if it lessens child poverty and reduces the social isolation of single parents and their children. Because the aid is provided in a form that is more palatable to taxpayer-donors and to low-income recipients than ordinary cash assistance, these programs may command broader public support than alternative reforms which simply raise public assistance payment standards. I should stress that the most worthwhile reforms will not save any taxpayer dollars, either in the short or long runs. Nor do I think it is even desirable to impose such a criterion when assessing particular reform proposals. Work programs and earnings subsidies are clearly insufficient by themselves to end poverty and dependency among single-parent families. But they represent modest and worthwhile first steps on the path to more fundamental reform.

Comment by Gary Walker

Gary Burtless has expertly reviewed the evidence about the impacts of various employment and training programs on welfare recipients. His review might be summarized as follows:

· Many types of strategies—including on-the-job training, job search, classroom training, supported work and work experience—improve in varying degrees the earnings and employment of AFDC recipients. Typically the improvement has not come from increasing hourly wage rates, but from increasing the hours worked. Typically the average increase is too modest to affect welfare or poverty status.

· More extensive and more costly interventions have larger impacts on income and employment than do less extensive, less costly interventions. Thus the estimated short-term earning increments projected for job search assistance interventions range from $150 to $700 per year, while the short-term earnings impacts of more extensive interventions, like on-the-job training, are estimated to range up to almost $2,000 (see Grossman, Maynard, and Roberts, 1985). For less extensive and cheaper programs the income impacts are down to $150–300 per year after two years; for more extensive ones the impacts are also significantly reduced. The program with the longest impact for which we have credible data is Supported Work; five years after the program, its participants were earning $300 a year more than the control group.

Why such modest results? There are several reasons why we should not have expected the impacts of public employment and training programs targeted to welfare recipients to have been anything but modest. The reasons I want to focus on fall into five broad categories.

Inadequate Funding. Each of these programs has been funded at levels that make it impossible to reach the whole caseload or provide intensive services even to a subset of the caseload. JTPA, for example, is funded to serve less than 5 percent of the eligible population. WIN has over the years consistently had funds to provide services to only a small fraction of its eligible population.

A recent example is the 1986 federal mandate for states to set up employment and training programs for Food Stamp recipients, in order to prepare them for regular jobs. The language of the Food Security Act of 1985 sounds as if this program is a major attempt to develop human capital by investing in educational literacy and skills development. In fact, the funding authorized under the act works out to approximately $50 for each participant.

The states' response has been predictable (see *Employment and Training Reporter,* 1987). First, they are exempting many clients from participation, often the most disadvantaged. Second, the services offered are usually job search assistance. As Georgia's chief of employment services for welfare clients sums it up: "The services fit the available funding."

Rewards for Modest Impacts. The pressures on local administrators which result in cheap services have historically been legitimized by the federal and state departments overseeing the programs. The JTPA system overseen by the Department of Labor, for example, originally set up performance standards for cost and placement rates that encourage low-cost, short-duration services, and the vast majority of states administer incentive funds to reward localities that can better those performance standards—that is, offer even cheaper services.

Poor Public Sector Coordination. Providing a recipient with the services and motivation to secure and maintain a decent-paying job may require the cooperation of several agencies over a long period of time. Support services, appropriate educational remediation, skills training, job-seeking skills, work experience—one agency could rarely provide or fund all these services even in the halcyon days of the early and mid-1970s; certainly none can in the 1980s. But neither boom nor bust in funding itself promotes public agency coordination, since neither changes an individual agency's protectiveness of its resources, or makes its policies, goals, performance measures, competence, and staff working styles more compatible with other agencies.

The best recent example is the federal JTPA program, endowed with more mandates and exhortation about coordination with other public agencies than any piece of public legislation in recent history. But such coordination has not occurred at anywhere near the expected level (see Grinker, Walker, and Associates, 1984, 1985, and 1986). In fact, JTPA has, at the local level, been a very insular system.

Poor Public-Private Sector Coordination. Most national training programs lack systematic or effective linkages with employers. CETA, for example, had a generally miserable reputation among businessmen. WIN has not fared much better. Only JTPA, which gives local businessmen the power to set policy and oversee local implementation, has achieved a notable level of public-private sector cooperation. But even that cooperation, produced by sharing authority and control over resources, has not resulted in much customized training, or in a focus on those who most need assistance, or in jobs much above the minimum wage, or in guaranteed jobs for successful program graduates. And giving authority to employers, who by all accounts are most disturbed by the education deficiencies of their current and future workforce, has resulted in only about 6 percent of JTPA expenditures going to remediation activities.

These results should not be surprising. Employers have always been resistant to guaranteed job arrangements, or even priority hiring, because they do not trust the products of social programs. Yet without structured access of some kind, only a modest proportion of welfare recipients can successfully compete for decent-paying jobs, even in relatively tight job markets.

Employers are also not well-versed in the mildly confusing primer lesson of impact research: that those groups for whom public training dollars have the greatest impact often do not have high placement rates into jobs, and require costly interventions; those groups with high placement rates at low costs most often do not produce high impacts. This lesson runs exactly counter to what most business managers aim for in their work.

Last, employers may complain bitterly about youthful illiteracy, but for the most part they want schools, not training programs, to remedy the problem. And most are not interested in being involved in programs that are lengthy, costly, and heavy with support services of any kind.

Thus public-private sector coordination, so essential to moving the most at-risk populations into jobs and off welfare, has not materialized. The group of recipients (about one-third of the total) who have long periods of dependence (ten years or more), and who account for 60 percent of welfare costs, are simply not going to secure and maintain decent paying jobs by being put into the job market along with everybody else, buttressed by some short-term job-readiness services. And without affecting that group, we are not going to accomplish major reductions in welfare rolls and costs.

Inadequate Infrastructure and Technology. There is no institutional infrastructure to offer intensive educational and skills training services and associated support services to more than a small percentage of welfare recipients. Certified day-care providers, for instance, fall far short of current need in most localities: if suddenly thousands of additional welfare recipients were going to school or training, there would be no care for their children.

Nonprofit agencies, which provided many of the motivational, support, and remedial education services to poor people just a decade ago, have seen their numbers and capacity decline significantly since the federal social service budget cuts began in the early 1980s. Educational institutions that can offer appropriate, flexible remedial services for significant numbers of single parents who are heads of households are rare. The educational establishment has problems meeting the needs of its current population. New capacity cannot be developed overnight, even if there were a sudden influx of resources.

This deficiency is especially serious, given projections that decent paying jobs of the future will require even greater literacy and computational skills than those of the recent past. Recent data indicate that the welfare population is especially deficient in these areas—three out of five participants in California's GAIN program were found to be in need of remediation, and the share of long-term recipients needing such remediation is almost certainly even higher.

The technology to deliver effective remediation services is perhaps even less developed than the institutional capacity. And the technology problem is complicated in at least three distinct areas: logistics, confidence, and content. The first means that mothers with young children need a flexible curriculum, and adequate and flexible support services like transportation and day care, to undertake learning and still carry out their maternal responsibilities well. They are not typical students.

Second, many individuals who need remediation are not confident that they can learn. For those who have not succeeded in a traditional school setting, a different setting, with a different approach and pedagogy, may be required. A recent example is the specialized curriculum for fourteen and fifteen-year-olds already significantly behind in educational achievement (Public/Private Ventures, 1986). The curriculum is getting positive results, but it took several years to develop, and needed substantial training for regular teachers to implement. There are a number of efforts around the country to develop curricula and teaching approaches that will stimulate successful learning in previously unsuccessful learners, but few have achieved scale, and even fewer can substantiate their effectiveness. The Comprehensive Competencies Program (CCP), developed by the Remediation Training Institute, is perhaps the most widespread of these newly developed approaches; CCP is now in 170 locations.

The third issue is one of content: what do people need to learn to secure and maintain decent paying jobs? This question is the subject of serious debate; some people think that the traditional approach to content is not sufficient for a service-oriented economy, either its entry-level or management jobs (Resnick, 1988). Scattered efforts are taking place to make learning more workplace-oriented.

In short, the challenge of structuring and delivering effective remedial services is both complex and daunting. It will take substantial investment, commitment, and patience to develop. There are no current public funders of size preparing to do it. A handful of national foundations have gotten involved, but their funds are limited compared to the task.

The obstacles outlined above have, in various combinations, confronted all major public efforts to provide education and training services to welfare recipients. The result is that only very small numbers of recipients ever receive the services that are necessary if they are actually to get good jobs, and get off welfare. The small achievements do show that having skills can lead to sizable income gains. A recent ten-site demonstration in intensive training of women, many of whom were welfare recipients, in construction skills, led to a wage differential of $4.00 per hour for those placed in jobs over women who received less intensive services. But this kind of effort is very expensive, and requires considerable skill and effort to mount and operate. Typically such efforts have high turnover rates, since the training is demanding. They rarely serve those recipients who are unlikely to get some kind of jobs on their own. And they are difficult to expand in size, because of the disproportionately high share of funds per trainee they absorb.

In short, the implementation obstacles to carrying out training and education for welfare recipients that can lead to decent wages, sufficient to get recipients off welfare, are considerable. There is little successful experience to build on. The investment and patience required are beyond what our public efforts have shown to date, and beyond the current welfare reform legislation being considered in Congress.

Targeting Long-Term Welfare Recipients

Douglas J. Besharov

Family breakdown is a now a major cause of welfare use. In 1983, the latest year for which statistics are available, 84 percent of children on AFDC were on the welfare rolls because of divorce, separation, and illegitimacy (U.S. Department of Health and Human Services, 1986). This is in sharp contrast to 1939, when AFDC was first established to support widows with children or families where the father was incapacitated. Then, about 71 percent of AFDC children were orphaned or had disabled fathers. (The corresponding figure for 1983 was only five percent; see Novak et al., 1987.) Senator Moynihan has described this historical transformation:

> What we *call* welfare is in point of fact Title IV of the Social Security Act of 1935. It addressed the problem of widows and orphans in an industrial society . . . [Over time this program] grew to the point where something like one child in three now being born can expect to be dependent on this form of public assistance before reaching age 18.
>
> This did not happen because of a great increase in the number of widows and orphans. It came about because of utterly unforeseen, utterly transforming change in American family life which took place in a brief period, roughly 1960–1980. A demographer has described this as "the earthquake that shuddered through the American family" in those years.[1]

Encapsulated in the phrase the "feminization of poverty," the poverty caused by the deterioration of family structures has been widely reported in the media. It was an issue in the last presidential campaign, and will likely be in the next. All major welfare reform proposals now before the Congress claim to address the needs of poor mothers and their children. The concept rightly generates great compassion—many single mothers

and their children are in truly distressing situations—but, as now formulated, it is fundamentally misleading.

Substantial differences among female-headed families are hidden by
aggregate statistics about their poverty and social dysfunction. Families
headed by divorced mothers are, in general, doing much better than
these aggregate statistics suggest, whereas families headed by never-
married mothers (the Census Bureau's term for mothers of children born
out of wedlock) are doing much worse. They experience much more
severe poverty for longer periods, and they go on welfare in far larger
proportion—and stay there.

In the pages that follow I describe the different needs of the two groups
and argue that lumping them together distorts public and political understanding of their problems. To assist female-headed families to become
financially self-sufficient, social welfare policies must distinguish between
these two types of families and the problems they face. There is growing
support for welfare policies that target on reducing the long-term
dependency of never-married mothers—so long as the policy is not
harshly punitive. Although current welfare reform bills attempt to target
long-term recipients, they could go much further in targeting young
never-married mothers and their needs.

The "Feminization" of Poverty

Income statistics for female-headed families with children under eighteen
paint a gloomy picture. Almost half of all such families are below the
poverty line (see U.S. Bureau of the Census, 1986a). Their poverty rate
is almost three times higher than the poverty rate of other families with
children.

The mean income of female-headed families is about one-third that of
intact families. In 1984, the mean family income for children living with
both parents was $33,182; for children living with their father only, mean
family income was $22,164; but for children living with their mother
only, it was $10,694 (U.S. Bureau of the Census, 1985a).[2] The median
income of female-headed families is about 26 percent of that of intact
families. In 1984, the median family income for children living with both
parents was $29,730; for children living with their father only, $20,024;
but for children living with their mother only, median family income was
$7,608 (U.S. Bureau of the Census, 1985a).[3]

Whether one looks at the total number of people (or of families) living below the official poverty line, female-headed families account for a disproportionate share of the poverty in this country. In 1985, of the 33,064,000 Americans living below the poverty line, about half were from female-headed families (16,365,000). This figure includes members of unrelated subfamilies living with female-headed families. When only related family members are counted, there are 11,600,000 poor persons in female-headed families—about a third of all poor persons in the country. Similarly, of the 7.2 million families that fell under the official poverty line in 1985, about half were headed by women (3,474,000). Ninety percent of these families (3,131,000) include children.[4]

In 1985, female-headed families with children under eighteen were almost three times as likely to be poor as other families with children. For all families with children, the poverty rate was 16.6 percent; for female-headed families with children, it was 45.4 percent.[5] While such families accounted for only about 21 percent of all families with children in 1985,[6] they made up 56 percent of all such families that fell below the poverty line.[7] As Garfinkel and McLanahan (1986) observe: "Families headed by single women with children are the poorest of all major demographic groups regardless of how poverty is measured. Their economic position relative to that of other groups, such as the aged and disabled, has actually declined during the past two decades" (p. 11).

The relative poverty of female-headed families should not be surprising. As a report of the U.S. House of Representatives, Committee on Ways and Means (1986) has pointed out: "Family composition . . . serves as a very rough proxy for the social, economic, and personal resources which the family as a whole can amass to meet its needs."

The poverty caused by family breakdown exacts a high toll of suffering from the mothers and children involved. But society also pays a high cost. Three-fourths of all spells on AFDC begin with the creation of a female-headed family (Bane and Ellwood, 1983). In 1984, about 60 percent of female-headed families were receiving AFDC or another means-tested benefit (U.S. Bureau of the Census, 1985b).

A New Form of Poverty

The "feminization of poverty" is a new form of poverty—not caused directly by racial discrimination nor by structural deficiencies in the economy, but rather by a major—and troubling—change in the behavior of American parents.

Over the past twenty-five years, the number of female-headed families tripled. According to the findings of the Working Seminar on the Family and American Welfare Policy, "Census Bureau data show that if the nation had the same proportion of female-headed households in 1985 as in 1959, there would have been about 5.2 million fewer persons in poverty. A special analysis by the Census Bureau showed that the poverty rate for black families would have been 20 percent in 1980, rather than its actual 29 percent, if black family composition had remained as it was in 1970."[8] After analyzing inequalities in wealth, Weicher and Wachter (1986) have concluded that "what appears to be an economic problem is probably better described as an economic manifestation of a social problem." This social problem has two separate components: divorce and illegitimacy.

Poverty after Divorce

During most of the past century, the divorce rate increased slowly but steadily. Then, about twenty-five years ago, it accelerated rapidly. Between 1960 and 1980, the annual number of divorces almost tripled, from nearly 400,000 to nearly 1.2 million. The annual divorce rate is twice that of twenty years ago. (After reaching a historic high in 1979, the divorce rate leveled off in 1980–81, dropped slightly in 1983, and has now begun to rise again.)[9] At present, one in eight marriages ends in divorce. If the current divorce rate continues, nearly half of all marriages established today will end in divorce.[10]

The third-party participants in this high divorce rate are the children. Since 1972, a million children a year have experienced a divorce in their family (U.S. Department of Health and Human Services, 1986a). By the 1990s, some estimate that one-third to one-half of all children born to married parents will have experienced parental divorce before they turn eighteen (Glick, 1979).[11]

Divorce can be a positive step in many families, for example, by ending a violent or hostile home atmosphere. But it can also have a devastating financial impact. Married women who became divorced or separated between 1971 and 1978 suffered an average drop in real family income of over $10,000 (Hill and Morgan, 1981). Duncan and Hoffman (1985) have reported that in "the first year following a change in marital status, the family income of women who do not remarry is 70 percent of its previous figure; five years after a divorce or separation, the ratio for those still unmarried is 71 percent. Especially hard hit by divorce are black women, whose incomes fell to 54 percent of their predivorce level."

"Because two separate households are more expensive to maintain than one, we would expect both parties to experience a drop in living standards after a divorce, but the drop for divorced mothers is much greater than the drop for divorced fathers," Garfinkel and McLanahan (1986) have explained. In fact, Weitzman's (1985) study of the economic consequences of divorce, based on California court records, found that divorced women and their children experienced a 73 percent decrease in living standards while the fathers enjoyed a 42 percent increase.

Out-of-Wedlock Poverty

If anything demonstrates the breakdown of the traditional family, it is the startling rise in out-of-wedlock births. The incidence of out-of-wedlock births is at the highest level ever observed, since national statistics were first collected on the subject in 1940 (U.S. Department of Health and Human Services, 1986b). The number of births to unwed mothers has more than quintupled, from 141,600 in 1950 to 770,355 in 1984 (see U.S. Bureau of the Census, 1985c, and U.S. Department of Health and Human Services, 1986b). The number of live births per thousand unmarried women of childbearing age has more than doubled since 1950, from 14.1 to 31.0. The fraction of children born out of wedlock rose from one in twenty-five in 1950 to one in five in 1984 (see U.S. Bureau of the Census, 1981 and 1985b).

Never-married mothers are much poorer than their divorced counterparts. In 1985, the mean family income for never-married mothers with children under the age of eighteen was $6,225; less than half the average income of divorced women with children, $13,281.[12] The median was $4,623, compared with $11,149 for divorced mothers (U.S. Bureau of the Census, 1985a and 1986a). In 1983, fully 69 percent of never-married women with children were below the poverty level, compared with 44 percent for divorced or separated mothers (U.S. House of Representatives, Committee on Ways and Means, 1986).

Family breakdown—and the poverty it causes—gives every indication of worsening. Of all children born in 1980, most predictions are that, if present trends continue, 60 percent will spend part of their childhood in a family headed by a mother who is divorced, separated, unwed, or widowed.[13] Some social scientists predict that things will be even worse in the next generation, with half of all children born out-of-wedlock, and one third to one half of all children born to married parents experiencing divorce before they are eighteen (see, for example, Hofferth, 1985).

Welfare Dependency

A much higher proportion of never-married mothers go on welfare than do divorced mothers. Eberstadt (1987) has calculated that, in 1982, almost three-fifths of all out-of-wedlock children in the United States were on AFDC, compared with just under a third of children of divorced mothers. Children of never-married mothers are three times more likely to be on welfare than are children of divorced mothers.

It has been clear for some time that there are two distinct categories of welfare recipients: those who use it as a stopgap, and those who become long-term dependents. According to a recent study by Ellwood (1986), about half the new entrants to AFDC will be off welfare within four years, most within two years. The other half are on for longer—on average, almost seven years. Moreover, nearly 25 percent of AFDC recipients stay on for ten or more years.

In an effort to understand the problem of long-term welfare dependency and to reduce AFDC program costs, a number of researchers have sought to identify the characteristics of long-term recipients. A study by Murray (1986) for the Working Seminar on the Family and American Welfare Policy examined the impact of age on poverty and welfare dependency rates. Using PSID data, he "found persistent signs that women who came onto AFDC as single women and those who came onto AFDC after a marital breakdown respond to AFDC in quite different ways." Murray's data set was not large enough to reach a definitive conclusion, but a calculation based on the data available to him indicated that never-married mothers spend an average of two and a half years longer on welfare than do mothers who had been married at some point. (And, again, many of the latter included unwed mothers who subsequently married, for however brief a time.)

Murray's findings are paralleled by those in the study by Ellwood (1986) which, going beyond the Bane and Ellwood (1983) study, looked at the aggregate impact of variables associated with long welfare spells as well as their marginal impact. In other words, he examined the effect of each variable when all other factors are not held constant as well as when they are. His purpose was to facilitate targeting long-term recipients, since in real life all other factors are never held constant.[14] Ellwood (1986) found that: "The single most powerful predictor of durations, when all else is not held constant, is marital status. Almost 40 percent of the women who have never been married when they begin to receive AFDC will have total welfare time of 10 or more years, while less than 15 percent of the divorced women have such long welfare times." He also estimated that never-married women who go on AFDC stay on for an average of 9.3 years, while divorced women stay on for an average of 4.9 years.

A recent study of welfare dynamics among teenage mothers by Adams of the U.S. Congressional Budget Office (1987) confirmed these findings. According to Adams,

> of the three characteristics examined [age, race, marital status at birth of first child], being unmarried at the time of the first birth is most consistently associated with both an increased likelihood of entering the welfare system within a few years of giving birth, and a decreased probability of leaving it within the first few years of welfare receipt . . . Half of the young mothers who were not married when their first child was born started receiving welfare within 12 months after they gave birth, compared to 7 percent of those who were married. These proportions rise to 73 percent and 22 percent, respectively, by the end of the fourth year after birth.[15]

Moreover, racial differences in poverty rates seem to all but disappear when the divorce versus out-of-wedlock issue is taken into account. According to the White House Working Group on the Family (1986), for example, the child of a never-married mother spends on the average six years in poverty if the mother is black, 6.2 if she is of another race.

Thus among female-headed families it is those that begin with an out-of-wedlock birth—usually teenagers—that result in the deepest poverty and form the bulk of long-term welfare dependency. This is not to say that postdivorce poverty is not a serious problem; it is. But much more than a divorce, an out-of-wedlock birth to a young mother is a direct path to long-term poverty and welfare dependency.

Demographic Differences between Never-Married and Divorced Mothers

An array of social, economic, and educational factors account for the differences in welfare dependency between divorced and never-married mothers.

Seventy percent of all out-of-wedlock births occur to young women between the ages of fifteen and twenty-four.[16] Never-married mothers are, on average, ten years younger than divorced mothers. The average

age range of never-married mothers is twenty and twenty-nine; for divorced mothers, the average range is thirty to thirty-nine.[17] (The age spread for this second group is lowered by the fact that many divorced mothers are formerly unwed mothers who are subsequently married, but for a short time.)

Never-married mothers are also, on average, much less educated. Only 53 percent of never-married mothers have a high school diploma, as compared with 77 percent of divorced mothers (U.S. Bureau of the Census, 1985a). Inexperience and lack of education thus combine to give these women much poorer job prospects.

Paid employment is the most telling difference between divorced and unwed mothers. While 63 percent of all divorced mothers work full time, only 29 percent of never-married mothers do so (Besharov and Dally, 1986). (An additional 11 percent of divorced mothers work part-time compared with 8 percent of never-married mothers.) Thus, never-married mothers work 54 percent less than divorced mothers. Since work is the primary source of income for female-headed families, the low employment rate of never-married mothers helps explain why their income is so low.

Child support is another difference. Never-married women are much less likely to receive child support from absent fathers than are divorced women. In 1983, 76 percent of divorced women received child-support awards, compared with only 18 percent of unwed mothers. Furthermore, the average award to never-married mothers was only $1,241 per year, while the average for divorced mothers was $2,641. The average amounts actually received were $860 and $1,901, respectively.[18]

This difference in awards and payments is largely explained by the fact that unwed fathers, like unwed mothers, are on average younger, less educated, and poorer than their divorced counterparts. In addition, courts systematically protect the unwed father's ability to start a new family at the expense of his first family—after all, there is always welfare to fill the gap.

Marriage is an important solution to the financial problems of single mothers. But here again, never-married women fare worse than divorced women. Never-married mothers do have a higher marriage rate than divorced mothers. (The House Ways and Means Committee has reported that "within two years after a first birth out of wedlock, more than 50 percent of women have married. But it is only after five years that nearly the same proportion of divorced or separated women have remarried.")[19]

Divorced mothers, however, have much more stable second marriages. As of 1985, only 16 percent of the divorced women who had remarried were divorced again, according to Norton and Moorman (1986), in comparison with 27 percent of the women who had married after an out-of-wedlock birth.

Furthermore, although never-married women in general are more likely than divorced women to marry, for women on welfare the situation is reversed. According to Bane and Ellwood (1983), "Women who enter AFDC after being wives are far more likely to exit by becoming a wife again than are unmarried women who enter when they have a child." And marriage is the principal means of getting off welfare. According to Ellwood, marriage accounts for 34.6 percent of all exits from welfare, while earnings increases account for only 21.3 percent.[20]

One need not be morally judgmental about our high illegitimacy rate in order to be deeply concerned about its economic consequences. It is one thing when a movie star has a baby without a husband to help support it. Cher once proclaimed: "A man is a luxury." But it is quite another when an unwed teenager or a young mother on welfare has a baby. The difference, to put it sharply, is money.

Many of these young families move out of poverty, but most do not. While divorced women typically use welfare as a temporary measure until they get back on their feet, unmarried mothers become trapped in long-term welfare dependency. They work less, receive less child support, and are less likely to marry and stay married to someone able to support them and their children. Indeed, the evidence is mounting that never-married mothers compose the majority of long-term welfare dependents—a permanent underclass. The plight of the women and children in these families is deeply distressing.

Targeting Never-Married Mothers

Welfare reform has been on the Washington policy agenda for the last two years. Although various groups wanted many particular changes, the primary objective for most was to find ways to reduce long-term welfare dependency.

Much of the concern over long-term dependency was based on new evidence that the AFDC program had, in effect, two different caseloads of female-headed families: one which receives "short-term relief," and one which receives "long-term income maintenance" (Ellwood, 1986). This understanding led to efforts to target employment and social services on the latter group, in order "to reduce their dependency, both for fiscal and humanitarian purposes" (Ellwood, 1986).

As we have seen, the substantial social and economic differences between divorced and unwed mothers translate into vastly different rates of AFDC use and duration and, in large part, define the two AFDC caseloads. The dichotomy between married and never-married mothers is not absolute, of course. Some unwed mothers are doing just fine. And some divorced mothers, especially if they were only married for a short time after having given birth to one or more out-of-wedlock children, are in dire straits. Nevertheless, the underlying distinction provides great heuristic insight.

The children of divorced mothers constitute about 40 percent of all children on AFDC (U.S. Department of Health and Human Services, Family Support Administration, 1986). Although the financial plight of divorced mothers is a matter of great national concern, most use welfare as a temporary support until they get back on their feet. Thus policy makers and the public are increasingly comfortable with the notion of welfare as a sort of social insurance for divorced mothers. Conservatives, for example, sense a lesser "moral hazard" when AFDC payments are made to divorced mothers, as the following passage by Murray (1986) illustrates:

> A woman who comes onto AFDC for the first time in her forties is in a profoundly different situation from that facing a woman who comes onto AFDC in her teens. Apart from the many inevitable differences that go with the age gap, there is an extremely important self-selection factor at work. The woman of 45 who has her first contact with the welfare system has demonstrated prima facie—by the very fact that she lived an adult life for that many years without needing welfare—her possession of experiential, psychological, and perhaps intellectual resources that cannot be assumed in the teenager with a baby and no husband. The teenager has demonstrated prima facie that she is unable to function in the adult world for any length of time at all. Moreover, the moral hazard associated with a woman who comes onto the AFDC rolls at 40 is much different than for a woman of 18. Her plasticity, if you will, is different. The woman of 40 is already more or less who and what she is ever going to be. The woman of 18 is at a moment that may decisively shape her identity and development. (p. 38)

Efforts to help ease and speed the economic recovery of divorced mothers should, of course, be made, but—all things considered—the present system roughly meets their needs.[21] For this reason, Novak and others (1987) concluded that welfare policies did not require major change in regard to divorced mothers: "For women of mature age thrown into temporary poverty by divorce or separation, transitional aid is in line with the purposes of AFDC. Many such women possess the educational resources, skills, and determination to enable them to become independent within a short time. Programs assisting them, accordingly, should not compromise their independence" (p. 114).

But, as we have seen, for never-married mothers welfare programs are not working—not even roughly. Although AFDC provides needed financial support (the importance of which should not be minimized), it does little to reduce the long-term dependency of never-married mothers, over 40 percent of whom spend ten or more years on AFDC (see Maynard and Maxfield, 1986). Consequently, most analysts and advocacy groups have argued that welfare reform should be targeted toward helping these mothers become more self-reliant. Summarizing the research, Maynard and Maxfield (1986) claim: "the never-married marital status is itself an effective method for targeting long-term recipients."

Growing Support for Targeting

Although out-of-wedlock births are still a sensitive subject, much has changed since Daniel Patrick Moynihan's 1965 report, "The Negro Family," which voiced his concern about the breakdown of black families and the poverty it created. Moynihan was branded a racist, and the subject was almost immediately moved off limits, for black leaders as well as social analysts. As time passed, however, the evidence of rising illegitimacy among blacks and its resultant social consequences have grown impossible to avoid. In 1984, 59 percent of all black births were out of wedlock, more than four times the white ratio, 13 percent. Nearly 90 percent of black teenage mothers were unmarried. Now, many black leaders identify illegitimacy, abandonment, and female-headed families as problems threatening the future of the black community.[22] The National Urban League's *The State of Black America, 1986,* for example, states that "teenage pregnancy in the black community is no longer . . . discussed in hushed tones among blacks."

Here is how the Tarrytown Group (thirty liberal black leaders meeting in Tarrytown, New York) and the Black Leadership Forum summarized these concerns in their 1983 pamphlet, *A Policy Framework for Racial Justice:* "teenagers and young men and women need to be encouraged to pursue training, work, and personal development while they delay pregnancy and family formation . . . for young people, there is a special need for sex education and education about the importance of delaying sex, pregnancy, and marriage." The Children's Defense Fund's ongoing nationwide campaign against teenage pregnancy is yet another demonstration of this developing consensus.

Ironically, now that the high out-of-wedlock birth rate among blacks can be discussed freely, race has become a less important factor in the illegitimacy problem. When income and education are taken into account, racial differences are cut in half. And the gap between black and white rates is closing rapidly.

In 1984, the black out-of-wedlock birth rate was 76.8, compared with 20.1 for whites. Although the black rate is almost four times that of whites, whites are catching up. The difference between the two races fell from about 7 to 1 (in 1970) to less than 4 to 1 (in 1984) (Besharov, Quin, and Zinmeister, 1987). Moreover, as the white rate has been increasing (up 45 percent since 1970), the black rate has been declining (down 20 percent in the same period). In fact, since 1981, there have been more white out-of-wedlock births than black ones.

Even these remaining differences in black and white illegitimacy are exaggerated by the failure to consider income and educational differences. About half of all out-of-wedlock births are to families with annual incomes under $10,000. Among families in this income range, the 1985 difference between the black and white out-of-wedlock birth rates drops from 4 to 1 to less than 2 to 1. If we had data holding other demographic variables (for instance, urban residence) constant, there would probably be an even smaller difference (Besharov, Quin, and Zinmeister, 1987). Hence illegitimacy—and the economic disaster that often follows—is not just a "black" problem. It is an American problem that increasingly cuts across all racial communities.

Building broad professional and public support for programs that target the welfare dependency of young, unwed mothers should be possible if a punitive or judgmental approach is avoided. Most Americans want compassionate social welfare policies. It will do no good to use the behavioral differences between divorced and never-married mothers to blame the latter—or to ignore their pressing needs. Both groups deserve our humane concern, but our response must be shaped by the realities of their differing life situations. There is no constitutional obstacle, such as the Equal Protection Clause, to such policies. They would be based on the age, educational status, and past work experience of welfare applicants, as this year's welfare reform bills demonstrate.

How Current Welfare Reform Bills Target

All three major welfare reform bills begin to target workfare-type services, broadly defined to include education, training, and work preparation programs, on never-married mothers. Each bill takes a slightly different approach, so that it is worth reviewing how each addresses the same underlying distinction.

The Downey bill, supported by many House Democrats and recently passed by the House, establishes the following "target populations":

· families with a teenage parent, and families with a parent who was under eighteen years of age when the first child was born;

· families that have been receiving AFDC or family support supplements continuously for two or more years;

· families with a parent who lacks a high school diploma or its equivalent;

· families in which the youngest child is within two years of being ineligible for family support supplements because of his or her age.[23]

The Michel bill, supported by many House Republicans, gives a bonus for successfully training and placing "high priority applicants and recipients." These are:

· individuals who have failed to complete high school (or an equivalent course of instruction);

· unwed mothers with children under three years of age;

· recipients of aid who are under twenty-two years of age.[24]

The Moynihan bill does not establish target populations per se, but it does require states to target 60 percent of their funds to what it calls "long-term dependents," defined as:

· persons who have received welfare payments for more than two and a half years;

· "recidivists," that is, persons who have received welfare for any 30 of the previous 60 months;

· recipients aged twenty-one or under who lack a high school diploma.[25]

Although not precisely welfare reform legislation, Senator Kennedy's bill (JEDI) gives a "incentive bonus" to those states that train and successfully place two groups:

- persons who: (a) have received aid for at least two years prior to participation in education, training, and supportive services designed to provide jobs for such individuals; and (b) have had no work experience for the year preceding the year for which the determination of eligibility is made; OR

- persons who: (a) are under twenty-two years of age, (b) have not completed secondary school or its equivalent, and (c) have no work experience for the year preceding the year for which the determination of eligibility is made.[26]

While each of these bills makes a significant—and laudable—departure from current policies, none goes as far as it could go—nor as far as the research suggests that it should go—in targeting "would-be" long term recipients.

The Timing of Intervention

As a way to identify would-be long-term recipients, some proposals—including elements of the welfare reform bills described above—suggest waiting up two years before imposing workfare requirements. However, recent research (Maynard and Maxfield, 1986) indicates that this is not a cost-effective targeting strategy: "Postponing the employment-related program for two years after a family enters AFDC does not clearly target the program towards those with relatively long *future* periods of welfare dependence. . . ." (p. xiii). "Virtually all of the targeting toward long-term recipients that is brought about by delaying the treatment is offset by the fact that the beneficial effects of the treatment begin later" (p. 37).

Moreover, breaking habits of dependent behavior is many times more difficult after they become entrenched. Using data from the NLS, O'Neill and her colleagues (1984) found that conditional exit probabilities decline over time. They report that

exit rates remained significantly related to duration—the longer a person had been on welfare, the less likely she was to exit in a particular year. One interpretation of this finding is that we have omitted important explanatory variables. Another is that welfare itself produces effects that induce longer duration. These potential effects include work disincentives which would not only lead to reduced current earnings but could lead to loss of skill development which would lower future wage rates. Another potential effect is on family size and structure. More generally, an individual may lose motivation and self-confidence as a result of being on welfare and these attitudes may perpetuate welfare dependency. (p. 84)

Early Intervention

Welfare agencies should, to borrow David Ellwood's phrase, target would-be long-term recipients when they first apply for assistance. From the first day that a young, unmarried mother applies for AFDC, welfare agencies know that she faces the likelihood of years of dependency, yet they do very little to help or encourage her to become self-reliant. They should focus intensive efforts at this crucial point in the lives of young, unwed mothers.

The major obstacle to early intervention, of course, is the problem of young children. For mothers with children under six, we presently have what amounts to a no-work policy. Ellwood (1986) has described the poor targeting that results when mothers with children under six are exempted from the WIN program:

> If the goal of the Work Incentive Program (WIN) is to serve groups that are most likely to be long-term recipients, its resources are not targeted most effectively. Only 25 percent of the women who enter AFDC for the first time do not have children younger than age 6; moreover, this 25 percent are likely to have relatively short stays on AFDC. By contrast, young women, particularly never-married women with young children, constitute a major portion of those who first begin a spell of AFDC, and they can be expected to have a relatively long duration of AFDC dependence. By waiting until these women no longer have young children, most will have already experienced relatively long episodes of AFDC and other disadvantages, such as the lack of recent work experience. (p. 64)

As Maynard and Maxfield (1986) conclude: "the length of recipiency drops substantially as the age of the youngest child is raised, indicating that lowering the minimum age of the youngest child is an effective way to target would-be long term recipients."

Welfare policy is in the midst of a major reversal on the subject of whether mothers of young children should be required to work, or at least to participate in educational or work-related activities. In part, this change has been fueled by the large increase in the proportion of non-welfare mothers in the labor force.

Mothers with Very Young Children

None of the welfare reform bills continues the WIN work exemption for mothers with children under six. The Moynihan bill only exempts mothers with children under three, with states authorized to lower the exemption to mothers with children under one.[27] The Downey bill does the same.[28] The Michel bill, on the other hand, only exempts mothers with children under six months, but it allows states to wait six months from the date of application before requiring the mother's participation.[29] (Since most mothers, even young, unmarried ones, do not go on welfare immediately, the difference between the Downey and Michel bills may be less that it first appears—assuming that states elect the lower age exemption.)

For targeting purposes, exempting mothers with children under three seems to be a mistake. On the other hand, no one seriously suggests that the mother of a newborn should be required to go out and find a job. The question is where to draw the line between the two. Given concerns about the conditional probabilities of exit described above, this writer would vote for the earliest possible intervention—at six months after the child's birth and, depending on the intervention, even before— because it sends the right signal about the importance of responsible behavior.

The Welfare Mother's Parental Responsibilities

A key argument in the debate about requiring welfare mothers to work is that, since so many nonwelfare mothers are now working, there is nothing wrong with expecting mothers on welfare to work. And in keeping with the careless way the statistics are used, the assumption is that welfare mothers should work full time. But except for divorced mothers, most mothers are not working full time and, for divorced mothers, full-time work is usually a question of economic necessity bred, in part, by current alimony and child-support policies (Besharov and Dally, 1986). Moreover, the divorced women and their children tend to be older than the average never-married mothers and their children on welfare. In imposing work and training requirements for welfare mothers, therefore, we should respect their role as parents. This does not mean that welfare mothers should not work; they should. But as we rightly push welfare mothers into the labor force, we need to remember that they are, after all, still mothers.

Participation requirements should vary depending on the age (and any special needs) of the children. On this issue, both the Downey and Moynihan bills seem unduly restrictive. For mothers with children under six, the Downey bill would limit required participation to twenty hours a week.[30] The Moynihan bill places a limit of twenty-four hours.[31] Such stringent limitations might be valid for parents with very young children, but they should be loosened as the child grows older. For example, the New York State Task Force on Poverty and Welfare (1986) recommended that: "For single parents with young children, the contract would require participation on at least a half time basis in a structured set of program activities. (Exceptions might be made, of course, for the parents of disabled children or others requiring special attention.) Single parents with school-age children would be expected to participate on a two-thirds to full-time basis." Similarly, the APWA has recommended that:

> In single-parent households with children under three years old, parents be required to complete high school and then to engage in some form of part-time out-of-home activity, which could be work-related, community service, parenting education, or further schooling, provided the activity improves employability or promotes stable, strong families. After the children reach three years of age, more intensive employment-related activity will be required of the parents, as noted above (see Heintz, 1986). (p. 19)

As the foregoing suggests, for mothers with very young children, the standard job-training program might not be suitable. In this vein, the Downey bill requires that the participation program for children between three and six "emphasize education and training including parenting and nutrition education (especially in the case of first-time parents)."[32] There is no reason why a state should be prohibited from mandating a young mother's greater participation in such activities.

Similarly, for mothers under eighteen, the requirement might be that she continue in school. Here again we see legislative hesitancy. The Moynihan bill, which requires mothers under eighteen to finish high school or complete remedial literacy training, for example, exempts them from this requirement if they have a child under three (or under one, if the state elects). Moreover, the attendance need only be part time, even though the school day is already part time.[33] The New York State Task Force (1986), on the other hand, was unequivocal on the need for young teenagers to stay in school: "Society, in return for public assistance, can insist that teenagers, including teen parents, must stay in school, or in an alternative learning environment if that is more appropriate."

Another major problem with requiring mothers to participate in education and work activities is child care: who will provide it and who will pay for it? All three welfare reform bills seek to ensure that the children are properly cared for, or at least that they are not left at home alone. The Downey bill exempts mothers of children under six years of age "unless day care is guaranteed";[34] the Moynihan bill limits required participation to "those with respect to whom the State assures child care";[35] and the Michel bill requires the state agency administering the program "to provide recipients who are assigned under the program with child-care services."[36] One recognizes the political and perhaps practical necessity for such provisions. Nevertheless, given the diversity of current child-care arrangements—especially the large-scale use of informal arrangements—this writer is uncomfortable with their seeming push toward inflexible—and more expensive—child-care programs.

Wisconsin has wrapped many of these concepts together in a program called Learnfare.[37] Under state law, as of February 1, 1988, all teenage parents on AFDC must attend school (broadly defined to include public, private, vocational schools and high school equivalency programs). As of September 1, 1988, all the teenage dependents of mothers on AFDC will also be required to attend school. The legislation authorizes the state agency to grant an exemption to mothers with very young children. At this writing, the department is considering exemptions ranging from age three months to three years. Moreover, the legislation also provides funding for child care and transportation for the teenage mother to assist her to comply.

Learnfare's school attendance requirements are enforced by reducing the family's AFDC grant by an amount proportional to the number of noncomplying family members. Thus if a teenage mother with a single child, making a grant unit of two, does not regularly attend school, her grant will be reduced to that of a grant unit of one. Similarly, a mother on AFDC with two teenagers would be considered a grant unit of three; but if one of her children does not attend school, the grant would be reduced to a grant unit of two.[38]

Conclusion

Divorce and out-of-wedlock births already impoverish hundreds of thousands of female-headed families. They are the root causes of the feminization of poverty, a serious national problem that requires sustained attention. There are, however, marked differences in the depth and duration of female-headed family poverty. These differences correspond to the different origins of the female-headed family. Divorced mothers and their children suffer less severe poverty for shorter periods than do never-married mothers and their children.

There is no panacea for long-term poverty and welfare dependency, and political and budgetary constraints severely narrow the range of possible options. But much more can be done if we develop policies that distinguish between the two types of female-headed families and the problems they face.

Too many past attempts to reform welfare have failed for this realist to suggest rushing headlong into a radically new program; too many questions remain unanswered. For example, are the public schools prepared to deal with large numbers of unwed mothers? Will workfare programs have success with them? So far, the answers to such questions are at best ambiguous. Workfare programs, for example, have not made substantial gains with these most dependent recipients (Friedlander, 1988). But clearly their ability to do so will determine the success of any policy designed to target never-married mothers. A certain humility is therefore required of policy makers—especially since we are tinkering with the lives of the least powerful and the most deprived. We should adopt a step-by-step approach, securing sound successes and avoiding over-promising and disillusionment. Programs should be neither massive nor designed for swift results, but rather for steady progress.

Support Services

Denise F. Polit and Joseph J. O'Hara

Recommendations for welfare reform are proliferating in response to an emerging consensus that something is fundamentally wrong with the way that public assistance to families with dependent children is being administered in this country. Both liberals and conservatives endorse the need for changes in the system in order to bring about reductions in long-term welfare dependency and increases in self-sufficiency. There is considerably less agreement as to how this can best be achieved. Nevertheless, the reform recommendations included in various bills and in the position papers of various study groups do share some common features and themes that suggest the likely direction that welfare reform policies will take. Our purpose in this chapter is to discuss the implications of the major welfare reform themes with regard to the role of support services, with particular emphasis on child care, medical assistance, family-planning and life-skills assistance, transportation, and counseling. We focus on support services within the context of welfare reform strategies, rather than within the context of broader anti-poverty policy reform.

It must be noted at the outset that, in contrast to a fairly extensive history of social experimentation with a variety of strategies to increase the work effort of recipients of AFDC, there is remarkably little research evidence that has a direct bearing on the central questions of this paper: What support services are essential to those who are trying to achieve self-sufficiency? Can these services be provided? Support services have generally been a secondary program component and have not been independently evaluated with regard to their effects on welfare dependency or their cost effectiveness. We must therefore draw upon a range of evidence that, while relevant, is largely indirect.

Major Themes in Welfare Reform

Since late 1986, various interest groups and organizations have issued reports with recommendations for the direction that welfare reform should take. Examples include the reports of the White House Domestic Policy Council (1986a, 1986b), the American Public Welfare Association (1986), the American Enterprise Institute (1987), the Project on the Welfare of Families (1986), the National Governor's Association (1987), the National Coalition on Women, Work, and Welfare Reform (1987), and the New York State Task Force on Poverty and Welfare (1986). Although these groups vary widely in terms of their ideological orientations and the specifics of their welfare reform recommendations, they have reached similar conclusions concerning some of the fundamental elements that must be addressed in conjunction with welfare reform. Three recurring themes that have particular relevance to the issue of support services are discussed below.

Employment and Employment Training

The cornerstone of most of the current welfare reform proposals is to help AFDC recipients become more employable. Because the welfare system has placed greater emphasis on work and self-support among welfare recipients during the past two decades, it seems safe to assume that efforts to improve their employability and employment will enjoy prominence in any reform measures that ultimately are enacted. This trend is consistent with a widely endorsed social value, namely that the able-bodied should work to support themselves and their families. The welfare reports generally emphasize that work is important not only in terms of cutting welfare costs but also because it has concomitant psychological rewards for the individual recipients and their families.

Most reformers recognize, however, that many recipients cannot fully and permanently participate in the labor force because they lack some of the resources that are needed for regular employment. In particular, they often lack the education and employment skills needed to enter the marketplace and to compete for jobs that pay wages sufficiently high to encourage them to leave the welfare rolls. Thus the core services mentioned most frequently in the welfare reform reports and in proposed legislation include a range of welfare-to-work services such as General Educational Development (GED) preparation, employability training, and skills training. Several reports also indicate the need for mechanisms to facilitate the use of these educational and employment services, such as support services.

The Target Population

During the past five years, we have experienced a growing appreciation of the diversity of the welfare population and of the need to treat different categories of recipients differently. This appreciation is largely the result of several studies that have examined characteristics of recipients in relation to the period of time that they are receiving AFDC. For example, data from the PSID have been used to show that the majority of individuals who have ever received welfare are recipients for relatively short periods of time. However, about 25 percent of AFDC recipients have total welfare terms in excess of nine years. These long-terms recipients account for almost 60 percent of those found on welfare at any one time, and they use a very disproportionate share of AFDC resources (Ellwood, 1986).

Ellwood's research has shown that young, never-married women who enter the welfare system when their children are three years old or younger are at highest risk of becoming long-term recipients. These findings have suggested to many concerned with welfare reform that this is an especially important group to target with programs designed to promote self-sufficiency. Many now believe that unless these women get appropriate intervention at a relatively early age, they will become entrenched in the welfare system and fall too far behind their peers in educational credentials and employment experience to escape long-term dependency.

This is a group, however, about which we know relatively little from an intervention standpoint because these women have traditionally been exempted from mandatory participation in the WIN program.[1] The current WIN policy exempting women with children under the age of six is in itself a much-discussed issue in the welfare reform reports because it was based on the now outmoded assumption that women with young children should stay home to devote their full-time energies to child-rearing. In a society where most mothers of young children work, many are now questioning the legitimacy of age of child as a criterion for exemption. Nearly all the current welfare reform reports recommend reducing or eliminating the age-of-youngest-child exemption, and these recommendations are reflected in the major reform bills now under consideration in Congress. For example, both H.R. 1720 and S. 1511 reduce the exemption to apply to mothers of children under age three; in the House Republican bill, the age-of-youngest-child exemption is six months.

Thus it seems highly likely that when welfare reforms are ultimately implemented, they will provide work-related services to women who are responsible for the care of preschool-age children. This in turn means that substantially younger women, including teenage mothers, will be included in the welfare-to-work programs. As a result, public assistance agencies are likely in the future to be dealing with groups of recipients that differ in many respects from the groups that they have attempted to serve through WIN in the past. It is therefore important to consider whether this group has special needs that must be addressed if the new welfare-to-work programs are to be fully implemented.

Social Contracts

Many proponents of welfare reform have emphasized "mutual obligations," "shared responsibility," and "reciprocity." This social contract theme, which has been endorsed by both liberals and conservatives, centers on the premise that while government has the responsibility to care for disadvantaged groups during times of distress through income maintenance and other social services programs, the recipients of this assistance also have an obligation to prepare themselves for self-sufficiency through education, training, or other forms of vocational preparation. Recent evidence from various state work-welfare demonstrations suggests that welfare recipients themselves view the notion of obligations on their part (here, in the form of work requirements) as fair and reasonable (Gueron, 1986).

The concept of shared responsibility is the rationale for support services in several of the welfare reform reports. That is, it is being argued or implied that the government would not be holding up its end of the bargain in expecting work-related effort on the part of welfare recipients unless it provides assistance in reducing or eliminating the barriers that interfere with such effort.

Potential Barriers in the Transition to Self-Sufficiency

Research on the correlates of long-term dependency, together with evaluations showing that programmatic interventions have different effects on different subgroups of recipients, clearly indicate that the welfare population is quite heterogeneous. The barriers that recipients face are likely to be diverse as well. Nevertheless, fairly extensive research and program experience suggest that many, if not most, AFDC mothers share numerous obstacles that interfere with progress toward self-sufficiency. If welfare reform initiatives are actually undertaken, personal barriers are likely to pose an even greater challenge to the welfare system than they have in the past, because many of the newly mandated recipients will be ones with especially complex problems. These include teenage mothers, mothers with preschool-age children, and older mothers who were teenage mothers when they left school and who have been on welfare for a number of years without working. These groups represent over 80 percent of the recipient population. They will face such problems as the following:

· *Poor educational credentials.* According to the 1975 survey of adult AFDC recipients, nearly two-thirds have less than a twelfth-grade education (Masters and Maynard, 1981), and among teen parent recipients the school profile is equally unfavorable. Research has consistently shown that the majority of teenage mothers drop out of school to have their babies and many others were already dropouts when they became pregnant (Mott and Marsiglio, 1985; Polit et al., 1982).

· *Basic skills deficits.* Many recipients are likely to require extensive remedial education. A recent analysis of the basic skills deficits of unmarried AFDC mothers aged seventeen to twenty-one (using data from the NLS) found that about 60 percent of this group scored in the bottom 20 percent of the test score distribution for all young adults (Sum and Goedicke, 1986).

· *Limited work experience.* In the 1975 AFDC survey, two-thirds of the adult sample had either never worked or had not worked at all in the twenty-four months prior to the survey (Masters and Maynard, 1981). Teenage AFDC mothers have little or no work experience, and little knowledge about the world of work (Polit et al., 1985).

· *Child-care needs.* The barrier that is perhaps the most self-evident is the child-care needs of AFDC mothers. If women with preschool-age children are required to make a work-related effort, they will need to make some arrangement for the care of those young children.

· *Health problems.* AFDC mothers and their children are generally less healthy than their counterparts who are not on welfare (Kasper, 1986).

Low-income women who give birth during their teen years are especially likely to have children with medical problems (Makinson, 1985; Strobino, 1987). Young AFDC mothers are also at very high risk of repeat pregnancies (Mosena, 1986; Polit et al., 1985).

Other problems. Poverty is associated with other types of experiences and stresses that interfere with progress toward self-sufficiency, including such problems as unstable personal relationships, physical abuse, depression, lack of self-confidence, and so on. A sizable proportion of young AFDC recipients experience such problems as unstable housing, turbulent home lives, and drug and alcohol abuse (Branch et al., 1984; Polit, 1986b), all of which can affect participation in special programs and subsequent work stability.

The authors of several of the welfare reform reports argue or imply that welfare agencies will be unsuccessful in carrying out the proposed reforms, to the extent that they fail to deal with these women's barriers to self-sufficiency. Support services are viewed by many as the primary means for tackling these barriers.

Arguments for and against Support Services

Advocates for the inclusion of support services in welfare reform programs argue that such services will play a critical role in the success of these programs. First, support services are considered to be enabling mechanisms—they enable people to cope with the problems or personal difficulties that interfere with the pursuit of some goal. People at all income levels need support services in order to keep working, but middle-income people usually either can afford to purchase these services directly (child care) or have employers who offer such services as fringe benefits (health benefits). The assumption underlying the recommendations for the provision of these support services as part of welfare reform programs is that people with limited resources cannot address their barriers to employment without some assistance. For example, a low-income mother with young children might be unable to find or afford, without some outside help, a suitable child care arrangement while she is in a job training program.

A second argument for providing support services is that the welfare system must be redesigned so as to ensure that work is more rewarding and less costly to the individual than dependency. If a mother with small children is worse off financially with earnings (because of medical expenses and work-related expenses such as child care and transportation) than she would be on welfare, then she is unlikely to be motivated to find and keep a job.

Those who oppose the provision or expansion of government-funded support services to AFDC recipients raise several arguments against them. The most notable objection is to the cost of these services and the problems of administering them. Support services can be quite expensive and, unlike skills training or job search programs, have a much less self-evident "payoff" in terms of movement toward employment. A second objection is that many of these services are seen as more properly the domain of other institutions, such as the family or private-sector employers. For example, relatives may be expected to play a role in the provision of child care, and employers could be called upon to provide health coverage to all workers. Finally, it is sometimes argued that too much support encourages further dependency. When the government makes all of the arrangements for child care, health care, and so on, is it in fact fostering the very type of dependency behavior that it is hoping to discourage?

Unfortunately, we really do not know a lot about the effects of adding support services to a program aimed at enhancing work effort among AFDC mothers because there have not been any evaluations that have focused specifically on the effects of different mixes and intensities of support services on eventual self-sufficiency. We do, however, have some isolated pieces of information that are suggestive of their effects.

Within the WIN program, for example, there is some evidence that the provision of support services and the availability of supportive agency staff have positive effects. In an organizational analysis, low-performing WIN offices were compared with high-performing sites, with performance defined in terms of registrants' success in securing job placements. The analysts found that low-performing offices offered very few support services; high-performing sites, conversely, were much more involved with all their clients, offering a variety of support services and intensive counseling on a range of personal issues (Mitchell, Chadwin, and Nightingale, 1980).

Some evidence from youth employment programs also suggests that support services are beneficial. Among youth programs, only the Job Corps programs have yielded reliable and replicable evidence of long-term success (Betsey et al., 1985). The Job Corps program, being residential in nature, is unparalleled in the degree of extra support that is provided to participants through counseling, recreational activities, and peer group sessions. Although it is not clear that the success of Job Corps is attributable to the availability of support services, the nature of the core program services, the residential character of the program, or some other factors, it is nevertheless noteworthy that the most successful youth employment model provides more than just employment and education services.

Relatively few low-income young mothers have been included (until very recently) in large-scale demonstrations aimed at improving their ability to enter the labor market, though there have been numerous "comprehensive" programs aimed at ameliorating the many negative consequences of early childbearing, and most of these programs have included substantial support services. The evaluations of these programs have not been as rigorous as might be desired (in particular, no major evaluation of a young-parent program has used an experimental design), but in the aggregate the major evaluations suggest that comprehensive programs do result in gains in a variety of outcome areas. The gains most notably have been in the areas of health and education, and appear to be especially strong for the teenage women entering the programs with the greatest degree of disadvantage, such as young women on AFDC (Polit, 1986a; Hofferth, 1987a).

Services in Support of Welfare to Work Programs

This section focuses on several specific types of support services, including child care, medical assistance,[2] family planning and life-skills assistance, transportation, and counseling. For each of these services, the main question we ask is: *To what extent is the provision of this service critical in assisting welfare-dependent women to gain entry into the labor market and maintain self-sufficiency?* To answer this question adequately, we would need results from studies in which a randomly assigned group of welfare mothers receiving the service were compared with another group who did not. Such studies have not been conducted. Because the information on the effects of specific support services is fairly limited, we will need to draw upon various pieces of indirect evidence, including self-report data on need for services from AFDC mothers and working women. In this section we also consider current sources for each support service, and the likely change in demand for these services if welfare reform proposals are implemented.

Child Care

If proposals to reduce or eliminate the age-of-youngest-child exemption are adopted, child care may well emerge as a key determinant of program success because the number of affected families would be enormous. According to projections based on Ellwood's (1986) work, about 82 percent of the AFDC recipients at any point in time have at least one child under the age of six, and about 60 percent have a child under the age of three. This means that if the exemption were lowered from six to three, the number of mothers who would be required to register for an employment-related intervention would more than double over current levels. All of the newly mandated recipients would, of course, need to make arrangements for the care of their preschool-age children during the time that they are employed or participating in a training or educational program. The critical policy questions for welfare reformers are the extent to which the government should provide or subsidize child care during training, and the nature, extent, and length of government assistance with child care once the mother is employed.[3]

Assistance with child care is currently provided to low-income families through a variety of federal programs. For the AFDC population, the primary federal funding sources for child care assistance are the Social Services Block Grant (SSBG, or Title XX), and the income-disregard provisions of AFDC and WIN (Title IV-A).[4]

Annually, the federal government spends about $700 million on child care subsidies through the SSBG. The passage of the OBRA in 1981 radically affected the level of federal funds available for such subsidies. As of 1986, SSBG funds were only 75 percent of what they would have been in 1982, in real dollars; thirty-five states spent less on child care subsidies in 1985 than in 1981 (Hofferth and Phillips, 1987). Child-care subsidies through the SSBG program are available to both AFDC recipients and other low-income families. There are no data regarding the number of AFDC recipients who are currently receiving subsidies through Title XX.

Title IV-A of the Social Security Act disregards child care expenses in calculating AFDC recipients' assistance payments. About $125 million annually are associated with this program. Although overall federal funds for Title IV-A remain uncapped, OBRA resulted in changes in the disregard formula. A maximum of $160 per month per child can now be disregarded as a child-care work expense. The disregard for earnings in order to maintain AFDC eligibility (the "$30-and-one-third" disregard) was limited to four months. Furthermore, a gross income limitation was set that makes recipients ineligible for AFDC when their gross income exceeds 150 percent of their state's needs standard. As a result of these changes, most mothers working full time quickly become ineligible for AFDC and the IV-A disregard, thereby putting more pressure on the limited Title XX funds.

Child-care arrangements presumably play a critical role in women's employment patterns and in participation in training programs, and therefore those involved in welfare reform must determine what the need for subsidized and market child care among welfare recipients would be under the new initiatives. This, unfortunately, is not an easy question to answer. There have been no major surveys of child care use and need among AFDC recipients since 1979 (a pre-OBRA survey), and in any event such a survey would probably fail to capture the needs of those yet-to-be-mandated recipients with young children. Several types of information, however, can be brought to bear in assessing child-care needs: self-reported information, reports of agency staff, correlational evidence regarding child-care costs and employment patterns, and information on existing utilization patterns.

Low-income women consistently have reported the need for child care in order to work. For example, in a CPS conducted in the late 1970s, about two out of ten women not working or looking for work said they would enter the labor force if satisfactory child care were available at a reasonable cost. The self-reported constraints of available child care on employment was found to be highest among the very groups that are of most concern in this paper: young mothers under the age of twenty-five, unmarried mothers, mothers without a high school diploma, and women whose annual family incomes were under $5,000 (Presser and Baldwin, 1980).

Findings similar to these survey results have also been reported in studies focusing on low-income families and WIN mothers. For example, in the Denver WIN Lab study, the exempt AFDC women (that is, primarily women with children under age six) who did not volunteer even after intensive recruitment efforts cited child care as their major reason (MDRC, 1980). In several studies of subsidized child-care voucher programs for low-income families, clients have consistently reported that child-care assistance was critical to their effort to obtain training or secure jobs (see Beyna et al., 1984; Dubnoff, 1986; Scoll and Engstrom, 1985).

Conversely, in studies of low-income teenage mothers, assistance with child care seldom emerges as a pressing need. For example, in the Project Redirection demonstration, the young mothers ranked child care as only their seventh greatest unmet service need, out of a list of twenty possible services (Polit et al., 1982). In a survey of 900 teen AFDC mothers in Chicago, Mosena (1986) found that child care was reported as a big problem by 14 percent of the sample; by contrast, finding a job was considered a big problem by 43 percent of those surveyed. It is unclear, however, whether this perception stems primarily from the young mothers' lack of involvement in activities requiring child care or from the availability of family members to meet their child-care needs.

Reports from within welfare agencies are also mixed. Various state needs-assessment reports generally indicate that the current gap between the supply of available subsidized child care and its need is substantial, and that waiting lists for available slots are long (Blank, 1986). WIN operators frequently comment that the unavailability of child care has impeded full participation among even the mandatory cases with older children. In the analysis of high-performing and low-performing WIN sites, the availability of adequate child care was found to be a problem in almost all sites (Mitchell et al., 1980). Yet some WIN staff believe that recipients who are highly motivated to work can usually arrange their own child care and that some mandatory WIN registrants use child-care problems as an excuse for not cooperating (Mitchell et al., 1980). This suspicion appears not to be totally unfounded. In the Supported Work demonstration for long-term AFDC recipients, more than three times as many control as experimental subjects reported that the unavailability of child care prohibited them from working (33 percent versus 10 percent), suggesting that most women were able to make acceptable child-care arrangements once a job placement was secured (Masters and Maynard, 1981).

Because of the limitations of self-report data, we must also consider other types of evidence about the role of child care and single mothers' self-sufficiency, such as the relation between child-care costs and women's labor-force participation. That is, to what extent does the cost of market child care inhibit women's entry into and sustained attachment to the labor force? In general, studies have found that when child-care costs rise, women's employment declines. For example, Stolzenberg and Waite (1984) found that both child-care costs and the availability of formal child-care providers in an area had positive effects on the percentage of mothers (especially mothers of very young children) who were in the labor force. Blau and Robins (1986) found that the cost of child care had a positive effect on working wives' rate of leaving employment and a negative effect on the rate at which nonemployed women entered jobs. Child-care subsidies, by contrast, had a positive effect on job entry and a negative effect on job exit.

Studies of actual utilization patterns also provide a line of evidence on child-care need. There is surprisingly little information from national samples regarding the types of child-care arrangements made by AFDC mothers who work or participate in educational or employment programs. The 1979 AFDC Recipient Survey had very limited information about child care and is, in any event, almost a decade old. National data on such arrangements from the 1984–85 SIPP show that employed female heads of households use substantially different types of child-care arrangements than employed women with husbands present. For example, for preschool-age children, relatives provide child care for about 40 percent of families with an employed female head, compared to about 20 percent of families with an employed wife. For school-aged children, relatives are the primary caretakers for 11 percent and 5 percent of these families, respectively (U.S. Bureau of the Census, 1987). A recent analysis of the SIPP data also indicated that relatives of AFDC recipients care for 58 percent of the youngest children under age six, compared to 44 percent for guardians never on AFDC (Brush, 1987). However, these analyses were based on a very small sample of employed parents on AFDC with preschool-age children (N = 50), and the percentage may not be very reliable.

A recent study of several hundred working AFDC mothers living in three large cities confirms that relatives play an especially important role in meeting the child-care needs of welfare families. Sonenstein (1984, 1987) found that relatives of employed recipients accounted for about half the child care arrangements for preschool-age children. Relative care was especially frequent for children under age four.

Reliance on relative-provided child care has been documented in several other studies of welfare recipients (see Klausner, 1978; Polit et al., 1982). These findings have led some commentators to suggest that the demand for market care and need for child-care subsidies in this population may not be very high. Some studies have found, in fact, that informal care by relatives is the preferred arrangement by many mothers (U.S. House of Representatives, 1984). However, such arrangements are often undependable and are not wholly satisfactory to the mothers. For example, Polit and White (1987), in a longitudinal study of disadvantaged women who had given birth as teens, found that the two most frequently voiced complaints were that care by relatives was unreliable and outside care was unaffordable.[5] In Sonenstein's (1987) survey, although 50 percent of the respondents used relatives as their main source of care, only 30 percent said that care by relatives was their first choice. Mothers who were most satisfied with their child-care arrangements were ones whose children were in licensed day-care centers or preschool programs, and those who were least satisfied were ones whose children were cared for by grandparents. In another study, Blau and Robins (1987) found that higher child-care costs (measured by the average weekly cost of market care) discouraged women from working even when informal child care was available, suggesting that relatives were not an acceptable source of child care for some of the women.

It appears, then, that child care by relatives is not enough to meet the needs of mothers of young children who will be involved in welfare-to-work programs. Many mothers do not have relatives available or willing to provide this service, and others appear to find such an arrangement undesirable or insufficiently reliable. Furthermore, such care is not always free. In Sonenstein's (1987) study of AFDC families, about one-third of relative-based arrangements involved payment.

The majority of welfare mothers who are employed must pay for their child care. Sonenstein found that the average weekly cost of child care in her sample represented 21 percent of the weekly wages of employed AFDC mothers. This is about double the percentage that has been reported in national samples of working parents (Hofferth, 1987b). In light of these disproportionately high child-care costs for low-income women, it seems plausible that subsidies could play a critical role in minimizing the disincentive that mothers may experience as they try to make a transition off the welfare rolls. Evidence from various demonstrations for the welfare population clearly indicate that many recipients do take advantage when they are included in special programs (for example, in Supported Work, the SIME/DIME negative income tax experiments, and so on). However, there is also considerable evidence that the standard subsidies that are now in place are not effectively utilized. According to data from the 1979 AFDC Recipient Survey, fewer than 40 percent of the full-time working mothers with children under age fourteen used the Title XX or the Title IV-A child-care subsidies (Hofferth and Sonenstein, 1983). In Sonenstein's recent study, only about 25 percent of the

AFDC mothers who worked had used the Title IV-A disregard for child-care expenses at any time during a fourteen-month study period. Evaluations of child-care voucher programs have also shown that AFDC recipients do not always understand services that are available to them. For example, in the Hennepin County voucher demonstration, almost all the recipients interviewed reported having had trouble finding out from the county welfare workers about the existence of the program (Scoll and Engstrom, 1985).

Overall, we can draw several tentative conclusions about the child-care needs of AFDC recipients. First, these women say they need affordable child care in order to work; and their claims are substantiated in part by findings that when child-care costs are lower, a higher percentage of them enter employment. (On the other hand, it seems likely that at least some recipients who report child-care problems are insufficiently motivated to resolve those problems in order to work or participate in work programs.) Second, many AFDC mothers—perhaps up to 50 percent—have access to free or low-cost child care by relatives and this may be the preferred arrangement for many. However, some mothers are unsatisfied with such arrangements and may prefer to stay home with their children; others who rely on relatives may be faced with problems at work if the unreliability of the arrangement leads to frequent absenteeism. Third, there are currently some mechanisms to offset or pay for child-care costs for AFDC mothers (Title XX and IV-A), but there are indications from various sources that available resources may not be adequate to meet even the current demand. Despite this, available subsidies and child-care assistance are not always used, at least in part owing to ignorance about existing resources.

If one assumes that this is a reasonably accurate portrayal of the current child-care situation, how is this picture likely to change if welfare reforms are enacted? First of all, the number of mothers who will need to make child-care arrangements will increase substantially if mothers of pre-school-age children are mandated to participate in welfare-to-work programs. Table 6.1 presents estimates of the number of AFDC recipients who would become mandated for some type of program participation, according to various "scenarios" based on age-of-youngest child exemptions. This table suggests that if the age of youngest child exemption is lowered to age three, the number of mandated recipients will double over the number mandated under the current WIN program, and if it is lowered to age one, the number will more than triple. Such changes

Table 6.1. Estimated number of AFDC mothers eligible for mandatory program participation, by age of youngest child exemption and years of welfare receipt

Age of youngest child exemption	Number of new recipients	Number of second year recipients	Number of third year recipients
<6	146,000	100,000	89,000
<3	247,000	192,000	184,000
<1	538,000	364,000	289,000

Source: Based on simulations reported in Maxfield and Rucci (1986), who used data from a sample of the 1984 AFDC Quality Control database.

would result in hundreds of thousands of women with preschool-age children newly mandated to participate in some program activity.

These figures suggest that there will be tremendous pressures to alter levels of governmental assistance for AFDC mothers while they are in programs and during the transition to regular employment. Available funding levels, if inadequate to meet current need, will clearly be much too low for the new demand that will be created, especially since there will be greater demand for the more expensive infant care. It is therefore important to consider the evidence on what the effects of child-care assistance might be in terms of incentives and disincentives for employment and self-sufficiency.

Although no rigorous evaluations have estimated the effect of subsidized child care on the work behavior of AFDC recipients, several studies conducted over the past decade have attempted to demonstrate that subsidized day care has income-enhancing potential for low-income families. One of the earliest was completed in 1979, based on a program operating in several Florida counties (Hosni and Donnan, 1979). These investigators concluded that the availability of child care on a sliding-fee-scale basis more than doubled employment and family income, and reduced welfare recipiency by about half. In an analysis of the effect of a subsidized child-care voucher program in a California community, Freis and Miller and Associates (1980) reported that the cost of welfare grants for families was reduced by about 50 percent, and that parent fees for child-care services increased by 65 percent over the study period. In a Massachusetts voucher demonstration, Gray and others (1984) reported that about half of the study participants were able to terminate AFDC, and that rates of employment increased from 64 percent at baseline to

93 percent for those who used the vouchers for twelve months or more. McMurray and Kazanjian (1982), in a study of the effect of reductions in New York City's subsidized child-care program, found that families who were able to retain their subsidized care were more likely to terminate welfare than those who remained on waiting lists.

Unfortunately, none of these studies used a rigorous evaluation methodology. Most of them were based on simple comparisons of families before and after the availability of child care subsidies. Since many people would have left the welfare rolls in any event, these findings do not by themselves provide conclusive evidence of the cost effectiveness of child-care subsidies. However, other findings based on more rigorous research support the view that subsidized care enhances the ability of low-income women to achieve self-sufficiency.

Robins (1987) recently completed a sophisticated economic analysis of child-care availability within public housing projects. Using data from a sample of 796 families in public housing projects with and without child-care centers on the premises, Robins found that the availability of on-site child-care centers serving a large fraction of public housing residents was associated with a considerable increase in the residents' employment probability, annual earnings, and number of hours worked, and with a decrease in their probability of receiving welfare. These effects were especially powerful among families with preschool age children. Although study subjects were not assigned to housing projects at random, Robins's analyses carefully controlled for background differences in the two groups that could account for the differences in employment and dependency patterns.

Burt and her colleagues (1984) studied hundreds of young mothers participating in comprehensive adolescent parent programs sponsored by the U.S. Office of Adolescent Pregnancy Programs. They also found that child-care assistance had positive effects on progress toward self-sufficiency. At twelve monts postpartum, mothers who received child-care assistance from the programs were significantly more likely than others to have better schooling outcomes, to be employed, or to be in a job training program. While it is possible that certain young mothers (that is, the most motivated) were most likely to seek out the assistance they needed, the analyses did control for many important background characteristics.

Evidence from one small study that investigated the effects of day-care provision is especially noteworthy because of its use of a true experimental design. The Abecedarian Project was an intense, multi-component intervention designed to provide free developmental day care to infants at risk of developmental delays (Ramey et al., 1982; Ramey and Campbell, 1984; Campbell et al., 1986). In this project, 100 economically disadvantaged families were randomly assigned to an experimental or control condition. Most of the families were headed by a single mother, and about one-third of these women were aged seventeen or younger. Mothers in the experimental group received free educational day care for their children from the time of birth until entry into public kindergarten, while control group mothers received no special child-care services. The results suggested sizable benefits to both the mothers and the children in the experimental group. For example, when the children were four-and-a-half years old, nearly 50 percent more of the control group mothers than experimental group mothers were receiving public assistance. Experimental group mothers were more than twice as likely as control group mothers to have received some training after high school, and significantly more had completed their basic schooling. On a test of cognitive abilities, the experimental group children scored a full standard deviation higher than control group children. The results for the subgroup of young teenage mothers were as promising as those for the entire sample.

Further evidence regarding the effects of child-care assistance comes from studies that have examined the impact of loss of Title XX child-care subsidies or reductions or losses of AFDC benefits. Several such studies were undertaken after the enactment of OBRA. This legislation resulted in major changes in the AFDC program, one of which was to drastically reduce the percentage of AFDC recipients with earnings who maintained eligibility (Griffith and Usher, 1986; Moffitt and Wolf, 1987). As a result, many employed recipients were terminated from AFDC and lost associated child-care benefits. A Massachusetts study revealed that almost half of the terminated families had to change their child-care arrangements, and one-fourth resorted to leaving their children alone or in the care of siblings. Furthermore, about 25 percent reported having to reduce their work hours, 10 percent said they quit their jobs, and nearly half reported missed days of work as a result of the change (Bass, 1984). This and other studies indicate that loss of access to child-care subsidies is associated with shifts to more informal arrangements, changes in work behavior, and, in a notable minority of cases, the placement of children in high-risk self-care arrangements (Marx, 1985).

Although these studies are suggestive, it must be acknowledged that our understanding of the complex interplay between child-care arrangements, employment, and welfare dependency is at this point quite meager. Furthermore, there are many questions this body of research evidence does not even address. For example, we know very little about the extent to which the availability of child-care assistance to recipients may actually serve as an incentive to stay on welfare.[6] Nor do we know whether the central child-care problem that would emerge in the context of welfare reform would be primarily one of supply or demand—that is, are child-care constraints most likely to arise because of availability, affordability, accessibility or acceptability of child care?

Nevertheless, despite these limitations, the current body of research taken collectively does lend support to the argument that child-care services help to remove an important barrier to employment among welfare-dependent mothers of young children. It therefore seems reasonable to conclude that successful welfare-to-work initiatives will need to address the child-care needs of affected recipients head-on, to learn how to tell the women about the available child-care options, and to help them make the necessary arrangements.

Medical Assistance

Medical care is categorically available to all AFDC recipients through the Medicaid program, and would therefore be available to all those participating in welfare-to-work programs. However, Medicaid coverage is typically terminated four months after recipients exit from welfare, and this is a policy that has been questioned in several of the welfare reform reports.

In the context of welfare reform proposals, two aspects of medical assistance are especially relevant. One is the extent to which health problems might be a barrier to employment and program participation in welfare-to-work programs. Second is the question of Medicaid: since the extension of its benefits has been recommended in several reform proposals, we will discuss the termination of medical benefits as a disincentive to leaving the welfare rolls.

With regard to the first question, there is reason to suspect that health issues are likely to pose some problems for those attempting to implement welfare-to-work programs, especially if large numbers of young mothers are mandated to participate. A recent review of the health problems of young disadvantaged mothers indicated that low-income adolescent mothers often suffer from chronic illnesses, poor nutrition, substance abuse, and poor hearing and vision (Klerman, 1986). This is not especially surprising, given the findings that the Medicaid population in general (both adults and children) is in poorer health than persons without Medicaid (see Kasper, 1986).

Health problems could therefore interfere with attendance in the core activities of welfare-to-work programs and, eventually, with employment itself. Good health and perceptions of good health among low-income single mothers are consistently found to be positively associated with participation in employment programs and in the labor force. For example, data from the study of the Denver WIN Lab, which focused intensive recruitment activities on the WIN exempt cases (that is, primarily mothers with young children), revealed that poor health was a frequently mentioned reason for not volunteering for WIN (MDRC, 1980). Similar results are reported in other studies of similar populations (see Dadkhah and Stromsdorfer, 1981; Goldman, 1981; Goldman et al., 1985).

Children's health problems are also relevant because they have been found to interfere with women's working patterns. For example, Salkever (1982) found that, even after statistically controlling numerous background factors, the presence of a child with a health problem or disability in a family significantly reduced the probability that the mother would be working; this was found to be especially true in low-income families.

In addition to health problems standing in the way of employment, we should ask whether current Medicaid policies result in a disincentive for these women to leave the welfare rolls. At issue here is the so-called "notch effect," which refers to the situation of women who leave AFDC because of employment and are actually worse off economically than they would have been had they remained on welfare. If a woman succeeds in earning enough to become ineligible for the cash grant through AFDC, she also loses other benefits associated with her welfare status. Medicaid, the most important of them, currently is terminated four months after AFDC eligibility ends. While AFDC recipients may not fully understand and use child-care subsidy programs, medical assistance through the Medicaid program is widely used by welfare mothers, and they apparently value it highly. In Gittell and Moore's (1985) study of AFDC mothers enrolled in employment training programs in three states, the prospect of losing medical benefits was the most frequently mentioned concern when women spoke about going off welfare.

Several of the welfare reports recommend extending Medicaid coverage beyond the current four-month period. An important question facing policy makers is whether the termination of these benefits (or the prospect of their termination) induces women to remain on the welfare rolls and inhibits their efforts to become employed. Unfortunately, this question is difficult to answer in a straightforward fashion. Since Medicaid is a universal program whose effects on work behavior have not been experimentally evaluated, we must consider some indirect evidence bearing on this question.[7]

One type of evidence concerns the extent to which working women are able to replace Medicaid benefits with other types of health insurance. This question is relevant to the overall health of this population, because it has repeatedly been found that health insurance increases access to and utilization of medical care (see Blank, 1987; Davis and Rowland, 1983). Outside of the Medicaid program, medical insurance is primarily available as a fringe benefit through employers. However, because many low-income women work only part time, discontinuously, or in entry-level jobs, this fringe benefit is not always available to them. In this regard, Blank (1987) found, on the basis of data from the National Medical Care Utilization and Expenditure Survey (NMCUES), that about one quarter of female-headed families with at least one child present had no medical insurance (either private or through Medicaid) for at least part of 1980, and that fewer than half of these families had private insurance available to them throughout the year. Even 17 percent of those who worked full time for the entire year did not have private year-round insurance. Fewer than half of the part-year workers and fewer than one-third of the part-time workers had year-round private insurance.

Many mothers who leave welfare for work may thus not be covered by private insurance through their jobs. This inference is consistent with findings from several studies that have examined OBRA's impact on medical coverage. As mentioned above, OBRA dramatically reduced the percentage of AFDC recipients with earnings who maintained their eligibility for AFDC, and consequently for Medicaid. Several analyses have been undertaken to determine whether these OBRA-related program changes affected the ability of former recipients to meet their health-care needs.

One such study, conducted in the Minneapolis area, found that substantial percentages of families failed to obtain private health insurance after termination from AFDC (Moscovice and Craig, 1984; Moscovice and Davidson, 1987). For example, two years after losing AFDC eligibility, 30 percent of the adults and 40 percent of the children had no health insurance coverage whatsoever. As a consequence, those who lost Medicaid benefits were significantly more likely to delay seeing physicians and dentists than those who remained on AFDC.

Similar findings from a national study have been reported by Long and Settle (1984, 1985). Using data from the NMCUES, they found that those who were successful in replacing Medicaid with private health insurance (about 55 percent of the newly ineligible population) did not experience a substantial decline in the use of major health services. However, those of the newly ineligibles who were unsuccessful in obtaining private insurance (45 percent) did experience significant declines in their use of basic health services. For example, the use of physician services and the purchase of prescription drugs declined by nearly 40 percent, and the use of inpatient hospital services declined by over 70 percent.

Interestingly, predictions that the OBRA-related changes would result in increased rates of welfare dependency have not been confirmed. Some critics of OBRA had expected that working AFDC recipients might respond to the legislation by quitting their jobs in order to maintain eligibility for Medicaid. The OBRA changes did not result in a substantial increase in the number of case reopenings (see Griffith and Usher, 1986; Moscovice and Davidson, 1987); however, those that did return to welfare tended to be the ones who did not have any private insurance in the pre-OBRA days.

If we could assume that those who became ineligible for AFDC through the OBRA changes resembled to some degree the recipients who might make a transition to work as a result of welfare reform employment programs, then we could predict, first, that substantial percentages would be successful in not returning to the welfare rolls; and second, that they would probably have less access to health care relative to what they had while on AFDC. However, it must be remembered that those families who became ineligible for AFDC as a result of OBRA were almost entirely ones who were already employed and had some attachment to the labor force when OBRA went into effect. Despite this work history, 45 percent of these recipients were unable to obtain private health insurance for themselves and their children. It seems likely that women with less prior work experience would have even greater difficulty in finding and maintaining a job with health benefits. They are therefore more likely to revert to welfare or to fail to receive appropriate medical services.

Only one other study has examined the effects of Medicaid coverage on employment and dependency patterns. Blank (1987) analyzed the effect of the Medically Needy program on AFDC status. In 21 states, Medicaid eligibility is determined by AFDC eligibility, but 29 states (and the District of Columbia) have a Medically Needy program that allows some families to receive Medicaid without participating in the AFDC program. Blank found that serious illness of the female head of household and perceptions of poor health had significant positive effects on AFDC participation, even after controlling for the woman's age, educational attainment, and number and ages of children. With all of these factors controlled, however, the presence of the Medically Needy program itself had little impact on AFDC participation. Thus Blank's analysis did not support the hypothesis that the Medically Needy program induces women to leave AFDC by providing them with medical insurance even while they are employed. However, as Blank points out, her analysis does not address the question of the effect of extending Medicaid benefits on rates of dependency, because the Medically Needy program has certain provisions (such as the low level of income eligibility set by most states with a Medically Needy program and a short spend-down period) that do not apply to the general Medicaid program. In fact, Blank's analysis suggests that the Medically Needy program primarily attracted participants who would otherwise have been uninsured. This analysis also indicated that participation in the Medically Needy Medicaid program was strongly related to the presence of small children in the household and to increased illness of the female head of household.

In summary, there is a dearth of empirical evidence to guide policy makers on the medical assistance issue. An extension of Medicaid coverage beyond the current four-month limit would apparently have a positive effect on access to health care among families exiting from welfare, but its effect on labor force participation and welfare dependency is difficult to determine. We have reason to believe, however, that health and welfare dependency are related in complex ways and that the link may be an especially important one among younger mothers and mothers with young children.

Family Planning Assistance

Several of the welfare reform reports discuss the need for family planning services, especially with regard to adolescent welfare mothers (for example, APWA, 1986; Project on the Welfare of Families, 1986). Young mothers are generally not very successful in regulating their fertility. Although few disadvantaged young mothers want to intend to have closely spaced births (Polit et al., 1982), early repeat pregnancies occur with great frequency. National surveys have revealed that by twelve months postpartum about one out of five women whose first birth occurred prior to their twentieth birthday become pregnant again (Ford, 1983; Mott, 1986). Even within comprehensive care programs designed to ameliorate the negative consequences of early parenthood, where the postponement of subsequent pregnancies is generally an explicit program goal, rates of repeat pregnancy tend to be very high (see Burt et al., 1984; Klerman and Jekel, 1973; Polit et al., 1985). As a result, women who begin their childbearing during their teenage years give birth to more children than women who delay their first birth, despite the fact that their family size preferences are similar (Moore et al., 1979; Millman and Hendershot, 1980).

The fertility behavior of young AFDC mothers has important implications for the success of welfare-to-work programs. Clearly, young women who have several closely spaced births will have difficulty in completing their basic schooling, participating in employment training programs, and finding and keeping a permanent job. In addition to the discontinuities resulting from the actual childbearing, problems of finding suitable child care and maintaining family health are exacerbated when there are several small children. As an example of the negative effects associated with closely spaced births, Polit et al. (1985) found in the Project Redirection evaluation that a repeat birth within 24 months of a baseline interview was associated with a 50 percent lower rate of employment among the experimental group mothers.

This finding is consistent with an extensive body of research literature that has documented the adverse effects of large family size on women's employment and dependency patterns. For example, even after controlling numerous background factors such as educational attainment, women with several children (in comparison with women with few or no children) spend less time in the labor force, have lower earnings, are more likely to be on welfare, and are more likely to be long-term welfare recipients (Bane and Ellwood, 1983; Cramer, 1980; Ellwood, 1986; Hofferth, 1981; Marini, 1978; Polgar and Hiday, 1974; Smith and Ward, 1980).[8]

There is some evidence, in fact, that improving birth control among welfare-dependent young mothers would be an especially promising way to lower rates of welfare dependency. Moore and Wertheimer (1984) performed several simulations of welfare dependency rates in the year 1990 under several different scenarios. In the baseline scenario (where current trends of adolescent childbearing, employment, school completion, and so on would continue), about 600,000 mothers aged twenty to twenty-nine who had first given birth in their teenage years are projected to be on AFDC. Simulations were then performed under several other scenarios. In one, for example, the fertility of teenage childbearers was made equal to the fertility of those who postponed first births, and in another the probability of completing school was made as high for teenage childbearers as that for other women. The results of these simulations suggested that reducing the family size of young childbearers would have a substantially greater negative effect on the size of the welfare population than increasing their educational attainment. Thus the evidence indicates that the fertility behavior of young mothers mandated to participate in the new welfare-to-work programs could undermine the entire intervention, and that successful efforts to postpone subsequent childbearing could have important payoffs in terms of eventual self-sufficiency. At this point, however, we must consider one further question: to what extent are efforts to offer assistance in the family planning area likely to be effective in reducing unintended fertility?

Unlike child-care subsidies and medical insurance, subsidized family-planning services are available to most low-income women in this country, regardless of their eligibility for AFDC. Title X makes family-planning services available to women on a sliding-fee basis at more than 5,000 clinic sites. In addition, family planning is available through Medicaid to all AFDC recipients.[9] Numerous researchers have found that public family-planning programs have been highly successful in helping low-income women avert unintended births (see Anderson and Cope, 1987; Cutright and Jaffe, 1977; Forrest et al., 1981). It has been estimated that for every dollar spent by government on family-planning clinic services, two dollars are saved in the first year on health and welfare costs; for teenagers, the savings are three dollars for every dollar spent (Chamie and Henshaw, 1981).

Despite the overall effectiveness of the family-planning programs, it is not clear that family-planning services are successful in helping those who are already mothers—especially young mothers who have many years of childbearing ahead to them—to avert or postpone second or subsequent births. This question has not been directly addressed in any major evaluation; but indirect findings suggest that young mothers are even more difficult to serve than never-pregnant young women, presumably because those who are already mothers are less motivated to avoid a pregnancy (see Benardik et al., 1982; Polit et al., 1981; Kalmuss, 1986).

As we noted earlier, comprehensive programs for adolescent mothers appear to have had little success in helping young mothers to delay a second birth. However, the family-planning component of these programs generally has not been a major program focus, and many among the program staff find the issues of sex and birth control difficult to deal with (see Branch et al., 1984). Nevertheless, family-planning services offered to low-income young mothers within the context of a comprehensive program do seem to have some positive effects. In Project Redirection, for example, teen mothers who received such services were more likely than others to have used a medically prescribed contraceptive (Polit et al., 1985). And in the evaluation of programs sponsored by the Office of Adolescent Pregnancy Programs, Burt and others (1984) found that providing family-planning services to those who entered the programs as mothers was associated with lower rates of repeat pregnancy twelve months postpartum. Of course, it may be that the teens who were most motivated to postpone subsequent childbearing were most aggressive in seeking out such services, but it also seems plausible that this particular access to family planning improved the beneficial outcome.

Other Support Services

Some of the welfare reform proposals and reports mention the need for other support services intended to reduce barriers to program participation. These include transportation, life-management skills, and personal counseling. There is even less empirical evidence to help us evaluate the effects of providing such services in terms of program participation and eventual self-sufficiency.

Transportation generally ranks as the third or fourth highest self-reported barrier to participation in special employment-focused programs for disadvantaged women, after health, child care, and (sometimes) personal or family problems. Transportation problems are generally reported for about 5 to 10 percent of WIN mandatory clients. For example, Wolfhagen and Goldman (1983) reported that 7 percent of the women who dropped out of a job search program in the Louisville WIN Lab cited transportation problems as the reason (personal illness, family illness, and child care were cited as the reasons for dropping out by 18 percent, 16 percent, and 16 percent of the women, respectively). Although transportation problems are not as pervasive as some of the other barriers we have described, it is likely that a fair number of women will be unable to participate in special programs without transportation assistance. In particular, transportation may constitute a formidable constraint in rural areas.

Instruction in life management is a support service of greatest relevance to young AFDC mothers. This service is generally offered to young disadvantaged parents in the context of comprehensive care programs, and is also a component in several of the new employment-focused demonstrations just getting underway (for example, the OFA Teen Parent Demonstration). Life-management instruction typically seeks to develop young mothers' skills in managing a household budget, using community resources and services, performing housekeeping tasks, and caring for the needs of young children. Such instruction is generally predicated on the assumption that the young age of these mothers, coupled with the absence of effective role models within their own families, results in difficulties in coping with the day-to-day responsibilities of parenthood. A further assumption is that, without such instruction, young mothers' inability to cope will have adverse effects on their attendance and full and active participation in special programs. These assumptions, however, have never been tested.

Finally, individual counseling is viewed as another service that can enhance the motivation and coping skills of disadvantaged women in their efforts to make a transition to self-sufficiency. Studies that have examined the characteristics and experiences of low-income mothers do suggest that many of them have complex and difficult lives with numerous problems, including abusive family situations, alcohol and drug problems, relationships with men involved in criminal activities, and depression and mental illness (see Polit et al., 1982; Gittell and Moore, 1985). These problems would presumably constitute substantial barriers to regular and active participation in employment programs and in the labor force. However, although counseling has been included in many programs designed to assist low-income mothers, little is known about how much of an effect such counseling has, and no study has documented the pervasiveness of these personal problems in the AFDC population.

Mechanisms for the Delivery of Support Services

If support services of the kinds described above are incorporated into new welfare-to-work programs, several administrative issues will need to be addressed, including the mechanisms through which the services would be paid for (for example, purchase of slots, direct reimbursement and vouchers) and the mechanisms through which they would actually be delivered. This section discusses the delivery vehicles.

Various models for delivering multiple support services have been discussed and experimented with in the social service community. One type of model involves a self-contained, comprehensive approach that includes all or most of the needed services on-site or within its directly controllable resources. An example is the New Chance Demonstration, aimed at disadvantaged mothers aged seventeen to twenty-one and currently in its pilot phase. A second model, exemplified by some of the programs in the New York State Comprehensive Employment Opportunity Support Centers Demonstration, involves co-location of several agencies that are directly providing services. A third model is a pure case-management model, wherein an agency representative (the case manager) puts together an appropriate mix of services for program participants, drawing upon services available in the community. The Teen Parent Demonstration of the OFA is an example of such a case-management approach to the delivery of multiple core and support services.

We focus on the case-management model, principally because it is the approach that is recommended by several of the welfare reform reports, and it has been incorporated into proposed federal welfare reform legislation (H.R. 1720). Furthermore, case management is not incompatible with the other models; comprehensive on-site programs and co-located service programs frequently include case managers to orchestrate the use of services. Finally, there is some research relating to case management.

Case management is a method of planning and delivering needed services to people who have diverse problems requiring assistance from several different sources. The case manager works with clients in an ongoing relationship to develop a suitable service plan, to facilitate access to services, to monitor client progress and service delivery, and to evaluate service outcomes and the need for modifications to the service plan. Among young clients, the role of the case manager as an instructor who models problem solving and interpersonal skills is also stressed (Brindis et al., 1987). Case management is not a new concept, but it has gained considerable ground in recent years as a model for working with vulnerable people with multiple needs because of the increasing complexity and bureaucratization of the human services delivery system.

Although the effectiveness of using case managers to orchestrate the delivery of support and training-educational services has not been rigorously evaluated, there is some modest evidence in support of this model of service delivery. In the organizational analysis of WIN programs (Mitchell et al., 1980), the high-performing offices emphasized personal counseling, referral to a range of needed support services, and individualized approaches toward job placement; in essence, those WIN offices that had good placement rates appeared to be using a case-management approach. Similarly, a recent analysis of successful employment programs for teenage parents concluded that case management was a salient characteristic of exemplary programs (Polit, 1986b). The evaluation of programs sponsored by the U.S. Office of Adolescent Pregnancy Programs revealed that strong case management was associated not only with the delivery of more services, but also with improved educational outcomes for young mothers (Burt et al., 1984).

One of the more compelling pieces of evidence about case management comes from the evaluation of the Prenatal/Early Infancy Project, designed primarily for high-risk infants (Olds et al., 1983). In the evaluation, which used an experimental design, 400 low-income families were randomly assigned to various treatments. The full treatment had visiting nurses pay home visits to experimental families from the time of the mother's pregnancy until the child was two years of age.[10] The nurses functioned essentially as case managers, providing information and referral to a range of health and community services, including educational programs, health services, job training programs, and child care. The evaluation indicated that mothers in the full treatment group were more likely to be employed, were more likely to have completed or returned to school, and relied on welfare for half as long as mothers who did not have the home visits. Although more evidence is needed within the context of programs explicitly focused on employment, it would appear that case management can have positive effects in assisting disadvantaged groups to move toward self-sufficiency.

In the social service arena, the function of case managers is perhaps most readily perceived as facilitating clients' access to services. Case management is sometimes viewed as a more costly social service delivery mechanism because of its visibility — that is, through the case manager more services might come to be in demand than would otherwise have been the case. However, case management is also hailed by some as cost effective because it allows for the identification and treatment of problems before they intensify. Moreover, it has been argued that this strategy ensures more effective and efficient use of services and avoids duplication. In fact, case-management models are being used in several Medicaid demonstrations to reduce costs (Freund and Hurley, 1987; Kern and Windham, 1986). In these demonstrations, the case manager is viewed as a gatekeeper of services, ensuring that the clients receive only those services that are truly needed. In welfare-to-work programs, a similar gatekeeping function might prove critical in ensuring that the limited supply of available support services (for instance, child-care subsidies) goes to those participants who most need them.

Conclusions

It is difficult to project what the actual demand for various support services will be if recommended welfare-to-work programs are implemented. Demand will be a function of a number of factors that are still unspecified, such as the age-of-youngest-child exemption, the extent to which targeting of special high-risk groups will be encouraged, and the period of time allotted for a transition from welfare to employment. Nevertheless, it seems clear that the demand for support services will increase substantially over current levels. Changes in exemption policies that require participation of mothers with preschool-age children are expected to put increased pressure on welfare agencies to supply a variety of support services, since the women who would become mandated for participation are younger, have children who require supervision, have more health problems, are more susceptible to subsequent unintended pregnancies, and are less experienced in getting services they need on their own than the current WIN-mandatory recipients.

Fiscal Issues

The most obvious implication of including support services in new welfare-to-work programs is that welfare reform will, in the short run, be expensive. Support services are generally costly, and costs are likely to rise as demand increases. Unfortunately, we do not have solid information on whether such services are cost effective. The evidence so far is consistent with the view that the AFDC population has numerous barriers to employment and that the removal of these barriers is related to progress toward self-sufficiency. To the extent that this is true, the inclusion of support services in new welfare-to-work programs could be considered an investment. Clearly, however, we need better evaluation data on whether such investments do, in fact, pay off in terms of eventual reductions in welfare dependency.

However, even if we knew for sure that future welfare dollars could be saved by offering interventions rich with support services, it is highly unlikely that policy makers could be persuaded to finance a full complement of services to all AFDC recipients. The problem is that the dollars spent would appear in today's tight budgets, while the dollars saved would accrue to the budgets of future policy makers. Thus those involved in welfare reform are going to have to make some decisions about how support services can best be provided at a reasonable cost. Some of the parameters of the decision are as follows:

· *Who should receive services?* One way of containing costs is to limit new interventions to those who can most benefit from them or to those who are at highest risk of long-term dependency. The research by Ellwood and others clearly indicates that substantial proportions of welfare recipients move off welfare after relatively short spells, and these women may therefore require limited or no services. Of course, focusing on would-be long-term recipients would mean targeting those whose needs for support services are most extensive and therefore most costly.

· *How long should services be available?* A major issue is whether support services should continue once the woman has left welfare for employment, and if so, for how long. The arguments for offering support services in the transition are: (1) such services would still be needed; (2) they are unlikely to be provided by the private sector in the type of jobs recipients move into; and (3) their withdrawal could create a disincentive for leaving welfare. On the other hand, extending services could also discourage self-sufficiency and increase reliance on government-sponsored services. Since there has been virtually no experimentation with variable service provision, the decision regarding length of services provided cannot be based primarily on empirical grounds.[11]

- *What services should be offered?* Policy makers may choose to include some but not all of the support services discussed in this chapter (for instance, child care but not counseling and life-skills instruction). From the point of view of cost effectiveness, family planning may well be the most justifiable support service, but it is too controversial to be universally endorsed. In any event, the full complement of support services would not be needed by all welfare recipients. Even if there is some targeting, individual needs for support services will vary, suggesting that substantial economies could be achieved with effective assessment and gatekeeping mechanisms.

- *What quality of services should be offered?* Creative ways of offering support services at reduced costs may need to be explored. For example, some services could be provided by nonprofessional staff, such as counseling and life-skills instruction by community mentors. Peer counseling (by recipients or recent ex-recipients themselves) is another possibility. With regard to child care, welfare agencies could train AFDC recipients to become child-care workers so that they could be employed as the caretakers of other recipients' children, a strategy that is being tested in several states.

- *Who should pay for the services?* The costs of offering support services need not be assumed entirely by welfare agencies. The private sector is an obvious target for some types of services, particularly health-related services through private insurance. Incentives could be offered to encourage more child care by relatives. Some costs could also be shifted elsewhere: for example, schools could be encouraged to offer free or low-cost preschool and after-school programs.

There is thus an array of possible ways to contain the overall costs of providing support services to participants in new welfare-to-work programs. Although the research is limited it provides some empirical support for targeting and for using a case-management approach to regulate the use of services. Clearly, further experimentation and evaluation are needed regarding the most effective ways to stretch dollars for removing barriers to self-sufficiency.

Administrative Issues

Welfare agencies are likely to experience various administrative pressures and constraints related to the provision of support services. First, even if funding were not an obstacle, it is likely to be difficult to find an adequate supply of services, at least in the short run. In particular, the availability of suitable child care (especially infant care) is likely to be problematic. Because of resource constraints, some triage may be necessary. Given the diversity of the welfare population, no single treatment is likely to be effective and no single support-service package will be useful. Welfare agencies are going to need to put into place mechanisms for assessing and monitoring participants' need for such services. Without adequate assessment tools and regular review of client needs, inefficiencies and improper utilization of the scarce resources are likely to occur.

Welfare agencies are also going to have to deal with the issue of agency staffing and organization. If case management-type models are adopted, who will these case managers be? Income maintenance workers in most welfare agencies are not trained to perform case management functions, although they are generally expected to make referrals to appropriate social service providers (Hagen, 1987). Welfare agencies might have to reorganize and retrain their staffs, or enter into new purchase-of-service arrangements for the case-management function.

As support services are expanded, additional burdens will be placed on the agencies in terms of licensing and monitoring functions (such as child-care licensing). These burdens will be especially intense if increased demand for services results in a lowering of the quality of services provided.

Finally, agencies may have to contend with problems that arise from developing collaborative arrangements with service providers and coordinating multiple core and support services. The experience of many communities that have tried to develop comprehensive service programs for young parents suggests that coordination is often quite difficult to achieve, even when concerted efforts are devoted to its attainment (see Weatherly et al., 1985).

Social Issues

Policy makers will also have to consider welfare reform and the support services it will entail in the light of broader social concerns. Two issues merit special comment. First, there will be some opposition to making participation in employment programs mandatory for mothers of preschool-age children. Critics will argue that it is unfair to make mothers leave their children to the care of strangers. Even though the majority of mothers of young children now work, those opposed to mandatory participation argue that their decision to work is voluntary. Critics will also summon up research evidence that suggests that early maternal employment and nonmaternal care are associated with adverse consequences in the socio-emotional development of the children (see Barglow et al., 1988; Schwartz, 1983; Rubinstein et al., 1981; Farber and Egeland, 1982; Haskins, 1985; Vaughn et al., 1980; Vlietstra, 1981).

In contrast, those who defend the inclusion of women with younger children in self-sufficiency programs will argue that it is important to provide disadvantaged children with role models of employed adults. They will also argue that offering AFDC mothers the opportunity to become self-sufficient and perhaps escape poverty is ultimately in the child's best interests. Advocates will also invoke studies that do not show any adverse social or emotional effects of being in nonmaternal care (see Brookhart and Hock, 1976; Blanchard and Main, 1979; Roopnarine and Lamb, 1980; Easterbrooks and Goldberg, 1985), and others that even found socio-emotional benefits associated with child care (see O'Connell and Farran, 1982; Schindler et al., 1987; Cochran, 1977). They will also point to the body of research that has shown that exposure to high-quality child care (including infant care) and preschool programs have positive effects on the cognitive development and educational attainment of low-income children (see Berrueta-Clement et al., 1984; Ramey and Campbell, 1984; Pierson et al., 1983; Garber and Heber, 1981). Because there is evidence to support the views of both critics and advocates, it seems unlikely that the resolution of this issue can be made on the basis of existing research. The controversy over the effects of early maternal employment and child care is one that is deeply rooted in values regarding women's roles, and is likely to persist under any version of welfare reform.

The second issue that policy makers will need to consider is that of social equity. If support services such as child care and medical assistance are linked to AFDC recipiency, the welfare reform programs are likely to be viewed as unfair—in fact, as rewarding welfare dependency and undermining the efforts of the working poor. This perception is especially likely to be held by the millions of low-income working mothers who lack access to low-cost child care and medical insurance. While broadening the eligibility for these support services will obviously entail additional costs, policy makers will have to consider the possible negative backlash associated with restricting eligibility to welfare recipients only.

In conclusion, it must be said that a disparity exists between current research evidence regarding the need for and effectiveness of support services and the perception of their need among front-line welfare workers and administrators. Few welfare commissioners or welfare staff would argue with the notion that support services such as child care are needed in order to have successful welfare-to-work programs, although they might disagree about such issues as targeting, length of service provision, type of support services, and so on. It is not that existing evidence undermines the importance of support services, but rather that research able to confirm unequivocally the perceptions of front-line workers simply has not been undertaken. Although the evidence taken as a whole does suggest that support services can help to promote the self-sufficiency of welfare recipients, we must acknowledge that the contribution of existing research to the policy debate on welfare reform is slim. This is unfortunate, because the success of welfare reform initiatives may well hinge on the nature and scope of policies relating to the provision of support services. With our current state of knowledge, decisions about these services are likely to be made primarily on the basis of personal values, political trade-offs, and budgetary constraints rather than on empirical evidence of what works. To the extent that support services are incorporated into welfare reform initiatives, the challenge for policy makers and analysts will be to develop ways to use these initiatives to evaluate the effects and cost effectiveness of such support services. Only when such evidence is available can we make more rational decisions about the utility of support services in the future.

Institutional Effects of Reform

Demetra Smith Nightingale

Over the past twenty years, federal welfare reform initiatives have sought to reduce the welfare rolls (or slow down their increase), to help more recipients become self-sufficient. Periodically, other objectives have also surfaced. In the 1960s and 1970s, policy proposals and changes focused mainly on standardizing the nation's welfare system, primarily through federal regulations governing eligibility and work-incentive provisions. During those two decades the welfare population greatly increased, and federal social and economic programs for economically disadvantaged persons proliferated. One result has been an extremely complex network of programs, agencies, organizations, institutions, and laws governing both recipients and services, each with its own set of mandates and incentives.

Today, welfare reform has once again become a priority issue. Two salient objectives in current proposals are: to improve the administrative efficiency of the welfare system; and to increase the rate at which individuals and families leave the welfare system permanently. All agree that these primary objectives must be accomplished with a minimum of federal funding, given the serious problem of the federal budget deficit. The means proposed for achieving these ends, however, vary considerably. Some proposals would increase benefit levels, expand eligibility for welfare, and provide for comprehensive training, employment, and social services to help clients become self-sufficient. Others are opposed to these types of potentially costly provisions and instead focus on strengthening the mandatory work requirements and individual obligations attached to welfare receipt. Some proposals reflect a combination of these two positions.

Given the increasing complexity of the nation's welfare network, current welfare reform proposals across the political spectrum would undoubtedly influence, and be influenced by, various public and private institutions and organizational entities at the federal, state, and local levels. The public welfare system would obviously be directly affected by any federal welfare legislation, but, beyond that, other systems would also be affected directly or indirectly.

This essay provides a framework for examining the institutional context surrounding welfare reform by addressing four questions:

· What programs and organizations might potentially be affected by federal welfare reform legislation?

· What administrative or programmatic changes might be expected?

· What changes to the current federal intergovernmental structure might occur?

· What effect might welfare reform have on the interactions among relevant programs, agencies, and other organizational entities?

The discussion is not meant to be a totally comprehensive assessment of the effects of welfare reform, but an attempt to structure and organize some of the numerous institutional issues that are raised by federal welfare reform proposals. One primary point to keep in mind is that the federal government has only limited direct influence over much of the complex network of welfare institutions. The current activity around welfare reform reflects institutional changes that either have already been initiated at the state level or have resulted from previous recent federal policy changes. Few of the reform proposals currently suggested would dramatically alter the trends that already are occurring or improve how the systems function.

The Welfare Network

The welfare network stretches well beyond the welfare agencies that traditionally have responsibility for administering public assistance. At the national, state, and local levels there are organizations, agencies, social institutions, and programs that are related to welfare in various ways. Figure 7.1 presents a general diagram of the major systems that make up the welfare network, all of which would be affected in some

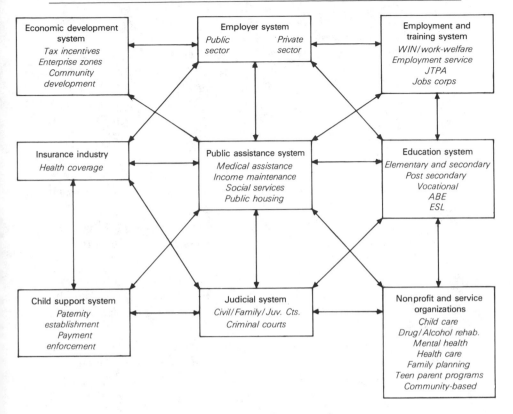

Fig. 7.1. The welfare network

way by federal welfare reform legislation. All are interrelated in that each might be involved as individuals and families move from public assistance to economic independence and self-sufficiency. Other systems not included in the diagram, such as immigration and refugee agencies or organized labor unions, may become more important actors in the welfare system over time.

The public assistance benefit system is at the center of the network and includes AFDC, Food Stamps, social services, Medicaid, and other income and benefit programs. Other significant systems that interact with welfare in serving both welfare recipients and nonwelfare poor are: employment and training system; education system; nonprofit service organizations; judicial system; child support system; insurance industry; economic development system; employers and labor market system.

We will see in more detail how the interaction and relations established among programs and organizations over the years have become increasingly complex. Moreover, the precise character of the broader welfare network varies by state and by community within states, and may vary by policy issue. Each system has its own set of programs, target populations, mandates, objectives, and incentives. Some systems interact extensively with others, some operate more autonomously, but each defines and addresses a given problem from its own perspective. Various programs operate under the direct authority of cities or states, while others are authorized by the federal government and subject to primarily federal regulations. Overlap inevitably exists among some systems and programs, in terms of the types of clients served (for example, welfare as well as nonwelfare population) or types of services provided, and coordination across related programs has become a major institutional activity.

This intricate and somewhat fluid intergovernmental and interorganizational web represents the current welfare network and provides the institutional context within which federal welfare reform legislation would have to be implemented. A simple example will demonstrate not only that the welfare network is intricate from the perspective of an individual client, but that numerous systems or entities within a community or state, including private employers and judicial units, become involved either directly or indirectly. Assume an unmarried female with one child applying for AFDC and Medicaid:

- She must assign her rights to child support to the state welfare agency, which means becoming a participant in the child-support enforcement program. The program will obtain information from her about the absent father.

- If the mother does not have a child-support order from the courts (usually through domestic, family, or civil courts) the program must petition for such an order.

- If she has never been married to the father, then legal paternity may not have been established. The child-support agency must first pursue paternity establishment, which is still generally handled in criminal rather than civil courts, before a child-support order can be established.

- If the mother does not know where the father is, the agency must attempt to locate him, which may mean contacting judicial or administrative officials in other states or substate jurisdictions.

- If the father is employed and has medical insurance coverage, then the agency must petition to include medical support in the child-support order. The medical support order then requires the Medicaid agency to consider the child as a third-party-liability case, which means coordinating with the private insurance company to assure that the private plan assumes all possible medical costs before any Medicaid payments are authorized.

- Once paternity and child support have been established, the absent father must make satisfactory arrangements for regular payments (make payments directly to the agency, to the court or another entity, or have his employer withhold the amount of the monthly payment from his wages and forward the payment to a designated state or local agency).

- If the absent father does not make regularly scheduled payments, then the child-support agency must take action to enforce the payment order, which could mean, among other options, obtaining court orders to attach his wages or tax returns or place liens on his property or issuing summonses to reappear in court.

- If the mother leaves the AFDC rolls, then the child-support case will probably be maintained as a nonpublic assistance case. The services available to the mother will be essentially unchanged, but the program will receive a different amount of federal incentive funds for the case.

Enforcing child support involves specific legalistic functions that require many linkages among programs, but it is a relatively straightforward part of the welfare system once the procedures have been defined. Other aspects of welfare, particularly those that are designed to provide social or human services to clients, are more complex because the interprogram linkages may vary depending on the characteristics of the client.

For example, if the mother's (only) child is six years old, she is required to register and cooperate with the WIN program (or the alternative WIN demonstration program), unless she lives in an area of the state that has been declared "remote." In a state with a comprehensive mandatory work-welfare program, she could be required to conduct an independent job search and go out on job interviews with local employers, participate in an organized group Job Club, be considered for training through the JTPA, be referred to an education agency or a community-based organization for remedial education, or be assigned to a workfare job in a public or private nonprofit agency. Depending on the state, she may be required to make her own child-care arrangements, or a social worker or other staff person might refer her to a subsidized day-care center, or she may be given a voucher to use with a day-care provider. If she and the agency cannot arrange adequate child care, then she may not be mandatorily required to participate in employment and training activities. If she obtains a job, she may lose her eligibility to subsidized child care, and will probably eventually lose eligibility for Medicaid. If she has another child, she is no longer required to participate in employment-related activities unless child care is available, but she may voluntarily choose to participate.

The complexity is obvious but the welfare network should not automatically be construed as unnecessarily or undesirably complex. Given the numerous dimensions of the problems associated with welfare dependency, it may well be that the network cannot be substantially simplified or consolidated. This suggests that program administrators and policy makers at the national and state level had best devote more attention to understanding the complexity of the institutional reality and attempt to improve program implementation within the realistic constraints.

Programmatic Effects of Welfare Reform

Over the years the nation's welfare system has been criticized on several fronts, but primarily because the welfare caseload continues to increase despite massive infusions of federal and state funds to address the problems of poverty and dependency. The administration of welfare programs has become exceedingly cumbersome. One reason is that welfare programs have multiple and often competing objectives (for example, accurate and efficient management of the income maintenance functions, versus enforcement of the work requirement provisions, versus human capital development to increase client employability). Another impediment to smooth functioning is that numerous federal regulations have been devised to both protect the rights of welfare clients and monitor client and agency compliance with federal rules. The administration and implementation of the nation's public assistance system could be affected in many ways by federal welfare reform measures, just as it is affected by any federal regulatory changes governing the various programs. Some programmatic effects that might be anticipated are related to program design, program objectives and priorities, and program caseload.

Program Design

The extent to which the design of welfare and welfare-related programs would be affected by welfare reform would in part depend on how broad the federal policy changes were. But even some of the minor changes being proposed would affect how states design various programs.

The most minimal type of federal welfare reform might focus on only one or two dimensions of the welfare system. For example, it is conceivable that the work-welfare provisions of AFDC (and perhaps Food Stamps) could be modified even if the more controversial benefits and income maintenance are not changed. A reform limited to this portion of the welfare system might be welcomed by states, since the national work-welfare system has, over the past eight years, experienced severe budget reductions and uncertainty about future policy directions.

In other words, the work-welfare portions of welfare reform proposals could be separated out from other provisions and enacted as permanent national legislation. Some of the programmatic changes currently being considered are: (1) shifting total responsibility for work-welfare programs to either DOL or HHS at the federal level; (2) possibly restricting unpaid workfare; and (3) requiring some welfare recipients to continue their education as a condition of eligibility. Given the way the work-welfare system has operated in the past several years, one might predict that the first two of these proposals would not result in major administrative changes, but the third would.

Advocates of the joint administrative structure of WIN, for instance, recognize that neither the welfare nor the Employment Security agencies can alone address all the problems welfare clients face. However, joint administration increases the problems of coordination and accountability. There is no reason to expect that mandating the single-agency structure would, in and of itself, improve work-welfare program administration.

Since 1981, state governors have had the flexibility to choose the welfare agency to administer the work-welfare program; and presumably, after seven years, at least some of the states that have not opted for the single-agency demonstration prefer the joint structure. In addition, the single-agency structure varies greatly from state to state in terms of program design. Several state welfare agencies have simply contracted back to the Employment Security agencies to have them perform the very same functions that they have handled in the past under the joint WIN program. Other states made major structural changes, but it generally took several years before the programs stabilized. Since about half the states have chosen the single-agency option already, only the other half of the states would be affected by federal legislation that would require a single-agency administration. In some of those that would be affected there would probably be few noticeable program changes, and in others there could be major changes, but only after a fairly long transitional period.

Some researchers have in fact found that successful programs can exist under either the joint or individual agency structure. Despite the drastic 70 percent reduction of federal funds for WIN and WIN demonstration programs since 1981, as of late 1986 eleven states had made substantial progress in the area of work-welfare by developing comprehensive employment and training initiatives for welfare recipients (California, Connecticut, Delaware, Maine, Massachusetts, Minnesota, New York, Ohio, Oklahoma, Utah, and Vermont). Six of these comprehensive programs are in single-agency WIN demonstration states, the other five are in dual-agency settings (see Nightingale and Burbridge, 1987).

A second program change being considered would restrict the use of workfare. Over the years, pure workfare for AFDC recipients (that is, requiring recipients to work a certain number of hours per month in unpaid jobs in exchange for their welfare check) has been very controversial. With the advent of the Reagan Administration, states were given the authority to require workfare of some AFDC recipients. About half the states have chosen to operate some type of workfare under the optional CWEP.

One would think that welfare reform provisions limiting CWEP would substantially change these state and local work-welfare programs. However, although about half the states have some type of workfare, in most places the component is either primarily restricted to men or designed to be developmental rather than punitive. Some states have been able to increase their total federal funds for work-welfare activities by implementing CWEP programs, which fall under the separate 50-50 funding provision of AFDC. The programs, though, are generally similar to traditional WIN work experience components and are designed to improve the employability of clients who have not had much or recent employment. Federal welfare reform proposals that would restrict workfare suggest doing so in a way that would allow the typical CWEP program to continue. Only the "pure" workfare programs that exist in a few jurisdictions would no longer be allowable. That is, most states, even those that currently have CWEP components, would not be affected by a federal restriction on workfare as described in major proposals.

The third possible work-welfare program change, requiring some recipients to participate in educational activities, would represent a major policy shift and could have substantial program effects on both the welfare and education systems. Although it makes intuitive sense to require welfare clients who have not attained a high school education to do so, it is not clear that implementing such a requirement would be straightforward, nor that it would improve the employability of welfare recipients.

In the first place, the public education system in most jurisdictions is not designed to serve large numbers of students with young children and the special circumstances they face, such as illness of the child, disruptions in day-care arrangements, or evening time required for parenting. Second, the welfare agencies would presumably be responsible for administering and monitoring compliance with the education participation requirement, but few jurisdictions have established procedures for welfare departments and schools to exchange information on individuals. Third, traditional educational programs may not be adequate to fully address the educational deficiencies of some welfare clients; new curricula and programs might have to be developed if remediation (and not just participation) is a desired outcome. A diploma may not necessarily result in competency, yet there is evidence that mastery of basic skills is needed to compete successfully in the labor market (see Levitan and Shapiro, 1987). Finally, the federal government has little authority over the education system; state welfare agencies would be called upon to establish the necessary linkages with a system with which they have had little contact in the past.

Overall, then, the program design effects of work-welfare components being considered for welfare reform would be minimal, since no new types of programs or services are suggested in any of the major proposals. A more significant programmatic effect would result from federal requirements that some welfare recipients participate in education activities as a condition of eligibility. Work-welfare legislation of any kind, though, even if the changes are nominal, would at least provide states with some assurance of federal funding beyond a few months at a time. This funding certainty alone would probably result in program changes in some states, particularly in those that have gradually reduced their activities or postponed planned initiatives.

Program Objectives and Priorities

Much of the current welfare reform debate at the national level has focused on whether the nation's welfare system can be (or should be) redirected from income-maintenance activities to a broader priority of moving individuals and families off welfare. On the surface, at least at the national level, there appears to be some consensus that welfare recipients, including mothers, should be required to participate in some form of employment-related activity as a condition of their eligibility for public assistance. Since 1967, national welfare policy has included both work incentives and work requirements. State programs must require recipients to work or register for work and assist them in becoming more employable.

Below the surface, however, there is less agreement about what that requirement should be. For example, a mandatory requirement can take different forms, from simple work registration to job search requirements, to active participation in education or training, to workfare. One low-cost way that many states have found to comply with federal work registration is to have "universal registration," where all or most public assistance applicants are automatically registered (on paper) with the work program. Because resources have been limited, many administrators and staff have chosen to spend more on the people who are most interested in participating, and less for enforcement of the federal priority on mandatory participation.

To some extent, the debate about the work requirement is directly related to the parallel controversies about the role of day care. Proponents of stricter work requirements argue that current federal policy that waives the work requirement for mothers with very young children is out of step with social reality, since most mothers even of young children are now in the paid work force. Since 1981 states have been encouraged to require more mothers with children under six years of age to participate in work activities, but most states have not done so partly because their programs cannot serve all those who fall under the current mandatory provisions.

In fact, the day-care controversy is quite heated. Some feel that this is perhaps the most serious problem working mothers face, and that work-welfare programs must include substantial resources for day care. The Massachusetts ET Choices Program and the California GAIN program are based on this premise. In both programs about half the budget is devoted to day care. Others feel that child care is not a very serious problem and cite statistics that indicate that the vast majority of children of working parents are cared for informally by friends, relatives, and neighbors, suggesting that adequate arrangements already exist (see Novak et al., 1987). The reality may be somewhere between the two extremes. If mandatory work program participation is conditional upon the public agency providing day care, one may see a relatively high proportion of clients who report that they need child care. Conversely, a high quality, successful, voluntary training program may be able to recruit large numbers of clients even without providing day care.

Similarly, requirements that clients conduct job search or unpaid workfare as a condition of their eligibility means that agencies must develop precise monitoring and tracking procedures to assure compliance. If compliance is not monitored or if there are too few workfare, work, or training assignments, then the viability of the requirement is undermined. Intensive job search and job-search training programs have also been criticized by employers in some areas who complain about being contacted by too many job seekers using the same "self-marketing scripts" they learned in a job search group. Although some group approaches have proved to be effective at helping clients find jobs, large-scale efforts are probably not an efficient means for implementing work requirement policy if they alienate employers.

In view of the complex nature of welfare, it would not seem that current reform proposals would alleviate the historic tension among objectives. In addition, it may well be that despite the objectives and priorities that are written into federal legislation, state and local administrators may have to set their own priorities when resources are limited.

Program Caseloads

The most extensive welfare reform proposals currently being considered would increase benefit levels for family financial assistance programs like AFDC, or provide incentives for states to increase benefit levels; require all states to provide assistance to two-parent families as well as single-parent families; expand the child-support enforcement activities for welfare and nonwelfare families; and revise the work-welfare system.

Reforms of this sort would have far-reaching administrative effects at the state and local levels, in terms of caseload and program scale. For example, some states may experience a significant increase in their public assistance caseload as a result of increasing the standard of need or expanding eligibility to two-parent families. Although the AFDC-U component currently is quite small (6.2 percent of all AFDC cases nationwide), states that presently do not offer the coverage may experience a caseload increase greater than 6.2 percent because they tend to have higher than average unemployment rates, little state or locally funded general assistance, relatively low AFDC grant levels, and limited work-welfare programs (see U.S. House of Representatives, 1988).

An increase in the AFDC-U caseload would in turn also affect the work-welfare programs, as they would be called upon to enforce the work requirement for a more able-bodied and employable population. Many states would have to increase their staffing levels simply to perform the routine income maintenance and work registration functions. If the state costs associated with these routine functions were substantial, less money would be available for expanding the work-welfare programs.

The work-welfare caseload would also increase if federal law lowered the age-of-youngest-child rule from six years of age to three, and if all states were required to operate work-welfare programs statewide.

It is quite conceivable, therefore, that some state work-welfare programs would experience an increase in the number of men, mothers with very young children, and nonurban residents. The effect would be greatest on those states that currently do not have an AFDC-U program, do not have a statewide work-welfare program, and do not serve many voluntary participants in the existing work program.

There could be similar caseload increases in the child-support enforcement programs if federal welfare reform requires immediate wage withholding for all absent parents with a child-support order. Current regulations allow states to encourage voluntary wage withholding and require mandatory wage withholding if a parent becomes delinquent in his or her regular payments. If automatic wage withholding is required, state child-support enforcement programs will have to handle far more payment or collection cases. Presumably, few of these new child support cases will be related to current AFDC cases, since current AFDC regulations already require applicants to cooperate with the child-support program. The main result of automatic wage withholding may be increased case-management costs for child-support programs, and increased total collections, but with little effect on long-term welfare families.

Finally, if welfare reform includes the education requirement, the education system, especially the adult basic education system, will have many more persons to whom it will have to provide remedial instruction.

The extent to which the education system is affected will vary depending on what clients are subject to the education requirement. Most of the national proposals that recommend education requirements limit mandatory participation to teenage parents; teenage dependents and older parents are not subject to it. But if a state does not have enough day-care resources for preschool children (and few do), then the mandatory education requirement for the parents would have to be waived, thus defeating the point.

Thus some programs could experience an increase in their caseload. Those programs that are likely to directly have the greatest caseload increase are the public assistance system, the employment and training system, and the child support system. Those that are likely to be indirectly affected include the education and child care systems.

Intergovernmental Effects of Welfare Reform

Some of the criticisms lodged against the present welfare system are related to the complex institutional character of the broader welfare network, and many of the current reform proposals include provisions to simplify that network by restructuring the responsibilities of government agencies or changing the incentive structure of the relevant programs.

Intergovernmental Authority

In the absence of a clear sense of federal direction in the last seven years, the major reform proposals related to welfare-employment policy acknowledge that states have been operating quite autonomously during this period and should continue to be given maximum flexibility, and at the same time recognize the need for an overarching federal policy direction to help welfare recipients become independent and self-sufficient.

An underlying theme of the current proposals is that the role of the federal government should decline and the role and discretion of states should increase. This theme is in keeping with the concerns about the federal budget deficit and the limited-government philosophy of the Reagan Administration. However, the shift toward the states obscures a very real danger. For the past thirty years, it is true, some states have been politically and fiscally in better positions to initiate and fund progressive and comprehensive social programs; currently, about a dozen states are in the forefront on work-welfare policy. They have been able to develop comprehensive work programs for welfare recipients that provide a broad range of employment, training, education, and social services. However, at least that many states are not actively interested in pursuing initiatives in this area. The critical differences among the various federal work-welfare proposals relate not to different types of programs or services, but rather to different funding levels and federal financial participation rates (matching rates).

Funding Incentives

All of the current welfare reform proposals would change the way welfare and work-welfare programs are funded. For example, WIN funding is 90 percent federal and 10 percent state, and the various AFDC work options such as CWEP and Work Supplementation are reimbursed by the federal government at a 50 percent rate. Economic theory suggests that one way to leverage federal resources and increase state commitment to a program is to increase the state financial participation requirement. Proposals recommend replacing the present 90 percent WIN funding with funding at a lower federal participation rate (at a ratio of 60-40, 75-25, or 70-30 for direct services; and about 50-50 for administrative costs); some would also allow unlimited federal funding above some base amount, but at a lower federal participation rate.

State legislatures, some of which have not been supportive of welfare assistance programs, would become essential in appropriating the additional revenues needed for an increased state match. Even if the federal government would provide uncapped funding for work-welfare programs, many states may not be able to obtain additional state funds beyond what the legislature has traditionally appropriated for AFDC and work programs (Nightingale and Burbridge, 1987). It should not be assumed that all (or even most) states would be inclined to expand their work programs after welfare reform if that means coming up with more state funds.

Hence, regardless of how attractive or open-ended the federal funding formula may look, some states will be hard-pressed to provide any more work-related activities than they currently provide. Because most states will continue to have limited resources, federal priorities will be modified at the state level. For example, federal legislation may target teen parents for priority services, but, if day care is limited, the education system is not prepared to serve this population, and the legislature has some other priority group, then state and local administrators may decide to limit their spending to groups that do not require extensive services (for instance, AFDC men or recently employed new AFDC applicants).

The challenges at the national level will be to devise federal funding mechanisms, program incentives, and policy requirements that will assure that all states operate a work-welfare program at some meaningful level, but at the same time not discourage states from continuing or developing new policy initiatives. At the state level, program administrators and policy makers who want to operate more comprehensive programs than are now in place will have to devote more attention to working with state legislatures, understanding the work and welfare-related issues that are important to legislators, and integrating those top state priorities with the federal mandates. Many states in the past few years have moved in this direction by integrating AFDC work programs with programs for general assistance recipients, since general welfare programs and costs are normally a high priority in state legislatures.

Federal financial provisions would have a different effect on child-support enforcement programs. The current child-support system is heavily influenced by the federal incentives states receive for actual amounts of support payments collected. To maximize collections and minimize administrative costs, some local programs place priority on those absent parents most likely to fulfill their financial obligations, and devote less effort to cases where the absent parent is chronically unemployed, where paternity has to be established, or where a court case would have to be reopened (see Sonenstein and Calhoun, 1987). If welfare reform legislation expects the child-support system to increase its efforts on all fronts (such as paternity, for example), the reformers must realize this will be difficult to accomplish without additional financial incentives. Without new funding incentives, the system will tend to continue to emphasize collections.

Federal funding thus clearly influences the balance of authority between the national and state governments. Work-welfare funding since 1981 has provided additional funds to states willing and able to increase state funds. The child-support system has become dominated by the strong federal financial incentives attached to "total collections." If welfare legislation changes the funding formula for work-welfare programs, it is possible that even open-ended funding will not provide enough impetus for some states to increase their funding level. Similarly, even if federal legislation mandates more aggressive efforts in establishing paternity, state programs will continue to emphasize collections unless new financial incentives are developed for paternity activities.

Interprogram Interaction and Coordination

The welfare system does not operate in isolation. Despite proposals that include open-ended funding, the federal deficit makes it unrealistic to expect that Congress will be willing or able to appropriate substantially more federal resources to welfare-related programs. If welfare reform legislation is enacted and if the costs substantially exceed current estimates, Congress will undoubtedly act to reduce costs—by capping work-welfare funds, for instance.

Coordination among various programs is one way that states might maximize and leverage potential resources available for services to welfare recipients. This is no simple task, however. Federal legislation routinely specifies objectives, mandates, and incentives for various programs, but conflicting incentives and bureaucratic hostility often limit interprogram cooperation. Welfare reform provisions that once again call for closer coordination in program planning are not likely to improve linkages.

For example, an ongoing controversy centers on where authority for the work-welfare programs should lie: in the DOL or HHS at the federal level, or in Employment Security agencies or welfare agencies at the state level. This debate, which reflects a long-standing bureaucratic and political rivalry, works against coordinating the various systems that formally and informally comprise the current welfare network. If welfare reform legislation is enacted, authority for all activities, including work-welfare programs, will probably be concentrated in state welfare agencies. Inevitably, they will face increasing pressure to coordinate more closely with other systems and to leverage the resources available through other systems to serve welfare recipients.

Individual agencies are not likely to coordinate with other agencies, however, unless they perceive some benefit from the collaboration, in terms of either improving their own performance or increasing the amount of funds over which they have control. Recent informal discussions with state administrators indicate that more coordination is beginning to occur in the employment and training area (see Nightingale and Burbridge, 1987). People are beginning to realize that federal funds are not likely to increase for any program and that the resources must be more closely coordinated.

JTPA provides an example of how the mandates of different programs may hinder coordination. The JTPA legislation simultaneously requires that AFDC clients be equitably served, and restricts the level of supportive services (such as child care and training allowances) to no more than 15 percent of all program funds. Clearly, the equitable service requirement was intended to encourage service to AFDC clients, and the limitation on supportive services would suggest that AFDC clients, who have access to income and social services, should be even more attractive to JTPA. Yet only about 20 percent of the JTPA enrollees are from AFDC families. One reason for this low figure may be that JTPA administrators, responding to federal emphasis on pleasing the private sector and placing participants into jobs as quickly as possible with the least cost, are forced to focus primarily on the most employable among the eligible persons. AFDC recipients typically have very low competency levels in reading and mathematics. An Educational Testing Service study of a national sample of WIN registrants (Goodison, 1982) found that 44 percent read below the ninth-grade level, and preliminary information from the Philadelphia Saturation Work Program (Nightingale, 1986) indicates that for those WIN mandatory clients who did not have a job in the previous two years, the average reading level was at about the seventh grade and the average math level was at the fourth grade. It is not very surprising, then, that AFDC clients are at the end of the JTPA queue.

Despite its federal incentive structure, JTPA has become an increasingly important part of state work-welfare programs. In about half the states, work-welfare administrators reportedly view JTPA as being more committed to welfare clients; and in nine states JTPA receives funds to operate certain components of the work-welfare program. Some governors have added welfare clients as targets for JTPA, and some work-welfare programs have shifted JTPA priorities toward welfare clients and expanded the number of training slots for them by contracting with JTPA to provide training for the participants (as in Massachusetts and New Hampshire). Other states contract with JTPA to actually operate the entire work-welfare program in some jurisdictions (Maryland and Tennessee).

But regardless of where welfare reform places administrative authority for relevant programs, and perhaps even without reform, state welfare and work-welfare programs will have to increase their coordination with other systems to maximize limited resources. Some states are already recognizing the benefits of such coordination. Funding, rather than new federal policy directions, is likely to provide the incentive for agencies and programs to coordinate.

Summary and Implications

Any type of major welfare reform would naturally affect many programs and organizations, just as changes in federal regulations affect programs. The most dramatic types of changes suggested under welfare reform would alter the federal-to-state share of funding, expand the eligibility criteria for receiving public assistance, expand the work requirement to mothers with preschool-age children, and target employment and training activities to certain client groups. It is not at all obvious, though, that any of the proposals would improve the nation's welfare system, at least not in the short-run.

A common complaint about the current system, for instance, is that funding limitations are a barrier to program effectiveness. It seems clear, though, that funding would still be limited even under the most liberal welfare reform proposals in view of the federal budget deficit. The new funding provisions are likely to have more of an effect than any proposed programmatic changes, in that they generally would require states to increase their commitment to welfare-related programs as the federal match is reduced. For states that have already increased their funding for special welfare initiatives and work-welfare programs, changes in the federal funding provisions will have only a minor effect on the administration of funds, and probably no effect on programs. However, many state legislatures are reportedly not willing or not able to increase their funding for welfare-related activities, regardless of how attractive or open-ended federal funding might be to welfare agencies.

Moreover, no new services are suggested in any of the major proposals, no substantially different types of programs are contemplated, and very little emphasis is placed on the working poor. Rather than designing program approaches to alleviate poverty and welfare dependency, the reform proponents would instead attempt to move the state systems in certain administrative directions by means of funding or performance incentives: expanding client eligibility (through financial incentives to states that increase their standard of need); or shifting more responsibility to states (via state demonstrations or uncapped funding for work programs).

Programmatic effects might, however, occur as a result of increased caseloads. For example, requiring mothers with preschool-age children to participate in education or employment activities as a condition of their public assistance eligibility could substantially increase the caseload of work-welfare programs, remedial education programs, social services, and day-care programs. Requiring all states to extend public assistance to two-parent families and enforcing the work requirement more aggressively could increase the number of clients in low-intensity work-welfare components (such as job search) that work-welfare programs must monitor. Tougher enforcement of child-support obligations could increase the active caseload of enforcement programs, as well as the number of absent parents who make payments to a central public agency. Most of these types of caseload increases would mean that states would have to devote more resources to routine case monitoring.

It is worth emphasizing that federal funds for work-welfare programs will continue to be very limited, with or without welfare reform. Even the most liberal proposals would, for example, raise federal funding for work-welfare programs only slightly above the WIN level in 1980. Limited funding means that if states are to increase their total resources above their 1980 levels, they would have to obtain additional state appropriations and focus more attention on interprogram coordination of resources. As state funds approach or exceed federal funds for specific programs or activities, it would become inevitable that state priorities and objectives would take precedence over federal objectives. If some state legislatures will not or cannot increase state appropriations, then substantial differences will remain among states.

More specifically, states without an AFDC-U component before welfare reform, those with relatively low AFDC grant levels, and those with minimal work-welfare programs can expect the most changes from welfare reform. Many of the states in these three categories are also the least likely to be willing or able to increase state funds for welfare programs.

The public assistance system and the broader public and private network of systems surrounding it have become very complex over the past twenty years as the number of people on welfare and the knowledge about the problems they face have grown. Complexity should not necessarily be construed as negative or counterproductive, but it makes interprogram coordination more difficult to achieve. Limited funding, however, makes coordination of resources ever more important. Yet federal legislation requiring coordination in planning will not result in substantive interaction among related programs or agencies, especially if the law is not binding on some of the programs (federal welfare laws have no jurisdiction over education agencies or state and local courts). The initiative should ideally come from the top elected officials in a jurisdiction, such as mayor or governor. It would be naive to expect that national legislative provisions in welfare reform would improve interprogram coordination.

Finally, the institutional effects of welfare reform should be considered within the broader context, both historically and in terms of the network of organizations that interact with public assistance programs in each state and community. A wave of welfare reform has been emanating from states over the past eight years, and little in any current federal proposals suggests that national legislation would dramatically change the direction some states have taken. The course for the next decade may already have been set. The national welfare reform that is currently being debated may not represent either a step forward or a step backward, but rather simply a side-step.

Child-Support Policies

Robert I. Lerman

Disturbing social trends lose their shock value within a short time. In the case of the breakdown of the American two-parent family, the flood of divorce and separation in the 1960s generated widespread concern, but it was soon submerged by other issues. Unfortunately, the shift away from two-parent families continued throughout the 1970s and early 1980s and reached unprecedented levels. By now the connections with child poverty, welfare dependency, and economic and social hardships of women and children are too great for the issue to be pushed aside.

With the renewed attention to the one-parent family has come a changing perspective about the nature of the problem. No longer are the financial difficulties of mothers heading families merely a matter of poverty and welfare policies. Instead, the income deficiencies of all one-parent families are increasingly viewed as resulting from an unfair division of resources that leaves mothers and children with too little and absent fathers with more than their appropriate share. Today, the child-support problem has become widespread, with millions of divorced, white middle-class mothers as well as low-income, black unmarried mothers receiving too little financial support from the fathers of their children.

Acceptance of the notion that absent fathers bear a major responsibility for the income deficiencies of mother-headed families is a recent phenomenon. The Moynihan report, which in 1965 dramatized the dissolution of the two-parent black family, said nothing about the problem of uncollected child-support payments. Daniel Moynihan's hope was to develop policies—particularly those designed to raise the employment and earnings of black men—that would strengthen two-parent black families and reverse the trends toward black families headed by women. Reforming the welfare system was viewed as another way of improving the economic viability of low-income, two-parent families and reducing the system's own contribution to the breakup of families. The approach embodied in the welfare proposals of Presidents Nixon and Carter was to extend benefits to two-parent families, not to increase the contribution of absent fathers.

In the early 1970s politicians and policy analysts began to take the child-support collection issue more seriously. At the time, illegitimate children in many states had either no right to claim support from fathers or rights that were narrower than those of legitimate children (Krause, 1973). Senator Russell Long spearheaded the drive to extract financial contributions from absent fathers. Although Senator Long freely admitted his goal was to have fathers' payments substitute for welfare costs, he argued vigorously for the policy on moral grounds. Welfare advocates variously rebuked or mocked Senator Long's approach as unfair to poor fathers and as wasteful because of the low amounts that would be collected relative to the costs of administering the program.

In 1975, when enacting the Title IV-D programs to stimulate states to increase child-support collections, the Congress recognized that nonpayment of child support affected middle-income as well as low-income mothers and provided states with new tools to help all custodial parents (whether on or off welfare) obtain support. The benign view that divorce and one-parenthood merely heralded new, valid family forms began to give way to a recognition that father abandonment was creating poverty among children and forcing middle-class mothers and children to accept sharp cuts in their living standard.[1]

Since 1975, federal legislation on child support has stimulated states to increase their collections substantially. Many current welfare reform proposals, including the Family Support Act of 1988, contain provisions that would require states to tighten further their enforcement of child-support obligations. Such efforts now command support from all segments of the political spectrum.

More controversial are proposals that states pay custodial parents some amount of support when the collection system is unable to obtain payments from the noncustodial parent. The *assured benefit* or *advanced maintenance* approach operates in a number of countries, including Austria, Sweden, Norway, and Israel. In 1986 Wisconsin began a demonstration project that is to include an assured benefit component.

Can expanded enforcement of child-support obligations and an assured child-support program reorient the U.S. welfare system? Can child-support policies significantly reduce the welfare rolls and poverty among one-parent families without major increases in government spending? To what extent can child-support policies encourage increased work effort and independence among families currently on welfare?

Before answering these questions, we consider the inherent economic difficulties that arise when intact families with children break up or two-parent families do not form. We then examine the potential impact of enforcement strategies, including increasing awards, obtaining support orders, and collecting the amounts due; we review existing estimates and construct new estimates of the effects of Child Support Assurance System (CSAS) programs. We also assess the impact of combining a CSAS program with a revenue-neutral refundable tax credit to replace the personal exemption and conclude by discussing the implications of the analysis for welfare reform policy.

Underlying Economic Problems of Parents Living Apart

When parents separate, the average dollar income per family member remains constant as long as parents earn as much living apart as they did living together. Nevertheless, economic difficulties arise as a result of the following: (1) The costs of achieving any given living standard are higher for two households than for one; (2) The income of the noncustodial parent (nearly always the father) is usually much higher than the income of the custodial parent; and (3) The need to preserve the work incentives of the noncustodial parent limits the government's ability to equalize living standards.

Figure 8.1 illustrates these points. Consider a married couple with two children in which the father earns $12,500 and the mother earns $5,500 per year (approximately 75 percent of the median income of men and women in 1986).[2] As a single unit, the family's income would equal $18,000 or 1.64 times the poverty line for a family of four. Now, suppose the husband moves away from the family, leaving the mother and two children as a separate household. Assuming the economies of scale used to construct the poverty line, the combined income required for both households to remain 64 percent above the poverty line would be about $23,700. Thus only if the parents increase their incomes can the two households avoid a reduction in their living standards.

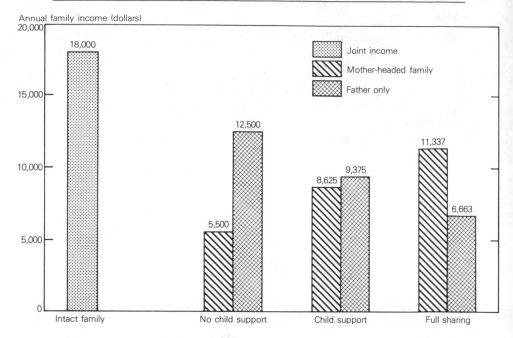

Fig. 8.1. Family incomes under alternative sharing patterns

Child-support payments can help but are unlikely to equalize the losses from the family's splitting. With no child-support payments at all, the husband's living standard would rise to 2.33 times the poverty line, while the mother and two children fall to 60 percent of the poverty line. Suppose instead that the father pays 25 percent of his income in child-support payments. The mother and two children would have enough income to live at 95 percent of the poverty line, while the father's remaining $9,375 would keep him 75 percent above poverty. To equalize living standards, the father would have to pay 47 percent of his income to the mother and child, leaving him with $6,663 and allowing both households to reach 24 percent above poverty.[3]

In practice courts rarely require payments of this magnitude, especially for fathers with a salary of only $12,500 per year. Even if courts insisted on equal sharing, the effort might prove counterproductive. The 47 percent child-support, 15 percent federal income tax, and 7 percent social security rates would cumulate to a 69 percent marginal tax rate, thereby encouraging the father to misreport income and avoid making support payments.

The fundamental problem is that *family breakup generally turns the father's spending on his children from a consumption good into a tax.* It is not simply that the father transfers some of his consumption to the mother and children. Rather, money spent on the children's consumption—especially when under the full control of the mother—loses its ability to bring satisfaction to both the children and the father.[4] Additional economic losses may occur if the support orders act as a distorting tax on the father's income.

Thus a breakup not only will impose losses on the family from economies of scale, but either the distribution of the loss will be highly unequal or the large child-support obligations will impose serious work disincentives on the noncustodial parent.[5] The size of actual economic burdens created by split families is an empirical issue. Some analysts have downplayed the importance of family splitting as a cause of poverty and of racial differentials in income. Bane (1986) finds that family breakup accounts for only 22 percent of the beginnings of poverty spells among black female heads and 49 percent among white female heads. Of the poverty induced by household composition change, Bane reports that loss of scale economies accounted for only 16 percent of the poverty among white female heads and 28 percent of black female heads. She concludes: "Although there has indeed been a dramatic and shocking increase in female-headed families among blacks and an equally dramatic feminization of black poverty, one cannot conclude it could have been avoided had families stayed together."

If Bane's conclusions are correct, it is hard to see how even the most far-reaching award and collection procedures could significantly reduce poverty. In fact, however, Bane overstates her case by looking only at the beginnings of poverty spells and by failing to examine directly the potential income contributions of absent fathers. Had the mother and father remained together, poverty begun before the household composition change might not have continued, and poverty begun after the change might have been avoided entirely.

Considerable evidence suggests that family breakup substantially reduces the incomes of mother-headed families. According to Weiss (1984), low-income mothers experienced an initial 25 percent income reduction immediately after a divorce and then had stagnant incomes over the next five years. Other parents, who started with similarly low incomes but who remained married, raised their incomes substantially over the next five years. Similar results emerged from a study by Duncan and Hoffman (1985).[6]

These comparisons may overstate the losses from family instability since parents that remained together may differ from parents who split in terms of income gains over time. The real question is: what would incomes of split families have been had those specific families remained together? The answer requires identifying absent fathers, calculating their incomes, and determining the incomes of mothers of their children. In addition, we must take account of the possibility that divorced, separated, or never-married fathers earn less than what they would have earned had they been married and living with their wife and children. Many absent fathers live with other relatives and do not feel the same responsibility for earning income as they would if they were resident fathers.[7]

Of all absent fathers, we would expect that young fathers are least capable of bringing their families above poverty. Do these fathers actually lack the resources to keep their children out of poverty? A mixed picture emerges from data on the incomes of 21–29 year-old absent fathers.[8] In 1985 the median income of these young fathers was $10,700, an amount above the poverty level for families of three; the typical black absent father had an income of $8,400. Although one of four young absent fathers earned less than $4,500, two-thirds had incomes of $7,000 or more. Among 25–29 year-olds, median incomes were $12,500 for all absent fathers and $9,500 for blacks. At these ages, two-thirds of black absent fathers had incomes above $6,700. Even fathers with an income at the bottom of this range would be making an important contribution to family income. Combining his income with such other sources as earnings of the mother, Food Stamps, and the EITC, the family would be able to attain an income above the poverty level.

Thus the vast majority of young absent fathers could alleviate their children's poverty if each pooled his income with the child's mother. When parents choose not to live together and pool income, the economic burden often unfairly falls on custodial parents and children. The mean family incomes of never-married mothers was only half the family income of unwed absent fathers. About 60 percent of never-married, 21–29 year-old mothers were poor in 1985, as compared to about 25 percent of never-married absent fathers.[9] Even more striking gaps show up among young divorced and separated parents; poverty beset over 50 percent of mothers but only 12 percent of absent fathers. It is important to determine, therefore, how far child support policies can go in relieving these unfair burdens, especially among the lowest income mother-headed families.

Impact of Current and Potential Child-Support Payments

Under any child-support system, there are limits to the claims on a father's income. Judges setting support awards must take account of the father's own living expenses and of disincentive effects on the work effort and reporting by fathers. Typically, support awards are no more than 20–25 percent of the father's income.

Census reports and other empirical research suggests that no single factor is responsible for the underpayments. The shortfall in support payments results from failure to establish a support award; nonpayment or underpayment of existing awards; and low award levels relative to the incomes of absent parents. Eliminating any individual gap while holding the others constant would accomplish little, but, as Garfinkel (1985) has pointed out, eliminating all three gaps would have a major impact on payments.

We can illustrate the potential for child-support payments with the following simple equation: $P = Y \times a \times b \times c$, where P represents mean support payments, Y is mean income, a is the percent of custodial mothers with awards, b is the percent of the award actually paid, and c is the award as a percent of income.[10] The b term depends on the percentage of men making payments and the percent they pay of their award amount.[11]

Were all the gaps eliminated, a and b would equal 1 and c would equal some appropriate proportion of income of absent fathers, say 24 percent. Existing studies provide good evidence about the proportion of mothers with awards, a, and the percent of money actually paid, b. Less clear is the average income of fathers, Y, and the award level as a percentage of income, c.

Patterns of Current Child-Support Awards and Payments

Data on the shortfall in child-support payments at the national level come mainly from surveys conducted by the U.S. Bureau of the Census. Using a questionnaire added to the CPS taken in April of 1979, 1982, 1984, and 1986, the Cenus Bureau asked only custodial mothers about their receipt of child-support and alimony payments.[12]

The CPS provides no data on payments to mothers who lack an agreement (voluntary, court-ordered, or other) that the father pay a specified amount. As a result, the Bureau reports ignore informal support payments that may have been received by 42 percent of all mothers with children of absent fathers and 58 percent of poor mothers. Reports by unwed fathers suggest that the Census procedures understate receipts of child-support payments.[13]

Detailed information on support payments is also available from the Census Bureau's SIPP. The SIPP data provide information on monthly child-support receipts as well as on awards and payments during the prior year. One SIPP module yields data on the amounts of child support reportedly paid by noncustodial parents, but only those who made a regular payment. The NLS provides comprehensive data on young absent fathers. Using the NLS, one can calculate actual child-support payments in relation to income for all absent fathers ages 21–29 in 1986.

Only limited information is available for the effect of property settlements on the level of child-support and alimony payments. If noncustodial parents were to trade off a large property settlement in return for a lower level of support payments, child-support payments would understate the contributions of noncustodial parents. But, as Weitzman (1985) reports, most divorcing couples have little property to divide. As of 1978, less than half the divorced women had any marital property and of those who received property, the median award was only $4,648. In 1983, 60 percent of divorced mothers living with their children received no property settlement at all (U.S. Bureau of the Census, 1986). Still, property distributions did seem to influence support payments. Of 3.7 million mothers who were not owed any support payments in 1983, about 3 percent said the reason was that a property settlement was paid in lieu of support payments.[14]

Table 8.1 reproduces estimates for 1978 to 1983 that Philip Robins developed by correcting for technical problems in the CPS data. The pattern of child-support awards has been remarkably stable, while real payment values actually declined. The unadjusted CPS figures show that the trends continued through 1985. Most disturbing is the decline in the real value of mean child-support payments from 1983 to 1985.

Improvements did occur for the fastest growing and most difficult to reach group—never-married mothers. Between 1978 and 1985, the proportion of mothers who were due payments nearly doubled from 8 to 15 percent; the percent receiving a payment jumped from 6 to almost 12 percent. In terms of the equation above, the average share of custodial mothers with support awards, a, was 46 percent, and the average proportion of awards received, b, was 65 percent.

Table 8.1. Child-support payments to one-parent families, 1978–1985

All one-parent families	1978	1981	1983	1985
Percent with awards and due payments during the year, according to adjusted estimates	46%	47%	45%	—
Percent for this group, according to unadjusted CPS reports	45%	44%	42%	46%
Percent receiving payments, according to adjusted estimates	35%	35%	35%	—
Percent for this group, according to unadjusted CPS reports	33%	36%	33%	35%
One-parent families due child support				
Percent receiving payment	75%	74%	77%	—
Percent of award received	64%	63%	68%	—
Mean award (1983 dollars)	$3,127	$2,676	$2,512	—
Mean payment (1983 dollars)	$2,176	$1,754	$1,804	—
One-parent families receiving payment				
Percent of award received	85%	85%	85%	—
Mean payment (1983 dollars)	$2,910	$2,358	$2,347	—
Mean payment according to unadjusted CPS reports (1983 dollars)	$2,711	$2,401	$2,419	$2,152

Sources: Unadjusted CPS reports are directly from tables published by the U.S. Bureau of the Census (1981, 1983, 1986, and 1987a). CPS figures for mean payments are given in 1983 dollars using the implicit GNP price deflator. All other numbers are drawn from Robins (1987), table 2.

What about the shortfall between legal obligations and actual payments? According to the CPS report, of the nearly 4 million mothers who were due payments in 1983, about half received the full amount from the father.[15] The average deficit between obligation and payment was $749, or 41 percent of the mean payment. However, if we exclude the mothers who did not receive any payment, the deficit is much smaller. Two-thirds of the mothers who obtained some child-support payment collected their full award. The mean shortfall among this group was only $180 per year, or 7 percent of actual payments. In general, then, absent fathers subject to support orders fall into two categories: payers—those who pay all or nearly all of their obligation—and nonpayers.

Table 8.2 shows how child-support awards and receipts vary by welfare

Table 8.2. Child support received by AFDC and non-AFDC mothers, 1983

	AFDC recipients	Not AFDC recipients
Percent with awards	40.0%	63.9%
Percent due child support	30.1%	50.9%
Percent receiving payments	17.6%	40.4%
Median payment	$1,214	$1,786
Mean payment	$1,515	$2,462

Source: U.S. Bureau of the Census (1986).

status. Clearly, AFDC recipients are less likely to receive child-support payments than mothers not on AFDC.[16] At the same time, it is equally clear that the lack of child-support payments alone does not lead to AFDC. Over 60 percent of mothers stayed off welfare even though they received no child-support payments.

Of all mothers who received child-support payments in 1983, AFDC recipients obtained less than others, but the differential is not enormous. Note in Table 8.2 that the median payment reported by AFDC mothers was about $1,200, or $100 per month.[17] But the median payment to mothers not on welfare was only $1,786, or about $150 per month. Thus even if welfare mothers received the median child-support payment received by mothers not on welfare, the $150 per month support payment, by itself, would be too low to push large numbers of families off welfare. Maximum AFDC payments to families of two were $258 in the typical state in 1984.

Among mothers on welfare who were supposed to receive child-support payments, only 5 percent obtained their full award while about 40 percent did not collect anything during 1983. On average, AFDC mothers who were due to receive payments obtained $905. If these mothers had received the full amounts awarded, the average support payment would have more than doubled to nearly $1,845; that is, the payment shortfall averaged about $940.

Estimates compiled from state agencies administering the enforcement of child support are broadly consistent with these figures. According to a recent report (OCSE, 1986), state agencies helped collect $2.70 billion in support payments in 1985, $1.09 billion of which was paid on behalf of AFDC recipients. The $1.09 billion reportedly collected in FY1984 is slightly less than the amounts reported to the CPS by AFDC families.[18]

Since 1984 states have allowed the first $50 per month of child-support payments to raise the mother's income and not reduce the AFDC grant. Administrative reports on the use of this provision between 1985 and 1987 indicate that as an incentive it had little effect on child support for AFDC mothers. Only 14.1 percent of mothers received child support in 1987 while on AFDC, up slightly from the 13.2 percent figure in 1985.[19]

What was the economic burden on fathers actually making support payments? Recent national data from SIPP permit direct calculations on the relation between support payments and incomes. Table 8.3 displays the payments reported by a national sample representing 3.6 million noncustodial parents. Note that the burdens on income are moderate and decline gradually with income.[20]

The CPS and SIPP data may understate the actual amounts received by mothers heading families, because they do not take account of payments by fathers who had not agreed to provide support. Unwed fathers—most of whom have no formal or informal support agreement— often report making payments. Table 8.4 presents my calculations (Lerman, 1986) of the percentage of absent fathers making payments and the amounts of payments by race and poverty status. Over half of the

Table 8.3. Child-support payments reported by noncustodial parents providing regular support in 1984

Income of noncustodial parent ($)	1984 child support payments ($)	Support payments as percent of income	Income distribution of noncustodial parents making payments (%)
1–4,999	1,567	59	4.8
5,000–7,499	984	16	4.8
7,500–9,999	1,519	17	6.6
10,000–12,499	2,057	18	6.5
12,500–14,999	1,601	12	7.8
15,000–19,999	2,176	13	16.8
20,000–24,999	2,602	12	15.0
25,000–29,999	3,009	11	11.8
30,000 and over	3,452	8	25.9
Median payment	1,975	—	—
Mean payment	2,477	12.4	100.0

Source: Tabulations from topical module 5 of the SIPP.

Table 8.4. Child-support payments by unwed absent fathers aged 21–29

Men (aged 21–29)	Child-support reports, 1984–85 averages		
	In poor families	Not in poor families	In all families
Percent paying child support			
All young men	20	48	41
Hispanic	13	38	28
Black	24	48	41
White	3	46	40
Mean payments (in dollars)			
All young men	920	2,535	2,280
Hispanic	1,170	1,300	1,380
Black	890	1,430	1,345
White	1,300	4,580	4,500

Source: Unpublished tabulations prepared from the NLS.

young unwed fathers report making some payment. Mean 1984 payments were nearly as high as the mean amount reportedly paid by all custodial parents. These estimates no doubt overstate average payments by unwed fathers, since many nonpayers fail to report that they have fathered a child.[21]

The Effects of Expanding Support Payments

The amount of child-support payments depends on the number of custodial parents with support awards, the size of the awards, and the percentage of the awards actually paid. The shortfalls in collection of existing support obligations and the low rates of establishing the obligations of many noncustodial parents are largely the fault of slack law enforcement. However, in many cases custodial parents themselves are responsible for the absence of a support order. In 1985, *over one in three (37 percent) mothers who were not awarded support awards reported that they did not want an award.*[22]

Raising the size of awards requires new policy measures and often new laws. Since 1975, state collection agencies have concentrated mostly on raising the proportion of child-support obligations that are actually paid. Recently, the strategy of increasing legal obligations—both through establishing paternity and support agreements and by increasing the size of the obligations—has become a high priority.

According to the OCSE, "increasing annual collections of child support means that more families have been helped to achieve self-sufficiency by either leaving or avoiding welfare." But in another part of the report, the OCSE reports that between 1981 and 1985 only about one percent of the caseload left AFDC because of child-support collections.[23]

State agencies managed to collect support payments worth about 7 percent of national AFDC payments in 1985, up from 5 percent in 1981. Between 1981 and 1985, the average payment per case jumped about 30 percent, from $1,224 in 1981 to $1,596 in 1985. In some states (Alabama, Idaho, and Utah) collections were over 20 percent of AFDC assistance payments.

A study conducted by MAXIMUS (1983) also revealed that support payments exerted only small effects on participation in welfare programs and on benefit payments. The MAXIMUS study found that support orders are generally below AFDC levels, so that even collecting the full support payment would leave most mothers on welfare.

A detailed, rigorous analysis by Robins (1986) estimates the effect of intervention by child-support services on the level of support payments and on the average payment amount.[24] Robins finds that services from state IV-D agencies significantly raised the likelihood of a mother receiving payments. About 38 percent of mothers who contacted the agencies obtained a support payment; without help from the agency, only 18 percent would have received a payment. The impacts on the average amount of child support were significant in a statistical sense, but small in absolute terms. On average, agency interventions raised support payments by $258 per year for all mothers. The payment increases were substantially higher among AFDC mothers (about $290 per year) than among those not on AFDC (about $208 per year).

Robins projects the effects on AFDC and poverty of expanding child-support collections and award. He compares seven alternatives: (1) no child support; (2) child support, but no enforcement program; (3) the existing enforcement program; (4) an extension of services to all families with a formal support award; (5) an extension of services to all families with or without a support award; (6) full collection of all support due to families with support awards; and (7) full collection of existing and subsequent support awards. For several of these alternatives, Robins takes into account that changes in child support payments may influence the work behavior of mothers.

His findings concerning the effect of the OCSE program are remarkably similar to the numbers drawn from OCSE reports. As against no child-support payments at all (the counterfactual used in the OCSE reports), the OCSE program raises child support collections to about 6.5 percent of AFDC benefits and reduces AFDC participation rates by about 1 percentage point. The enforcement program does reduce poverty rates from 51 to 48 percent of the sample.

Under the most ambitious case—full collection of existing awards and establishing and collecting support orders for all mothers on AFDC—collections would jump to 32 percent of benefits, would reduce AFDC participation rates by 2 percentage points from 34 percent to 32 percent of mothers, and would lower their poverty rates from 51 to 45 percent.

As Robins notes, the modest impacts of expanded enforcement result from low support awards. In 1982 the average obligation of absent fathers amounted to only $86 per child on AFDC and $127 per child not on AFDC. Since average AFDC benefits per family well exceed average support awards, and since only a small proportion of AFDC mothers work, the low impact of enforcement on welfare are not surprising. More recently, Robins (1987) found a similar lack of correlation between AFDC participation and overall child-support collections. Between 1978 and 1981, the 17 percent decline in the real value of collections induced only a 1 percent increase in AFDC participation. Slight increases in collections between 1981 and 1983 had no discernible impact on the AFDC rolls.[25]

Trends in costs also cast doubt on the efficacy of a collections strategy for reforming welfare. Between 1984 and 1987, administrative costs in the child-support enforcement program increased by $337 million, almost as much the $359 million rise in support payments collected for AFDC recipients. In one sense, this comparison understates the net gains from the enforcement program because state IV-D agencies collect payments for non-AFDC custodial parents. On the other hand, some of the amounts reportedly collected by IV-D agencies would have been paid without the program.

Another concern is that the enforcement strategy may not succeed because of the declining proportion of mothers who want support awards. Among never-married mothers, the largest group lacking a support order, the proportion who said they did not want an award jumped from 27 percent in 1983 to 42 percent in 1985. One possible explanation for this attitude is that mothers feared that in obtaining support awards they might have to give up their authority over child-rearing and visitation by fathers.[26] Alternatively, more custodial mothers might have chosen to try to receive intermittent amounts that they can keep, instead of giving the government the chance to obtain support payments that largely offset the costs of welfare programs. A third possibility is that expanded enforcement caused fathers to pressure custodial mothers not to seek an formal award.

If support payments based on existing awards would do little to reduce welfare dependency, what about the potential impact of increased support awards as well as collections?

Haskins and others (1985) used a small national sample and a North Carolina survey of absent fathers to estimate potential collections. From the national sample they calculated that the national potential for child support was about $27 billion in 1984, as compared to the approximately $10.4 billion reported by the U.S. Census as currently owed to custodial mothers. However, data from a North Carolina survey of absent fathers with active case records in the state's IV-D system indicated that absent fathers had mean earnings of only about $10,000. Unfortunately, the authors did not explore whether their national estimates of child-support potential could be consistent with such low incomes based on state data.

Garfinkel and Oellerich (1986) also developed estimates of absent fathers' incomes based on the incomes of all men and various payment formulas. Their projection of the collection potential using the Wisconsin formula is $27 billion in 1983, an amount identical to the above estimate.[27] Garfinkel and Oellerich project awards at $22 billion under the Delaware approach, a figure somewhat lower than the estimates of Haskins and colleagues.

Extrapolating from these studies, it appears that raising potential collections would have only a moderate effect on the welfare rolls. First, the Garfinkel-Oellerich equations indicate that absent fathers of AFDC children have incomes about 43–45 percent below the average incomes of other absent fathers. Thus if the incomes of absent fathers averaged $20,000, absent fathers of AFDC children would have incomes of about $12,700. Payments based on the Wisconsin or Delaware formulas would provide amounts well below the AFDC payment levels in most states. As we have seen, historical OCSE data and the Robins analysis indicate that increased collections have little impact on AFDC rolls. Furthermore, a rising share of AFDC families are headed by never-married mothers.

The incomes of never-married absent fathers are lower than incomes of other groups.

Summary of Shortfall in Support Payments

If awards averaged 25 percent of income and all fathers had obligations which they fully paid, AFDC mothers would receive about $3,000 per year in support payments. In fact, they received an average of $225 in 1984. Combining Census data on child-support awards and payments with estimates of incomes of absent fathers, Table 8.5 shows that actual payments fall short of potential payments.

Collections amount to only about 1.9 percent of incomes of absent fathers. Note that it would take dramatic improvements in all the award and collection areas to produce a significant dent in the AFDC rolls. Increasing awards to 25 percent of income and leaving other factors unchanged would raise support payments only to 3 percent of the average father's income. If all custodial parents had awards and nothing else changed, support payments would rise to 6.5 percent of the father's income. Collecting all that fathers with awards now owe would raise average payments to about $535 per year (or 4.5 percent of income).

Table 8.5. Child-support payments

Based on SIPP data			
Annual mean payment	Percent with awards and due payments during the year	Amount supposed to receive	Amount received
$225	28.7	$1,873	$777

Based on SIPP data with projected incomes of absent fathers				
Income of father	Award as percent of father's income	Percent with awards and due payments during the year	Percent of award collected	Payment as percent of father's income
$12,000	15.6	28.7	41.5	1.9
$10,000	18.7	28.7	41.5	2.2

Source: Support awards and support payment amounts tabulated from topical module 5 of the 1984 SIPP.

It is only when we accomplish all three goals that dramatic increases in payments take place. Achieving all enforcement targets would raise support payments to welfare mothers by over 13 times their current levels.[28]

Mandating Payment Standards and the CSAS

Turning the full potential for increased payments into reality requires extraordinary policy and administrative measures as well as substantial increases in administrative costs. Although the federal and state governments have improved procedures and increased collections, the size of the support payments actually received by mothers heading families has declined in real terms.

The passage of 1984 amendments to Title IV-D of the Social Security Act has pushed states to adopt additional enforcement measures, including automatic wage withholding and property liens, and to make more serious efforts to establish paternity. Another provision calls on governors to form State Commissions on Child Support that would examine the functioning of child-support systems and consider the establishment of objective standards for support. Unfortunately, it is likely to take a long time before these provisions result in substantial increases in child-support payments for current AFDC recipients. Meanwhile, the proposal to develop a complementary program that would assure at least a minimum support payment to custodial parents is receiving serious consideration.

Under the CSAS custodial parents would receive a payment equal to the difference between the noncustodial parent's payments and some minimum level. The idea is that custodial parents should not have to bear the entire burden of the noncustodial parents' unwillingness to pay support and the government's inability to collect. Such programs, sometimes called *advanced maintenance*, have operated for many years in a number of European countries and Israel (Kamerman and Kahn, 1987).

One approach is to combine a high assured benefit with expanded enforcement under new standards for relating support obligations to income. Wisconsin is currently testing a plan of this type. An alternative proposal is to provide a modest assured benefit, supplemented by a refundable tax credit for all children, which would replace the personal exemptions (see Lerman, 1985).

Aspects of the New Child-Support Strategies

Two of the new strategies involve policy changes that go beyond enforcing existing laws and court decisions: requiring judges to use formulas as presumptive rules for determining child support obligations; and providing government payments to custodial parents who receive less in collections than some minimum amount.

Current child-support obligations are inequitable in two ways. Because support orders rarely keep pace with inflation or with increases in the living standards of noncustodial parents, custodial mothers and children often receive too little by almost any standard. The tendency for judges to set obligations in absolute terms has played an important role in the erosion of support obligations with inflation and increased real wages. The other inequity is: some noncustodial fathers end up having to pay much more than others, who may simply be lucky enough to have their cases decided by judges who give unusually high weight to the needs of noncustodial parents. The purpose of standardized benefit formulas is to reduce both types of inequities.

Formulas and guidelines are likely to raise average support obligations in large part by indexing them to inflation. This will improve equity by raising payments to custodial parents. But reducing or eliminating the discretion of judges might prevent them from adjusting for special circumstances that justifiably alter the equitable level of support payments. Income formulas do not capture differences in wealth or in factors that affect the costs of attaining a given level of living. A noncustodial parent may amass great wealth (after a divorce) but have low measured income. Alternatively, a child from the noncustodial parent's new family may suffer a physical impairment that requires high medical outlays. Presumptive standards would not necessarily prevent judges from making adjustments in extreme cases. But how does one determine an extreme case? If standards are to mean anything, they will have to reduce the ability of judges to respond to every special circumstance. The real question is whether wide judicial discretion—both for a particular judge and for all judges—produces more unfairness than a simple formula would.

A clear advantage for standards is the probable reduction in administrative costs. Deciding on the basis of a formula should take less time than making judgments based on diverse criteria limited only by the imagination of enterprising lawyers. Legal costs for the parents should decline for similar reasons. Whatever the method for allocating support payments, the economics of family splitting creates difficult trade-offs between maintaining equality of sacrifice and preserving work and reporting incentives. States have tried to address these issues in developing their standards. The goals of a support system might be: (1) to minimize the gap between the actual living standard of children and what their living standard would have been if the father had remained; (2) to minimize the gap between the living standards of the custodial-parent family and the noncustodial-parent family; (3) to minimize work disincentives imposed on custodial and noncustodial parents; and (4) to encourage the noncustodial parent to stay involved with the children.

Goals 1 and 2 have very different implications for contributions by noncustodial parents. Under 1, the standard would require as much as the noncustodial parent would have spent on his family, independently of his needs and of the income of the custodial parent. Noncustodial parents would not be able to reduce their obligations by starting a second family. Amounts might vary little by number of children, since a father of one child might spend almost as much of his income to provide that child with a high living standard as he would if he had two children.[29] Goal 2 would relate support obligations to the income and resources of the custodial parent's family and to the needs of the noncustodial parent's family. In this case, noncustodial parents might end up contributing no money at all if their potential living standards were lower than those of the custodial parent.

However states determine payment standards, they may want to encourage in-kind contributions and joint custody, so that the noncustodial parent's contribution looks more like a consumption good (as it does when the parent remains with the family) and less like a tax. The consumption aspects could arise from the joint enjoyment of a nicer home and the child's well-being, or from the increased ability to regulate outlays for children. On the other hand, in-kind contributions could limit savings in welfare outlays and delay the movement of families off welfare.

The Child Support Assurance System (CSAS). In the case of the CSAS, one ideological consequence would be to move the country away from its reliance on means-tested programs as a way of helping low-income, one-parent families. The legislation might also stimulate increased collection efforts, as the public sees more clearly the direct cost associated with enforcement breakdowns. Unlike AFDC, CSAS would be a universal program, not one providing benefits on the basis of the family's poverty. Government spending on CSAS would result not from the mother's inability to support her family, but rather from the payment shortfall by absent fathers and from child-support enforcement deficiencies. This characteristic of the program should reduce the stigma currently associated with receiving AFDC. A practical advantage of CSAS is that states could decide against spending large amounts on tough cases with low-payment potential without imposing high costs on mothers.

CSAS could be used to help mothers avoid AFDC's high marginal tax rates on work effort. In fact, the hope is that CSAS would stimulate increased work by AFDC recipients. Combining CSAS with modest earnings would help families have a realistic chance of leaving welfare and raising their total incomes. Even for women who usually receive support payments, CSAS would reduce their risks of leaving welfare because it insures a stable payment.

Critics of the CSAS concept see the program simply as a disguise for welfare. After all, the government does not usually reimburse parties who lose income as a result of slack law enforcement. A further objection is that, in the absence of an income test, the CSAS approach would be less target-efficient than other welfare programs. Too many government dollars would flow to nonpoor families. In my view, the ability to distinguish the CSAS concept from welfare depends mainly on the credibility of the claim that CSAS compensates only for slack enforcement policies; this implies that states could escape CSAS outlays in nearly all cases if they collected a reasonable proportion of the incomes of absent fathers. Another way to distinguish CSAS from welfare is to avoid income and asset tests.

In what share of cases should states be able to avoid any CSAS spending by effective enforcement policies? Should it be 10 percent, 20 percent, or 5 percent? A threshold of 10 percent would imply an assured benefit equal to the obligation of fathers with incomes at the tenth percentile in the overall distribution. Decisions on the appropriate threshold will depend partly on the costs and feasibility of achieving high collection rates and the net costs of alternative levels. The size of legal support obligations will partly determine the cost and impact of an assured benefit. If awards are low, then a CSAS benefit set at the payment obligation of low-income parents might be so small as to have little impact on mother-headed families. This is why efforts to raise legal award levels complement proposals for assured benefits.

Regardless of enforcement capabilities, setting the benefits too high (say at the thirtieth percentile of father's income) would convert CSAS into a transfer program, since custodial parents would end up receiving far more under CSAS than they would have if they received the child-support payment that represented an equitable payment from the non-custodial parent. High assured-benefit levels might also increase the strain on the enforcement system, by increasing the incentive for custodial and noncustodial parents to collude. A high-payment CSAS would give more mothers the same incentive that AFDC mothers now have of helping the absent father evade official payments so that he will provide more informal payments.

The eligibility for benefits of custodial parents who have not obtained legal awards is a difficult issue. If the CSAS is to preserve the concept that the program compensates for ineffective state collection policies, then the payment policy might depend on the reasons mothers have no awards. In cases where mothers make a good-faith effort to assist in establishing paternity and locating fathers, state agencies may be responsible for the absence of the award and thus should provide CSAS. Given the difficulties of applying criteria of cooperation, the program might have to use a single policy for all custodial parents without support awards.

One argument for excluding them is the evidence that mothers without awards are not especially eager to obtain them. Of mothers lacking awards in 1985, 37 percent said the reason was they did not seek an award (U.S. Bureau of the Census, 1987a). Although nearly 50 percent did want an award, there is anecdotal evidence that AFDC mothers often do little to help identify and locate fathers. Any decision will have incentive effects. If mothers without awards have access to CSAS, then those with low-income fathers will continue to have (as currently under AFDC) little incentive to cooperate in establishing an award. But excluding mothers without awards from CSAS will reduce the incentive for states to spend the resources necessary to obtain a support order on behalf of mothers not on AFDC. As under current law, states would still save outlays by establishing awards and collecting money from fathers of AFDC children.

The Wisconsin Child-Support Demonstration. The Wisconsin state government is currently implementing a multifaceted child-support demonstration project. The overall project includes:

- the adoption of guidelines under which child-support awards would equal a proportion of the absent parent's income;

- improved procedures (including automatic wage withholding) for collecting support payments;

- an assured child-support benefit equal to some specified level ($3,000 to $4,500 per year) less the amount paid by the absent parent and a reduction for incomes of the custodial parent;
- $1 to $1.75 per hour wage subsidy that would phase slightly below median family income.

The guidelines call for noncustodial parents to pay 17 percent of their incomes for one child and 25, 29, 31, and 34 percent for two, three, four, and five or more children. If the noncustodial parent's payment falls short of the CSAS minimum, then the state would pay the difference between the minimum and the actual payment. Custodial parents who receive a CSAS benefit would be subject to a surtax on their earnings that would reduce the CSAS payment; the rate at which the CSAS declines with the custodial parent's income would be equal to the percentages applied to the noncustodial income. A custodial parent with two children and $400 per month in income would thus receive a CSAS payment of $233 per month ($333 − .25 × $400). The wage subsidy included in the plan would also decline with income beyond a certain point, phasing out gradually over the annual income range of $8,000 to $16,000.

The Wisconsin CSAS program diverges somewhat from the pure, nonwelfare concept. The main difference is that the payment schedule is set higher than what the state could expect to collect from many absent fathers. With the minimum for a one-parent family with one child at $3,000 per year, the CSAS amount would be fully offset by the noncustodial parent's payments only if his earnings were at least $17,647 ($17,647 times the 17 percent support standard equals $3,000).[30] The $3,000 figure for one child is 73 percent higher than the mean payment currently provided by contributing noncustodial parents.[31]

Garfinkel, Robins, and Wong (1987) simulated the impact of all components of the child-support demonstration on the AFDC program and on the earnings and total incomes of custodial parents in Wisconsin. They take direct account of the program's impact on the work effort of custodial parents, but do not consider the possible effects on the work patterns of noncustodial parents. According to their results, the proposed system would generate dramatic increases in work by AFDC recipients along with reductions in work effort by nonrecipients. At high levels ($3,500 per year) of the assured benefit, the program would by itself raise the work effort by AFDC mothers by 350 hours per year, a percentage increase of over 300. Even low assured-benefit levels would lead to work increases averaging more than 100 percent. The proposed system would also reduce work hours by mothers not currently receiving AFDC. The primary reason is that the added income from the program would allow mothers to reduce work hours without experiencing a drop in their families' income. Although the work reductions among these mothers are smaller than the work increases among AFDC mothers, combined earnings from the two groups would fall. Because of the higher wage rates of non-AFDC mothers, a reduction in their work hours translates into a larger decline in earnings than a reduction in work hours of AFDC mothers.

Garfinkel, Robins, and Wong project the increased costs of the plan at $38 million, at current award and collection rates.[32] Under the assumption of moderate improvements in enforcement policies, the costs would fall to $1 million. The benefits would be considerable: the poverty gap would fall from $292 to $209 million; and the proportion of custodial mothers on AFDC would fall from 46 to 39 percent, a reduction of about 15 percent. One explanation for only a modest decline in AFDC participation is that about one-third of recipients do not have child-support awards and thus do not qualify for the program.

Although these results show larger impacts on AFDC mothers and welfare caseloads than the earlier Robins analysis, comparisons are difficult to make because Garfinkel and coauthors did not isolate the separate impacts of each change. For example, the $1 per hour wage subsidy together with assured-benefit levels that lower the cost of leaving AFDC could make the major difference. Improved enforcement might show up as having equally weak impacts. Another difference may be related to the specifics of the Wisconsin caseload. Nationally, it is much less common for AFDC mothers to have a support award than it is in Wisconsin. This implies that the impact on Wisconsin mothers probably overstates the national impact. On the other hand, the impact on the welfare rolls and poverty would be higher in other states, because Wisconsin's welfare benefits are much higher than those in other states.

There are reasons to believe that the three authors understate the long-term effects. The induced short-term increases in employment may generate investment gains and reduce the proportion of people who return to welfare. The certainty of support payments (or assured benefits) may lessen the concern of recipients about the insecurity of support payments.

The CSAS in the Wisconsin demonstration could achieve a number of desirable goals, but it moves away from the concept of a nonwelfare alternative. With its high minimum benefits, a large proportion of custodial parents will qualify for payments that are well above the support obligations of absent fathers. For these cases, the CSAS would be making payments on the basis of income deficiencies, as do standard welfare programs. Further, the surtax on custodial parent earnings would exclude middle-income custodial parents, thereby lessening the universal nature of the program.

An alternative approach is to adopt a CSAS with a minimum benefit low enough to assure states that they can escape their payment obligations if they collect a reasonable proportion of income from noncustodial parents. Suppose, for example, that 90 percent of noncustodial parents (mostly absent fathers) had incomes of $10,000 or more per year. Then, by getting all fathers of single children to pay at least 11 percent of their incomes, the states would be able to eliminate CSAS costs for all but 10 percent of mothers.[33] To achieve a similar result for fathers of two children, the state would have to make sure that payments are at least 20.8 percent. I have chosen these low benefit levels partly to keep program costs low and partly to ensure the integrity of the program. Doing away with the surtax is another way for the CSAS to avoid traditional welfare approaches. To limit the value of CSAS benefits to high-income families, the government would count such benefits as taxable income.

By itself, a low-benefit CSAS would exert only a moderate impact on the welfare rolls and poverty. However, combining the CSAS with a refundable tax credit could reshape today's welfare system. The credit would replace the $2,000 personal exemption for children and heads of families and would involve minimal or zero net revenue costs. A credit of $350, or 17.5 percent of the exemption, would leave total tax revenues approximately constant. This change in the tax code could target benefits on low-income families fairly and without stigma or serious incentive effects. Allowing credits only for children and heads of families would limit the administrative burden of providing refundable credits. The decline in the top marginal rate to 28 percent substantially reduces the tax losses of middle- and high-income families in shifting from the exemption to the credit.[34] Finally, the EITC has already broken the precedent against making credits refundable.

For a mother and two children, the maximum credit and child-support assurance payments would equal $260 per month. These two amounts alone would well exceed AFDC levels in 10–12 states. In the other states, even a moderate amount of earnings would move people off welfare.

Mothers able to work half time at $4 per hour would be off welfare in all but a few states and have a total income of over $600 per month.

One may implement each of the CSAS approaches in a variety of ways. We simulate the impact of four alternatives shown in Table 8.6. The simulations assume no improvement in establishing child-support awards, in collecting payments, and in work effort induced by the program. If we expect progress over time in the establishment of awards, then we can interpret the low restricted plan as the short-run case and the low general plans as taking place in the long run, when nearly all mothers have awards.[35]

A major difficulty with estimating CSAS plans is the under-reporting of AFDC and child-support benefits. AFDC outlays for benefits were about $15.1 billion, or about $3 billion more than reported to Census interviewers. The $3 billion shortfall implies nonreporting (that more mother heads of families received AFDC), underreporting (the size of AFDC benefits were higher than reported), or both. Comparing Census with administrative data indicates that about 400,000–600,000 female heads of families received AFDC but did not report the benefits.[36] The vast majority of AFDC mothers not reporting benefits would show up in the simulations as receiving full or nearly full CSAS benefits with no AFDC reductions. In reality, these CSAS benefits would be almost entirely offset by AFDC reductions. Another upward bias results from underreporting of benefits by those who report receiving some AFDC payments. In the low general plan, adjusting for these sources of bias could reduce net outlays by about $1.7 billion.[37]

Table 8.6. Alternative child-support assured payment plans

Plan	Guarantee level	Surtax	Tax credit	Eligibility
Wisconsin model	High, $250/month, first child	Yes	No	Limited to those with awards
Low restricted	Low, $90/month, first child	No	No	Limited to those with awards
Low general	Low, $90/month, first child	No	No	All mothers with children from absent fathers
Low with credit	Low, $90/month, first child	No	Yes $90/month, mother and two children	All mothers with children from absent fathers

The estimates in Table 8.7 overstate net outlays for the following additional reasons:

· The CSAS could help persuade state legislatures and the public to adopt tougher enforcement mechanisms that can increase collections. However, the rise in support payments would be partly offset by increased collection costs.

· The CSAS would generate other savings, such as reductions in public housing costs and rent subsidies, and increased state income taxes.

· Under-reporting of child-support payments in the SIPP data would probably exceed the amount not discovered as part of the CSAS program.

· Less than 100 percent of eligible custodial parents would actually participate.

All the CSAS plans would reduce the poverty gap, the numbers of poor families and families on AFDC, and AFDC expenditures. Not surprisingly, approaches that exclude mothers with no support orders can be implemented at much lower cost, but have a lesser impact on poverty and welfare use. Of the three pure CSAS plans, the high-benefit Wisconsin plan channels the highest proportion of net outlays to poor families.

Table 8.7. Cost and impact of alternative CSAS approaches

Costs / benefits	Wisconsin model	Low restricted	Low general	Low general and tax credit
Net outlays[a]	$ 1.6	$ 1.1	$ 3.6	$ 2.5
Gross cost of CSAS component[a]	3.3	2.4	8.5	8.5
Reduction in AFDC outlays[a]	1.7	1.0	4.0	6.0
Reduction in poverty gap[a]	0.9	0.4	1.3	11.3
Reduction in number of poor families[b]	153	81	209	1,075
Reduction in number of AFDC families[b]	306	104	328	737

Source: Tabulations from the SIPP, waves 4–6.
a. In billions of dollars.
b. In thousands of families.

It reduces the AFDC rolls as much as the low general plan costing twice as much. The main drawbacks of the Wisconsin plan are that the benefit levels go beyond replacing what most fathers would owe and that the program's surtax adds a form of income testing to the program.

Combining the low-benefit CSAS with a revenue-neutral refundable tax credit would generate the largest impact on poverty, the poverty gap, and the welfare rolls. The two components would reshape the welfare system. Outlays on AFDC benefits would fall to about half of their current levels. AFDC rolls would decline by about 30 percent, and the remaining recipients would need much lower earnings to escape welfare. The two components would fill 45 percent of the poverty gap and reduce the proportion of families in poverty by 19 percent. And, despite the absence of direct income testing in either of the two components, the income gains to the poor would be over 5 times the net change in federal budget costs. Of the total income gains received by families who are net gainers from the program, over 60 percent would go to families below the poverty line.

Policy Implications

Child-support enforcement is an important tool for implementing the new consensus about welfare policy. Liberals and conservatives agree that absent fathers should pay more to support their children and that state governments should intensify their collection efforts. The question is, how can policy makers build on this consensus to achieve significant reductions in poverty and reliance on welfare programs?

Certainly, any increase in support payments makes work and independence from welfare more attractive to mothers heading families. Unlike welfare benefits, child-support payments do not decline with the mother's earnings, so they supplement the incomes of working mothers. Moreover, the potential for increased collections is large. If all absent fathers of welfare families paid 25 percent of their incomes in child support, payments to welfare mothers would increase thirteen-fold.

Unfortunately, incremental changes in enforcement procedures and in administrative resources can achieve only a modest improvement in the situation of poor one-parent families, whether on welfare or not. This is because child-support obligations are low and a high proportion of mothers lack any support award. Until now, state agencies have concentrated on collecting the amounts due under current awards. The job of establishing awards has proved far more difficult and costly.

The continuing effort to enforce existing obligations and establish new ones is necessary, but not sufficient. To reorient the welfare system and improve the income options of poor one-parent families, the country must move beyond the pure enforcement strategy. One step already under way is the development of income-related standards for setting support obligations. Requiring judges to impose awards in line with these standards will raise support payments and thus the incomes and independence of mothers heading families. Yet even this new policy will not bring about dramatic changes.

The best hope for achieving immediate and significant effects is to institute a CSAS program. Under it mothers would no longer have to bear the entire burden of the failure to collect on existing or potential obligations of the father. Custodial parents would receive some minimum assured benefit in lieu of support payments, and it would go to mothers not on the basis of their poverty, but because it was theirs by law. To insure the program remains distinct from welfare, assured benefits should not exceed what the vast majority (say, 70 to 90 percent) of mothers would have collected if the enforcement system operated effectively. This low-benefit program could accomplish much. If all mothers with absent parents were eligible, expenditures on the AFDC program would fall by one-third and 200,000 families would move out of poverty.

More promising results would derive from linking the CSAS with the substitution of a refundable personal tax credit that replaces and costs no more than the existing personal exemptions. Such a combined program could achieve much more dramatic effects while lowering the net costs to the government. Although the shift from exemptions to credits would involve a sizable redistribution of the tax burden, the net cost would be about $2.5 billion or less. The combined approach would move about 1 million families out of poverty, reduce the income deficit of the poor by $11 billion, and cause 30 percent of AFDC recipients to leave the rolls. Those left on AFDC would find it much easier to earn their way off welfare.

A breakthrough in welfare reform is politically and economically feasible. But it will require stretching the new consensus beyond child-support enforcement to include a modest assured-benefit program augmented by the replacement of personal exemptions with refundable tax credits.

Costs of Welfare Programs

Craig Thornton

Costs have always been a central concern in debates over welfare reform. This is to be expected given the growing pressures on government budgets, the resulting demands for program accountability, and the fact that annual expenditures for assisting able-bodied poor persons of working age and their children now exceed $90 billion. This concern is bolstered by the recognition that the costs of government assistance programs go well beyond directly measured program expenditures.

Today's policy makers face a major challenge in determining the relevant price tags for alternative reform proposals. The reform options are often complex and the cost implications uncertain. The budget estimates generally begin with evidence on costs and program impacts from ongoing or past programs or demonstrations. These estimates must be adjusted to reflect the anticipated changes in program design, context, targeting, and other program elements that will affect total expenditures. The uncertainty in the specification of reform options and in the available cost estimates renders the entire budgeting process more of an art than a science.

It is therefore useful, in this volume on welfare reform, to consider some basic issues of cost measurement as they apply to welfare policy and to summarize the best available estimates of the direct budgetary costs of the reform under consideration. This chapter summarizes some basic issues of cost measurement as they apply to welfare policy; presents estimates of the direct budgetary costs of the major components of welfare reform options; and concludes with discussions of some special issues in cost estimation and the role of this analysis in the policy debate.

Measuring the Costs of Welfare Policy

In estimating the costs of welfare policy options, analysts must focus on three basic cost elements: (1) the direct program expenditures, (2) expenditures on complementary programs (programs whose use follows from the use of the program under consideration), and (3) expenditures on substitute programs (the old programs to be displaced by the program under consideration). Total costs will equal the direct costs plus an increase in complementary-program costs less any reductions in costs to substitute programs.

In estimating the direct, complementary, and substitute costs of policy and program changes, it is important to consider these basic propositions: programs and policies are interrelated in ways that affect the costs of reform options; targeting decisions may affect both the level and time pattern of costs; programs are dynamic and thus the magnitude and nature of program costs may change over time; costs are relative; and there are important distributional issues in the allocation of costs across groups in society.

Interrelating. Program impacts and costs depend on each other in a variety of ways. Some links result from formal program regulations, while others work through the effects programs have on the decisions and actions of participants and taxpayers. For example, program regulations link the AFDC and Food Stamp programs in that the calculation of Food Stamp benefits is based on all household income, including AFDC payments. Training programs and job-search requirements affect the employment choices and opportunities of participants and, thus, the participation rates in income-support programs and in substitute and complementary education and employment services.

In addition, plans to expand services offered through one program may affect the level of services participants will receive through other sources. Many WIN programs, for example, rely on JTPA-funded programs to provide training to WIN participants. Budgets for an expansion of WIN must therefore consider whether there will be parallel increases in JTPA expenditures or whether additional WIN monies will be needed to pay for the desired service expansion. Because of these program interrelationships, the total costs of a program or policy change go beyond the direct expenditures made to implement that program or policy.

Targeting. The clientele of a program will affect costs in two ways. First, direct program costs will reflect the needs and abilities of the persons served. This is particularly true for education and training programs where costs can often be reduced by directing services toward those applicants who appear most ready or by screening out those persons who will need extensive remedial or support services. It is also true for transfer programs where attempts to target payments by changing eligibility criteria or benefit levels will affect program participation and exit rates. Second, targeting by one program can affect the costs of other programs. For example, increasing efforts to exclude the more employable applicants from the welfare rolls will increase the costs of training programs for welfare recipients.

The Dynamic Nature of Programs. Changes in welfare policies can have long-lasting impacts on recipients and government budgets and may thereby alter the time pattern of welfare participation and costs. Such policy changes also can affect the general level of economic growth by influencing the economic actions of welfare recipients and taxpayers. Furthermore, changing economic conditions, demographics, and social attitudes all affect participation in welfare and related programs, even in the absence of changes in program regulations.

Costs Are Relative. Throughout all budgeting efforts, costs must be measured against a specific alternative. Particular uses of resources count as costs only if those uses require that some other uses must be foregone. Generally, the costs of the proposed welfare reforms are measured relative to the costs that would be incurred under the status quo. However, costs can also be measured relative to other specific policy alternatives.

Distribution. The way costs are spread across groups in society is critical for assessing costs. Each group affected by welfare policy—federal, state, and local governments, welfare recipients, employers, and other persons in the economy—will view specific welfare expenditures differently. Allocations of costs among levels of government are particularly important because efforts by one level of government to reduce its costs may impose costs or savings on other levels. Such situations are most likely to arise when governments share the costs of a program (as in the case of the AFDC, Medicaid, and WIN programs) and changes in the federal matching rate are used to influence the actions and expenditures of state and local governments. In such cases, the cost estimates of any proposed change must account not only for the changing federal share of expenditures but also for the extent to which states will alter their expenditures in response to the new matching formula.

These issues imply that efforts to budget welfare reforms must follow a complex and multistep process. The particular components of the reforms, the conditions prevailing in the absence of any reform, and the ways in which recipients and potential recipients respond to the incentives and opportunities created by the reforms have been discussed in other chapters. I therefore turn here to estimates of the average operating costs for the principal welfare programs.

Estimates of Average Direct Budgetary Costs

The average direct budgetary cost of a program intervention describes the general level of resources needed to operate that program. This figure provides a useful basis for comparing the general intensity and scope of alternative programs and figures for several interventions can be combined to estimate the budgetary effects of potential changes in the welfare system. However, direct budgetary estimates alone are insufficient for judging the relative merits of various alternatives, because they ignore the indirect benefits and costs that are generated by the intervention, and they represent gross costs in the sense that they are not measured relative to any specific alternative.[1]

This section presents information about the estimated cost of three general categories of welfare reform policies: (1) benefit formulas and coverage policies of the major transfer programs; (2) other welfare policy interventions (employment, education and training, and related support services), and (3) nonwelfare policies (tax-based policies and child-support enforcement). Within each group, I have indicated the general level of direct expenditures needed to operate programs and noted the special issues pertaining to the costs of that type of program.[2]

Benefit Formula and Coverage Changes

Most persons associate welfare with the major transfer programs: AFDC, Food Stamps, and Medicaid.[3] These programs provide cash or in-kind benefits to eligible persons, with the level of benefits generally depending on the income and other circumstances of the household. Debate over welfare always addresses the benefit levels and coverage for these transfer programs. In FY1985 the seven transfer programs listed in Table 9.1 accounted for almost $50 billion in government expenditures. Thus the budgetary costs implied by changes in benefits or coverage for these programs attract considerable attention. For example, it would cost almost one-half billion dollars just to pay an additional $10 per month to all families currently receiving benefits from AFDC.

At the most basic level, costs for these programs are determined by the number of recipients and the average level of benefits. The number of recipients will depend on program entrance and exit rates, which in turn depend on the relative magnitudes of benefit levels and alternative employment opportunities as well as on general demographic trends. The average level of benefits is largely set by program regulations, although it can change in response to changes in household size and composition and to shifts in the average levels of earned and unearned income. Cost analysts need to consider how these factors might change over time with and without the proposed reform in order to estimate the net budgetary costs of the reform. Given the large number of factors and the complexity of modeling individuals' behavior (see Chapter 4 for a review of attempts to model how policy changes affect the employment decisions of recipients and potential recipients), it is clearly a difficult challenge to forecast the long-term costs of proposed reforms.

Further complicating this estimation process is the uncertainty about how some reforms will alter the structure of transfer programs. This is particularly true when the reforms are in the form of changes in the shares of program costs to be borne by various levels of government. For example, some efforts to increase AFDC benefits have sought to increase the share of benefit costs paid by the federal government, thereby inducing the states to pass along this increase in the form of higher benefits. Such a change has a direct effect that makes welfare benefits look cheaper to states, since states now receive more federal funds per state dollar expended. There is also an indirect effect because taxpayers in the state will have to contribute to the federal taxes needed to fund the federal share of any state benefit increases. The extent to which the offer of an increased federal share will lower the price of welfare benefits to a state, and hence lead to an expansion of benefits, will depend on the relative magnitudes of the direct and indirect effects as they are perceived by state governments.[4] Furthermore, the extent to which states will respond to such financial incentives is unclear. It is the need to estimate the net price and price elasticity of state demand for welfare payments that complicates the cost analyst's task.

Gramlich (1982) has estimated the extent to which states will respond to changes in the share of AFDC benefits paid by the federal government.

Table 9.1. Average gross budgetary costs of major transfer programs

Program	Number of participants (1000s)	Unit for cost estimate	Estimated average gross costs (1986 $)[a]			Base year[c]	Source
			Average cost	Low estimate[b]	High estimate[b]		
AFDC							
Cash benefits	3,747[d]	Family month	$ 352	$114	$ 569	CY86	U.S. House of Representatives (1987a), section 7, tables 13, 20
Emergency assistance	32.1	Family month	293	0	760	CY84	Social Security Adm. (1986), tables 204, 205
Food Stamps	19,910	Recipient month	46	—	—	FY85	Social Security Adm. (1986), table 206
General assistance	1,364	Recipient month	169	N.A.	N.A.	CY80	Social Security Adm. (1986), table 211
Medicaid[e]	15,234	Recipient month	51	N.A.	N.A.	FY85	Social Security Adm. (1986), tables 162, 164
School lunch[f]	23,700	Student school year	134	47	287	FY86	U.S. House of Representatives (1987a), p. 704

Energy Assistance							
Heating assistance	6,360	Household year	213	63	668	FY86	U.S. Department of Health and Human Services (1987), p. ix, table 12
Weatherization assistance[g]	191	Household assisted	1,011	N.A.	3,000	FY86	U.S. Department of Health and Human Services (1987), pp. 11, 26, and table 12

a. Costs have been adjusted to 1986 dollars using the implicit price deflator for gross national product.

b. The low and high estimates indicate the variation in average costs across programs. The range in costs across individual participants is generally larger than the range in the program estimates.

c. The year shown is the one for which the participation and original (unadjusted) cost estimates were made. FY indicates that the estimate was made for a fiscal year, CY indicates calendar year, and PY indicates program year.

d. The participation figure is average monthly enrollment. Because of caseload turnover, the number of families in a year will be larger.

e. The average costs and participation figures for Medicaid pertain to dependent children and adults in families with dependent children who received Medicaid benefits. The insurance value of Medicaid per person who receives AFDC benefits is less than the figures reported in the table.

f. School lunch subsidies depend on household income. Approximately half of the participants are from households with incomes below 130 percent of the poverty level. The average shown is the total expenditure divided by the number of children served. The high estimate is the total that would be received over a 9-month school year by a low-income student, given the fiscal 1986 subsidy level of $1.47 per lunch.

g. Because of the ways states treat administrative and other costs, the average benefit levels reported for weatherization assistance understate total expenditures. Minimum-benefit information is unavailable.

He estimated that if the federal government cut the effective price states had to pay for welfare benefits by a certain percentage, the states would respond by increasing their expenditures by the same percentage. However, such estimates are subject to considerable uncertainty that correspondingly introduces uncertainty in the overall budget estimates. Furthermore, the states' responses are likely to differ substantially between income transfer programs and service programs. In addition, as the recent state welfare reforms have shown, the responses can be strongly influenced by the political aspirations of state and local politicians and the level of attention focused on welfare issues in general.

Additional Welfare Interventions

Other important welfare policies and proposals are those that promote economic self-sufficiency through increasing employability and satisfactory performance on the job. They include incentives and regulations with regard to education, training and employment programs, and support services to facilitate participation in these activities. For the most part, these services require an up-front investment by the government. Table 9.2 indicates current available services and provides some estimates of their costs. The benefits of such investments are expected to accrue over the subsequent working lifetime of the participants. This time pattern of costs and benefits requires funders to use a long time horizon (five years or longer) to assess the true net budgetary costs of the investment.

Education and Training. Public schools represent our most extensive investment in human capital and provide a good reference point for assessing the direct expenditures for welfare-oriented education and training programs. Schools are generally available to all persons interested in getting a public education. Furthermore, funding for public education is high relative to the more remedial intervention services. However, many of those who constitute the poor and welfare-dependent populations have been rejected by the schools or have themselves rejected public education. Thus while public schools may be an important component of a welfare reform strategy, other education and training services will tend to predominate in the overall service plans associated with welfare reform.

The largest such initiatives for the disadvantaged and welfare dependent populations are those funded under CETA and JTPA. These pro-

Table 9.2. Average gross budgetary costs of education, training, and employment programs

Program	Number of participants (1000s)	Unit for cost estimate	Estimated average gross costs (1986 $)[a]			Base year[c]	Source
			Average cost	Low estimate[b]	High estimate[b]		
Public schools							
High school	12,357	Student year	$ 4,051	$2,400	$ 8,500	1985–86	U.S. Department of Education (1987), tables, 2, 98, 99
Post-secondary vocational[d]	1,687	Student	2,046	326	10,053	1980–81	U.S. Department of Education (1987), table 222
College, public 4-year	5,198	Student year	7,347	n.a.	n.a.	1983–84	U.S. Department of Education (1987), tables 122, 211
College, public 2-year	4,279	Student year	3,637	n.a.	n.a.	1983–84	U.S. Department of Education (1987), tables 122, 211
Education and training programs							
JTPA, title II-A programs	1,077	Participant	1,725	n.a.	n.a.	PY85	National Commission for Employment and Policy (1987), table C-1

Table 9.2 (continued)

Program	Number of participants (1000s)	Unit for cost estimate	Estimated average gross costs (1986 $)[a]			Base year[c]	Source
			Average cost	Low estimate[b]	High estimate[b]		
Job Corps[e]	103	Participant	9,288	7,000	17,000	PY86	U.S. Department of Labor (1987), section E
CETA[f]	626	Participant	2,863	n.a.	n.a.	FY80	Taggart (1981), pp. 24–25
NETWork[g]	—	Participant	1,737	—	—	FY88	U.S. House of Representatives (1987), p. 93
Job search assistance programs							
Title IV-A programs	36.9	Participant	188	41	549	FY85	U.S. General Accounting Office (1987), tables 3.2, 4.4
EOPP demonstration, job search only[h]	15.8	Participant	645	n.a.	n.a.	CY80	Long (1983), p. 91

Work experience programs

Program						
CWEP programs	19.5	Participant	439	56	6,977	FY85	U.S. General Accounting Office (1987), tables 3.2, 4.4
CETA, public service employment	378.2	Participant	4,603	n.a.	n.a.	FY80	Taggart (1981), p. 25
Supported work demonstration	2.5	Participant	13,045	n.a.	n.a.	1977–78	Manpower Demonstration Research Corporation (1980), table 2–7
West Virginia CWEP[i]	1.8	Participant	1,369	n.a.	n.a.	CY84	Friedlander, Erickson, Hamilton, and Knox (1986), p. 128

Targeted jobs tax credit

| Administration | 622 | Qualifying employee | 46 | n.a. | n.a. | FY85 | Levitan and Gallo (1986) |
| Tax-expenditures | 622 | Qualifying employee | 660 | 1[j] | 2,040[j] | FY85 | Levitan and Gallo (1986) |

Child care

| Cash expenditure employed mothers | 5,299 | Week of care, all children | 39 | n.a. | n.a. | 1984–85 | U.S. Bureau of the Census (1987), table 8 |

Table 9.2 (continued)

Program	Number of participants (1000s)	Unit for cost estimate	Estimated average gross costs (1986 $)[a]			Base year[c]	Source
			Average cost	Low estimate[b]	High estimate[b]		
WIN child care subsidies	714.4	Participant	34	0	416	FY1985	U.S. General Accounting Office (1987), tables 3.2, 5.3
EOPP child care expenditures	15.8	Participant week	30	5	76	CY80	Long (1983), p. 91–95

a. Costs have been adjusted to 1986 dollars using the implicit price deflator for gross national product.

b. The low and high estimates indicate the variation in average costs across programs. The range in costs across individual participants is generally larger than the range in the program estimates.

c. The year shown is the one for which the participation and original (unadjusted) cost estimates were made. FY indicates that the estimate was made for a fiscal year, CY indicates calendar year, and PY indicates program year.

d. Postsecondary vocational education costs are estimated on the basis of average charges for a course study. Because of subsidies to public programs, actual costs may exceed charges.

e. Job Corps data are for program year 1986 (PY86), July 2, 1986–June 30, 1987. The capital costs of Job Corps centers are not included in the average cost estimates.

f. CETA classroom and on-the-job training under Titles II-B and II-C.

g. These estimates were used by the CBO to estimate the budgetary costs of the NETwork program, a program that was anticipated to provide education, training, and other employment and support services to welfare recipients (see U.S. House of Representatives, 1987).

h. EOPP tested a welfare reform program that provided job-search assistance along with support services and limited subsidized employment for persons who did not find jobs in the private sector. Long (1983) estimated that the job-search assistance services could be provided at a cost of $645 per participant (1986 dollars) by an ongoing program. Actual job-search expenditures in the demonstration were approximately $1,270 per participant.

i. The West Virginia Community Work Experience Demonstration required able-bodied AFDC recipients to perform public service in exchange for their welfare payments. This program focused on men receiving benefits under the AFDC-U program and it required ongoing participation by welfare recipients.

j. These high and low estimates are for individual qualifying employees rather than different programs.

grams have been targeted primarily at disadvantaged adults and out-of-school youth, and have generally operated outside of the traditional school setting. As seen in Table 9.2, their average costs are in the range of $2,000 to $3,000 per participant, with the Job Corps Program standing out at over $9,000 per participant. The reasons for the high cost of the Job Corps are its residential setting and comprehensiveness. It also targets a particularly disadvantaged population.

Recent state welfare reform initiatives have emphasized increasing the use of employment and training programs for welfare recipients. While at this time there are no published cost estimates for these new initiatives, we have been able to tease out some estimates. The widely publicized ET program operating in Massachusetts estimates the costs per placement and provides data on placements, from which I have estimated that costs in FY1986 were about $1,100 per participant. However, the ET program has been serving an increasingly disadvantaged population over time, so the average cost per placement has nearly tripled (presumably producing a similar change in cost per participant).[5] Data from the Maryland Employment Initiatives program (Friedlander et al., 1985) suggest that average costs for those who participated in employment and training averaged at least $2,500.

These cost estimates from recent employment and training initiatives can be very helpful in assessing the likely costs of new education and training interventions. However, it is important to consider the implications of the characteristics of those who would receive services under the new programs with respect to the nature, intensity, and duration of services needed and the likely outcomes of the services. For example, the average costs for a program that attempts to serve a broad range of AFDC recipients are likely to exceed those observed for JTPA programs, which serve, in general, a more job-ready population.[6]

Furthermore, in assessing the reasonableness of investments in education and training, we should not judge them solely on the basis of their short-term direct costs. The use of limited-duration time horizons will understate or ignore potential long-term savings generated by program impacts on participants' employment and welfare receipt.

Employment Services and Programs. A variety of employment services and programs have been designed for low-income and welfare-dependent individuals. The three most common of these include job search assistance, work experience, and employer incentives to hire disadvantaged persons.

Job search assistance has been very popular, largely because of its relatively low cost. The assistance ranges from brief classroom instruction on job search techniques to job clubs and supervised job search, sometimes with a rich array of support services that include child care and transportation. The evidence as to the effectiveness of these programs is encouraging. First, because the programs are inexpensive, only modest impacts are needed to justify the programs on cost-benefit grounds. Second, the evidence suggests that many welfare recipients can obtain employment with only a small amount of assistance. The savings these programs can generate in the form of reduced welfare payments, increased tax payments, and reductions in the use of alternative social programs are important and should be considered in any policy decision regarding the role of job-search assistance programs in our welfare policy.

The costs of the programs funded under Title IV-A of the Social Security Act represent the best index of the costs of current job-search assistance programs. These costs, as reported in Table 9.2, range from a low of about $40 per participant to a high of $550 per participant, with the average program cost per participant being around $190. However, the figures reflect the limited funds available and the fact that the states (which operate these programs) must bear a higher fraction of their costs than they do for other work-related programs for welfare recipients. The average costs may thus reflect responses to available resources rather than explicit decisions about the level of resources needed to operate an effective job search program.

For budgeting future initiatives, it may be more appropriate to rely on some of the recent demonstration programs that have shown evidence of generating budgetary savings. The San Diego demonstration (Goldman et al., 1986) and the job search component of the EOPP demonstration (Brown et al., 1983) were newly designed programs targeted primarily at AFDC recipients. The costs of both programs exceeded even the most expensive of the Title IV-A programs, averaging $650 to $700.[7]

In judging the relevance of these different cost estimates for future program planning, cost analysts and policy makers must consider whether the greater costs of the newly designed programs are offset by even greater benefits as compared with the costs and benefits of the current (less expensive) programs. With a five-year time horizon, both of the demonstration programs appear to at least break even and may produce some budgetary savings. The lack of information about the impacts of the Title IV-A programs, however, makes it impossible to compare the net costs of the various models.

Work experience programs, the second major type of employment service, vary substantially in content and cost. The intent of these programs is to provide some employment experience so as to enhance the participants' employability and to enable welfare recipients to fulfill their reciprocal responsibility to the government by earning their grant.

Community Work Experience Programs (CWEP) are limited in duration and generally modest in scope. Their costs average between $500 and $1,500 per participant; these figures appear to correspond principally to the available resources. Other more extensive work experience programs, such as those funded under CETA and Supported Work programs, have been of longer duration, paid substantial stipends or wages, and sometimes included sizable support services. The costs of these more intensive interventions are orders of magnitude larger than those of the community work experience program.

In addition to the intensity of the intervention, the direct budgetary costs of work experience depend on whether the program pays wages or merely requires participants to work off their welfare grants. Costs also depend on the length of the intervention. Many of the state CWEP programs require thirteen weeks of participation. In contrast, the more expensive CWEP program in West Virginia required ongoing participation. Finally, costs depend on administrative decisions about who will be served and the degree to which participation will be mandatory. For example, it will be more expensive to serve mothers with young children because of the higher child-care costs, and efforts to enforce mandatory participation requirements will likely increase the costs of administration and services because a greater number of severely disadvantaged and unmotivated individuals must participate.

As in the case of job-search assistance interventions, the various work experience programs also lack comparable impact and cost information, making it difficult to measure relative program costs. For example, we have good evidence from the Supported Work demonstration (Kemper, Long, and Thornton, 1984) that the costly, structured work experience provided to AFDC recipients in that demonstration led to net budgetary savings. What we do not know is whether a more modest effort also would have generated net savings.

Quite a different strategy for promoting work experience among welfare recipients has been the use of the Targeted Jobs Tax Credit. This is in effect a subsidy paid to employers who hire disadvantaged workers. The credit equals a fraction of a worker's wages up to a ceiling of $6,000. Because the credit reduces the normal deduction an employer would take for wages paid to employees, its value (and cost to the government) depends on the marginal tax rate of the employer. Levitan and Gallo (1986) report that the best available evidence suggests that the average cost is about $700 per qualifying employee. They add, however, that this estimate is imprecise since the various published estimates of expenditures and participation are inconsistent. The effectiveness of these credits is clouded further by lack of evidence as to their ability to increase employment and reduce welfare dependence.

A variety of support services is needed to enable low-income persons to participate and succeed in employment and in education and training programs. The most critical such services are child care and transportation. However, other services that have been provided include case management, health services, counseling, mental health services, family planning assistance, emergency assistance, provision of work uniforms and tools, and substance-abuse counseling. Depending on how many services and how much of each service the program participants use, these support services can add substantially to education, employment, and training program costs.

Child care in particular can increase the costs. Among employed mothers in general, the average weekly cash expenditure for child care is approximately $40.[8] For employment and training programs, which may emphasize center-based child care to a greater extent than within the general population of working mothers, the costs are likely to be greater. For example, the ET program in Massachusetts, which spends approximately 40 percent of its budget on child care, allocates almost $3,600 per child-care slot (Massachusetts Taxpayers Foundation, 1987). Obviously, if many program participants do not need child care or find alternative arrangements, the costs of offering child care can be modest. In the current WIN programs, child-care costs averaged across all participants were generally less than $50. In the EOPP demonstration (Long, 1983), child-care costs for persons in job search assistance average almost $30 a week (in 1986 dollars), but were as low as $5 per week in one of the ten EOPP projects.

While child care is likely to be the major support service provided by employment and training programs for welfare populations, other supports can also be substantial, although such costs are likely to vary greatly. Again, the EOPP demonstration provides some useful estimates. Long (1983) found that the average expenditure for transportation and other support services (excluding child care) was almost $100 per month of enrollment. However, the range for the ten projects was from zero to $220 per month.

Nonwelfare Policies

Nonwelfare interventions to mitigate the nation's poverty and welfare dependency problems include tax-relief policies and child-support payment reforms. Table 9.3 contains cost estimates relevant to these types of reform options.

The major welfare tax-based policy is the EITC, a refundable credit available to low-income workers with at least one child. Workers can choose to receive the credit in a lump sum tax refund or may file to have a prorated amount added to their regular paychecks. The other major tax credit program is the Dependent Care Credit, although this credit is not widely used by low-income taxpayers (U.S. House of Representatives, 1987a).[9]

Costs for tax-credit programs are determined by the earning and expenditure patterns of eligible taxpayers, the amount of the credit, and the rate at which the credit is faded out as income rises. The credit equals 14 percent of eligible earnings and is phased out once earnings exceed a specified level. Both the level of eligible earnings and the phase-out level are indexed to inflation. In 1984 the maximum credit was $550, and the average value of the credit received by the more than 6 million households who benefited from this program was approximately $250.

In developing program budgets, analysts also need to determine what fraction of the credit will be refunded to individuals and what fraction will offset taxes owed by individuals. The first amount will constitute an outlay of cash, while the second is a tax expenditure that reduces government revenues. Currently, 80 percent of the credit is actually paid out as refunds. In addition, analysts will have to consider how the tax credit affects expenditures for other programs. The EITC is counted as income by the AFDC and Food Stamp programs and will therefore reduce those benefits to households that receive the credit.

As Lerman mentioned in Chapter 8 above, there has been a growing interest in enforcing child-support payments as a component of welfare policy. Through such enforcement the government assists custodial parents to obtain court-ordered support payments from absent parents. States can use a variety of methods to obtain the payments, including withholdings from the absent parent's paycheck or tax refund. These programs serve virtually all AFDC recipients and can serve other parents with formal support awards or agreements. AFDC recipients must assign their rights to support to the welfare agency as a condition of eligibility, and the amounts collected can be used by states to offset the costs for AFDC payments.

Table 9.3. Average gross budgetary costs of nonwelfare reform options

Program	Number of participants (1000s)	Unit for cost estimate	Estimated average gross costs (1986 $)[a]			Base year[c]	Source
			Average cost	Low estimate[b]	High estimate[b]		
Tax policies							
Earned-income tax credit[d]	6,376	Family year	$239.00	$1.00	$800.00	CY84	U.S. House of Representatives (1987a), p. 610
Child support enforcement							
Paternity determination	245	Determination	460.00	n.a.	n.a.	FY86	U.S. House of Representatives (1987a), p. 475, and (1987b), p. 99
Enforcement, AFDC families[e]	609	AFDC dollar collected[f]	0.76	0.23	3.70	FY86	U.S. House of Representatives (1987a), pp. 472, 483.

a. Costs have been adjusted to 1986 dollars using the implicit price deflator for gross national product.

b. The low and high estimates indicate the variation in average costs across programs. The range in costs across individual participants is generally larger than the range in the program estimates.

c. The year shown is the one for which the participation and original (unadjusted) cost estimates were made. FY indicates that the estimate was made for a fiscal year, CY indicates calendar year, and PY indicates program year.

d. The EITC is a national program; the high and low estimates indicate the range for individual taxpayers, not for programs.

e. Although this program serves AFDC and non-AFDC households, the figures in the table pertain to AFDC families. The number of participants shown is the average number of AFDC child-support enforcement cases in which a collection was made. In fiscal 1986, these collections totaled $1.2 billion. Published estimates are unavailable, but these figures suggest that the average amount collected for an AFDC family would be approximately $168 per month in those cases where a collection was made. Collections are made for about 16 percent of AFDC cases.

f. The overall program spends 30 cents for every support dollar collected, when all collections are combined. Because two-thirds of collections go to non-AFDC households, the administrative cost per dollar of AFDC child-support collections is higher (as shown in the table).

Child-support payment enforcement has become a major activity. In FY1986 the CSEP spent almost $940 million to collect over $3 billion in support payments. On average, collections are made for 1.4 million individual awards (AFDC and other cases) and these collections offset over 7 percent of the AFDC payments. Overall, the program spends about 30 cents to collect a dollar of support. However, because almost two-thirds of the collections go to non-AFDC parents, the administrative cost per dollar collected for an AFDC family is approximately 75 cents.

Many factors influence program costs and the ability to recover payments from absent parents. These include the level of support awards, the costs of determining paternity and obtaining support awards, the extent to which absent parents voluntarily comply with the support orders, the number of absent parents located and forced to comply, and the effects of the enforcement actions on the labor-market activities of custodial and absent parents. Issues of distribution may arise to the extent that the federal government provides incentive payments to the states to expand their enforcement practices.

Because of the AFDC offsets of child-support payments, enforcement programs have the potential of creating net budgetary savings, even though child support will not eliminate the need for welfare expenditures by government. In addition, Garfinkel (1988) indicates that these programs have the potential to generate sufficient savings so that support enforcement could be combined with assured minimum benefit levels and still operate at a net savings to the government.

Special Issues in Cost Estimation

Two special issues relate to the methods for developing reasonable cost estimates for the types of reform options currently under consideration—the relevant time period over which the costs and impacts of reforms should be considered and the fixed costs associated with the start-up of a new program or policy.

Appropriate Time Periods

Welfare policies are implemented over time and can have long-lasting impacts on recipients and government budgets. This is true of education and training programs that invest in the recipients and of income-maintenance programs that affect the decisions recipients make about their schooling and labor-force participation. As a result, estimates of costs need to consider how changes in the welfare system will manifest themselves over time.

In making cost estimates for proposed changes to welfare (or other government programs), the CBO is mandated to use a five-year time horizon. This is a reasonable procedure given the difficulty in estimating what a program will look like over time and in estimating the alternative situation into the future. Furthermore, the dynamic nature of public policy makes a five-year span reasonable, since it is a rare program that goes more than five years without modification.

Nevertheless, programs may have far-reaching effects even if the program is eliminated before the five years are over. Education and training programs aim to influence the overall employability of participants over their remaining work life. Similarly, the decisions individuals make about marriage and family formation, decisions that are influenced by welfare programs, will have impacts lasting long into the future.

Thus while limits on the time period used to assess the cost implications of policy changes render the estimation process tractable, they may also make it difficult to capture the true long-term effects of programs.[10] This limitation on the estimation process is generally recognized and is sometimes exploited, as when supporters of a new program design it so that its major costs will not appear until the sixth year after implementation.

It should also be noted that the cost estimates need to account for inflation over time. This is generally done based on projections of a broad-based price index like the implicit price deflator for gross national product, or components of this index such as the one for government services (these estimates are regularly reported by the Council of Economic Advisers in *Economic Indicators*).

Another issue involving time is that of discounting future costs; that is, accounting for the potential return from invested funds that could be earned over time. Because of these potential returns, expenditures that do not have to be made until some date in the future are less costly than the same expenditures made in the present period. Discounting is particularly important when one is comparing several alternative programs that have different time patterns of expenditures.[11]

Although the effect of discounting expenditures over a five-year period is not huge, it can make a difference. A single payment made immediately would cost approximately 13 percent more than a similar nominal expenditure spread out over five years (assuming that the rate of interest, net of inflation, is 5 percent per annum). Such a difference could influence decisions about the relative merits of alternative programs.

Start-Up Costs

A clear problem for program budgeters is to estimate the one-time costs involved in initiating a new program. These can be substantial. For example, the Social Security Administration worked for fourteen months on setting up the SSI program before making any payments. The cost of the preparation is difficult to estimate, since start-up costs were certainly incurred even after payments began.[12] However, if only the costs incurred during the preparatory phase are included, over $45 million (in 1975 dollars) were spent on start-up.

A similar problem arises from the use of cost estimates based on demonstration or prototype programs. These programs will experience the typical array of start-up costs as they begin operations. However, even after a demonstration is operational, its costs may exceed those of non-demonstration programs that provide the same services. The extra costs may be imposed by the research and evaluation activities of the demonstration or may reflect other features of a demonstration that would not be replicated in an ongoing program. For example, demonstrations often must expend greater than normal outreach and recruiting costs in order to convince eligible persons to enroll in a new and essentially untried program. Such demonstration-specific costs must be taken into account when budgeting from the cost experience of a demonstration or prototype program.

The Role of Cost Estimation in the Policy Debate

The challenge facing budget analysts is to provide point estimates of program costs that accurately capture the trade-offs implicit in decisions about welfare reform (or other public policy). Such estimates can be of enormous value to policy makers responsible for using government resources to satisfy the needs and desires of the public, because the estimates serve as a convenient shorthand for characterizing the magnitude of different alternatives.

In the last ten years policy makers have come to rely on cost and evaluation information, and the quality of the cost and impact estimates has risen. Today, the various congressional and administration budget analysts regularly produce cost estimates based on an impressively broad range of data and analyses. Given the number of alternative policies and programs whose costs must be estimated, the limitations of currently available data, and the rapid turnaround often needed in the estimation process, this is a remarkable accomplishment, one that only other researchers who work with cost issues can appreciate fully. In part, improvements in cost estimates are due to the increased availability of rigorously derived cost and impact data from the social experiments and analyses of the last twenty-five years. This has increased the precision of cost estimates (at least when compared with other information about the policy options) so that such estimates are more widely accepted and used. The greater use of cost estimates also reflects the growing use of budget targets as means of monitoring and controlling the overall spending of governments.

Despite these improvements, substantial uncertainty remains in the cost estimation process. Even the best available evidence is still deficient in many areas, particularly when programs are being extended to populations that those programs have not served previously. Also, many assumptions and approximations are necessary to render the estimation process tractable, but their use can bias the estimates. In general, the estimates are sufficiently precise to compare policies or programs of a similar nature. However, they are less reliable measures for comparing proposals with substantially different mixes of programs, due to the differences in the sources and degrees of uncertainty in cost estimates for different types of programs.

Demands for improving cost estimates will continue. Analysts need better information about many program effects and costs, particularly those for complementary and substitute programs. There is a continuing need for good information about the responses of states and local governments to changes in federal regulations and matching rates. More disaggregated cost information that indicates how costs vary for specific program components and target populations would be valuable for extrapolating beyond the specific programs that have been tested.

Beside estimates, we need information about the real benefits and costs of the various programs, particularly those that occur beyond the first two years following a person's enrollment in a program. This benefit-cost information includes the net effects on budgetary costs and the net effects on recipients and other persons in society. Moving beyond budgetary costs is particularly important, so as to avoid the dangerously exclusive focus on costs and benefits that accrue to the government. Policy makers will have to be careful to keep in mind the humanitarian objectives of social programs if they are to make good judgments about the appropriate course of welfare reform.

Conclusion

David T. Ellwood

Fifteen years ago, the primary focus of these essays might have been on the negative income tax, with worries of guarantees, tax rates, incentives, and cost in the forefront. In the pages above the negative income tax hardly even came up. Indeed, in policy discussions today, it often seems that the most damaging attack that one can make on some new plan is to call it just a negative income tax in disguise. And surprisingly little attention was given to guarantees, tax rates, or even incentives. Cost remained ever-present. Fiscal limits, indeed, probably loomed even larger than they might have a decade and a half previously. Even so, the predominant focus was on welfare dependency and ways in which to help people move into positions of self-support. The authors often invoked American values, of work and responsibility and obligations. To be sure, such matters were at the head of much political and popular debate in the early 1970s, but were not discussed so overtly and directly by academics and policy analysts.

Goals, Dilemmas, and Directions

The question of goals was raised several times, by the authors and in the discussion surrounding them, often in the context of a difficult choice: "Are we trying to reduce poverty or are we trying to reduce dependency?" In a context of traditional income support through means tested programs, this question poses the almost hopeless dilemma of adequacy versus dependency. The obvious way to reduce poverty is to raise welfare benefits. But higher benefits almost inevitably increase welfare use and the length of time people are on welfare, and they do lead to some reduction in work. And even if they did not, more generous benefits would mean that applicants with somewhat higher incomes would qualify for assistance, thereby increasing welfare use. Conversely, the obvious antidote to dependence is to cut back dramatically on welfare. So we apparently must decide whether to worry about current poverty or longer dependency.

Rather than wrestle with this dilemma, most authors side-stepped it by setting the combined goal of reducing both poverty and dependence on welfare. The ideal appears to be a world where people can realistically support themselves above the poverty line without the need for welfare. The notion of moving healthy welfare recipients toward a more transitional program seemed remarkably uncontroversial, at least in principle. The real questions were not what we sought to achieve, but how we might proceed, whether one or another program would work, and the like. This implicit agreement on the basic goal of social policy should not be passed over lightly, for broad agreement on the goals makes for a more productive debate. Pragmatism and empirical evidence may be able to play a much more powerful role if success can be measured by a uniform yardstick.

But is it really possible to avoid the adequacy/dependency dilemma? In the end the authors reveal more than a little skepticism about how far we could really move in the direction of reducing both poverty and welfare use. And if there are no magic bullets, or if the bullets cost a great deal, then the weakness of the consensus in principle becomes readily apparent. Those who worry mostly about poverty are willing to talk of obligations as a way of increasing future earning potential and legitimizing more generous welfare benefits. Those who worry about dependency talk about the need to deter welfare use. If obligations seem to serve little role in increasing earnings, then the need to fight over the benefit levels arises just as before. Yet the authors did share some ideas that could genuinely change the dimensions of poverty and welfare. Let me review some key themes.

Three Policy Streams

The first set of alternatives amounted to a strategy of fixing the welfare system. Its proponents explored mixing work and welfare, adding more training, imposing new obligations, altering case-management methods, adding more support services, targeting services more effectively, or making some other adjustment in hopes of transforming welfare into a more transitional and more politically acceptable form of support.

The second set of ideas involved reliance on nonwelfare supports. These included expanded health benefits outside the welfare system, wage subsidies, expanded EITC, child-support assurance policies, making the child-care tax credit refundable, and changing the personal exemption into a refundable tax credit. Generally, those favoring the first line emphasized the incremental nature and the direct and immediate applicability of their approach. Those favoring the second stream talked about the limitations of the first to reduce either poverty or welfare use.

Loïc Wacquant and William Julius Wilson introduced a third theme. They argued eloquently that unless far more ambitious reforms were made in macroeconomic policies, in the number and types of jobs that were available, and in the social and educational structure of our cities, the problems of poverty—especially ghetto poverty—would remain. The third stream then involved reorientation in overall economic, educational, and social policies.

In evaluating these strategies, the authors had to consider more than the primary goal—to reduce poverty and welfare use and increase earnings. In addition, political and fiscal feasibility were much discussed, as they always are in any examination of welfare reform proposals. And happily, more than lip service was paid to administrative feasibility as well. In Chapter 7 Nightingale faced the issue head on, and forced consideration not only of what is involved in changing the operation of a particular agency or bureaucracy, but also of how the nature of poverty problems created complex interactions among agencies and institutions that would interfere with any attempted changes.

Two other goals or criteria that are not so often discussed commanded a remarkable amount of attention. The normative message that the system conveyed about what the society valued and condemned struck many authors and conference participants as vital. And several chapters touched on the psychological and social perception of recipients—the feel of the system for those who are in it. These insights did suggest a move away from what some have labelled a purely technocratic approach to one that also explores more difficult questions involving ethics, philosophy, and social norms. Let me now explore each of the three streams in more detail.

Stream 1: Fix the Welfare System

Education and Training

Chapter 4 and the comment following it looked specifically at the use of education and training for welfare recipients. The appeal of human investment strategies is transparent. If we can train people so that they fare better in the marketplace, we can encourage work and reduce dependency simultaneously. The critical question, though, is: do training programs really work?

A wide variety of education and training strategies have been tried. They range from relatively inexpensive job-search or job-club strategies designed to help people be more effective and confident in their attempts to locate employment, to the intensive and expensive supported-work program where people faced gradually escalating goals and expectations. The authors reviewed a large literature on the costs and impacts of experimental and nonexperimental programs.

Many strategies have had some positive effect, and more expensive interventions typically had larger impacts than less costly ones. Still by many measures the impacts were modest. The much heralded work-welfare demonstrations rarely produced annual average earnings gains of more than a few hundred dollars. Even the supported-work program, which costs, according to Thornton (Chapter 9), over $13,000 per participant, produced earnings gains of about $1,500 per year. This is a substantial gain relative to the $3,300 earnings of the control group, yet the average combined earnings would still leave a family of three with income at only half the poverty line. And the programs that are currently contemplated in most welfare reform proposals look far more like the work-welfare demonstrations than supported work.

A strong macroeconomic picture also seemed critical if the programs were to achieve any real success. Otherwise, even if welfare recipients do find jobs, they may only push other disadvantaged persons into unemployment. But it is hard to know how to achieve an economy of high growth and low unemployment. Thus some authors expressed considerable skepticism about whether the current incremental welfare reform strategies are likely to reduce poverty or dependence.

Others saw in the data a basis for some optimism. In a host of experimental results, benefits have exceeded costs. Even though not too many lives were transformed, the process of converting welfare into a transitional system did begin. Past efforts have been deficient in a number of ways, including low funding, poor public and private coordination, perverse incentives, and the like. Such programs are rarely allowed the years of stability necessary to operate effectively and efficiently. The programs with small average benefits often served only a small fraction of the "treatment" group; and gains (and costs) per actual participant would be higher.

Perhaps the most forceful argument for investing in training was the lack of a real alternative. Should people be left to languish in poverty and welfare with little hope for the future simply because the cost-benefit ratio wasn't high enough? Some authors noted that sending the signal that the system cared about the poor and wanted and expected people to eventually regain economic control of their lives would in itself be a remarkable reform indeed.

Targeting

Douglas Besharov (Chapter 5) summarizes the existing studies on long-term welfare use and targeting. There seems to be a large degree of consensus in the literature that for many people welfare is already a relatively short-term, transitional program. But a smaller group stays on welfare for quite a long time. And this long-term group consumes a very disproportionate share of the resources spent on welfare. The durations of welfare receipt follow predictable patterns. Divorced women, those with previous work experience, good educations, and smaller and older families seem far less likely to be long-term users. By contrast, women who enter welfare as young, never-married mothers and have limited education or experience, typically fare much worse. If one could target the prospectively long-term recipient, one might both help the most disadvantaged and reduce the expenditures of the most expensive subgroup.

The potential benefits of targeting were raised repeatedly. Unfortunately, the programmatic evidence that can be used to decide whether it really works is very limited. Besharov places particular emphasis on the problems of never-married mothers with young children. Past efforts have typically exempted persons with young children from participation requirements, so there is little basis for deciding just what is the best way to help. Social and supportive services may be quite critical for this group, yet very little is known about their effectiveness. Moreover, the kind of intensive training and services, including preschool day care, could be expensive. Fortunately, a major experiment is now getting under way, and it is designed to see what programs work for young mothers.

One issue relevant to targeting merits special concern. Some states, notably Massachusetts and California, have begun to impose rules on their staff or contractors regarding the wage level of jobs that people could be placed into. Administrators properly noted that low-paying jobs often are not economically secure enough to provide a long-term alternative to welfare. Yet the pressure to place people in higher-paying jobs will almost inevitably push the system toward trying to place the least needy—the people who would be relatively short-term recipients anyway—and short-circuit the targeting efforts for the most disadvantaged.

Likewise, efforts to serve AFDC recipients must address their low basic skills. For example, it is estimated that 61 percent of the California caseload lacks the basic literacy skills necessary to move directly into job training or employment. Especially given the modest results of training and education programs, it is likely to be very hard to place such people in $5 or $6 or $7 per-hour jobs with good medical protection.

A second issue concerns the dangers of singling out some groups for special attention. Those who work with young mothers reported that they often lack contact and are isolated from the so-called mainstream. Unless it is done carefully, targeting could serve to increase the sense of isolation. It may be quite important to have mothers who are likely to move off welfare quickly mixed with those who are unlikely to do so, because the former group can serve as role models and provide job contacts. Programs targeted only on the most needy may stigmatize as they seek to aid. And the political viability of aid focused strictly on this group is also questionable.

Obligations

The imposition of some new obligations or responsibilities on those receiving welfare in exchange for greater training or other support is now a common theme in welfare reform proposals. Terms like "social contract" or "mutual obligations" pepper nearly all the recent task force reports on welfare. The American Enterprise Institute task force went so far as to claim that there is a new consensus among liberals and conservatives to this effect. The hope is that by asking everyone to do more, welfare will move in a more transitional direction. Yet the consensus wears thin when one actually determines what is to be mandated on each party. Concerns about dignity on the one hand and fiscal realities on the other seem to temper the actual proposals.

Surprisingly, there is little disagreement about the issue of obligations in this volume. In part that may reflect the fact that truly mandatory programs in which everyone actually did some demanding activity have never really been implemented in the AFDC program. Modest participation requirements have a long history, but there have always been ways to escape the requirements. Current mandatory programs allow far less avoidance, but they still do not look particularly onerous. Indeed, it might be argued that they place greater burdens on administrators than on recipients. Some experimental evidence seems to show that clients do not resent requirements and thus might well participate in many of the activities voluntarily. If "hard workfare" were ever seriously proposed, of course, it might be more controversial.

Support Services

Denise Polit and Joseph O'Hara did what many might have considered impossible—they summarized what we know about the role of support services and social services in helping to move welfare toward a more transitional system. Positions on whether such services are essential or peripheral are held with almost religious fervor, yet the available research is limited indeed. The only point of general agreement is that the direct costs of quality support services, especially for women with young children, can be extremely high.

Those who advocate support services argue that common sense and even a brief exposure to real clients ought to convince skeptics of the need. How can a woman go to work if she has no day care for her child or if the fear of medical catastrophe lurks in the background? Those who denigrate the notion that government must provide such services point out that millions of low-income mothers are already working without government help. The logic behind both positions seems solid, so strong evidence is needed to help make decisions. Polit and O'Hara (Chapter 6) identified a considerable number of studies that do meet at least a minimal level of scientific standards.

In the child-care area, they pointed to one randomized controlled experiment and a variety of less rigorous studies that suggested day care might indeed play a key role in employment; at the conference,

New York City work-welfare experience suggested day care was critical, but welfare administrators in other states did not always use all the money allocated for child care in specific programs. Several authors also hinted that failure to provide day care could give clients a way to avoid mandatory participation requirements, since courts will often refuse to allow programs to sanction a woman for noncompliance if she can claim she could not get adequate child care.

Nearly everyone seemed to agree that there is little hard evidence to date to support or refute the anecdotal information suggesting that lack of medical protection may be a serious deterrent to work. Transportation services got relatively little attention and there was even less evidence on their importance.

In many respects the appeal of support services is the same as the appeal of training: if effective, they may significantly enhance income and independence. The idea of support has great normative and psychological appeal. Medical protection and help for children is an integrating rather than isolating policy. And some among us pointed out that medical protection and child care could be done outside the welfare system entirely—a move that appeals to the advocates of nonwelfare supports (Stream 2). Medical protection doesn't have to be tied to the welfare system—indeed, this is the only industrialized country where it is. It was also suggested that Head Start or other preschool education programs could serve the dual role of aiding children and promoting the long-term work success of mothers.

Case management is a way to coordinate a diverse set of services and support and to insure that a single person is available to monitor and reinforce the efforts of a client in the welfare system. Case managers are to perform many of the duties expected of social workers in a previous generation: offering help, being the primary point of contact with the system, perhaps even providing a role model.

Welfare administrators have expressed considerable interest in the case-management concept. The various training and support services might work far more effectively under this more comprehensive approach. At the same time, they emphasize what a significant change this system would be from the current system in most states, where specialists handle each aspect of a client's case. The administrators expressed a fear that current personnel is not equipped to handle such new responsibilities. Given the considerable difficulty and cost in switching to such a system, evidence on its effectiveness and proper management would be quite helpful. Polit and O'Hara (Chapter 6) note that there is some positive evidence on the impact of case management. Generally it seemed to be a promising but yet unproven avenue.

One area worthy of much greater attention is the problems of serving the increasingly large Hispanic population. Hispanics now constitute 50% of New York City's caseload, and this group is growing rapidly as a proportion of the caseload in Massachusetts. Considerable uncertainty apparently remains about how to best help these persons, about what services they need, about the efficacy of English as a second language programs. Moreover, there appears to be a shortage of providers able to serve them. Arguably, training and employment services might be more effective if they were designed to meet the specific needs of this group.

Expanded Benefits and Eligibility

I have already noted the rather remarkable fact that expansion of benefits and eligibility standards hardly arose here. Reischauer certainly noted the issue, and expansion remains important in the current welfare reform proposals. A few people mentioned the desirability of moving to more uniform levels of AFDC benefits across states and the need to extend welfare benefits to two-parent families with an unemployed parent. Yet there was little talk of indexing, of extending welfare to working poor families, or even of reinstating the work incentives which were removed during the 1981 OBRA legislation.

Overall, little enthusiasm was voiced for welfare as the primary tool for income support of the poor; welfare seemed desirable only because there was not much of an alternative. The poor ought to be aided and protected. At the same time, few voices argued for a more reasonable, less invasive, more generous, less stigmatizing system. One can speculate that such debates make little sense in a political environment so hostile to welfare expansion. But certainly among those emphasizing nonwelfare (Stream 2) approaches, and even among those favoring reformist (Stream 1) approaches, there seemed to be a deeper suspicion that welfare, if not part of the problem, was not really a large part of the solution either. The welfare battles this group wanted to fight had to do with ways to help people off welfare, not ways to make welfare more humane or more adequate.

Taken together, the reform proposals clearly would have some immediate and measurable effect in increasing earnings and reducing welfare use. In terms of demonstrated improvements and alterations in the basic structure of the welfare system, Reischauer (Chapter 1) is no doubt correct when he dubs the package "welfare revision" more than welfare reform—a term that even the most vocal proponents of this approach could accept.

The appeal of these improvements runs deeper, though, than their demonstrated yet modest effect in reducing dependency. They mark the beginning of what could be a rather profound change in the nature of the welfare system—a change that begins the process of converting public assistance from a passive income support system to a more active system designed to move people into positions of greater independence. Clients may have a different view of the system and a different set of expectations for themselves if put in a more proactive environment. They may begin to take more responsibility for, and have greater hope and expectations of, themselves. Welfare might even become less stigmatizing.

In states like Massachusetts there is clear evidence that the public's perception of welfare has changed now that the system seems to be helping people help themselves rather than merely providing income to those who are poor. This good will may translate into increased generosity. In Massachusetts, for example, benefits have been raised by nearly 50 percent over the past few years. And nationally, in the final years of an extremely conservative administration and in a period of unprecedented fiscal pressures, we may yet pass welfare reforms that commit the government to greater support for the poor. Thornton (Chapter 9) makes it clear that Stream 1 approaches come in a wide variety of shapes and costs. The political process can, therefore, pick and choose among them and still make some difference. Indeed, the strongest argument for the reformist approaches may be that they are practical and incremental.

If the money provided is modest and the mandated changes are limited to those discussed under Stream 1, welfare will not be fundamentally changed into the transitional system that constitutes the collective dream of many current reformers. Nightingale (Chapter 7) shows very clearly how many actors and constituencies are involved. Welfare reformed, when it is sifted through this administrative filter, may not look or feel all that different. But there is hope that it may be the first step of a longer process. And frankly, even if reforms do nothing more than improve the public perception and increase our investments in the poor, these are more positive steps than we have taken in quite some time.

Stream 2: Nonwelfare Alternatives

Many of the authors favored an agenda that extended far beyond welfare revision, by promoting nonwelfare approaches to reform. Logically, a very wide range of policies could legitimately be classified as nonwelfare aid—including wage subsidies, expanded tax credits, child support, medical protection (if provided outside the welfare system), Head Start, and macroeconomic reform. For descriptive purposes, I will classify as Stream 2 all policies that would bring immediate aid to at least some segment of the poverty population. Thus changes in the Earned Income Tax Credit or expansion of the child support system, even expanded medical protection, would count as nonwelfare approaches. Reserved for Stream 3 would be social, educational, and economic reforms that would seek to strengthen the position of the poor over the long run.

Support for the wider approach emanated from three rather different frustrations with Stream 1 policies. First, there is little evidence that the fix-welfare programs alone will substantially improve the earning prospects of those on welfare. Second, Danziger (Chapter 2) emphasizes that a large fraction of the poor are not even in the welfare system. So even if the changes were extremely successful, they would not help a majority of the poor. Moreover, the left-out groups, notably the working poor, are generally considered to present a far more sympathetic face than the welfare poor. Finally, welfare-based policies seem to create major value conflicts, whereas broader strategies may be far more likely to garner long-term public support. According to this view, programs like Social Security have been very successful in reducing poverty among the elderly precisely because some redistribution was embedded in a broader program which aided the middle class.

Those who opposed the wider approach argued the reforms were expensive and impractical, and often were just disguised versions of old and defeated ideas like the negative income tax. Their fear was that pie-in-the-sky reform proposals would again derail practical, though more modest, improvements in the system. Let us examine some of those proposals.

Policies Designed Specifically to Help the Working Poor

The working poor were not the primary focus of this volume, but a number of the writers emphasized the dilemmas posed by ignoring them. Danziger (Chapter 2) points out that poverty among married couples and their families worsened because of falling market income and tax changes between 1979 and 1985. Many of these families are poor even though they have a full time worker. Indeed, even one full-time and one half-time job at the minimum wage will not push a family of four out of poverty.

Poverty among the working poor is particularly hard to justify at a time when we are trying to encourage those on welfare to begin working. What normative messages do our social policies send if single parents on welfare are often as well or better off than two-parent families with someone working? And how can we ask welfare recipients to work if work does not guarantee a route out of poverty?

According to Reischauer, help to the working poor often seems far more palatable to the body politic than aid for other groups. Witness the massive improvements in tax policies for this group that came out of the last set of tax reforms. Still, in evaluating claims that this group commands a high level of political respect, one cannot miss the fact that the working poor qualify for very little cash or near-cash aid (other than Food Stamps) or in-kind aid such as medical protection.

Although policies to aid this group were not the focus of any specific chapter, I will briefly review the most prominent ones.

Wage Subsidies. If people are working and remain poor, certainly one interpretation is that their wages are too low. Most economists are trained from a very early age to be suspicious and troubled by direct measures like raising the minimum wage. The most natural way to help the working poor, they believe, is through a wage subsidy. One way might be to offer a subsidy equal to half the difference between a person's hourly wage and, say, $6 per hour. Such policies directly tackle the problem of low wages and increase the incentive for low-wage workers. Lerman (Chapter 8) particularly emphasized the appeal of wage subsidies and added that, according to his calculations, a substantial wage subsidy could do more than the current EITC at the same cost.

Burtless (Chapter 4) raises the perpetual problem with such subsidies: they are very hard to administer. He also notes that even though such subsidies raise the effective wage rate, they do not appear to increase work effort by the poor and may even reduce it, according to simulation models. (Still, the negative income tax experiments unquestionably found that welfare-like benefits lead to very real reductions in work. The wage subsidies look good in comparison to almost any alternative form of support.) Wage subsidies can also lead to the perception (and reality) of low-wage employers being subsidized by the government.

Expanded Earned Income Tax Credit. An EITC is an earnings rather than a wage subsidy. For instance, a family might receive a refundable tax credit of, say, 15 percent of any earnings below some limit such as $7,000. The credit is gradually phased out for people above that level. For persons with earnings below $7,000, the EITC amounts to a 15 percent pay increase. Unlike a wage subsidy, an EITC is comparatively easy to administer. One is already in place, and it was expanded under the recent tax reform. Unfortunately, the EITC is more costly than a wage subsidy, and it does create some work disincentives over the middle-income range as it is phased out. There was considerable support for expanding the existing EITC and adjusting it for family size. Its comparative simplicity and the potential for incremental expansions in existing policy make it an attractive alternative. Still, it too has uncertain labor supply impacts (though again it would surely do far better than a welfare system or a negative income tax). And the costs are troubling.

Increased Minimum Wage. The final and most controversial way to influence earnings of at least some of the working poor is by raising the minimum wage. Though the minimum wage was mentioned only briefly, discussion of the pros and cons of raising it was spirited if somewhat predictable. A higher minimum wage ought to get more working families out of poverty. Its costs are "off budget" (something many economists might regard as a negative rather than a positive feature). And other policies alone are unlikely to be sufficient to insure that people who work can avoid poverty. The disadvantages are that there will be some reduction in employment and that most people who are paid the minimum wage are not in poor households.

The Urban Institute's recent study provides helpful new findings relevant to this debate showing that raising the minimum wage to adjust for inflation since 1970 (also considering disemployment effects) would reduce the poverty gap by $1 billion and push 200,000 working families out of poverty. A modest increase in the minimum wage might be combined with the EITC to achieve increased security for working families.

Refundable Child Care Tax Credit. Danziger (Chapter 2) emphasizes that the current child care tax credit (equal to roughly 30 percent of actual child-care costs, though the credit varies by income level) is not refundable. Thus it does not help those who owe no taxes. Since tax reform essentially removed all taxes from the working poor, the credit is of no help to this group and thus benefits only middle- and upper-income families. Making it refundable seems an obvious reform, but it is not clear just how much help a refundable credit would actually provide, since working poor families often use informal child-care arrangements.

Child-Support Payments

Collecting more money from absent parents seems to appeal to almost everyone along the political spectrum, since such payments potentially enforce responsibility, help single parents, and reduce welfare costs and dependency. Lerman (Chapter 8) gives a good sense of just how little child support is collected now and of the potential gain if a much larger fraction of absent parents paid according to a more "reasonable" formula. He also tries to assess the impact various child-support enforcement policies would have on welfare use.

According to the reports of single mothers, only one-third get any court-ordered child support, and payments average just over $2,000 for those lucky enough to get them. Fathers, however, report that they pay more than that (outside the formal court mandate), and many who did not pay but acknowledge having had a child seem to have sufficient income to make a reasonable contribution to the mother.

Expanded Child-Support Collection. To get more child-support payments, we must identify more absent parents (here referred to as "fathers"), set larger and more uniform awards, and collect more of the money from those with awards in place. Most states are now moving (under some federal pressure) toward a more formula-based system for setting awards. For example, the Wisconsin formula requires child-support payments equal to 17 percent of the absent parent's income for one child, and ranges to 34 percent for five or more children. And collection could be vastly improved with automatic wage withholding. Doubts remain about the feasibility of identifying virtually all fathers. Irwin Garfinkel argued at the conference that once some threshold percentage was reached (perhaps 80 percent), all fathers would be quickly identified because the ethic and expectations regarding paternal identification would change. Others were less optimistic. Nightingale (Chapter 7) emphasized just how disparate were the institutions involved in child support and how they would have to converge if a truly major overhaul were implemented. If the courts refused to cooperate, for instance, the reform would almost certainly fail.

Under optimal circumstances, a dramatic increase in collections seems likely. A variety of studies have suggested that child-support collections of between $20 and $30 billion (rather than the current $7 billion) are possible if a Wisconsin-type formula were applied to all or nearly all absent parents. But just how much difference such a system would make for poor women on welfare is uncertain, especially for young never-married mothers. Lerman provided a surprisingly large expectation of $3,000 per AFDC mother on average; his critics suggested that his estimates of fathers' incomes were overly optimistic, because they were based on reports of fathers who admitted having children. Yet even if Lerman's optimistic estimate is correct, that sum alone will push very few women off AFDC. It would significantly reduce welfare costs, since those on welfare can keep only $50 per month; but unless women supplemented the child support with work, most would still require welfare support. And Lerman worries that excessive enforcement of child support would turn even voluntary payments into a penalizing tax, increase tension, and possibly reduce contact among absent parents and their children.

Interestingly, even those who were skeptical about the potential of absent fathers to contribute nevertheless seemed to feel that stronger enforcement would be quite desirable. Some felt that Lerman significantly overstated the actual links between never-married mothers and the fathers of their children, and argued that child support enforcement might increase rather than decrease contact between father and child. Generally there seemed broad agreement that expanded child-support enforcement is essential, not only because of its potential for helping poor mothers, but also because of the signals it sends regarding responsibility and support.

Child-Support Assurance. In addition to the expanded child-support payments, the "Wisconsin plan" also calls for a guaranteed minimum child-support payment—a far more controversial feature. All child-support payments would be collected by the government, but when collections from a particular father were less than some specified amount, the government would provide a supplement to maintain a minimal level. Thus a single mother could count on getting, for example, $100 per child per month in child-support payments even if the father became unemployed.

The supporters of this plan emphasized that it would have much of the appeal of the Social Security system. Child-support enforcement alone would benefit mostly middle-class families in which absent fathers have higher incomes. But if child-support assurance were added, poor mothers would benefit also. Just like Social Security, this would be a middle-class program with a redistributive element and no stigma attached. Mothers could count on a stable source of income and might then be in a better position to achieve a reasonable standard of living through work. Proponents of the assured benefit seemed to agree that it should be kept rather low to prevent the impression that it was a replacement for public assistance. And the success of the program might require that the vast majority of fathers pay enough so that supplementation was unnecessary. Only when fathers were unemployed, or had very low earnings, would government help be used.

The most vocal opponents of such a plan at the conference claimed that child support assurance was nothing more than Nixon's Family Assistance Plan—a variant on the negative income tax—in disguise (something proponents denied vehemently). Less vehement opponents noted that these payments alone would not push many women off welfare, so it would not really change the position of poor women anyway; that it seemed a decidedly nonincremental change; and that it was an untested and unproven idea.

The question of support brings up the issue of family integrity. If we really do come up with policies that make it feasible for single mothers to realistically support themselves, will we weaken the position of men and increase the number of single-parent families? Ought we instead to leave single-parent families in a difficult and dependent position in hopes that we can reduce their frequency? My own reading of the evidence is that the notion that a child-support assurance system will weaken traditional families is quite far-fetched.

Additional Nonwelfare Proposals

Danziger (Chapter 2) and Lerman (Chapter 8) emphasized the benefits of converting the current personal exemption for each individual into a refundable tax credit of perhaps $400 per person. Instead of taking an exemption for each family member on its tax form, every family would start with a tax credit of $400 per person annually, which could be kept if the family owed no taxes or used to offset any taxes that were owed. This low level of support would especially help poor families, serving as a base they could supplement with earnings. It would be similar to the children's allowances popular elsewhere in the world. Moreover, this would be revenue-neutral, or nearly so.

Critics of this idea said that it looked like a guaranteed annual income; a family of four would start with $1,600 in income even if none of them worked. Moreover, even though the proposal might be revenue-neutral overall, it certainly wouldn't be by income class. This plan would represent significant redistribution from rich to poor, a fact that would not be lost on the body politic. It looked similar, they suggested, to the highly unpopular "demogrant" proposed by George McGovern.

The problem of health care did not receive enough attention in my estimation. The authors who commented on it made the point that lack of medical protection is a particularly serious problem for the working poor, made even more invidious because those on AFDC, mostly not working, have relatively generous coverage. More universal coverage seems unlikely to damage values regarding work or family or to promote dependency. It will cost more, but we are already paying a great deal for public and uncompensated care—often only after families find themselves drained of both assets and dignity. Especially as we move to a more competitive health system, some way of insuring the uninsured seems the only sensible and humane route.

Do the Nonwelfare Reforms Make Sense?

The proponents of this type of reform emphasized that their ideas typically were more universal, hence more integrating and less stigmatizing, and they seemed likely to garner more long-term public support. Nonwelfare reforms could help the working poor and they often reinforce traditional values like work and parental responsibility. But the critics argued that large expenditures were involved, that taken together these were nothing but incremental proposals. If a new president took this path, a chance to do the clearly beneficial things under Stream 1 might be lost. For too long welfare reformers have sought to do everything and come up with nothing.

To my mind there is no reason both approaches cannot or should not be pursued simultaneously. Indeed, I am absolutely convinced that Stream 1 approaches will never work very well until Stream 2 changes are in place. Danziger offered perhaps the simplest yet most profound observation: that the goal of Stream 1 proposals was to convert the welfare poor into the working poor. He is absolutely right. A far more appealing agenda would be to convert the welfare poor into the working *non*poor. If work offered a realistic alternative to welfare and provided some real power and control over one's life, then welfare really could be changed into a temporary support system. But if we adopt only a melioristic approach, the real choices people face will change little.

Let me offer two examples of the best programs in the country. Massachusetts has mounted the ET/Choices program, which has really changed the atmosphere and mentality of welfare offices. Now the talk is of jobs and independence, and some day care and training go with the talk. Because the state economy is strong, jobs are relatively plentiful. Many people have been placed into jobs. The public is pleased. And the state has been able to raise benefits by almost 50 percent since the program started—not up to the poverty line, but a lot closer than they used to be. California, which is the only state in the country that indexes AFDC benefits, has adopted the GAIN program. GAIN too has liberal child care, a considerable educational commitment, and a variety of mandatory participation requirements. And there has been considerable excitement surrounding its introduction.

Yet behind all the excitement, the caseload in Massachusetts has fallen by only 5 to 10 percent. In part this is because other trends—a greater number of single-parent families, immigration of certain groups, and higher benefits—have pulled more people onto welfare. Still, even a terrific program in a healthy economy has not dramatically reduced the caseload. And in California, a San Diego work/welfare program that preceded GAIN and is like it in some ways showed only modest gains as was mentioned above.

Why does it seem so hard to reduce dependency? I think the answer is simple. For people to move from welfare to work, work must be an economically realistic alternative. How much does it take to do as well working as on welfare in these states? For work to really make sense, you must be able to work full time at a job paying $5 or $6 or even $7 per hour. That is why both Massachusetts and California have rules strongly favoring placements in higher-paying jobs. The people who get lower-paying jobs often return to welfare.

But research has shown that the long-term problem cases consume the bulk of the resources and these are the people who are going to have the hardest time in the labor market. Carl Williams, Deputy Director of GAIN External Affairs, noted that the majority of AFDC recipients in California have literacy problems. Many of these people will be lucky to get jobs paying $4 per hour.

And is it reasonable to expect full-time work from a mother with young children? Only about a quarter of all married mothers with children of any age work full year, full time. And they have other resources to draw on for help with emergencies, child care, and the like. A small problem can easily cause a woman to miss some work, especially if she is working full time. She may lose her low-pay, low-security job and return to welfare. It shouldn't come as a big surprise that the existing interventions have only a modest impact because they don't make work pay more than welfare or help mothers wrestle with their dual role of provider and nurturer.

If we adopted measures to raise the pay for poor workers, work at the minimum wage would be more attractive. It is not hard to find a combination of measures to create an effective minimum wage (including wage subsidies or tax breaks) of $5 to $5.50 per hour. If medical protection were available outside the welfare system, then full-time work would offer a decent living. If a child assurance plan were adopted that assured, say, just $1,750 annually per child, then a mother of two could work half time at the $5.50 hour job, and with her $3,500 in child support escape both poverty and welfare.

Absent nonwelfare programs, Stream 1 ideas still are sensible and ought to be pursued. But they will inevitably yield small and disappointing results; we will not have transformed the welfare system, and the over-promising necessary to get the policies sold will come back to haunt the program. As today, we will always have to worry about whether we should raise welfare benefits to be fair and decent or keep them low to discourage dependency.

Stream 3: Reorient Economic, Educational, and Social Policies

Wacquant and Wilson (Chapter 3) focus on the ghetto poor, especially in Chicago. They alone provide a clear sense of the complexity of the problems in the ghetto and the impossibility of getting modest changes in the welfare system to redress that situation. Among a host of difficulties, Wacquant and Wilson point to the growing isolation and concentration of ghetto residents, to general increases in joblessness, and to the deindustrialization and general deterioration of the so-called rustbelt cities. There are concomitant declines in the social buffers and role models provided by working-class families, in the educational system, in job networks that are often crucial in finding and securing relatively well-paying jobs, and in the subjective expectations of people about their futures and aspirations. In the light of such major social and economic factors and the attendant decay in critical institutions, the authors emphasize that welfare reform of the types usually contemplated can have only a minor impact at best; even nonwelfare reforms might have little effect.

Unfortunately, there was very little discussion of policies for the ghetto poor outside Chapter 3. Perhaps for most of the authors the goal was to help a group far larger than the ghetto poor. Although all of the authors would surely agree that the problems of the ghetto poor ought to command considerable attention in their own right, most researchers suggest that the ghetto poor represent no more than 10–15 percent of the poor; many estimate less. Clearly, the desperation of the ghetto is not representative of poverty generally, but it warrants full-time emphasis in many future research projects and conferences.

In discussing the ghetto, Wacquant and Wilson highlighted that welfare reform cannot be seen in isolation. The success or failure of social policies to do more than simply give money to those who would otherwise have very low incomes will depend ultimately on forces largely outside the welfare system.

The economy's critical role was emphasized throughout the conference. Danziger (Chapter 2) shows that, especially for the working poor, growth and low unemployment are absolutely critical in influencing poverty outcomes. When jobs are scarce, programs that put welfare mothers into a job could be displacing others who might work. I would trade away many of my favorite ideas for welfare reform for a guarantee of the 2–3 percent unemployment and high growth one finds in Massachusetts today. Growth not only raises many (but not all) ships; it also seems to create a more generous and fiscally sympathetic public.

Similarly, the crucial role that the educational system needs to play over the long run has been a favorite yet legitimate truism from the very earliest efforts designed to help the poor. There is evidence that some kinds of educational interventions, such as Head Start, may make a big difference in the long run. Likewise, a host of social problems from drugs to discrimination to disease and disability clearly need continued close attention. Yet none of our authors dwelled on reforms of this sort. To be sure, few are expert on macroeconomic policy or education or social policies designed to deal with deeper individual or societal ills. Moreover, broad social policies alone will not solve the poverty problem. Still, it is clear that efforts to "solve" poverty through work, opportunity, and nonwelfare supports must rest critically on the progress that the larger society makes in these areas.

Looking for Meaning and Direction

A number of issues that weren't addressed deserve closer attention in any debate over welfare reform. I have already mentioned a few. There was not enough discussion about ways to help the working poor, the ghetto poor, Hispanics, or the rural poor. In some sense, these all represent perhaps a larger failing of much of the discussion, which focused far more on the who and what of poverty than the why. Much has been learned about why people are poor in recent years and a look at these lessons would go a long way toward informing policy. If we asked why people are poor, we could not avoid considering the working poor or those in the ghetto.

Many questions remain to be answered about administrative and implementation issues. We need to bring administrative practice and academic theories closer together.

Many of the principal controversies centered on whether an idea was politically feasible, or whether we ought to expend the very limited political and economic resources currently available on one plan rather than another. The broad outlines of a direction to move, which ultimately would involve all three streams, really did seem to emerge. There was a clear desire to work toward a system where most currently poor citizens can take more control and responsibility over their lives and achieve a measure of independence. I really do believe that a concerted effort could profoundly change the situation for poor Americans. Thus I see reason for real optimism for the first time in a long while.

The fact that fiscal resources are so terribly constrained right now might be reason for pessimism. Reischauer suggests that the next president can't have too much on his mind other than the budget deficit. With little money to spend, it is very clear that we can only take small steps, and those steps may be determined by the current political forces which have already shaped the debate. Yet I'd like to believe that conference discussant Laurence Lynn was right when he argued the new president could transform the debate. And most of the participants would no doubt hope the new president takes Lynn's advice and take a "risk with respect to welfare reform . . . [and] to do so with an imagination and verve that six Congressional subcommittees can never hope to muster."

References

1. The Welfare Reform Legislation

Bane, M. J., and D. T. Ellwood. 1986. "Slipping into and out of Poverty: The Dynamics of Spells." *Journal of Human Resources,* 21(1), pp. 1–23.

———1983. *The Dynamics of Dependence: Routes to Self-Sufficiency.* Cambridge, Mass.: Urban Systems Research.

Barnow, B. S. 1987. "The Impact of CETA Programs on Earnings." *Journal of Human Resources,* 22(2), pp. 157–193.

Bishop, J. H. 1980. "Jobs, Cash Transfers, and Marital Instability: A Review and Synthesis of the Evidence." *The Journal of Human Resources,* 15(3), pp. 301–334.

Bumpass, L. L. 1984. "Children and Marital Disruption: A Replication and an Update." *Demography,* 21(1), pp. 71–82.

Butler, S., and A. Kondratas. 1987. "Reactivating Federalism." In *Out of the Poverty Trap.* New York: Free Press.

Cain, G. 1987. "Negative Income Tax Experiments and the Issues of Marital Stability and Family Composition." In *Lessons from the Income Maintenance Experiments,* ed. A. H. Munnell. Boston: Federal Reserve Bank of Boston Conference Series, no. 30.

Children's Defense Fund. 1987. *Child Care: The Time Is Now.* Washington, D.C.: CDF.

Dionne, E. J., Jr. "Poll Finds Iowa Voters More Liberal Than Nation." *New York Times,* sect. A, p. 36, November 1, 1987.

Duncan, G. 1984. *Years of Poverty, Years of Plenty.* Ann Arbor: Survey Research Center, University of Michigan.

Ellwood, D. T. 1986. "Targeting 'Would-Be' Long-Term Recipients of AFDC." Report. Princeton, N.J.: Mathematica Policy Research, Inc.

Ellwood D. T., and M. J. Bane. 1985. "The Impact of AFDC on Family Structure and Living Arrangements." *Research in Labor Economics,* 7, pp. 137–149.

Freeman, R. B., and B. Hall. 1986. "Permanent Homelessness in America?" Working Paper 2013. Cambridge, Mass.: National Bureau of Economic Research.

Friedlander, D., and D. Long. 1987. *A Study of Performance Measures and Subgroup Impacts in Three Welfare Employment Programs.* New York: Manpower Demonstration Research Corporation.

Friedlander, D., M. Erickson, G. Hamilton, and V. Knox. 1986. *West Virginia: Final Report on the Community Work Experience Demonstration.* New York: Manpower Demonstration Research Corporation.

Friedlander, D., S. Freedman, G. Hamilton, and J. Quint. 1987. *Final Report on the Illinois WIN Demonstration Program in Cook County.* New York: Manpower Demonstration Research Corporation.

Friedlander, D., G. Hoerz, D. Long, and J. Quint. 1985. *Maryland: Final Report on the Employment Initiatives Evaluation.* New York: Manpower Demonstration Research Corporation.

Garfinkel, I., and P. Wong. 1987. "Child Support and Public Policy." Paper presented at the OECD Conference of National Experts, "Lone-Parents: The Economic Challenge of Changing Family Structure," December 15–17.

Goldman, B., D. Friedlander, and D. Long. 1986. *Final Report on the San Diego Job Search and Work Experience Demonstration.* New York: Manpower Demonstration Research Corporation.

Gramlich, E. M. 1982. "An Econometric Examination of the New Federalism." *Brookings Papers on Economic Activity,* vol. 2. Washington, D.C.: Brookings Institution, pp. 327–370.

Grossman, J. B., R. Maynard, and J. Roberts. 1985. "Reanalysis of the Effects of Selected Employment and Training Programs for Welfare Recipients." Report. Princeton, N.J.: Mathematica Policy Research, Inc.

Gueron, J. M. 1987. "State Welfare Employment Programs: Lessons from the 1980's." Paper presented at the annual meeting of the American Economics Association, Chicago, December.

Hofferth, S. L. 1985. "Updating Children's Life Course." *Journal of Marriage and the Family,* 47, February, pp. 93–115.

Institute for Cultural Conservatism. 1987. *Cultural Conservatism: Toward a New National Agenda.* Washington, D.C.: ICC.

Lewis, I. A., and W. Schneider. 1985. "Hard Times: The Public on Poverty" and "Opinion Roundup: Poverty in America." *Public Opinion,* June/July, pp. 3–7, 59–60.

Manpower Demonstration Research Corporation. 1980. *Summary and Findings of the National Supported Work Demonstration.* New York: Ballinger.

Melville, K., and J. Doble. 1988. "The Public's Perspective on Social Welfare Reform." Report. New York: Public Agenda Foundation.

Minarik, J. J., and R. S. Goldfarb. 1976. "AFDC Income, Recipient Rates, and Family Dissolution: A Comment." *Journal of Human Resources,* 11(2), pp. 243–250.

Moffitt, R. 1984. "The Effects of Grants-in-Aid on State and Local Expenditures." *Journal of Public Economics,* no. 3, pp. 279–305.

———1987. "Has State Redistribution Policy Grown More Conservative?" Providence, R.I.: Department of Economics, Brown University. Mimeo.

Murray, C. 1984. *Losing Ground: American Social Policy, 1950–1980.* New York: Basic Books.

Norton, A. J., and J. E. Moorman. 1987. "Current Trends in Marriage and Divorce among American Women." *Journal of Marriage and the Family,* 49, February, pp. 3–14.

Orr, L. 1987. "Income Transfers as a Public Good: An Application to AFDC." *American Economic Review,* 66, (3), 359–371.

Peterson, P. E., and M. C. Rom. 1987. "Federalism and Welfare Reform: The Determinants of Interstate Differences in Poverty Rates and Benefit Levels." In *Brookings Discussion Papers in Governmental Studies.* Washington, D.C.: Brookings Institution.

Plotnick, R. D. 1987. "Welfare and Other Determinants of Teenage Out-of-Wedlock Childbearing." Paper presented at the APPAM Research Conference, Washington, D.C., October.

Reischauer, R. D. 1987a. "Welfare Reform: Will Consensus be Enough?" *Brookings Review,* Summer, 3–8.

———1987b. "Welfare Reform and the Working Poor." In *Work and Welfare: The Case for New Directions in National Policy,* no. 22, *Alternatives for the 1980's,* pp. 35–46. Washington, D.C.: Center for National Policy.

Schram, S., and M. Wiseman. 1988. "Should Families Be Protected from AFDC-UP?" Berkeley: University of California at Berkeley. Mimeo.

Shapiro, R. Y., K. D. Patterson, J. Russell, and J. T. Young. 1987. "The Polls: Public Assistance." *Public Opinion Quarterly,* 51, spring, pp. 120–130.

Simon, P. 1987. *Let's Put America Back to Work,* chap. 4. Chicago: Bonus Books.

Smith, T. W. 1987. "That Which We Call Welfare by Any Other Name Would Smell Sweeter." *Public Opinion Quarterly,* 51, spring, pp. 75–83.

U.S. Department of Health and Human Services. 1986. *Characteristics and Financial Circumstances of AFDC Recipients, 1986.* Washington, D.C.: HHS Office of Family Assistance.

U.S. House of Representatives, Committee on Ways and Means. 1987. *Background Material and Data on Programs within the Jurisdiction of the Committee on Ways and Means: 1987 Edition.* Washington, D.C.: Government Printing Office.

2. Fighting Poverty and Reducing Welfare Dependency

Aaron, H. 1984. "Six Welfare Questions Still Searching for Answers." *Brookings Review,* 3, fall, pp. 12–17.

Adams, T., and G. J. Duncan. 1987. "The Prevalence and Correlates of Persistent Urban Poverty." Ann Arbor: Institute for Social Research, University of Michigan. Mimeo.

Danziger, S. 1986. "Tax Reform, Poverty and Inequality." Discussion Paper no. 829-86, Madison: University of Wisconsin–Madison, Institute for Research on Poverty.

Danziger, S., and P. Gottschalk. 1985. "The Poverty of Losing Ground." *Challenge,* May/June, pp. 32–38.

———1986. "How Have Families with Children Been Faring?" Discussion Paper no. 801-86, Madison: University of Wisconsin–Madison, Institute for Research on Poverty.

Danziger, S., and D. Weinberg, eds. 1986. *Fighting Poverty: What Works and What Doesn't.* Cambridge, Mass.: Harvard University Press.

Duncan, G. J., and S. D. Hoffman. 1988. "The Use and Effects of Welfare: A Survey of Recent Evidence." *Social Service Review,* forthcoming.

Duncan, G. J., and W. L. Rodgers. 1988. "Longitudinal Aspects of Childhood Poverty." *Journal of Marriage and the Family,* forthcoming.

Duncan, G. J., et al. 1984. *Years of Poverty, Years of Plenty.* Ann Arbor: Institute for Social Research, University of Michigan.

Ellwood, D. 1986. "Targeting 'Would-Be' Long-Term Recipients of AFDC." Report. Princeton, N.J.: Mathematica Policy Research, Inc.

————1987. "Poverty through the Eyes of Children." Harvard University, John F. Kennedy School of Government. Mimeo.

Ellwood, D., and L. Summers. 1986. "Poverty in America: Is Welfare the Answer or the Problem?" In *Fighting Poverty: What Works and What Doesn't,* ed. S. Danziger and D. Weinberg. Cambridge, Mass.: Harvard University Press, pp. 78–105.

Garfinkel, I., and S. McLanahan. 1987. *Single Mothers and Their Children: A New American Dilemma.* Washington, D.C.: Urban Institute Press.

Hill, M. 1983. "Trends in the Economic Situation of U.S. Families with Children: 1970–1980." In *American Families and the Economy,* ed. R. Nelson and F. Skidmore. Washington, D.C.: National Academy Press, pp. 9–53.

Lerman, R. 1987. "The Costs and Income Gains of Nonwelfare Approaches to Helping the Poor." Paper presented at the annual meeting of the Society for Governmental Economics, Waltham, Mass., Heller Graduate School, Brandeis University. Mimeo.

Murray, C. 1984. *Losing Ground: American Social Policy, 1950–1980.* New York: Basic Books.

Plotnick, R., and F. Skidmore. 1975. *Progress against Poverty: A Review of the 1964–1974 Decade.* New York: Academic Press.

Smolensky, E., S. Danziger, and P. Gottschalk. 1988. "The Declining Significance of Age: Trends in the Well-Being of Children and the Elderly Since 1939." In *The Vulnerable,* ed. J. Palmer, T. Smeeding, and B. Torrey, pp. 29–54. Washington, D.C.: Urban Institute Press.

Tobin, J. 1969. "Raising the Incomes of the Poor." In *Agenda for the Nation,* ed. K. Gordon, pp. 77–116. Garden City, N.Y.: Doubleday.

U.S. Bureau of the Census. 1987a. *Alternative Methods of Valuing Selected In-Kind Transfer Benefits and Measuring Their Effects on Poverty.* Technical Paper no. 57. Washington, D.C.: U.S. Government Printing Office.

————1987b. *Money Income and Poverty Status of Families and Persons in the United States: 1986.* Current Population Reports, P-60, no. 157. Washington, D.C.: U.S. Government Printing Office.

U.S. Congressional Budget Office. 1988. *Trends in Family Income: 1970–1986.* Washington, D.C.

U.S. Council of Economic Advisers. 1988. *Economic Report of the President, 1988.* Washington, D.C.: U.S. Government Printing Office.

U.S. House of Representatives, Committee on Ways and Means. 1985. *Children in Poverty.* Washington, D.C.: U.S. Government Printing Office.

————1987 and 1988. *Background Material and Data on Programs within the Juris-diction of the Committee on Ways and Means*. Washington, D.C.: U.S. Government Printing Office.

Weinberg, D. 1987. "Filling the 'Poverty Gap': 1979–84." *Journal of Human Resources*, 24, fall, pp. 563–573.

3. Poverty, Joblessness, and the Social Transformation of the Inner City

Anderson, M. 1978. *Welfare: The Political Economy of Welfare Reform in the United States*. Stanford, Calif.: Hoover Institution.

Bane, M. J., and P. A. Jargowski. 1988. "Urban Poverty and the Underclass: Basic Questions." Paper presented at the Urban Poverty Workshop, The University of Chicago, January.

Barton, M., G. Farkas, K. Kushner, and L. McCreary. 1985. "White, Black, and Hispanic Youth in Central City Labor Markets." *Social Science Research*, 14, pp. 266–285.

Blank, R. M., and A. S. Blinder. 1986. "Macroeconomics, Income Distribution, and Poverty." In *Fighting Poverty: What Works and What Doesn't*, ed. S. H. Danziger and D. H. Weinberg. Cambridge, Mass.: Harvard University Press.

Blau, P. M. 1987. "Contrasting Theoretical Perspectives." In *The Micro-Macro Link*, ed. J. C. Alexander, B. Giessen, R. Munch, and N. J. Smelser. Berkeley: University of California Press.

Blau, P. M., and J. E. Schwartz. 1984. *Crosscutting Social Circles*. Orlando, Fla.: Academic Press.

Blinder, A. S., and H. Y. Esaki. 1978. "Macroeconomic Activity and Income Distribution in the Postwar United States." *Review of Economics and Statistics*, 60, pp. 604–609.

Bluestone, B., and B. Harrison. 1982. *The Deindustrialization of America: Plant Closings, Community Abandonment, and the Dismantling of Basic Industry*. New York: Harper Colophon Books.

————1987. *The Great American Job Machine: The Proliferation of Low-Wage Employment in the U.S. Economy*. Washington, D.C.: Joint Economic Committee.

————1988. *The Great U-Turn Corporate Restructuring and the Polarization of America*. New York: Basic Books.

Blumberg, P. 1980. *Inequality in an Age of Decline*. New York: Oxford University Press.

Bourdieu, P. 1974. "Avenir de classe et causalité du probable." *Revue française de sociologie*, 15-1, January/March, pp. 3–40.

————1979. "Les trois états du capital culturel." *Actes de la recherche en sciences sociales*, 30, November, pp. 3–6.

————1980. *Questions de sociologie*. Paris: Editions de Minuit.

Boyas, G. J., and M. Tienda, eds. 1985. *Hispanics in the U.S. Economy*. New York: Academic Press.

Brune, T., and E. Camacho. 1983. *A Special Report: Race and Poverty in Chicago*. Chicago: The Chicago Reporter and the Center for Community Research and Assistance.

Burtless, G. 1986. "Public Spending for the Poor: Trends, Prospects and Economic Limits." In *Fighting Poverty: What Works and What Doesn't,* ed. S. H. Danziger and D. H. Weinberg. Cambridge, Mass.: Harvard University Press.

Castel, R. 1978. "La 'guerre à la pauvreté' en Amérique: Le statut de l'indigence dans une société d'abondance." *Actes de la recherche en sciences sociales,* 19, January, pp. 47–60.

Chicago Fact Book Consortium. 1984. *Local Community Fact Book: Chicago Metropolitan Area.* Chicago: Chicago Review Press.

Chicago Tribune. 1985. *The American Millstone: An Examination of the Nation's Permanent Underclass.* Chicago and New York: Contemporary Books.

City of Chicago. 1973. *Chicago Statistical Abstract, Part 1: 1970 Census, Community Area Summary Tables.* Chicago: Department of Development and Planning, July.

Coleman, J. S., and T. Hoffer. 1987. *Public and Private Schools: The Impact of Communities.* New York: Basic Books.

Danziger, S. H., and P. P. Gottschalk. 1985. "The Poverty of Losing Ground." *Challenge,* May/June, pp. 31–38.

Designs for Change. 1985. *The Bottom Line: Chicago's Failing Schools and How to Save Them.* Chicago: Chicago School Watch, Research Report no. 1.

Drake, St. C., and H. R. Cayton. 1962 (orig. 1945). *Black Metropolis: A Study of Negro Life in a Northern City.* 2 vols. New York: Harper and Row.

Ellwood, D. T., and M. J. Bane. 1985. "The Impact of AFDC on Family Structure and Living Arrangements." *Research in Labor Economics,* 7, pp. 137–149.

Ellwood, D. T., and L. H. Summers. 1986. "Poverty in America: Is Welfare the Answer or the Problem?" In *Fighting Poverty: What Works and What Doesn't,* ed. by S. H. Danziger and D. H. Weinberg. Cambridge, Mass.: Harvard University Press.

Friedland, R. 1976. "Class Power and Social Control: The War on Poverty," *Politics and Society,* 6-4, pp. 459–490.

Gueron, J. M. 1987. "Reforming Welfare with Work." *Public Welfare,* Fall, pp. 14–25.

Harrison, B., C. Tilly, and B. Bluestone. 1986. "Wage Inequality Takes a Great U-Turn," *Challenge,* 29-1, March/April, pp. 26–33.

Hirsch, A. 1983. *Making the Second Ghetto: Race and Housing in Chicago, 1940–60.* Cambridge: Cambridge University Press.

Hirschman, A. O. 1970. *Exit, Voice, and Loyalty: Responses to Decline in Firms, Organizations, and States.* Cambridge, Mass.: Harvard University Press.

———1986. *Vers une economie politique élargie.* Paris: Editions de Minuit.

Holzer, H. J. 1987. "Informal Job Search and Black Youth Unemployment." Paper presented at the Urban Poverty Seminar, The University of Chicago, May.

Isaac, L., and W. R. Kelly. 1981. "Racial Insurgency, the State and Welfare Expansion." *American Journal of Sociology,* 86, July, pp. 1348–86.

Jennings, E. T. 1979. "Civil Turmoil and the Growth of Welfare Rolls: A Comparative State Analysis." *Policy Studies Journal,* 17, Summer, pp. 739–745.

Kasarda, J. D. 1983. "Entry Level Jobs, Mobility, and Minority Unemployment." *Urban Affairs Quarterly,* 19, pp. 21–40.

Katz, M. B. 1986. *In the Shadow of the Poorhouse: A Social History of Welfare in America.* New York: Basic Books.

Katznelson, I., and M. Weir. 1985. *Schooling for All: Class, Race, and the Decline of the Democratic Ideal.* New York: Basic Books.

Kaus, M. 1986. "The Work Ethic State." *New Republic,* July 7, pp. 22–33.

Levitan, S. A., and I. Shapiro. 1987. "The Fall of the Minimum Wage." Unpublished paper. George Washington University Center for Social Policy Studies, February.

Levy, F. 1987. *Dollars and Dreams: The Changing American Income Distribution.* New York: Russell Sage Foundation and Basic Books.

Lichter, D. T. 1988. "Racial Differences in Underemployment in American Cities." *American Journal of Sociology,* 93-4, January, pp. 771–793.

Massey, D. S., and N. A. Denton. 1987. "Trends in the Residential Segregation of Blacks, Hispanics and Asians: 1970–1980." *American Sociological Review,* 52-6, December, pp. 802–825.

Mead, L. M. 1985. *Beyond Entitlement: The Social Obligations of Citizenship.* New York: Free Press.

Melman, S. 1983. *Profits without Production.* New York: Alfred A. Knopf.

Murray, C. 1984. *Losing Ground: American Social Policy, 1950–1980.* New York: Basic Books.

Neckerman, K. M., and W. J. Wilson. 1987. "Schools and Poor Communities." Paper presented at the Summer Institute of the Council of Chief State School Officers, Whitefish, Mont., August.

Neckerman, K. M., R. Aponte, and W. J. Wilson. 1988. "Family Structure, Black Unemployment and American Social Policy." In *The Politics of Social Policy in the United States,* ed. M. Weir, A. S. Orloff, and T. R. Skocpol, pp. 379–420. Princeton, N.J.: Princeton University Press.

New York State Task Force. 1986. "A New Social Contract Rethinking the Nature and Purpose of Public Assistance." Report of the Task Force on Poverty and Welfare, submitted to Governor Mario Cuomo, Albany, N.Y.

Offe, C. 1985. *Disorganized Capitalism: Contemporary Transformations of Work and Politics.* Cambridge, Mass.: MIT Press.

Piven, F. F., and R. A. Cloward. 1971. *Regulating the Poor: The Social Functions of Public Welfare.* New York: Pantheon Books.

———1977. *Poor People's Movements: Why They Succeed, How They Fail.* New York: Vintage Books.

———1987a. "The Contemporary Relief Debate." In *The Mean Season: The Attack on the Welfare State,* F. Block, R. A. Cloward, B. Ehrenreich, and F. F. Piven, pp. 45–108. New York: Pantheon Books.

———1987b. "Sources of the Contemporary Relief Debate." In *The Mean Season,* pp. 3–43.

Portes, A., and C. Truelove. 1987. "Making Sense of Diversity: Recent Research on Hispanic Minorities in the United States." *Annual Review of Sociology,* 13, pp. 359–385.

Reischauer, R. D. 1987a. "The Geographic Concentration of Poverty: What Do We Know?" Unpublished paper. Washington, D.C.: Brookings Institution.

———1987b. "Welform: Will Consensus Be Enough," *The Brookings Review,* 5, Summer, pp. 3–8.

Sampson, R. J. 1987. "Urban Black Violence: The Effects of Male Joblessness and Family Disruption." *American Journal of Sociology,* 93-2, September, pp. 348–382.

Sarbanes, P., ed. 1986. *The Changing American Economy*. London: Basil Blackwell.

Sawers, L., and W. Tabb, eds. 1984. *Sunbelt-Snowbelt*. New York: Oxford University Press.

Schiller, B. R. 1970. "Stratified Opportunities: The Essence of the Vicious Circle." *American Journal of Sociology*, 76-3, November, pp. 426–442.

Shram, S. F., and J. P. Turbot. 1983. "Civil Disorder and the Welfare Explosion." *American Sociological Review*, 48, May, pp. 408–414.

Spear, A. H. 1967. *Black Chicago: The Making of a Negro Ghetto, 1890–1920*. Chicago: University of Chicago Press.

Thurow, L. 1986. "A General Tendency toward Inequality." *American Economic Association Papers and Proceedings*. Menasha, Wis.

Tilly, C., B. Bluestone, and B. Harrison. 1988. "The Reasons for Increasing Wage and Salary Inequality, 1978–1984." John W. McCormack Institute of Public Affairs, Boston, February. Mimeo.

U.S. Bureau of the Census. *County and City Data Book*. Washington, D.C.: U.S. Government Printing Office, 1962, 1972, 1977, 1983.

———1973. *Low-Income Areas in Large Cities*. Census of the Population, 1970, Subject Reports, PC(2)-9b, 3 vols. Washington D.C.: U.S. Government Printing Office.

———1985. *Poverty Areas in Large Cities*. Census of the Population, 1980, Subject Reports, PC80-2-8D. Washington, D.C.: U.S. Government Printing Office.

———1986a. *Money Income and the Poverty Status of Families and Persons in the United States: 1985*. Current Population Reports, P-60, no. 154. Washington, D.C.: U.S. Government Printing Office.

———1986b. *State and Metropolitan Area Data Book*. Washington, D.C.: U.S. Government Printing Office.

U.S. Department of Commerce and Industry. 1982. *Census of Service Industries*, SC82-A, vols. 1–50. Washington D.C.: U.S. Government Printing Office.

U.S. General Accounting Office. 1987. *Welfare: Income and Relative Poverty Studies of AFDC Families*. Publication no. HRD 88-9. Washington, D.C.: U.S. General Accounting Office, November.

U.S. News and World Report. "America's Hidden Poor." January 11, 1988, pp. 18–25.

Wilson, W. J. 1980. *The Declining Significance of Race*. 2nd ed. Chicago: University of Chicago Press.

———1987. *The Truly Disadvantaged: The Inner City and Public Policy*. Chicago: University of Chicago Press.

Wilson, W. J., and K. M. Neckerman. 1986. "Poverty and Family Structure: The Widening Gap between Evidence and Public Policy Issues." In *Fighting Poverty: What Works and What Doesn't*, ed. S. H. Danziger and D. H. Weinberg. Cambridge, Mass.: Harvard University Press.

Wilson, W. J., R. Aponte, J. Kirschenman, and L. J. D. Wacquant. 1988. "The Ghetto Underclass and the Changing Structure of Urban Poverty." In *Quiet Riots: Race and Poverty in the United States*, ed. F. Harris and R. Wilkins. New York: Pantheon Books.

4. The Effect of Reform on Employment, Earnings, and Income

Auspos, P. 1986. *Bibliography and Review of Research Findings Relevant to Employment and Training Programs for Food Stamp Recipients.* New York: Manpower Demonstration Research Corporation.

Bane, M. J., and D. T. Ellwood. 1983. *The Dynamics of Dependence: The Routes to Self-Sufficiency.* Cambridge, Mass.: Urban Systems Research.

Barnow, B. 1987. "The Impact of CETA Programs on Earnings: A Review of the Literature." *Journal of Human Resources,* 22, Spring, pp. 157–193.

Bell, S. H. 1986. "AFDC Homemaker-Home Health Aide Demonstrations: Trainee Public Program Benefits." Report. Cambridge, Mass.: Abt Associates.

Betson, D. M., and J. H. Bishop. 1982. "Wage Incentive and Distributional Effects." In *Jobs for Disadvantaged Workers: The Economics of Employment Subsidies,* ed. R. H. Haveman and J. L. Palmer. Washington, D.C.: Brookings Institution.

Burtless, G. 1987. "The Work Response to a Guaranteed Income: A Survey of Experimental Evidence." In *Lessons from the Income Maintenance Experiments,* ed. A. H. Munnell. Boston: Federal Reserve Bank of Boston.

Danziger, S., R. H. Haveman, and R. Plotnick. 1981. "How Income Transfers Affect Work, Savings, and the Income Distribution: A Critical Review." *Journal of Economic Literature,* 19, September, pp. 975–1028.

Enns, J. H., K. L. Flanagan, and S. H. Bell. 1986. "AFDC Homemaker-Home Health Aide Demonstrations: Trainee Employment and Earnings." Report. Cambridge, Mass.: Abt Associates.

Fraker, T., R. Moffitt, and D. Wolf. 1985. "Effective Tax Rates and Guarantees in the AFDC Program, 1967–82." *Journal of Human Resources,* 20, spring, pp. 264–277.

Friedlander, D., and D. Long. 1987. *A Study of Performance Measures and Subgroup Impacts in Three Welfare Programs.* New York: Manpower Demonstration Research Corporation.

Grossman, J. B., R. Maynard, and J. Roberts. 1985. "Reanalysis of the Effects of Selected Employment and Training Programs for Welfare Recipients." Report. Princeton, N.J.: Mathematica Policy Research, Inc.

Kemper, P., D. A. Long, and C. Thornton. 1981. *The Supported Work Evaluation: Final Benefit-Cost Analysis.* New York: Manpower Demonstration Research Corporation.

Ketron, Inc. 1980. "The Long-Term Impact of WIN II: A Longitudinal Evaluation of the Employment Experiences of Participants in the Work Incentive Program." Report. Wayne, Penn.: Ketron, Inc.

Levy, F. 1979. "The Labor Supply of Female Heads, or AFDC Work Incentives Don't Work Too Well." *Journal of Human Resources,* 14, Winter, pp. 76–97.

Manpower Demonstration Research Corporation. 1980. *Summary and Findings of the National Supported Work Demonstration.* Cambridge, Mass.: Ballinger.

Mathematica Policy Research. 1983. "Final Report: Employment Opportunity Pilot Project—Analysis of Program Impacts." Princeton, N.J.: Mathematica Policy Research, Inc.

Mead, L. M. 1987. "The Potential for Work Enforcement: A Study of WIN." New York: Department of Politics, New York University. Mimeo.

Moffitt, R. 1985. "A Problem with the Negative Income Tax." *Economics Letters,* 17, pp. 261–265.

———1987. "Work and the U.S. Welfare System: A Review." Providence, R. I.: Department of Economics, Brown University. Mimeo.

Nightingale, D. S., and L. C. Burbridge. 1987. "The Status of State Work-Welfare Programs in 1986: Implications for Welfare Reform." Project Report to the Ford Foundation. Washington, D.C.: Urban Institute.

Orr, L. L. 1986. "AFDC Homemaker-Home Health Aide Demonstrations: Benefits and Costs." Report. Cambridge, Mass.: Abt Associates.

Rea, S. A., Jr. 1974. "Trade-Offs between Alternative Income Maintenance Programs." In *Studies in Public Welfare,* paper no. 13, *How Income Supplements Can Affect Work Behavior,* pp. 33–63. Prepared for the Subcommittee on Fiscal Policy, Joint Economic Committee, 93d Cong., 2d sess. Washington, D.C.: U.S. Government Printing Office.

Reischauer, R. D. "Testimony." 1987. Presented before the Subcommittee on Social Security and Family Policy, Committee on Finance, U.S. Senate, February 23.

U.S. Congressional Budget Office. 1987. *Work-Related Programs for Welfare Recipients.* Washington, D.C.: Congressional Budget Office.

U.S. General Accounting Office. 1987. *Work and Welfare: Current AFDC Work Programs and Implications for Federal Policy.* Washington, D.C.: U.S. Government Printing Office.

U.S. House of Representatives, Committee on Ways and Means. 1987. *Background Material and Data on Programs within the Jurisdiction of the Committee on Ways and Means.* Washington, D.C.: U.S. Government Printing Office.

Comment on Chapter 4

Employment and Training Reporter, December 16, 1987, pp. 314–316.

Grossman, J., R. Maynard, and J. Roberts. 1985. "Reanalysis of the Effects of Selected Employment and Training Programs for Welfare Recipients." Report. Princeton, N.J.: Mathematica Policy Research, Inc.

Grinker, Walker, and Associates. 1984, 1985, 1986. *An Assessment of JTPA Implementation,* vols. 1, 2, 3. New York: GWA.

Public/Private Ventures. 1986. *The Summer Training and Education Program: 1986 Findings.* Philadelphia: P/PV.

Resnick, L. B. 1988. *Education and Learning to Think.* Washington, D.C.: National Academy of Sciences, 1988.

5. Targeting Long-Term Welfare Recipients

Adams, G. 1987. "The Dynamics of Welfare Recipiency among Adolescent Mothers." Draft of paper prepared for the Congressional Budget Office, Washington, D.C.

Bane, M. J. 1984. "Household Composition and Poverty." Conference paper, Institute for Research on Poverty, presented at Williamsburg, Va., December 6–8.

Bane, M. J., and D. T. Ellwood. 1983. *The Dynamics of Dependence: The Routes to Self-Sufficiency.* Cambridge, Mass.: Urban Systems Research.

Besharov, D., and M. Dally. 1986. "How Much Are Working Mothers Working?" *Public Opinion,* November/December, pp. 48–51.

Besharov, D., A. Quin, and K. Zinmeister. 1987. "A Portrait in Black and White: Out-of-Wedlock Births." *Public Opinion,* May/June, p. 43.

Duncan, G. J., and S. D. Hoffman. 1985. "A Reconsideration of the Economic Consequences of Marital Dissolution." *Demography,* 22(4), pp. 485–497.

Eberstadt, N. 1987. "Economic and Material Poverty in Modern America." Revised version of paper presented at the Working Seminar on the Family and American Welfare Policy, Washington, D.C., American Enterprise Institute for Public Policy Research, April 30.

Ellwood, D. 1986. "Targeting 'Would-Be' Long-Term Recipients of AFDC." Report. Princeton, N.J.: Mathematica Policy Research, Inc.

Friedlander, D. 1988. *Subgroup Impacts and Performance Indicators for Selected Welfare Employment Programs.* New York: Manpower Demonstration Research Corporation.

Garfinkel, I., and S. McLanahan. 1986. *Single Mothers and Their Children.* Washington, D.C.: Urban Institute.

Glick, P. C. 1979. "Children of Divorced Parents in Demographic Perspective." *Journal of Social Issues,* 35.

Green, G., and E. Welniak. 1982. "Changing Family Composition and Income Differentials." Washington, D.C.: U.S. Department of Commerce, Bureau of the Census.

Heintz, S. 1986. In APWA, *Investing in Poor Families and Their Children: A Matter of Commitment,* Final Report Part I: "One Child in Four." Washington, D.C.: American Public Welfare Association.

Hill, M. S., and J. N. Morgan, eds. 1981. *Five Thousand American Families: Patterns of Economic Progress.* Ann Arbor: Institute for Social Research, University of Michigan.

Hofferth, S. 1985. "Updating Children's Life Course." *Journal of Marriage and Family,* 93, February.

Loury, G. C. 1985. "The Moral Quandary of the Black Community." *The Public Interest,* 79, Spring, 9–22.

Maynard, R., and M. Maxfield. 1986. "The Design of a Social Demonstration of Targeted Employment Services for AFDC Recipients." Report. Princeton, N.J.: Mathematica Policy Research, Inc.

McCarthy, J., and J. Menken. 1979. "Marriage, Remarriage, Marital Disruption, and Age at First Birth." *Family Planning Perspectives,* 11(1).

Moynihan, D. P. 1987. "The Family Security Act." Speech before the National Press Club, July 23, pp. 1–3.

Murray, C. 1986. "According to Age: Longitudinal Profiles of AFDC Recipients and the Poor by Age Group." Paper presented at the Working Seminar on the Family and American Welfare Policy, Washington, D.C., American Enterprise Institute for Public Policy Research, September.

Newberger, C., L. Melnicoe, and E. Newberger. 1986. "The American Family in Crisis: Implications for Children." *Current Problems in Pediatrics,* 20(12), pp. 670–721.

New York State Task Force. 1986. "A New Social Contract—Rethinking the Nature and Purpose of Public Assistance." Report of the Task Force on Poverty and Welfare, submitted to Governor Mario Cuomo, Albany, N.Y., December.

Norton, A. J., and P. C. Glick. 1986. "One-Parent Families: A Social and Economic Profile." *Family Relations,* 35(9).

Norton, A. J., and J. E. Moorman. 1986. "Marriage and Divorce Patterns of U.S. Women." Revised version of paper presented at the annual meeting of the Population Association of America, San Francisco, April.

Novak, M., et al. 1987. *A Community of Self-Reliance: The New Consensus on Family and Welfare.* Washington, D.C.: American Enterprise Institute for Public Policy Research.

O'Neill, J., D. A. Wolf, L. J. Bassi, and M. T. Hannan. 1984. "An Analysis of Time on Welfare." Contract no. HHS-100-83-0048. Washington, D.C.: Urban Institute.

U.S. Bureau of the Census. (1932–1981). *Vital Statistics of the United States: Natality,* 1981 ed. Washington, D.C.: U.S. Government Printing Office.

————1985a. "Living Arrangements of Children, by Characteristics of the Parent, by Marital Status of the Parent: March 1985." Unpublished data.

————1985b. "Economic Characteristics of Households in the United States: First Quarter 1984." *Current Population Reports,* P-70, no. 3. Washington D.C.: U.S. Government Printing Office.

————1985c. *Statistical Abstract of the United States: 1986,* 106th ed. Washington, D.C.: U.S. Government Printing Office.

————1986a. "Money Income and Poverty Status of Families and Persons in the United States: 1985." *Current Population Reports,* P-60, no. 154. Washington, D.C.: U.S. Government Printing Office.

————1986b. "Child Support and Alimony: 1983." *Current Population Reports,* P-23, no. 148. Washington D.C.: U.S. Government Printing Office.

U.S. Congressional Research Service. 1987. "Families at Risk." *Congressional Research Service Review: The 100th Congress—Major Issues.*

U.S. Department of Health and Human Services. 1986. *1983 Recipient Characteristics and Financial Circumstances of AFDC Recipients.* Washington, D.C.: U.S. Government Printing Office.

U.S. Department of Health and Human Services, Family Support Administration, Office of Family Assistance and Office of Policy and Evaluation. 1986. *Recipient Characteristics and Financial Circumstances of AFDC Recipients: 1983.* Washington, D.C.: U.S. Government Printing Office.

U.S. Department of Health and Human Services, National Center for Health Statistics. 1980. "National Estimates of Marriage Dissolution and Survivorship: United States." DHHS (PHS) 81-1403. Hyattsville, Md.: Public Health Service.

————1986a. "Advance Report of Final Divorce Statistics: 1984." *Monthly Vital Statistics Report,* 35(6), supp. DHHS (PHS) 86-1120. Hyattsville, Md.: Public Health Service.

————1986b. "Advance Report of Final Natality Statistics, 1984." *Monthly Vital Statistics Report*, 35 (4), supp. DHHS (PHS) 86-1120. Hyattsville, Md.: Public Health Service. 1986.

U.S. House of Representatives, Committee on Ways and Means. 1986. *Children in Poverty*. Washington, D.C.: U.S. Government Printing Office.

Weicher, J., and S. Wachter. 1986. "The Distribution of Wealth among Families: Increasing Inequality." Paper presented at the Working Seminar on the Family and American Welfare Policy, Washington, D.C., American Enterprise Institute for Public Policy Research.

Weitzman, L. 1985. *The Divorce Revolution*. New York: Free Press.

White House Working Group on the Family. 1986. *The Family: Preserving America's Future*. Washington, D.C.: WHWGF.

Wilson, W. J., and K. Neckerman. 1984. "Poverty and Family Structure: The Widening Gap between Evidence and Public Policy Issues." Conference paper, University of Wisconsin–Madison, Institute for Research on Poverty.

6. Support Services

American Enterprise Institute for Public Policy Research. 1987. *The New Consensus on Family and Welfare*. Washington, D.C.: American Enterprise Institute.

American Public Welfare Association. 1986. *Investing in Poor Families and Their Children: A Matter of Commitment*, Final Report Part I: "One Child in Four," by S. Heintz. Washington, D.C.: APWA.

Anderson, J. E., and L. G. Cope. 1987. "The Impact of Family Planning Program Activity on Fertility." *Family Planning Perspectives*, 19, pp. 152–157.

Bane, M. J., and D. Ellwood. 1983. *The Dynamics of Welfare Dependence: The Routes to Self-Sufficiency*. Cambridge, Mass.: Urban Systems and Research.

Barglow, P., B. E. Vaughn, and J. Molitor. 1988. "Effects of Maternal Absence due to Employment on the Quality of Infant-Mother Attachment in a Low-Risk Sample." *Child Development*, in press.

Bass, S. 1984. "A Closer Look at the Safety Net: The Human and Social Impact of Selected Welfare Changes in Massachusetts." Boston: Massachusetts Department of Social Services.

Benardik, E., P. Namerow, and M. Weinstein. 1982. "Does a Prior Pregnancy Affect Choice of Contraceptive Method or Effectiveness of Use?" Paper presented at the annual meeting of the American Public Health Association, Montreal.

Berrueta-Clement, J. R., L. J. Schweinhard, W. S. Barnett, A. S. Epstein, and D. P. Weikart. 1984. "Changed Lives: The Effects of the Perry Preschool Program on Youths through Age 19." Monographs of the High/Scope Educational Research Foundation, no. 8. Ypsilanti, Mich.: High/Scope Press.

Betsey, C. L., et al. 1985. *Youth Employment and Training Programs: The YEDPA Years*. Washington, D.C.: National Academy Press.

Beyna, L., J. Bell, and J. Trutko. 1984. *Six-Month Evaluation of the Maryland Day Care Voucher Demonstration*. Arlington, Va.: James Bell and Associates.

Blanchard, M., and M. Main. 1979. "Avoidance of the Attachment Figure and Social-Emotional Adjustment in Day Care Infants." *Developmental Psychology,* 15, pp. 445–446.

Blank, H. 1986. "The Special Needs of Single-Parent and Low-Income Families." In *Group Care for Young Children,* ed. N. Gunzenhauser and B. M. Caldwell. Key Biscayne, Fla.: Johnson and Johnson Baby Products Co.

Blank, R. 1987. "The Effect of Medical Need on AFDC and Medicaid Participation." Discussion paper no. 831-87, Madison: University of Wisconsin–Madison, Institute for Research on Poverty.

Blau, P. M., and P. K. Robins. 1986. "Fertility, Employment, and Child Care Costs: A Dynamic Analysis." Paper presented at the annual meeting of the Population Association of America, San Francisco.

————1987. "Child Care Costs and Family Labor Supply." Paper presented at the annual meeting of the Population Association of America, Chicago.

Branch, A., J. Riccio, and J. Quint. 1984. *Building Self-Sufficiency in Pregnant and Parenting Teens.* New York: Manpower Demonstration Research Corporation.

Brindis, C., R. P. Barth, and A. Loomis (prepared 1987). "Continuous Counseling: Case Management in a Comprehensive Teenage Pregnancy and Parenting Project." *Social Casework,* forthcoming.

Brookhart, J., and E. Hock. 1976. "The Effects of Experimental Context and Experiential Background on Infants' Behavior toward Their Mothers and a Stranger." *Child Development,* 47, pp. 333–340.

Brush, L., 1987. "Child Care Used by Working Women in the AFDC Population: An Analysis of the SIPP Data Base." Paper prepared for the Office of Social Services Policy, DHHS.

Burt, M., M. Kimmick, J. Goldmuntz, and F. Sonenstein. 1984. *Helping Pregnant Adolescents: Outcomes and Costs of Service Delivery.* Final report to the Office of Adolescent Pregnancy Programs. Washington, D.C.: Urban Institute.

Campbell, F. A., B. Breitmayer, and C. T. Ramey. 1986. "Disadvantaged Single Teenage Mothers and Their Children: Consequences of Free Educational Day Care." *Family Relations,* 35, pp. 63–68.

Chamie, M., and S. K. Henshaw. 1981. "The Costs and Benefits of Government Expenditures for Family Planning Programs." *Family Planning Perspectives,* 13, pp. 117–124.

Cochran, M. M. 1977. "A Comparison of Group Care and Family Childrearing Patterns in Sweden." *Child Development,* 48, pp. 702–707.

Cramer, J. C. 1980. "Fertility and Female Employment." *American Sociological Review,* 45, pp. 167–190.

Cutright, P., and F. S. Jaffe. 1977. *Impact of Family Planning Programs on Fertility: The U.S. Experience.* New York: Praeger Press.

Dadkhah, K. M., and W. Stromsdorfer. 1981. "The Decision of Welfare Clients to Volunteer for Work and Training." Report. Cambridge, Mass.: Abt Associates.

Davis, K., and D. Rowland. 1983. "Uninsured and Underserved: Inequities in Health Care in the U.S." *Milbank Memorial Fund Quarterly,* 61, pp. 149–176.

Dubnoff, S. 1986. "Work Related Day Care: A Survey of Parents." In *FY '86 Day Care Report.* Boston: Massachusetts Department of Social Services.

Easterbrooks, M. A., and W. A. Goldberg. 1985. "Effects of Early Maternal Employment on Toddlers, Mothers, and Fathers." *Developmental Psychology,* 21, pp. 774–783.

Ellwood, D. 1986. "Targeting the 'Would-Be' Long-Term Welfare Recipient." Report. Princeton, N.J.: Mathematica Policy Research, Inc.

Ellwood, D., and M. J. Bane. 1985. "The Impact of AFDC on Family Structure and Living Arrangements." *Research in Labor Economics,* 7, pp. 137–149.

Farber, E. B., and B. Egeland. 1982. "Developmental Consequences of Out-of-Home Care for Infants in a Low-Income Population." In *Day Care: Scientific and Social Policy Issues,* ed. E. F. Zigler and D. W. Gordon. Boston: Auburn House.

Ford, K. 1983. "Second Pregnancies among Teenage Mothers." *Family Planning Perspectives,* 15, pp. 268–272.

Forrest, J. D., A. I. Hermalin, and S. Henshaw. 1981. "The Impact of Family Planning Clinic Programs on Adolescent Pregnancy." *Family Planning Perspectives,* 13, pp. 109–116.

Freis and Miller and Associates. 1980. "The Economic Impact of Subsidized Child Care." Livermore, Calif.: Freis and Miller.

Freund, D. A., and R. E. Hurley. 1987. "Managed Care in Medicaid." *Annual Review of Public Health,* 8, pp. 137–163.

Garber, H. L., and R. Heber. 1981. "The Efficacy of Early Intervention with Family Rehabilitation." In *Psychosocial Influences in Retarded Performance,* vol. 2, *Strategies for Improving Competence,* ed. M. J. Begab, H. C. Haywood, and H. L. Garber. Baltimore: University Park Press.

Gittell, M., and J. Moore. 1985. *Women on Welfare: Education and Work.* New York: Ford Foundation.

Goldman, B. 1981. *Impacts of the Immediate Job Search Assistance Experiment.* Louisville WIN Research Laboratory Project. New York: Manpower Demonstration Research Corporation.

Goldman, B., D. Friedlander, J. Gueron, and D. Long. 1985. *Findings from the San Diego Job Search and Work Experience Demonstration.* New York: Manpower Demonstration Research Corporation.

Gray, W., L. Kafalas, and D. Knight. 1984. "An Evaluation of the Massachusetts Voucher Day Care." Boston: Massachusetts Department of Social Services.

Griffith, J. D., and C. L. Usher. 1986. "A Quasi-Experimental Assessment of the National Impact of the 1981 Omnibus Budget Reconciliation Act (OBRA) on the Aid to Families with Dependent Children (AFDC) Program." *Evaluation Review,* 10, pp. 313–333.

Gueron, J. 1986. *Work Initiatives for Welfare Recipients: Lessons from a Multi-State Experiment.* New York: Manpower Demonstration Research Corporation.

Hagen, J. L. 1987. "Income Maintenance Workers: Technicians or Service Providers." *Social Services Review,* 61, pp. 261–271.

Haskins, R. 1985. "Public School Aggression among Children with Varying Day-Care Experience." *Child Development,* 56, pp. 689–703.

Hofferth, S. 1981. *Effects of Number and Timing of Births on Family Well-Being over the Life Cycle.* Final report to NICHD. Washington, D.C.: Urban Institute.

————1987a. "The Effects of Programs and Policies on Adolescent Pregnancy and Childbearing." In *Risking the Future: Adolescent Sexuality, Pregnancy, and Childbearing,* vol. 2, ed. S. L. Hofferth and C. D. Hayes. Washington, D.C.: National Academy Press.

————1987b. "Child Care in the U.S." Statement made before the U.S. House of Representatives, Select Committee on Children, Youth, and Families, July 1.

Hofferth, S., and D. A. Phillips. 1987. "Child Care in the United States: 1970 to 1985." *Journal of Marriage and the Family,* 49, pp. 559–571.

Hofferth, S. L., and F. L. Sonenstein. 1983. *An Examination of the Effects of Alternative Approaches to Financing Day Care for AFDC Children.* Washington, D.C.: Urban Institute.

Hosni, D., and B. Donnan. 1979. "An Economic Analysis of Child Care Supports to Low-Income Mothers." Orlando: University of Central Florida Press.

Kalmuss, D. 1986. "Contraceptive Use: A Comparison Between Ever- and Never-Pregnant Adolescents." *Journal of Adolescent Health Care,* 7, pp. 332–337.

Kasper, J. D. 1986. "Health Status and Utilization: Differences by Medicaid Coverage and Income." *Health Care Financing Review,* 4, pp. 1–14.

Keefe, D. E. 1983. "Governor Reagan, Welfare Reform, and AFDC Fertility." *Social Service Review,* 57, pp. 234–253.

Kern, R. G., and S. R. Windham. 1986. *Medicaid and Other Experiments in State Health Policy.* Washington, D.C.: American Enterprise Institute for Public Policy Research.

Klausner, S. Z. 1978. *Six Years in the Lives of the Impoverished: An Examination of the WIN Thesis.* Washington, D.C.: U.S. Department of Labor.

Klerman, L. 1986. "Health Care Component of the New Chance Demonstration." New York: Manpower Demonstration Research Corporation.

Klerman, L., and J. F. Jekel. 1983. *School-Age Mothers: Problems, Programs, and Policy.* Hamden, Conn.: Linnet Books.

Long, S. H., and R. F. Settle. 1984. "The Impact of Eligibility Changes under the Omnibus Budget Reconciliation Act of 1981 on the Characteristics of the Medicaid Population." Syracuse, N.Y.: Maxwell School, Syracuse University.

————1985. "Cutbacks in Medicaid Eligibility under the Omnibus Budget Reconciliation Act of 1981: Implications for Access to Health Care Services among the Newly Ineligible." Syracuse, N.Y.: Maxwell School, Syracuse University.

Macrae, J. W., and E. Herbert-Jackson. 1976. "Are Behavioral Effects of Infant Day Care Program Specific?" *Developmental Psychology,* 12, pp. 269–270.

Makinson, C. 1985. "The Health Consequences of Teenage Fertility." *Family Planning Perspectives,* 17, pp. 132–139.

Manpower Demonstration Research Corporation. 1980. *Preliminary Research Findings: WIN Research Laboratory Project.* New York: MDRC.

Marini, M. M. 1978. *Consequences of Childbearing and Childspacing Patterns for Parents.* Final report to NICHD. Seattle, Wash.: Battelle Human Affairs Research Center.

Marx, F. 1985. "Child Care." In *Services to Young Families,* ed. H. McAdoo and T. M. J. Parham. Washington, D.C.: American Public Welfare Association.

Masters, S., and R. Maynard. 1981. *The Impact of Supported Work on Long-Term Recipients of AFDC Benefits.* New York: Manpower Demonstration Research Corporation.

Maxfield, M., and M. Rucci. 1986. "A Simulation Model of Employment and Training Programs for Long-Term Welfare Recipients: Technical Documentation." Report. Princeton, N.J.: Mathematica Policy Research, Inc.

McMurray, G., and D. Kazanjian. 1982. *Day Care and the Working Poor: The Struggle for Self-Sufficiency.* New York: Community Service Society of New York.

Millman, S. R., and G. Hendershot. 1980. "Early Fertility and Lifetime Fertility." *Family Planning Perspectives,* 12, pp. 139–149.

Mitchell, J. J., M. L. Chadwin, and D. S. Nightingale. 1980. *Implementing Welfare-Employment Programs: An Institutional Analysis of the Work Incentive (WIN) Program.* Washington, D.C.: U.S. Department of Labor.

Moffitt, R., and D. A. Wolf. 1987. "The Effect of the 1981 Omnibus Budget Reconciliation Act on Welfare Recipients and Work Incentives." *Social Service Review,* 61, pp. 247–260.

Moore, K. A., and S. Caldwell. 1977. "The Effect of Government Policies on Out-of-Wedlock Sex and Pregnancy." *Family Planning Perspectives,* 9, pp. 164–169.

Moore, K. A., and R. F. Wertheimer. 1984. "Teenage Childbearing and Welfare: Preventive and Ameliorative Strategies." *Family Planning Perspectives,* 16, pp. 285–289.

Moore, K. A., S. Hofferth, S. Caldwell, and L. Waite. 1979. *Teenage Motherhood: Social and Economic Consequences.* Washington, D.C.: Urban Institute.

Moscovice, I., and W. Craig. 1984. "The Omnibus Budget Reconciliation Act and the Working Poor." *Social Service Review,* 58, pp. 49–62.

Moscovice, I., and G. Davidson. 1987. "Health Care and Insurance Loss of Working AFDC Recipients." *Medical Care,* 25, pp. 413–425.

Mosena, P. 1986. "Adolescent Parent Outreach Follow-Up Survey." Unpublished paper. Chicago: University of Chicago.

Mott, F. L. 1986. "The Pace of Repeated Childbearing among Young American Mothers." *Family Planning Perspectives,* 58, pp. 5–12.

Mott, F. L., and W. Marsiglio. 1985. "Early Childbearing and Completion of High School." *Family Planning Perspectives,* 17, pp. 234–237.

National Coalition on Women, Work and Welfare Reform. 1987. *Changing Welfare: An Investment in Women and Children in Poverty.* Washington, D.C.: National Coalition.

National Governor's Association. 1987. *NGA Welfare Reform Policy.* Washington, D.C. NGA.

New York State Task Force on Poverty and Welfare. 1986. "A New Social Contract: Rethinking the Nature and Purpose of Public Assistance." Report of the Task Force on Poverty and Welfare, submitted to Governor Mario Cuomo, Albany, N.Y., December.

O'Connell, J. C., and D. C. Farran. 1982. "Effects of Day-Care Experience on the Use of Intentional Communicative Behaviors in a Sample of Socioeconomically Depressed Infants." *Developmental Psychology,* 18, pp. 22–29.

Olds, D., C. Henderson, M. Birmingham, and R. Chamberlain. 1983. "Prenatal/ Early Infancy Project: Final Report to Health Resource Service Administration." Rochester, N.Y.: University of Rochester.

Orr, M. T., and L. Brenner. 1981. "Medicaid Funding of Family Planning Clinic Services." *Family Planning Perspectives,* 13, pp. 280–287.

Pierson, D., M. Bronson, E. Dromey, J. Schwarz, T. Tivnan, and D. Walker. 1983. "The Impact of Early Education." *Evaluation Review,* 7, pp. 191–216

Placek, P. J., and G. Hendershot. 1974. "Public Welfare and Family Planning: An Empirical Study of the 'Brood Sow' Myth." *Social Problems,* 21, pp. 658–673.

Polgar, S., and V. A. Hiday. 1974. "The Effect of an Additional Birth on Low-Income Urban Families." *Population Studies,* 28, pp. 463–471.

Polit, D. F. 1986a. *Comprehensive Programs for Pregnant and Parenting Teens.* New York: Manpower Demonstration Research Corporation.

——1986b. *Building Self-Sufficiency: A Guide to Vocational and Employment Services for Teenage Parents.* Saratoga Springs, N.Y.: Humanalysis, Inc.

Polit, D. F., and C. M. White. 1987. *Parenting among Low-Income Teenage Mothers.* Saratoga Springs, N.Y.: Humanalysis, Inc.

Polit, D. F., J. R. Kahn, and G. Enman. 1981. *Contraceptive Decision-Making in Adolescent Couples.* Final report to NICHD. Cambridge, Mass.: American Institutes for Research.

Polit, D. F., J. R. Kahn, and D. Stevenson. 1985. *Final Impacts in Project Redirection.* New York: Manpower Demonstration Research Corporation.

Polit, D. F., J. Kahn, C. A. Murray, and K. Smith. 1982. *Needs and Characteristics of Pregnant and Parenting Teens.* New York: Manpower Demonstration Research Corporation.

Presser, H., and W. Baldwin. 1980. "Child Care as a Constraint on Employment: Prevalence, Correlates, and Bearing on the Work and Fertility Nexus." *American Journal of Sociology,* 85, pp. 1202–13.

Project on the Welfare of Families. 1986. *Ladders Out of Poverty.* Washington, D.C.: American Horizons Foundation.

Ramey, C. T., and F. A. Campbell. 1984. "Preventive Education for High-Risk Children: Cognitive Consequences of the Carolina Abecederian Project." *American Journal of Mental Deficiency,* 8, pp. 515–523.

Ramey, C. T., D. MacPhee, and K. O. Yeates. 1982. "Preventing Developmental Retardation: A General Systems Model." In *Facilitating Infant and Early Childhood Development,* ed. L. A. Bond and J. M. Joffe. Hanover, N.H.: University Press of New England.

Robins, P. K. (prepared 1987). "Child Care and Convenience: The Effects of Labor Market Entry Costs on Economic Self-Sufficiency among Public Housing Residents." *Social Science Quarterly,* forthcoming.

Roopnarine, J. L., and M. E. Lamb. 1980. "Peer and Parent-Child Interaction before and after Enrollment in Nursery School." *Journal of Applied Developmental Psychology,* 1, pp. 77–81.

Rubinstein, J. L., C. Howes, and P. Boyle. 1981. "A Two-Year Follow-Up of Infants in Community-Based Day Care." *Journal of Child Psychology and Psychiatry,* 22, pp. 209–218.

Salkever, D. S. 1982. "Children's Health Problems and Maternal Work Status." *The Journal of Human Resources,* 17, pp. 94–109.

Schindler, P. J., B. E. Moely, and A. L. Frank. 1987. "Time in Day Care and Social Participation in Young Children." *Developmental Psychology,* 23, pp. 255–261.

Schwarz, J. C. 1983. "Length of Day Care Attendance and Attachment Behavior in Eighteen-Month-Old Infants." *Child Development,* 54, pp. 1073–78.

Scoll, B., and R. Engstrom. 1985. "Final Report of the Hennepin County Grant Purchase of Child Day Care through a Voucher System." Minneapolis: Hennepin County Community Services Department.

Smith, J. P., and M. P. Ward. 1980. "Asset Accumulation and Family Size." *Demography,* 17, pp. 243–260.

Sonenstein, F. L. 1984. "Federal Child Care Subsidization Policies: Their Impact on Child Care Services Used by AFDC Recipients." Paper presented to the National Council on Family Relations, San Francisco.

———1987. "Caring for the Children of Welfare Mothers." Paper presented at the Maryland Governor's Conference on Work and Welfare, July.

Stolzenberg, R. M., and L. J. Waite. 1984. "Local Labor Markets, Children and Labor Force Participation of Wives." *Demography,* 21, pp. 157–170.

Strobino, D. 1987. "The Health and Medical Consequences of Adolescent Sexuality and Pregnancy." In *Risking the Future: Adolescent Sexuality, Pregnancy, and Childbearing,* Vol. 2, ed. S. L. Hofferth and C. D. Hayes. Washington, D.C.: National Academy Press.

Sum, A., and B. Goedicke. 1986. "Basic Academic Skill Deficiencies of Young Women Potentially Eligible for Participation in Project New Chance: Implications for Educational Remediation and Training." Boston: Center for Labor Market Studies.

U.S. Bureau of the Census. 1987. *Who's Minding the Kids?* Current Population Reports, P-70, no. 9.

U.S. House of Representatives, Select Committee on Children, Youth and Families. 1984. *Families and Child Care: Improving the Options.* Washington, D.C.: Government Printing Office.

Vaughn, B., F. Gove, and B. Egeland. 1980. "The Relationship between Out-of-Home Care and the Quality of Infant-Mother Attachment in an Economically Deprived Population." *Child Development,* 51, pp. 1203–14.

Vlietstra, A. 1981. "Full- Versus Half-Day Preschool Attendance: Effects in Young Children as Assessed by Teacher Ratings and Behavioral Observations." *Child Development,* 52, pp. 603–610.

Weatherley, R., S. Perlman, M. Levine, and L. Klerman. 1985. "Patchwork Programs: Comprehensive Services for Pregnant and Parenting Adolescents." Seattle: University of Washington.

White House Domestic Policy Council. 1986a. Low Income Opportunity Working Group, *Up from Dependency: A New National Public Assistance Strategy.* Washington, D.C.: Domestic Policy Council.

———1986b. Working Group on the Family, *The Family: Preserving America's Future.* Washington, D.C.: Domestic Policy Council.

Wolfhagen, C., and B. Goldman. 1983. *Job Search Strategies: Lessons from the Louis-ville WIN Laboratory*. New York: Manpower Demonstration Research Corporation.

7. Institutional Effects of Reform

Goodison, M. 1982. "Testing Literacy Levels in the WIN Population." Project Report to U.S. Department of Labor, Employment and Training Administration. Princeton, N.J.: Center for Occupational and Professional Assessment, Educational Testing Service.

Levitan, S. A., and I. Shapiro. 1987. *Working But Poor*. Baltimore: Johns Hopkins University Press.

Nightingale, D. S. 1986. "Assessing the Employability of Welfare Clients." Paper prepared for the New York State Department of Social Services 1986 Employment Training Conference, Albany, N.Y., May 22. Washington, D.C.: Urban Institute.

Nightingale, D. S., and L. C. Burbridge. 1987. "The Status of State Work-Welfare Programs in 1986: Implications for Welfare Reform." Project Report to the Ford Foundation. Washington, D.C.: Urban Institute.

Novak, W., et al. 1987. *A Community of Self-Reliance: The New Consensus on the Family and Welfare*. Washington, D.C.: American Enterprise Institute for Public Policy Research.

Sonenstein, F., and C. Calhoun. 1987. "Results of Pilot Studies of the Survey of Absent Parents." Project Report to U.S. Department of Health and Human Services, Asst. Secy. for Policy and Evaluation. Washington, D.C.: Urban Institute.

U.S. House of Representatives, Committee on Ways and Means. 1988. *Background Material and Data on Programs within the Jurisdiction of the Committee on Ways and Means*. Washington, D.C.: U.S. Government Printing Office.

8. Child-Support Policies

Bane, M. J. 1986. "Household Composition and Poverty." In *Fighting Poverty: What Works and What Doesn't*, ed. S. H. Danzinger and D. H. Weinberg. Cambridge, Mass.: Harvard University Press.

Duncan, G., and S. Hoffman. 1985. "Economic Consequences of Marital Instability." In *Horizontal Equity, Uncertainty, and Economic Well-Being*, ed. M. David and T. Smeeding. Chicago: University of Chicago Press.

Garfinkel, I. 1985. "The Role of Child Support Insurance in Antipoverty Policy." *Annals of the American Academy of Political and Social Science*, 479, May, pp. 119–131.

Garfinkel, I., P. Robins, and P. Wong. 1987. "The Wisconsin Child Support Assurance System: Estimated Effects on Participants." Discussion Paper no. 833-87. Madison: University of Wisconsin–Madison, Institute for Research on Poverty.

Garfinkel I., P. Robins, and P Wong. 1987. "The Wisconsin Child Support Assurance System: Estimated Effects on Participants." Discussion Paper no. 833-87. Madison: University of Wisconsin–Madison, Institute for Research on Poverty.

Graham, J., and A. Beller. 1985. "A Note on the Number and Living Arrangements of Women with Children under 21 from an Absent Father: Revised Estimates for the April 1979 and 1982 Current Population Surveys." *Journal of Economic and Social Measurement*, 13, pp. 209–214.

Haskins, R., A. Dobelsten, J. Akin, and J. B. Schwartz. 1985. "Estimates of National Child Support Collections Potential and the Income Security of Female-Headed Families." Final Report to the Office of Child Support Enforcement, Social Security Administration. Bush Institute for Child and Family Policy, University of North Carolina at Chapel Hill, April.

Kamerman, S., and A. Kahn. 1987. "Mother-Only Families in Western Europe." Report prepared for the German Marshall Fund of the United States. New York: Columbia University School of Social Work. Mimeo.

Krause, H. 1973. "Child Welfare, Parental Responsibility, and the State." In *The Family, Poverty, and Welfare Programs: Household Patterns and Government Policies*, prepared for the Subcommittee on Fiscal Policy, Joint Economic Committee, Paper No. 12, Part II, in the series *Studies in Public Welfare*. Washington, D.C.: U.S. Government Printing Office.

Lerman, R. 1985. "Separating Income Support from Income Supplementation." *Journal of the Institute of Socioeconomic Studies*, Autumn, pp. 101–125.

———1986. "A National Profile of Young Unwed Fathers: Who Are They and How Are They Parenting?" Paper presented at the Conference on Unwed Fathers, Family Impact Seminar, Catholic University, Washington, D.C., October.

MAXIMUS. 1983. "Evaluation of the Child Support Enforcement Program: Final Report." Technical Report, Office of Research and Statistics, Social Security Administration, U.S. Department of Health and Human Services, McLean, Va., April.

Nakosteen, R., and M. Zimmer. 1987. "Marital Status and the Earnings of Young Men." *Journal of Human Resources*, Spring, pp. 248–268.

Oellerich, D., and I. Garfinkel. 1983. "Distributional Impacts of Existing and Alternative Child Support Systems." *Policy Studies Journal*, Spring, pp. 119–130.

Office of Child Support Enforcement. 1986. *10th Annual Report to Congress*, vol. 2, *Child Support Enforcement Statistics, Fiscal Year 1985*. Washington, D.C.: U.S. Department of Health and Human Services.

O'Neill, J. 1986. "Determinants of Child Support." Final report prepared for the Center for Population Research, National Institute of Child Health and Human Development. Washington, D.C: Urban Institute.

Robins, P. 1986. "Child Support, Welfare Dependency, and Poverty." *American Economic Review*, September, pp. 768–788.

———1987. "An Analysis of Trends in Child Support and AFDC from 1979 to 1983." Discussion Paper DP 842-84. Madison: University of Wisconsin–Madison, Institute for Research on Poverty.

U.S. Bureau of the Census. 1981. "Child Support and Alimony: 1978." Current Population Reports, P-23, vol. 112. Washington, D.C.: U.S. Government Printing Office.

———1983. "Child Support and Alimony: 1981 (Advance Report)." Current Population Reports, P-23, vol. 124. Washington, D.C.: U.S. Government Printing Office.

————1986. "Child Support and Alimony: 1983 (Supplemental Report)." Current Population Reports, P-23, vol. 148. Washington, D.C.: U.S. Government Printing Office.

————1987a. "Child Support and Alimony: 1985 (Advance Report)." Current Population Reports, P-23, vol. 152. Washington, D.C.: U.S. Government Printing Office.

————1987b. "Money Income of Households, Families, and Persons in the United States: 1986." Current Population Reports, P-60. Washington, D.C.: U.S. Government Printing Office.

U.S. House of Representatives, Committee on Ways and Means. 1987. *Background Material and Data on Programs within the Jurisdiction of the Committee on Ways and Means.* Washington, D.C.: U.S. Government Printing Office.

Weiss, R. 1984. "The Impact of Marital Dissolution on Income and Consumption in Single-Parent Households." *Journal of Marriage and the Family,* February, pp. 115–127.

Weitzman, L. 1985. *The Divorce Revolution: The Unexpected Social and Economic Consequences of Women and Children in America.* Chicago: Free Press.

9. Costs of Welfare Programs

Brown, R., et al. 1983. *Final Report, Employment Opportunity Pilot Project: Analysis of Program Impacts.* Princeton, N.J.: Mathematica Policy Research, Inc.

Council of Economic Advisors. 1987. *Economic Indicators.* Washington, D.C.: U.S. Government Printing Office.

Friedlander, D., et al. 1985. *Final Report on the Employment Initiatives Evaluation.* New York: Manpower Demonstration Research Corporation.

Friedlander, D., M. Erickson, G. Hamilton, and V. Knox. 1986. *Final Report on the Community Work Experience Demonstration.* New York: Manpower Demonstration Research Corporation.

Garfinkel, I. 1988. "Child Support Assurance: A New Tool for Achieving Social Security." In *Child Support: From Debt Collection to Social Policy,* ed. A. Kahn and S. Kamerman. Beverly Hills, Calif.: Sage Publications.

Goldman, B., D. Friedlander, and D. Long. 1986. *Final Report of the San Diego Job Search and Work Experience Demonstration.* New York: Manpower Demonstration Research Corporation.

Gramlich, E. 1982. "An Econometric Examination of the New Federalism." *Brookings Papers on Economic Activity,* 2, pp. 327–360.

Kemper, P., D. Long, and C. Thornton. 1984. "A Benefit-Cost Analysis of the Supported Work Program." In *The National Supported Work Demonstration,* ed. R. Hollister, P. Kemper, and R. Maynard. Madison: University of Wisconsin Press.

Levitan, S., and F. Gallo. 1986. "The Targeted Jobs Tax Credit: An Uncertain and Unfinished Experiment." Washington, D.C.: Center for Social Policy Studies, George Washington University, September. Mimeo.

Long, D. 1983. "An Analysis of the Costs of the Employment Opportunity Pilot Project." Report. Princeton, N.J.: Mathematica Policy Research, Inc.

Long, D., C. Mallar, and C. Thornton. 1981. "Evaluating the Benefits and Costs of the Job Corps." *Journal of Policy Analysis and Management,* 1(1), pp. 55–76.

Manpower Demonstration Research Corporation. 1980. *Summary and Findings of the National Supported Work Demonstration.* Cambridge, Mass.: Ballinger.

Massachusetts Taxpayers Foundation. 1987. "Training People to Live Without Welfare." Boston: Massachusetts Taxpayers Foundation. Mimeo.

National Commission for Employment Policy. 1987. *The Job Training Partnership Act.* Washington, D.C.: National Commission for Employment Policy.

Social Security Administration. 1986. *Social Security Bulletin. Annual Statistical Supplement, 1986.* Washington, D.C.: U.S. Government Printing Office.

Taggart, Robert. 1981. *A Fisherman's Guide: An Assessment of Training and Remedial Strategies.* Kalamazoo, Mich.: W.E. Upjohn Institute for Employment Research.

U.S. Bureau of the Census. 1987. *Who's Minding the Kids?* Current Population Report, P-70, no. 9. Washington, D.C.: U.S. Bureau of the Census.

U.S. Department of Education. 1987. *Digest of Education Statistics, 1987.* Washington, D.C.: U.S. Department of Education, Center for Education Statistics.

U.S. Department of Health and Human Services. 1987. *Low Income Home Energy Assistance Program, Report to Congress for Fiscal Year 1986.* Washington, D.C.: U.S. Department of Health and Human Services, Family Support Administration.

U.S. Department of Labor, Employment and Training Administration. 1987. *Job Corps in Brief.* Washington, D.C.: U.S. Department of Labor.

U.S. General Accounting Office. 1987. *Work and Welfare: Current AFDC Work Programs and Implications for Federal Policy.* Washington, D.C.: U.S. General Accounting Office.

U.S. House of Representatives, Committee on Ways and Means. 1987a. *Background Material and Data on Programs within the Jurisdiction of the Committee of Ways and Means, 1987 Edition.* Washington, D.C.: U.S. Government Printing Office.

U.S. House of Representatives, Committee on Ways and Means. 1987b. *Family Welfare Reform Act of 1987: Report, Parts 1, 2, and 3.* Report 100–159. Washington, D.C.: U.S. House of Representatives.

Notes

1. The Welfare Reform Legislation

1. The principal groups were the National Governors' Association, the American Public Welfare Association, the Task Force on Poverty and Welfare convened by Governor Mario Cuomo, the Project on the Welfare of Families convened by Governor Bruce Babbitt and Arthur Flemming, and the Working Seminar on Family and American Welfare Policy convened by Marquette University and the American Enterprise Institute. For a review of the reports they issued, see Reischauer (1987a).

2. The major legislative proposals introduced in 1987 were the Administration's Low Income Opportunity Improvement Act (H.R. 1288 and S. 610); the Family Welfare Reform Act of 1987 (H.R. 1720) which was passed by the House of Representatives with Food Stamp amendments as H.R. 3644; H.R. 3200, the AFDC Employment and Training Reorganization Act drafted by the House Republicans as a substitute to H.R. 1720; and the Family Security Act of 1987 of Senator Moynihan (S. 1511), which was passed by the Senate.

3. For more on public attitudes about the poor and welfare, see Smith (1987) and Lewis and Schneider (1985).

4. A recent *New York Times*/CBS News poll (see *New York Times,* 1987) directed at methods of reducing the deficit found that Americans favored spending as follows:

    On programs for the poor, 54 percent for higher, 9 percent for lower, 34 percent for unchanged; on defense, 18 percent for higher, 28 percent for lower, 51 percent for unchanged; on agriculture, 55 percent for higher, 14 percent for lower, and 27 percent for unchanged.

5. For estimates of the size of the homeless population, see Freeman and Hall (1986).

6. While the poverty rate among children has risen since the early 1970s, the fraction of all poor who are children has fallen slightly:

%	1959	1970	1980	1983	1987
Children who are poor	26.9	14.9	17.9	21.8	20.0

Poor who
are children   43.6   40.3   38.0   37.9   38.2

7. This conclusion derives from comparing the fraction of the population that is poor in a single year to the fraction that is poor over an extended period such as ten years. The PSID estimates that while 6.8 percent of the population was poor in 1978 (11.0 percent below 1.25 percent of the poverty threshold), 24.4 percent (32.5 percent below 1.25 percent of poverty) were poor at least one year during the 1969 to 1978 period (see Duncan, 1984).

8. For estimates of the fraction of children who will spend part of their childhood in a single-parent family, see Hofferth (1985) and Bumpass (1984). For estimates of the fraction of marriages that will end in divorce, see Norton and Moorman (1987).

9. For further information, see Bane and Ellwood (1983), Bane and Ellwood (1986), Ellwood (1986), and Duncan (1984).

10. Much of this evidence is contained in MDRC evaluations of state welfare-employment initiatives. For a summary of this literature, see Gueron (1987). For reviews of the effectiveness of other employment and training programs, see Barnow (1987), Grossman, Maynard, and Roberts (1985), and MDRC (1980).

11. The state of Wisconsin is engaged in a major restructuring of child support along these lines. For a description of the problem and the range of policy responses, see Garfinkel and Wong (1987).

12. In April 1988 Massachusetts enacted a program of this sort that will be phased in by 1992. See also Reischauer (1987b).

13. The Family Support Act of 1988 requires states to establish and periodically update uniform child-support guidelines for use as rebuttable presumptions in setting child-support awards. It also calls on states to make a greater effort to determine the paternity of children born out of wedlock, and to institute the automatic withholding of child-support payments from the wages of noncustodial parents.

It should be noted that the Catastrophic Health Insurance Act of 1988 requires that states provide by July 1990 prenatal care to pregnant women and full Medicaid coverage to infants up to the age of one if they live in a family with income below the federal poverty threshold.

14. The Family Support Act increased benefits slightly for recipients who work by increasing the standard earned income disregard from $75 to $90 per month and the disregard for child care costs from $160 to $175. It also altered the treatment of the EITC so that EITC payments will no longer reduce AFDC benefits.

15. The interaction with the Food Stamp program makes the state share even larger than the nominal federal AFDC matching rate implies. For example, if a state with a 50 percent matching rate wanted to improve the combined AFDC and Food Stamp benefits of a family by $10, it would have to spend $7.14 of its own money, not $5.00, to achieve this objective.

16. The welfare reform proposal passed by the House of Representatives (H.R. 1720) in 1987 would have increased the federal matching share for costs associated with benefit increases implemented during the fiscal year 1988 through 1991 period.

17. Estimates for the late 1960s and early 1970s showed that states would not change their benefit levels a great deal if matching rates were increased. Estimates for more recent years suggest that states would be significantly more responsive to changes in matching rates today. Nevertheless, some significant portion (about one-third) of any increase in the federal match for marginal benefit increases will find its way into state fiscal relief or the support of other state spending. For estimates for the early period, see Moffitt (1986) and Orr (1976). For estimates for the more recent period, see Moffitt (1987) and Gramlich (1982).

18. For the relevant research, see Bishop (1980), Ellwood and Bane (1985), Plotnick (1987), and Minarik and Goldfarb (1976).

19. For a statement of the conservative argument, see Murray (1984). The reevaluation of the Seattle-Denver evidence is presented in Cain (1987). For some recent evidence that the AFDC-U program may not have positive or benign effects on families, see Schram and Wiseman (1988).

20. States that offer benefits for less than twelve months will be required to provide Medicaid coverage for the family during the months when cash benefits are not paid because of the time limit.

21. For a recent review of the literature dealing with the impact of AFDC on migration, see Peterson and Rom (1987).

22. For a moderate statement of these arguments, see Butler and Kondratas (1987).

23. Edward M. Gramlich (1982) concludes that the existing variation in the matching rate, which is based on the square of the ratio of each state's per capita income to that of the nation, successfully compensates for state income differences.

24. The version of H.R. 1720 reported out of the Subcommittee on Public Assistance in the 100th Congress called for the establishment of minimum benefit levels that varied according to the income level in each state. After a five-year phase-in period, states would have been required to keep their AFDC-Food Stamp benefit levels at 15 percent of the state's median family income for each family size. The provision was dropped because of its cost (some $1.7 billion five years after implementation) and opposition from some of the 18 affected states. An earlier draft version of the bill (October 1, 1986) called for a minimum combined AFDC-Food Stamp benefit level equal to 55 percent of the poverty level. This minimum would have risen to 70 percent of the poverty threshold over five years.

25. The descriptions that follow relate to proposals that have been part of the current debate. A number of more radical conservative and liberal approaches to the welfare problem have been proposed but they are not under serious consideration at this time. For an example on the conservative side, see the Institute for Cultural Conservatism (1987).

26. Unpublished Bureau of Labor Statistics data show that for 1986 the labor force participation rate of married women with children under one year was 49.8 percent, for divorced women with children under three was 64.3 percent, and for never-married women with children under three was 44.4 percent.

27. These figures represent rough estimates for high-quality services per participant per year. Not all participants utilize every service and there is a considerable range in the cost of providing acceptable programs and services. For example,

one survey estimated that the average annual cost of providing care for three-to five-year-olds in large city day-care centers was $3,696 per year (see Children's Defense Fund, 1987). However, Census Bureau data suggest that the median out-of-pocket expenditure on day care by working women was roughly $2,000 per year. For more refined child care cost estimates, see Chapter 9 above.

28. For a review of this evidence on support services and case management, see Chapter 6 above. In 1989, the MDRC evaluation of California's GAIN program and the Urban Institute's evaluation of the Massachusetts ET Choices program should provide valuable information on the costs and effectiveness of substantial, multidimensional interventions to enhance the self-sufficiency of welfare recipients.

29. For examples, see Goldman, Friedlander, and Long (1986) and Friedlander et al. (1985).

30. States have the option of requiring participation by those whose youngest child is at least one year old. Recipients can be exempted because they are ill, aged, incapacitated, caring for an incapacitated household member, employed more than thirty hours a week, under sixteen years of age, attending school full-time, pregnant, or residing in an area where the JOBS program is unavailable.

31. A compromise was impossible because of the extreme difference between the conservative and liberal proposals. The Republican proposal (H.R. 3200) provided unlimited waiver authority for states to establish demonstrations involving up to 22 federal programs. These included Food Stamps, WIC, TEFAP, low-income housing, Medicaid, rent supplements, CDBG, Head Start, JTPA, WIN, Vocational Education, Vocational Rehabilitation, Adult Education, Chapter 1, LIHEAP, Maternal and Child Health, AFDC, SSI, Social Services, Block Grant, Child-Support Enforcement, U.S. Employment Service, and Emergency Assistance.

At the other end of the spectrum, the more liberal bill passed by the House (H.R. 1720) provided no broad waiver authority for major experimentation but authorized a large number of demonstration projects covering a variety of modifications in existing approaches, most of which were rather narrow. Demonstration authority under Section 1115 would have been broadened in the areas of work, education, and training. In addition, this bill authorized demonstrations to test incentives to reduce school dropouts, the feasibility of using welfare mothers as paid day care providers, the effect of changes in the "100-hour" rule, the efficacy of volunteer-based early childhood education programs, the impact of using Food Stamp vehicle-value limits in AFDC, the feasibility of reducing Emergency Assistance by expanding housing for the homeless and the feasibility of encouraging noncustodial parents who can't pay child support to participate in employment and training programs. Most of these demonstrations were included in the Family Support Act.

The bill that initially passed in the Senate (S. 1511) took a middle position. It provided authority to grant up to ten waivers to states that wanted to experiment with new approaches. This waiver authority covered the eight programs under the jurisdiction of the Finance Committee (AFDC, JOBS (WIN), Child Welfare Services, Child-Support Enforcement, Foster Care and Adoption Assistance, Emergency Assistance, and the Social Services Block Grant). The federal government would exercise a moderate amount of control over these experiments and would evaluate their results. S. 1511 also authorized a range of narrow demonstration projects similar to those contained in H.R. 1720.

32. The major state experiments that have been given authority to proceed have all been fairly liberal in structure. The OBRA for FY1988 (P.L. 100–203) provided authority for Washington to conduct its Family Independence program and New York to implement its Child-Support demonstration. New Jersey's REACH program, California's GAIN program, and Wisconsin's Child Support Assurance program also represent major new approaches.

33. The only exception to this is stronger child-support efforts.

34. AFDC falls under the jurisdiction of the Subcommittee on Public Assistance and Unemployment Compensation of the House Ways and Means Committee, and the Subcommittee on Social Security and Income Maintenance of the Senate Finance Committee. Legislation affecting Food Stamps is under the jurisdiction of the Subcommittee on Domestic Marketing, Consumer Relations and Nutrition of the House Committee on Agriculture, and the Subcommittee on Nutrition and Investigations of the Senate Agriculture Committee. The responsibility for the Medicaid program is in the Subcommittee on Health and Environment of the House Committee on Energy and Commerce, and the Subcommittee on Health of the Senate Finance Committee. Work-related programs in the House fall under the jurisdiction of the Subcommittee on Employment Opportunity of the Education and Labor Committee. In the Senate, jurisdiction is split between the Senate Finance Committee (WIN) and the Committee on Labor and Human Resources (JTPA). Other committees are responsible for LIHEAP, low-income housing, and other programs directed at the poor.

35. For a discussion of the public's attitudes about some of these policies and its willingness to pay higher taxes to support such programs, see Melville and Doble (1988).

2. Fighting Poverty

1. Aaron (1984) emphasizes this point: "What is most striking about the emphasis on welfare in those early days of the antipoverty campaign is that there wasn't any . . . In fact, welfare developed into a prominent issue only after it became clear that millions of Americans would remain poor despite government's best efforts to add to their human capital, to lower the barriers of discrimination, and to cultivate a strong economy" (p. 12).

2. Irwin Garfinkel spoke of the need to fight poverty and reduce welfare dependency simultaneously in his comments at the Rockefeller Foundation conference.

3. The Family Support Act of 1988 mandated that all states implement a program of assistance for families with two unemployed parents (AFDC-U). The number of additional welfare recipients resulting from this mandate will be only a small fraction of the number that FAP or PBJI would have added.

4. Whether or not replacing a mother's welfare check with a payroll check of the same amount will be beneficial for her children obviously depends on the type of child care and other services made available as part of the welfare reform.

5. The Family Support Act will increase welfare spending by less than a billion dollars per year. The expansion of the EITC included in the Tax Reform Act

will annually provide about $5.4 billion of additional tax relief to an additional 7.5 million families by 1990 (U.S. House of Representatives, Committee on Ways and Means, 1988, p. 611).

6. Both the median family income and official poverty series are adjusted for inflation with the CPI. See the Appendix for a discussion of alternative measures of poverty and an alternative price index.

7. The CBO (1988) series on "adjusted family income" shows a 20 percent increase for the period from 1970 to 1986 in contrast to the 4 percent decline for the median family income series shown in column 1. The CBO series uses the CPI-XI to correct for inflation and the equivalence scales implicit in the official poverty lines to correct for differences in family size. Median family income does not account for differences in family size—a family of four with an income of $25,000 is counted as well-off as a family of two with the same income. Because average family size fell over this period, any series that adjusts incomes for family-size differences will show a greater growth rate than the census series. Nonetheless, by the standards of the 1949–1969 period, even the growth since 1970 in adjusted family income was disappointing.

8. Pretransfer poverty overstates the extent to which private market incomes fail to keep people out of poverty. Because transfers induce labor supply reductions and may lower private savings, private income in the absence of transfers would exceed measured pretransfer income.

Transfers may also induce changes in living arrangements that increase pretransfer poverty and overstate their measured antipoverty effects. For example, consider a teenage mother who would live with her nonpoor parents if welfare were not available. With welfare, she might set up a separate household, have a pretransfer income below the poverty line, and receive enough in benefits to escape poverty. She would then be counted as pretransfer poor and as having been taken out of poverty by transfers. But without welfare, she would not have belonged in that category. If she moves out of her parents' house but does not receive enough in benefits to escape poverty, then the antipoverty impact of transfers is not overstated, but the poverty rate is.

I conclude, on the basis of the existing literature, that though transfers do increase pretransfer poverty via the labor supply route, the effect is relatively small and that few of the demographic changes that have increased poverty in recent years occurred in response to rising transfers (Ellwood and Summers, 1986). The charges that poverty programs actually increase poverty have no foundation in the data. Most of the recent increase in poverty is attributable to changes in economic, demographic, and social conditions that largely operated independently of the transfer system. Certainly the rise in pretransfer poverty since the mid-1970s cannot be blamed on transfers because, as noted earlier, real transfers have declined during this period.

However, because transfers do not raise the incomes of the pretransfer poor at a dollar-for-dollar rate, Table 2.2 and Figure 2.2 overstate the antipoverty impact of transfers in each year. Nonetheless, the trends of rising and then falling antipoverty effects for families with children would hold even if adjustments were made for behavioral responses.

9. The poverty rates in Tables 2.2 and 2.3 are not directly comparable, as the

demographic groups are defined and incomes are measured somewhat differently. The decomposition in Table 2.3 treats each of the four changes as independent and assumes that they did not elicit labor supply or family structure responses.

10. A recent simulation by the CBO (U.S. House of Representatives, Committee on Ways and Means, 1988) shows that if the policies enacted in the Tax Reform Act of 1986 had been in place by 1986, then 1.14 million fewer persons would have been poor. For all persons living in families with children, the poverty rate would have been 14.9 instead of 15.8 percent. The number of persons removed from poverty by the Act was about the same as the number added to poverty by the tax changes that occurred between 1979 and 1986.

11. The increase in single-parent families has been an important contributor to child poverty. However, the rise in child poverty since the late 1960s was primarily due to the impact of poor national economic performance on parents' incomes. A demographic standardization (Smolensky, Danziger, and Gottschalk, 1988) shows that if children's living arrangements were the same in 1985 as they were in 1969—that is, if 12 instead of 24 percent of all children lived in single-parent families—but the poverty rates for children in single-parent and two-parent families were at their 1985 levels, then the child poverty rate in 1985 would have been 16.1 instead of 20.1 percent. A similar standardization, also based on 1969 living arrangements, shows that if the poverty rate for all children had declined between 1969 and 1985 at the same rate as between 1959 and 1969, then the 1985 rate would have been 6.3 percent. The actual child poverty rate in 1985, 20.1 percent, was 13.8 percentage points higher than this standardized rate. About one-third of the difference was due to the increased propensity of children to live in single-parent families, while about two-thirds was due to the failure of poverty rates to decline at their pre-1969 rates. The poverty-increasing impact of the trend toward single-mother families has received so much attention, in part, because the causes of the recent disappointing economic performance are not well understood.

12. The CPS data used in Table 2.4 are presented only on an annual basis. It is probably the case that these parents work only during part of the year and receive transfers during part of the period when they are not working.

13. Burtless (Chapter 4) suggests that gains of about $1,000 per recipient per year can be expected from the most successful of current workfare programs. Garfinkel and McLanahan (1987) expect larger effects from the Wisconsin Child Support Assurance program, but their estimate is based on the inclusion of an assured minimum payment. Such a benefit has not been proposed by Congress.

14. This large difference between the two measures of persistence implies that many of those who were poor in only some of the years, and hence were not classified as poor by the first measure, had incomes in their nonpoverty years that were relatively close to the poverty line. Consider this hypothetical example for two single individuals for whom the poverty line was $5,000. The first individual earned $4,500 in each of the years. The second, $5,500 in five years and $3,500 in the other five. Here, the first measure of persistence would find that only the first person was persistently poor; the second person would not be counted as persistently poor because she or he was poor in only five of the ten

years. But the second measure would classify both persons as persistently poor, as the average annual income of each over the ten-year period ($4,500) was below the poverty line.

15. These estimates of persistent poverty and persistent welfare receipt should not be taken as indicators of the size of the underclass. The underclass concept generally depends on some definition of spatial concentration—for example, those who are persistently poor and receive welfare and live in neighborhoods with high concentrations of poverty (see Adams and Duncan, 1987, and Chapter 3 above).

16. An example of a policy that would have taxed the implicit subsidy in Medicare can be found in the version of H.R. 2470, the Medicare Catastrophic Protection Act of 1987, which was passed only by the Subcommittee on Health of the Committee on Ways and Means.

17. There are obvious administrative problems in providing such large refundable credits. If they were available only as part of the annual income tax filing, they would not effectively aid the poor. Administrative procedures would have to be developed for providing them on a regular basis to the nonworking poor and through reduced payroll deductions for the working poor.

18. Increasing the Food Stamp participation rate of the poor above its current 50 percent level has proved difficult. If this rate could be increased, a stronger case could be made for choosing the $560 refundable credit and not replacing the Food Stamp program.

19. For most people any base-broadening will have only an income effect (reduced income), promoting greater work effort; only a small number will have an altered substitution effect (since fewer shift to higher tax brackets), promoting lower work effort. For the beneficiaries of such expanded credits, the income effect will lead to less work, but the substitution effect will lead to more work, because the credits will take the place of a welfare program, which had higher marginal tax rates.

3. Poverty, Joblessness, and the Inner City

1. On the notion of field, see Bourdieu (1980). The literature on the role of politics and social-racial struggles in the determination of welfare policy is extensive. For the recent period, see, among others, Piven and Cloward (1971 and 1977, especially Chapter 5); Friedland (1976); Isaac and Kelly (1981); Jennings (1979); Shram and Turbot (1983); and Katz (1986, especially Chapters 9 and 10).

2. For a penetrating discussion of this characteristic contraction of both research and policy arguments, see Piven and Cloward (1987a).

3. See in particular the recent writings of conservative and neoconservative scholars and policy analysts (for example, Anderson, 1978; Murray, 1984; Mead, 1985; and Kaus, 1986). Reasons for the recent preeminence of conservative theses in American public debate are discussed in Wilson (1987).

4. There are several reasons for this choice. First, welfare receipt, like poverty, covers a wide diversity of situations. We find it more sensible to address consistently a clearly circumscribed one than to gloss over trends that have no

concrete referent other than the statistical aggregates which measure them. Second, while there is no question that the inner-city underclass forms a minority of the total poverty population, it is growing and its plight is clearly worsening. Furthermore, it comprises the "hard core" of welfare recipients. Finally, we believe that the dominant forces at play in the ongoing formation of the black underclass are the same ones that act, albeit with less adverse and visible effects, and through different mediations, upon a large fraction of the poor, notably the fast-growing ranks of the working poor. In this sense, the inner-city constitutes a sort of litmus test for the scientific analysis of poverty as well as for the policy debate over welfare.

5. This is particularly true of concentrated poverty, that is, high spatial and social densities of households or individuals living under the official poverty line. The phenomenon of the concentration of poverty has recently been highlighted by Reischauer (1987a) and Bane and Jargowski (1988).

6. That is, the ten central cities with the largest population as of 1970. One decade is a relatively short time span but, as will be seen, changes were so swift during this period that it will suffice to highlight them. For this analysis, we rely mainly on data published in U.S. Bureau of the Census (1973 and 1985).

7. Another motive for disaggregating these figures is the disproportional contribution of New York City to the ten-city averages: the nation's largest metropolis contributes over one-third of the ten-city total population, 36.5 percent of the total poor population, and 12.8 percent of all poor blacks.

8. Furthermore, these "whites" include a large and growing number of Hispanics. It appears that the population of non-Hispanic whites already shrank to less than half of the residents of the ten largest central cities of the country by 1980 (although changes in coding procedures used to count and allocate "Hispanics" into racial categories make data from the 1970 and 1980 censuses difficult to compare on this).

9. In this city, the number of poor fell by a modest 3 percent compared to a overall population drop of 24 percent.

10. Trends in Indianapolis are somewhat difficult to interpret since data are not strictly comparable over time, due to the incorporation of the outlying Marion county into the city after 1970.

11. Poverty areas and extreme poverty areas are census tracts containing at least 20 percent and 40 percent poor persons, respectively.

12. We cannot address here the varied situation encapsulated under the label "Hispanic." For a state-of-the-art review of the problem, see Portes and Truelove (1987), as well as Boyas and Tienda (1985).

13. Percentages ranged from 2.5 in Los Angeles to 4 percent in Chicago, 8 percent in New York City and Philadelphia, to a high of 14 percent in Detroit.

14. Employment rates are given by the number of employed adults (sixteen years and older) over the total number of adults of a given area.

15. These data measure the incidence of means-tested cash assistance, not in-kind benefits, and do not include Social Insurance income, both of which grew much faster than the former over this decade (see Burtless, 1986).

16. Everything suggests that the proportion of welfare families living in poverty areas decreased noticeably among non-Hispanic whites.

17. This period, it should be emphasized, stops before the most severe depression of the postwar era, which came in 1981–1983.

18. Indeed, recent research by Bane and Jargowski (1988) on the growth and concentration of extreme poverty in the 50 largest central cities of the country over the same period supports this hypothesis (although Bane and Jargowski themselves seem to conclude otherwise). Their work shows conclusively that concentrated urban poverty has worsened dramatically in the 1970s, with increases in 34 of the 50 largest cities, particularly in older, industrial, racially divided cities. Of the 12 cities that fared worse (above average initial levels of black poverty concentration and above average growth of concentration), 8 are declining industrial centers of the Northeast and North Central regions of the country, including New York, Newark, Philadelphia, Buffalo, Pittsburgh, Cleveland, Cincinnati, and Chicago, while Columbus, Rochester, Milwaukee, and Detroit also posted above average growth in black poverty concentration. It is worth emphasizing that these cities are also among those with the highest degrees of racial segregation and isolation in the country (see Massey and Denton, 1987).

19. The high unemployment anti-inflationary policies of the past decade are thus one of the chief causes of the expansion of poverty and welfare need throughout the country, since such policies effectively tip the cost of economic reorganization in favor of upper- and middle-class families at the expense of poor ones.

20. There is mounting evidence of the structural linkages between unemployment, economic deprivation, family disruption, and crime among urban blacks. Sampson (1987) has recently articulated how black male joblessness increases the prevalence of female-headed households, which in turn directly increases the incidence of crimes such as murder and robbery.

21. On the causes and consequences of deindustrialization, see Bluestone and Harrison (1982 and 1988), as well as Melman (1983). Regional shifts in employment and industrial activities are discussed in Sawers and Tabb (1984) and Sarbanes (1986). We cannot explore here the causes behind these structural shifts in the American economy, nor the mechanisms, political and social, that determine the *social allocation* of their costs and benefits. Suffice it to say that such trends as deindustrialization, plant relocation, and the growth of low-wage service employment are not "natural" phenomena that must be taken as givens: they too must be subjected to sociological analysis.

22. The category "selected services" given in column 4 is the best proxy readily available for noncredentialized services, since it excludes mostly (but not most) professional and middle-class oriented services. This category, as defined by the U.S. Bureau of Census, includes all taxable services except the following for all years: health (with the exception of dental laboratories which are included); special educational services; accounting, auditing, and bookkeeping; and "social and other" services. Prior to 1977, personal services are not included, thus leading to an overestimate of the actual growth of these selected services over time (see U.S. Bureau of the Census, 1962, 1972, 1977, and 1983; U.S. Bureau of the Census, 1986b; and U.S. Department of Commerce and Industry, 1982).

23. With the apparent exception of Indianapolis, but see note 10 above.

24. Study reported in the *The New York Times* of February 7, 1985, cited in Piven and Cloward (1987).

49. For a recent account in the popular media, see *U.S. News and World Report* (1988).
50. Put otherwise: the value of the minimum wage in 1968 was, in terms of 1986 dollars, about $5, far above the $3.35 now in force (see Levitan and Shapiro, 1987).
51. On this point, see Danziger, chapter 2 above.

4. The Effect of Reform on Employment, Earnings, and Income

1. Both figures are taken from the respective U.S. budgets and are measured in constant 1986 dollars.
2. Earnings changes are measured in 1985 prices (see U.S. Congressional Budget Office, 1987, p. 46).
3. See Auspos (1986, p. 31). Figures are converted into 1985 dollars.
4. Federal grants appropriated under Title II-A are used by states to finance training and related services for economically disadvantaged people, including AFDC recipients (see U.S. Congressional Budget Office, 1987, pp. 18–19).
5. The employment rate in the absence of EOPP would have been about 36 to 38 percent. Hence a rise of 3 to 4 percentage points represents a gain in employment of 8 to 11 percent. Mathematica formed this estimate by comparing employment trends in the EOPP sites with similar trends in nearby comparison sites. The reliability of this type of estimate may be questionable.
6. Mathematica Policy Research (1983), pp. 181 and 212. The MPR estimate has been adjusted to reflect annual earnings gains measured in 1985 dollars.
7. A good brief summary of findings is presented in U.S. Congressional Budget Office (1987).
8. The factors that lead to long spells of welfare dependency are examined by Bane and Ellwood (1983).
9. I should emphasize that the high costs and large earnings gains per participant were partly the result of the small number of AFDC beneficiaries served in these programs. If the costs and benefits of the programs were spread across the entire eligible population of AFDC beneficiaries, rather than only across program participants, both benefits and costs would of course look a great deal smaller.
10. See Moffitt (1987), Table 3. Benefit levels are converted to constant 1985 dollars.
11. Note that this $30 and one-third exemption is less generous than the one in effect between 1968 and 1981. The earlier exemption was computed using gross monthly earnings before work-related expenses; the latter one used net monthly earnings after work-related expenses.
12. From 1971 to 1975, 62 percent of female heads of household with children under eighteen received AFDC benefits sometime within a year. From 1977 through 1981, the percentage receiving benefits ranged between 52 and 57 percent. Since the OBRA legislation became effective in 1982, only 43 to 45 percent of single mothers have received AFDC (see Moffitt, 1987, Table 3).
13. The wage-rate subsidy is also open to obvious fraud and abuse on the part of workers and their employers. Since the hourly subsidy actually rises as the

wage rate falls, while the total subsidy rises with the number of hours worked, employees would be tempted to exaggerate their hours and minimize their wage rates in order to qualify for a larger subsidy. Employers would be inclined to cooperate in this deception, for it costs them nothing and it makes their workers better off. Even if obvious fraud could be prevented, workers and employers would presumably collude to achieve the same purpose, for example, by counting coffee and meal breaks as paid hours in order to raise nominal weekly hours and reduce reported wage rates.

14. By "most successful" and "more effective" programs I mean those that produced the largest earnings gains per participant. Different programs might be judged successful or effective by a criterion that ranks programs by the level of earnings gain produced per dollar spent on the program.

5. Targeting Long-Term Welfare Recipients

1. Moynihan (1987) was quoting Samuel H. Preston, Presidential Address to the Population Association of America, 1984.
2. U.S. Bureau of the Census (1985a): unpublished data graciously provided by Arlene Saluter.
3. Ibid.
4. The figures in these two paragraphs come from U.S. Bureau of the Census (1986a).
5. Derived from U.S. Bureau of the Census (1986a).
6. In 1985, there were 33,536,000 families with children. Of these, 6,893,000 were female-headed families (U.S. Bureau of the Census, 1986a).
7. In 1985, there were 5,586,000 families with children living below the poverty line. 3,131,000 of these were headed by females (U.S. Bureau of the Census, 1986a).
8. Novak et al. (1987, p. 48), citing for the first estimate U.S. Bureau of the Census (1986a, pp. 22–23, Table 16), and citing for the second estimate Green and Welniak (1982). However, such estimates are fraught with methodological difficulties and subjective assumptions. They are presented here to demonstrate the effect of the increase in female-headed families, not to establish its exact effect on poverty rates. (See U.S. Bureau of the Census, 1986a, citing Bane, 1984.)
9. For these figures, see U.S. Department of Health and Human Services (1986a).
10. See U.S. Department of Health and Human Services (1980), projecting that 49.2 percent of those married in 1973 will eventually divorce.
11. Glick (1979) projects that by 1990 half of all children will spend some time in their childhood (under eighteen) living in a single-parent household. One-third of all children will have experienced a parental divorce before they reach the age of eighteen.
12. See U.S. Bureau of the Census (1986a). The income difference between divorced and never-married women does not appear attributable to a difference in average household size. The mean number of siblings in households headed by divorced women was 1.09, while for those headed by never-married women it was 1.21.

13. See, for example, U.S. Congressional Research Service (1987), Newberger et al. (1986), and Norton and Glick (1986).

14. Maynard and Maxfield (1986) stated: "When measured by total correlations rather than by partial correlations, marital status, race, education, age of the youngest child, and age of the mother are the best predictors of welfare dependency. This set of welfare characteristics differs from those that are most strongly associated with dependency when measured by partial correlations." [p. XIV]

15. The Adams (1987) study is based on data from the NLS.

16. Derived from U.S. Department of Health and Human Services (1986b), p. 31, Table 18.

17. Derived from U.S. Bureau of the Census (1985a).

18. The numbers in this paragraph were derived from U.S. Bureau of the Census (1986b), Table 1, p. 17.

19. See U.S. House of Representatives, Committee on Ways and Means (1986), citing McCarthy and Menken (1979), p. 23.

20. The other major reasons women leave AFDC are that their children reach an age beyond eligibility (11 percent) and their income from other transfers increases (14 percent) (see Ellwood, 1986).

21. The cold cost-benefit analysis also suggests that job training and other services should not be targeted on divorced mothers. See Maynard and Maxfield (1986), who state that "a dollar spent through an employment-related program to move a potential, or 'would be,' long-term recipient off the rolls is more cost-effective than a dollar spent to move off the rolls a case which would have left the rolls quickly in the absence of the program."

22. See, for example, Wilson and Neckerman (1984) and Loury (1985).

23. 133 Congressional Record H11537 (daily ed. Dec. 16, 1987), Section 101, amending Social Security Act sec. 416(c)(3). The bill then establishes a priority for volunteers. And, of course, the mandate to participate is only as broad as the funds available for programs.

24. H.R. 3200, 100th Cong., 1st Sess., Sec. 203, amending Social Security Act sec. 417(h)(3)(C)(i) (1987).

25. 133 Congressional Record S10402 (daily ed. July 21, 1987) (statement of Sen. Moynihan).

26. S. 514, 100th Cong., 1st Sess., Sec. 2, amending Job Training Partnership Act sec. 502(a)(2)(B) (1987).

27. S. 1511, 100th Cong., 1st Sess., Sec. 201, amending Social Security Act sec. 416(c)(2)(A) (1987).

28. 133 Congressional Record H11537, Sec. 102, amending Social Security Act sec. 416(c)(4)-(6) (1987).

29. H.R. 3200, 100th Congress, 1st Sess., Sec. 102, amending Social Security Act sec. 416(b)-(c) (1987).

30. 133 Congressional Record H11537 (daily ed. Dec. 16, 1987), Sec. 102, amending Social Security Act sec. 416(c)(6)(A).

31. S. 1511, 100th Congress, 1st Sess., Sec. 201, amending Social Security Act sec. 416(c)(3) (1987).

32. 133 Congressional Record H11537 (daily ed. December 16, 1987), Sec. 102, amending Social Security Act sec. 416(c)(6)(B).
33. S. 1511, 100th Congress, 1st Sess., Sec. 401, amending Social Security Act sec. 402(a) (1987).
34. 133 Congressional Record H11537 (daily ed. December 16, 1987), Sec. 102, amending Social Security Act sec. 416 (c)(6)(A).
35. S. 1511, 100th Congress., 1st Sess., Sec. 201, amending Social Security Act sec. 416(c)(1)(A)(i) (1987).
36. H.R. 3200, 100th Congress, 1st Sess., Sec. 102, amending Social Security Act sec. 417(e) (1987).
37. Telephone interview with Susan Felker-Donsing, Budget Section Chief, Department of Health and Social Services, Madison, Wisconsin, January 27, 1988.
38. Apparently, Missouri and Washington are considering similar legislation.

6. Support Services

1. Several demonstration projects that are currently under way attempt to find the best ways to meet the needs of young, unmarried welfare mothers with young children (see the OFA Teen Parent Demonstration, the New Chance Demonstration initiated by MDRC, the Rockefeller Foundation Minority Female Single Parent Demonstration, and the New York State Comprehensive Employment Opportunity Support Centers). However, all of these efforts are too recent to have yielded any evaluative information as of yet.
2. Medical assistance is not traditionally categorized as a support service. However, we include it here because it is among the services needed to remove potential barriers to participation in welfare-to-work programs and in the labor force. Medical assistance supports the recipient's ability to move toward self-sufficiency. Remedial education services, which also address an important barrier to employment (that is, poor basic skills), are not covered in this chapter because they are part of "core" services in welfare-to-work programs—a subject discussed in other chapters in this volume.
3. Two other important policy questions—the extent to which government agencies should play a role in expanding the supply of market child care for low-income mothers and the extent to which the government should encourage employers to offer on-site child care—are not considered in this chapter.
4. The federal funding source that represents the biggest outlay for child care is the Dependent Care Tax Credit. Annually this federal program costs about $1.5 million, which is about twice the federal share of expenditures for child care under the SSBG. However, this subsidy program has not been used very much by low-income families; of the 4.6 million families claiming the credit, only 7 percent had incomes below $10,000. This program, in its current form, will probably be used even less now because tax reform has reduced the tax liability of low-income families. However, some proposals would make child-care costs refundable like the earned income tax credit, which would clearly have a substantial impact on low-income families.

5. Indeed, according to the 1984–85 SIPP survey, the most unreliable forms of child care (in terms of employed mothers' loss of time from work) are arrangements where relatives care for the child in his or her own home or in another home (U.S. Bureau of the Census, 1987).

6. There has been some speculation that the tendency for service-rich programs (that is, ones that offer child care and an array of other support services) to have a bigger impact on employment and earnings than on rates of welfare dependency stems from the attractiveness of the services to some of the recipients and their reluctance to leave welfare. See Chapter 4 above.

7. Although no researchers have studied the effect of varying the length of Medicaid coverage as yet, a current demonstration in Wisconsin, funded by the Health Care Financing Administration, is just getting under way and should yield important information about the effects of extending Medicaid coverage beyond the current four-month limit.

8. One of the more persistent beliefs about the welfare population is that welfare mothers deliberately bear additional children to increase the size of their welfare grant—a reversed direction of causality between fertility and welfare than that suggested here. However, numerous researchers have failed to find support for this belief (see Keefe, 1983; Moore and Caldwell, 1977; Ellwood and Bane, 1985). Placek and Hendershot (1974), in fact, found that low-income women were more likely to use birth control and avoid a pregnancy during a spell of welfare dependency than when they were not receiving AFDC.

9. To our knowledge, there have been no national studies of the manner in which family planning is utilized within the Medicaid program. However, Orr and Brenner (1981) have reported that Medicaid accounts for only 10 percent of federal expenditures for family-planning services, and that fewer than one-third of the Medicaid-eligible women at risk of unintended child-bearing are served by organized family-planning providers.

10. The other groups received more limited services. One group received only screening, a second received screening and transportation, and a third received screening, transportation, and nurse home-visitors during pregnancy only. The full treatment group received all services, including continuing home visits.

11. A fairly substantial body of research evidence indicates that longer periods of service receipt are associated with greater gains among disadvantaged women (see Masters and Maynard, 1981; Polit et al., 1985). It is not clear whether this relation reflects primarily the incremental effect of receiving more services, or the characteristics of participants who remain in programs for longer periods of time, although most evaluations have controlled for factors thought to result in self-selection biases.

8. Child-Support Policies

1. The work of Irwin Garfinkel and of Lenore Weitzman have helped persuade the public, political leaders, and the policy community that failure to pay for child support constitutes a major and general problem.

2. The median income figures come from U.S. Bureau of the Census (1987b, p. 20).

3. Even with full financial sharing, the mother might lose if unpaid child care was formerly provided by the father.

4. Of course, in some cases, noncustodial fathers stay in close touch with the children and contribute whatever they would have provided had they continued living with the children. These are the cases in which child-support awards are least necessary and even payments that are proportional to income may not be viewed as a tax.

5. These economic impacts of splitting would be less serious if custodial mothers earned more than shown in the example. However, were mothers merely to substitute market work for home work, their dollar income might well stay the same after paying for child care and other household work. Figure 8.1 also overstates the economic losses from family splitting when fathers have very little income. In this case, the father's absence may even reduce the needs of the family by as much as it lowers the family's income.

6. Immediately after the marital breakup, the children of women who remained unmarried endured a one-third decline in their living standard and saw little change over the next few years. Among the black children with mothers who did not remarry, poverty rates jumped from 24 percent before the breakup to the 40–60 percent range over the next five years. Meanwhile, black intact couples experienced significant reductions in poverty.

7. Although a number of studies indicate that marriage increases earnings, Nakosteen and Zimmer (1987) recently cast doubt on the notion that marriage itself rather than the types of people who choose marriage exerts the positive impact. Their study dealt with young white 18–24 year-olds. Our concern is with fathers of all ages, not with differences between young married and unmarried men.

8. I calculated the figures discussed below using data from the 1986 wave of the NLS.

9. The mean family income of all never-married young mothers was $11,000 in 1985. A large portion of never-married mothers were able to escape poverty because they live with a parent or other relative.

10. By "those with awards" we mean only custodial parents who are due child support in the relevant year. This excludes those who obtained awards that are no longer applicable.

11. It is not the simple product of the two terms because the parents not making payments may have lower award obligations than those making payments.

12. Specifically, the mothers in the sample consisted of women living with own children under twenty-one from an absent father. Asking only the custodial mother is likely to lead to under-reporting. As Robins (1987) and Graham and Beller (1985) point out, the Census Bureau sample is not precisely the most appropriate one. It includes women who have only grandchildren in the household and excludes married women who were never divorced but had children prior to their first marriage. Timing is also a problem since some women who were divorced at the time of the survey were married during the prior year, the period when they were asked about child-support payments. Conversely, some currently married women may have been divorced during the prior year. The figures calculated by Robins and reported in Table 8.1 correct for several of these problems.

13. In a 1987 paper using NLS data (1986) I found that over one-third of unwed fathers report making child-support payments. Very few of these unwed fathers have made formal agreements to do so.

14. Over 800,000 divorced mothers with children present obtained property settlements but did not receive child-support payments in 1983. Of course, this does not imply any formal or informal trade-off.

15. See U.S. Bureau of the Census (1986, Table 7, p. 38).

16. The CPS data are unlikely to include payments made by fathers of AFDC children to state agencies collecting payments as a partial offset to welfare benefits. However, as we shall see below, child support paid directly to the government does not add much to these levels.

17. These numbers come directly from the U.S. Bureau of the Census (1986) report on CPS data. Amounts reported to SIPP show even lower mean ($1,326) and median ($960) payments.

18. The actual disparity may be greater, since many AFDC families are not recorded as having received AFDC during the prior year.

19. The proportion of AFDC recipients who received child support in the average month was much smaller, only 3 percent in 1986. These figures come from U.S. House of Representatives, Committee on Ways and Means (1987, pp. 435 and 472).

20. These calculations do not take account of the apparent underestimates of imputed incomes performed by the Census for low income persons. I am grateful to Alice Robbin for pointing out this imputation problem.

21. It is difficult to determine the size of the bias partly because we cannot determine the age gaps between unmarried men and their women partners. Using a gap of two years, I found that unmarried men ages 21–26 who reported having children accounted for only about 60 percent of the children reported by unmarried women, ages 19–24 (see Lerman, 1986, for details).

22. See U.S. Bureau of the Census (1987a, p. 3).

23. In its FY1986 reports, OCSE changed the definition to include all cases closed in which former participants received a support payment. Not surprisingly, the figure for the number removed because of support collections jumped from 34,000 to 248,000.

24. Robins uses data on 2,543 mothers from the April 1982 CPS. He encounters and adjusts for statistical problems associated with the fact that parents using state Title IV-D agencies face more difficulties in obtaining support payments than do parents who do not require IV-D services. Robins recognizes that the differences vary by AFDC status, since state IV-D agencies automatically become involved in collections for AFDC mothers while mothers not on AFDC typically come to the agencies when other methods of collecting payments fail.

25. A study of O'Neill (1986) yields results broadly consistent with the Robins analysis.

26. State Title IV-D agencies do not provide legal representation to custodial mothers with regard to custody matters.

27. Using SIPP data on noncustodial parents actually making a payment, I estimated the increase in child-support payments that would take place if the Wisconsin formula were applied and all obligated payments were collected. In 1984 these

changes would nearly double the amount of support payments, from about $9 to almost $18 billion.

28. Because these estimates do not take account of payments to custodial parents who do not have court orders or voluntary agreements, they probably overstate the potential increases in contributions by absent fathers.

    Oellerich and Garfinkel (1983) give the following estimates of increased payments in Wisconsin that would result from filling the individual payment gaps: obtaining awards for those with no award ($19 million); collecting 100 percent of existing awards ($26 million); and raising the award levels to the Wisconsin standard ($16 million). Achieving all three together would increase payments by $141 million.

29. Much of the spending affecting a child's living standard would involve joint consumption, especially the quality of the home. The total amount a father would spend for an item like children's clothing may remain almost the same; having one child instead of two might simply lead to higher quality without any major change in total spending.

30. The $3,000 figure is the lowest of the minimums to be applied in Wisconsin.

31. According to reports by noncustodial parents, the mean payment for those supporting one child was $1,738.

32. We limit the discussion to the case of a minimum CSAS of $3,000 for the first child.

33. The minimum payment for one child is $90 per month, or $1,080 per year, or 10.8 percent of $10,000. Even if the income at the tenth percentile of absent fathers were as low as $7,000, states could cover expenses in 90 percent of cases by collecting only 15 percent of income.

34. Taxpayers with the highest incomes would neither lose nor gain from the change, since the new tax law already phases out the value of their exemptions.

35. The presence of a CSAS restricted to those with awards may itself be important in raising the share of custodial mothers with awards.

36. The extent of actual nonreporting exceeds these figures, since the Census Bureau itself allocates AFDC benefits to some families that fail to report benefits.

37. We derive the nonreporting adjustment as follows: (1) the average AFDC savings for the 2.4 million families reporting AFDC was about $1,670 per year; (2) multiplying $1,670 times the 500,000 families not reporting AFDC yields about $830 million. The under-reporting adjustment involved multiplying the approximately $360 annual shortfall times the 2.5 million AFDC families also receiving CSAS.

9. Costs of Welfare Programs

1. Assessments of the desirability of undertaking modifications to the welfare system should account for both the direct and indirect effects of the programs on each other and the programs' effects on the labor-market and other activities of participants. A number of studies exist for employment, education, and training programs, but empirical studies of other alternatives (including tax credits, transfer programs, support services, and child-support enforcement efforts) are generally missing.

2. The policies and programs listed in the tables that accompany this discussion are sufficiently complex that they cannot be fully described here. The Ways and Means Committee of the U.S. House of Representatives (1987a) provides total cost estimates and general descriptive information about virtually all programs intended to assist the poor. The Social Security Administration (1986) also provides detailed program statistics for most of the relevant programs.

3. Housing assistance also constitutes a major in-kind transfer program. In FY1985, federal housing assistance programs aided over 4 million persons and incurred expenditures in excess of $11 billion. However, these programs were omitted from the table because of the variety of programs, the lack of detailed participation and cost data, and the difficulty in estimating average costs in a meaningful way.

4. Given the current AFDC cost-sharing regulations, an increase in the federal matching rate will increase the total cost of welfare payments to rich states and will lower costs for poorer states.

5. Conversations with Massachusetts officials indicated that costs per placement increased from $2,000 in FY1986 to $6,300 in FY1987. Assuming placement rates remain in the 50 percent range, this increase in costs per *placement* implies that per *participant* costs may be nearly $3,000.

6. In fiscal 1985, only 21 percent of the participants in JTPA education and training programs were welfare recipients. A much smaller fraction of these participants were AFDC-R recipients.

7. Goldman et al. (1986) report costs per experiment participant, net of the costs of services received by controls, of about $640. Since about 90 percent of the people in the experiment received job-search assistance, the average cost per participant is estimated at around $700.

8. This cost estimate, developed by the U.S. Bureau of the Census (1987), is the median weekly cash payment made by employed mothers who made any such payment as reported in the SIPP. Fifty-four percent of these mothers had more than one child. Public and private subsidies are excluded from the estimate, as are any costs of care provided by family members (even if payments were made). Thus these estimates under-represent actual resource costs.

9. The Targeted Jobs Tax Credit available to employers who hire disadvantaged workers was discussed above with the employment programs.

10. Consider decisions about the Job Corps, a residential program that provides intensive education and training services to disadvantaged youths. Long, Mallar, and Thornton (1981) found that this program yielded net benefits to society as a whole, when evaluated over the expected work years of corpsmembers. However, since many of the benefits of Job Corps accrue to the corpsmembers as nonbudgetary costs and benefits, the program operates at a net cost to the government budget. The net budgetary costs for operating the Job Corps for five years would be $597 million (in 1977 dollars) assuming that the program had 20,000 slots. If the longer-term benefits of the training investments Job Corps made in the corpsmembers are included in the analysis, the cost of operating the program for five years would be 40 percent less ($360 million in 1977 dollars). In this case, the truncated time horizon thus results in a substantial overstatement of the budgetary costs. Of course, neither of these budgetary

net cost estimates considers the benefits to the corpsmembers or the cost and benefits that do not directly affect the government budget.

11. The CBO does not discount expenditures that occur in the future when making their cost estimates, so no distinction is made among programs that have different time distributions of costs.

12. One such start-up cost was the programming error that resulted in paying recipients an amount equal to their ZIP code divided by 100 rather than the SSI payment to which they were entitled. Problems of this nature are almost impossible to avoid during program initiation. The costs involved in resolving them and refining procedures should be included in the start-up costs.

Acknowledgments

The chapters in this volume are revised versions of papers prepared for a Rockefeller Foundation conference on welfare reform held at Historic Colonial Williamsburg in February 1988. Almost eighty researchers, public policy makers, and civic leaders heard Haynes Johnson's opening address on the political climate surrounding welfare reform, synopses and critiques of each paper by assigned discussants, and presentations by state welfare officials and others on current state initiatives and goals for welfare reform. A summary of the reactions to the papers and floor discussion was written by David Ellwood, and appears as the concluding chapter of this book.

The papers were commissioned and the conference funded by the Equal Opportunity Program of the Rockefeller Foundation. Rebecca Maynard originally proposed the idea of the conference and worked closely with Foundation officers in developing the substantive issues for the conference papers. Early on, Felicity Skidmore joined the conference planning team and helped the authors prepare their papers for the conference as well as for publication. The conference and this volume would not have crystallized into the serious endeavor it became without the sustained and thoughtful contributions of both Rebecca and Felicity.

Similarly, it would not have been possible to carry out such a multifaceted and strenuous project without the strong dedication and teamwork by staff at both the Foundation and Mathematica Policy Research. Audrey J. Mirsky, in Mathematica's Washington office, worked tirelessly on the conference arrangements, assisted by Sharon Corbin-Jallow, and by Rosa Cervera at the Foundation. Tom Good provided editorial assistance. Aida Rodriguez helped review the papers and identify conference participants.

James O. Gibson, Director of Equal Opportunity at the Foundation, moderated the two-day conference. Four state welfare commissioners (Charles M. Atkins, Massachusetts; Robert Fulton, Oklahoma; James L. Solomon, Jr., South Carolina; Carl B. Williams, California) and Alicia C. Smith gave panel presentations on current state initiatives, moderated by Judith M. Gueron. Irwin Garfinkel moderated a panel discussion focused on the values underlying the welfare reform debate that brought thoughtful commentary by Angela Glover Blackwell, Lawrence M. Mead, Ronald B. Mincy, and Hugh Heclo.

Views expressed in this book are those of the authors and should not be construed as representing the official position or policy of the Rockefeller Foundation, Mathematica Policy Research, Harvard University, or the other institutions with which individual authors are affiliated.

The acknowledgments of the contributors are listed below, by chapter number and title.

1. The Welfare Reform Legislation

The views expressed in this paper are those of the author and should not be attributed to the Brookings Institution, its staff, trustees, or sponsors. The author thanks Erica B. Baum, Vee Burke, Deborah Colton, Irwin Garfinkel, Ron Haskins, Audrey Mirsky, Wendell E. Primus, and James A. Rotherham for their valuable comments.

2. Fighting Poverty

This paper was written while the author was Director, Institute for Research on Poverty, Public Policy Studies, University of Wisconsin-Madison. Support from the Graduate School Research Committee of the University of Wisconsin-Madison is gratefully acknowledged. Computational support was provided by a grant from the U.S. Department of Health and Human Services to the Institute for Research on Poverty. I have benefited from the comments of Gary Burtless, Mary Corcoran, Greg Duncan, David Ellwood, Irwin Garfinkel, Martha Hill, Wendell Primus, Timothy Smeeding, and Daniel Weinberg. The opinions expressed are my own.

3. Poverty, Joblessness, and the Inner City

We gratefully acknowledge the financial support of the Rockefeller Foundation, the Ford Foundation, the Carnegie Corporation, the U.S. Department of Health and Human Services, the Institute for Research on Poverty, the Joyce Foundation, the Lloyd A. Fry Foundation, the Spencer Foundation, the William T. Grant Foundation, the Woods Charitable Fund, and the Chicago Community Trust.

4. The Effect of Reform

I gratefully acknowledge the helpful comments of Judith Gueron, Frank Levy, Rebecca Maynard, Lawrence Mead, Isabel Sawhill, and Felicity Skidmore on an earlier version of this paper. The views expressed in this paper are the author's alone and do not reflect those of the staff or trustees of the Brookings Institution.

5. Targeting Long-Term Welfare Recipients

Parts of this paper are based on "Not All Female-Headed Families Are Created Equal," an article written with Alison J. Quin for *The Public Interest*, 89(Fall 1987):48–56. Harvetta M. Asamoah, Paul Tramontozzi, and Matthew L. Biben provided research assistance.

7. Institutional Effects of Reform

Useful comments and suggestions were offered by Lee Bawden, Barbara Blum, Lynn Burbridge, Sar Levitan, Cesar Perales, and Sue Poppink. The essay also benefited from the discussions with the authors of other chapters in this volume.

8. Child-Support Policies

The author thanks the Ford and Rockefeller Foundations for research support and Robert Williams, Irwin Garfinkel, and Diane Dodson for helpful comments.

9. Costs of Welfare Programs

In preparing this paper, I have benefited from the comments of David Long, Rebecca Maynard, Charles Metcalf, Reuben Snipper, Janice Peskin, Ralph Smith, William Prosser, and Janine Matton.

Contributors

Douglas Besharov, Resident Scholar, American Enterprise Institute for Public Policy Research

Gary Burtless, Senior Fellow of Economic Studies Program, The Brookings Institution

Phoebe H. Cottingham, Associate Director, Equal Opportunity Program, The Rockefeller Foundation

Sheldon Danziger, Professor of Social Work and Public Policy and Faculty Associate, Population Studies Center, University of Michigan

David Ellwood, Professor of Public Policy, John F. Kennedy School of Government, Harvard University

Robert I. Lerman, Senior Research Associate/Lecturer, The Heller School, Brandeis University

Demetra Smith Nightingale, Senior Research Associate, The Urban Institute

Joseph O'Hara, President, Institutes for Health and Human Services, Inc.

Denise Polit, President, Humanalysis, Inc.

Robert D. Reischauer, Senior Fellow of Economic Studies Program, The Brookings Institution

Craig Thornton, Senior Economist, Mathematica Policy Research, Inc.

Loïc J. D. Wacquant, Doctoral candidate, the Department of Sociology, The University of Chicago, and Ecole des Hautes Etudes en Sciences Sociales, Paris.

Gary Walker, Executive Vice President, Public/Private Ventures

William Julius Wilson, Lucy Flower Distinguished Services Professor of Sociology and Public Policy, The University of Chicago

Index